THE GREENHAVEN ENCYCLOPEDIA OF

GREEK AND ROMAN MYTHOLOGY

Don Nardo, *Author*

Barbette Spaeth, Associate Professor,
Department of Classical Languages,
Tulane University, *Consulting Editor*

Daniel Leone, *President*
Bonnie Szumski, *Publisher*
Scott Barbour, *Managing Editor*

Greenhaven Press, Inc., San Diego, California

OTHER TITLES IN THE
GREENHAVEN ENCYCLOPEDIA OF SERIES:

Ancient Rome
Witchcraft

*The author wishes to express his sincere thanks to Tulane
University scholar Barbette Spaeth for her assistance in
selecting the topics for this volume.*

Library of Congress Cataloging-in-Publication Data

Greek and Roman mythology / Don Nardo.
   p. cm.—(The Greenhaven encyclopedia of)
 Includes bibliographical references and index.
 ISBN 0-7377-0719-4 (lib. bdg. : alk. paper)
  1. Mythology, Classical—Juvenile literature. I. Nardo,
Don, 1947– II. Series.

BL725 .G74 2002
398.2'0938—dc21

                               2001040864

Cover photo credit: Scala/Art Resource, NY

CONTENTS

Chapter 2:
Major and Minor Gods

**Chapter 3:
Animals, Monsters,
Spirits, and Forces**

PREFACE

The modern reader may well ask why new books about the ancient Greek and Roman myths continue to appear on a fairly regular basis. How can the enduring fascination for these archaic tales be explained, and what benefit can be reaped from studying them and passing them on to new generations? On the one hand, these stories are a kind of window into the past. In many ways, they go beyond ruins and other surviving physical artifacts, which can only tell so much about long-dead societies, and reveal some of what was in the minds of the Greeks and Romans, the founders of our Western culture. As noted classical scholar Michael Grant puts it, these myths

> are as important as history for our understanding of what these peoples, ancestors of our own civilization, believed and thought and felt, and expressed in writing and in visual art. For their mythologies were inextricably interwoven, to an extent far beyond anything in our own experience, with the whole fabric of their public and private lives.

At the same time, and perhaps more importantly, the Greek and Roman myths are not simply old artifacts that were forgotten, buried, and later rediscovered, ending up as quaint curiosities on some museum shelf. Quite to the contrary, these stories remained alive and vibrant after their makers died. They have been endlessly retold, translated, adapted, visualized, and memorialized; and thereby, gifted minds and hands have intricately interwoven them into the literary and artistic fabric of Western civilization. In this process, one still ongoing, these stories not only survived

the extinction of the classical civilization that created them, but also shaped and colored the cultures and world views of later Western societies, including our own. For this reason, they remain essential reading for every thoughtful person. Classical scholar Max Herzberg writes, "We are bound to the past in innumerable ways, and it is well to know the old myths in order that we may understand our own times."

Indeed, examples of the West's cultural absorption of the classical myths abound. The medieval Italian writer Dante, great Elizabethan dramatist Shakespeare, and seventeenth-century English poet John Milton, to name only a few literary figures, were both fascinated by and steeped in the old mythological stories and characters. Merely listing Milton's references to mythology would consume dozens of pages; as for Shakespeare, entire volumes have been written about his uses of classical mythology, which number in the thousands.

Modern literature is no less replete with references to ancient myths. Nineteenth-century American writer Edgar Allan Poe spoke of "the glory that was Greece, and the grandeur that was Rome" in his salute to the mythical Helen of Troy. Twentieth-century Irishman James Joyce based his acclaimed novel *Ulysses* on Homer's epic poem the *Odyssey*. And American playwright Eugene O'Neill reset the murderous saga of the Greek house of Atreus in a post–Civil War New England setting in his *Mourning Becomes Electra.*

In the same way that they inspired playwrights, poets, and novelists, the classical myths also became rich sources of material for artists, musicians, and filmmakers. These range from *The Birth of Venus,* the classic painting by Italy's Sandro Botticelli; to Frenchman Hector Berlioz's opera, *The Trojans;* to Lerner and Loewe's Broadway musical *My Fair Lady* (based on the myth of Pygmalion); to the multimillion dollar Hollywood film, *Clash of the Titans,* about the hero Perseus killing the monster Medusa.

In short, the classical myths have become so integrated into our culture that their images and ideas inundate us. And the average person cannot be expected to recognize, identify, or sort out all of the heroes, villains, gods, monsters, exotic locales, and fantastic events of these stories without some kind of aid. The *Greenhaven Encyclopedia of Greek and Roman Mythology* provides both students and general readers with that aid in the form of this thorough nonscholarly compilation. For the reader's convenience, the hundreds of topics are divided into chapters, each covering a major aspect of the myths—for example, a chapter on human characters, one on gods, another on monsters and other creatures, and so on. Also included is a chapter on the sources of these tales— the mythtellers and their works, including Homer and his *Iliad,* Sophocles and his *Oedipus the King,* and Ovid and his *Meta-*

morphoses. Most entries are carefully cross-referenced, guiding the interested reader to related topics or expanded discussions. In addition, the fulsome bibliography directs the serious reader to further exploration of classical mythology in the works of the leading scholars in the field as well as the ancient authors.

Finally, this book includes an unusual feature for an encyclopedia, namely a section in which the twelve major Greek and Roman myths are retold in extended narrative form. Alphabetical lists of entries can tell the main facts about heroes, gods, and monsters, but we must always remember that the ancients learned about these things in story form, usually by hearing them recited aloud. And their enduring strength and charm cannot be sufficiently appreciated without some good old-fashioned storytelling. In this manner, for at least a few fleeting moments we can attempt to feel the power of these tales as the Greeks and Romans did, not simply as quaint fiction but as a potent combination of fiction and fact. Then, in our imaginations, can we enter, in the words of classicist Stewart Perowne, "that realm of which they will forever be masters, where reality and fantasy dissolve, and come together again as immortal poetry."

CHAPTER 1
RULERS, HEROES, AND OTHER HUMAN CHARACTERS

Acastus

The son of King Pelias of Iolcos (or Jolcos). Acastus sailed with Jason and the Argonauts in search of the Golden Fleece; and after Jason returned with the fleece, the sorceress Medea killed Pelias, and Acastus became king. The new monarch promptly ordered Jason and Medea to leave Iolcos, and he married a woman named Astydamia. When one of the other Argonauts, Peleus, arrived in Iolcos, Astydamia falsely accused him of making advances toward her. Acastus retaliated by taking Peleus hunting on Mt. Pelion and abandoning him while he slept. With the aid of the kindly centaur Chiron, Peleus survived and later returned and killed both Acastus and Astydamia. **See** Peleus; **also** Chiron (Chapter 3); Iolcos (Chapter 4); The Quest for the Golden Fleece (Chapter 6).

Achates

In the story of Aeneas's adventures, as told in Virgil's *Aeneid,* Aeneas's close friend, often called "faithful Achates." Some writers have compared their relationship to that between Achilles and Patroclus in Homer's *Iliad.* **See** *Aeneid* (Chapter 5).

Achilles

One of the major Greek heroes of the Trojan War and the central figure in Homer's epic poem the *Iliad.* Achilles was the son of a sea nymph, Thetis, and a mortal man, Peleus, king of Phthia (in Thessaly). According to legend, Thetis dipped the infant Achilles into the River Styx, which made him invulnerable to wounds, except in the heel by which she held him. Later, when he was a young man and the Greek forces were gathering to attack Troy, she hid her son to keep him from going to Troy because an oracle had predicted that he would die on the expedition. However, the Greek hero Odysseus discovered Achilles' hiding place and convinced him to go to Troy.

Achilles sailed for Troy at the head of a contingent of fifty ships and a group of loyal followers called the Myrmidons. According to the *Iliad,* in the ninth year of the siege, Achilles quarreled with the leader of the Greek forces, Agamemnon, then retired to his tent, refusing to fight. But when the Trojan champion Hector killed Achilles' close friend Patroclus, Achilles reentered the fray and slew Hector. Later, an arrow shot by Troy's Prince Paris struck Achilles' vulnerable heel, killing him. **See** Hector; Patroclus; Peleus; **also** Thetis (Chapter 2); *Iliad* (Chapter 5); and, for a more detailed account of Achilles' exploits, **see** The Trojan War (Chapter 6).

Acontius

A young man who hailed from the island of Ceos and fell in love with an Athenian maiden named Cydippe during a religious festival on the sacred island of Delos. Because he was poor and she came from a wealthy family, he dared not ask for her hand in marriage directly. Instead, he wrote the message "I swear by the goddess Artemis that I will marry no man but Acontius" and dropped it where she would see it. She picked it up and read it aloud; later, the Delphic Oracle said that Cydippe was bound by the oath she had recited. To Acontius's delight, her parents felt that they had no choice but to allow the marriage.

Acrisius

A king of Argos who played an important role in the life of the hero Perseus. When the god Zeus impregnated Acrisius's daughter, Danae, and she gave birth to Perseus, the king set both mother and child adrift in the sea on a wooden chest. Later, Perseus ended up killing Acrisius by accident. For a more detailed account, **see** Perseus and Medusa (Chapter 6).

Actaeon

The son of Aristaeus (Apollo's son) and Autonoe (daughter of Cadmus, founder of Thebes). As a youth, Actaeon was trained to hunt either by his father or by the kindly centaur Chiron. The young man was famous for making the mistake of glimpsing the goddess Artemis naked while she was bathing. As a punishment, she turned him into a stag. His own dogs then mistook him for that animal and tore him

apart. **See** The Theban Myth Cycle (Chapter 6).

Admetus

One of Jason's Argonauts and the son of Pheres, king of Thessaly. After Pheres abdicated the throne, Admetus became king and quickly gained a reputation for kindness and justice. Hearing of this reputation, the god Apollo, whom Zeus had condemned to become the slave of a human for a year, chose Admetus as a master. Admetus treated Apollo (who was disguised as a farmhand) so well that the god helped him win the hand of Alcestis, daughter of King Pelias of Iolcos. Apollo also made it possible for Admetus to escape death by substituting another mortal for himself when it was time for him to die. As it turned out, no one would trade places with Admetus except his wife, Alcestis, who saved him by offering to die in his place. (Luckily, she was saved from death's clutches.) **See** Alcestis.

Adonis

An unusually handsome youth famed for his affair with the love goddess, Aphrodite. Adonis was born to a Cypriate (or Egyptian or Assyrian) woman, Myrrha, and her own father, a twisted union brought about

Aphrodite's favorite, the handsome Adonis, reclines in this ornate sculpture on the lid of a sarcophagus.

by Aphrodite to punish the woman for refusing to worship her. Other gods subsequently turned Myrrha into a myrrh tree. After Adonis was born from the tree, Aphrodite fell in love with him at first sight. Persephone, queen of the Underworld, also came to love him, and Zeus (or, in another version, the muse Calliope) decreed that he should spend half of each year with Aphrodite and the other half with Persephone. While with Aphrodite, Adonis was killed by a wild boar; she was so saddened by the loss that she made the blood he had shed turn into the blood-red sea anemone. Adonis was worshiped as a minor god by some Greeks beginning in the fifth century B.C. **See** Aphrodite; Persephone (Chapter 2).

Adrastus

A king of Argos (in the eastern Peloponnesus) and an important character in the mythical tale told in Aeschylus's *Seven Against Thebes* and Euripides' *The Suppliant Women.* One day two young men—Polynices and Tydeus—arrived in the city wearing animal skins. Because an oracle had said that Adrastus should have his daughter marry a lion and a boar, he gave the young men her hand in marriage. Adrastus then tried to help one of his new sons-in-law, Polynices, gain the throne of Thebes by leading an army against that city. When the attack failed, Adrastus escaped. A later attempt to conquer Thebes succeeded, but Adrastus lost his son in the fighting and soon afterward died of grief. **See** Polynices; **also** *Seven Against Thebes* (Chapter 5); The Theban Myth Cycle (Chapter 6).

Aeacus

One of the many sons of the god Zeus and king of the island of Aegina (lying in the Saronic Gulf, directly south of Megara and southwest of Athens). After wedding Endeis, a princess of Megara, Aeacus fathered Telamon and Peleus, and was

therefore the grandfather of their famous sons, Ajax and Achilles, respectively. Aeacus became known for his honesty and piety. According to legend, his prayers ended a severe drought, and he aided the gods Apollo and Poseidon in erecting the walls of Troy. (In one story, a snake was able to get through a gap in the section Aeacus built, and Apollo predicted that the man's descendants would end up destroying the city; this came true, for Ajax and Achilles were among the leaders of the Greek expedition against Troy.) As a result of Aeacus's goodness, Zeus did him two major favors. First, when Aegina's population was wiped out by a plague, the god repopulated it by turning ants into people. (They became known as the Myrmidons, some of whom Homer mentions in the *Iliad* as followers of Aeacus's grandson, Achilles.) Second, after Aeacus died, Zeus made him one of the three judges of the Underworld (along with Minos and Rhadamanthys). **See** Achilles; Ajax 1; Peleus; Telamon; **also** The Trojan War (Chapter 6).

Aedon

The daughter of Pandareos, king of Miletus (on the southwestern coast of Asia Minor), and the wife of Zethus, the son of Zeus and a ruler of Thebes. Because Aedon had only two children, she envied Niobe (wife of Zethus's brother and coruler, Amphion), who had many children. Deciding to kill Niobe's eldest son, Aedon sneaked into the boy's room in the middle of the night and stabbed the form lying in the bed. Unfortunately for her, it turned out to be her own son, Itylus, who was spending the night in the other boy's chamber. Aedon was so grief-stricken that Zeus changed her into a nightingale so that she would no longer feel human pain.

Aeetes

A noted king of Colchis, a land on the southeastern rim of the Black Sea, and the father of the famous sorceress Medea. When a Greek named Phryxus arrived in Colchis riding a fabulous talking ram with a golden fleece, Aeetes welcomed him and allowed him to marry his daughter Chalciope. But later, after an oracle told the king that Phryxus would bring about his death, Aeetes executed Phryxus and retained possession of the ram's fleece until the hero Jason arrived to retrieve it. Aeetes tried but failed to prevent Jason from taking the fleece. Later, Aeetes' own brother, Perseus of Tauri, deposed him. Later still, Medea, having returned to Colchis from Greece, restored her father to the throne, and he presumably died of old age. **See** Medea; **also** Golden Fleece (Chapter 4); and, for a full account of Jason's exploits, **see** The Quest for the Golden Fleece (Chapter 6).

Aegeus

A king of Athens during the Age of Heroes and the father of Athens's national hero, Theseus. After the Delphic Oracle foretold the coming of a great Athenian hero, Aegeus visited Pittheus, king of the neighboring state of Troezen. Hearing of the prediction, Pittheus endeavored to ensure a link between his own family and the prophesied hero. He summoned his daughter, Aethra, got Aegeus drunk, and arranged for the girl to sleep with the intoxicated man. Theseus, who was born of this union, lived much of his childhood with his mother in Pittheus's court. Meanwhile, Aegeus returned to Athens and married the sorceress Medea, whom he had given sanctuary after she had fled from Corinth. She bore Aegeus a son named Medus.

When the grown-up Theseus traveled to Athens and met his father, Aegeus accepted the younger man's offer to go to Crete to put an end to that island's demand that seven Athenian boys and seven Athenian girls be handed over each year for sacrifice to the monstrous Minotaur (a creature half-man and half-bull). But when Theseus returned triumphant, he forgot to

substitute a white sail (signifying success) for a black one (signifying his failure and death); and Aegeus committed suicide, out of grief, by throwing himself into the sea (or, in another version, off the Acropolis). Thereafter, the sea was called the Aegean in his honor. **See** Medea; Theseus; and, for a full account of Theseus's expedition to Crete, **see** The Exploits of Theseus (Chapter 6).

Aegimius

As king of the city of Doris (north of Delphi), Aegimius enlisted the aid of the legendary strongman Heracles to expel the Lapiths, a Greek tribe from Thessaly, who had overrun his land. As a reward, Heracles asked that Aegimius allow his descendants, the Heracleidae, to permanently settle there. Among these descendants were several kings of Doris, who later became known as the Dorians. (The classical Greeks had a tradition that a Greek-speaking people from northern Greece—the Dorians—had invaded and settled in southern Greece two generations after the Trojan War. Modern scholars now believe that the Dorians did not invade but rather migrated into the area after a series of upheavals that had destroyed the Mycenaean kingdoms that had controlled the Greek mainland for several centuries.) **See** Dorians; Heracles; Lapiths.

Aegisthus

The son of Thyestes, who was the brother of the Mycenaen king Atreus. Before Aegisthus's birth, Atreus had banished Thyestes from Mycenae, and Thyestes had retaliated by placing a terrible curse on Atreus's house. Thyestes then raped his own daughter, Pelopia, who later gave birth to Aegisthus. Pelopia left the child outside to die, but some shepherds found him, and later Atreus heard of his existence and brought him up in Mycenae. The king tried to get Aegisthus to kill Thyestes. But the plan failed when Thyestes recognized Aegisthus as his son, and Aegisthus refused to slay his father. The two then conspired to kill Atreus, and Aegisthus carried out the deed. However, though Atreus was dead, the curse on his house was still in effect and it now proceeded to affect others, including Aegisthus. When Atreus's son, Agamemnon (Aegisthus's cousin), left to fight in the Trojan War, Aegisthus stayed behind in Mycenae and seduced Agamemnon's wife, Clytemnestra; the lovers then murdered Agamemnon when he returned from the war ten years later. Aegisthus then met death himself at the hands of Agamemnon's son, Orestes. For a more detailed account of these bloody happenings, **see** *Agamemnon; Libation Bearers* (Chapter 5); **also** The Curse of the House of Atreus (Chapter 6).

Aeneas

A legendary prince of the city of Troy, Roman tradition viewed him as the founder of the Roman race. According to the legend, as told most completely in Virgil's epic poem the *Aeneid*, when the Greeks sacked Troy Aeneas escaped and sailed to southwestern Italy. There, he met and married the daughter of a local king, and from their union sprang the lineage that later led to Romulus, founder of the city of Rome. **See** Anchises; Latinus; Lavinia; Romulus; Sibyl; Turnus; **also** *Aeneid;* Virgil (Chapter 5); and, for a complete description of Aeneas's adventures, **see** Aeneas's Journey to Italy (Chapter 6).

Aeolus

1. A mortal who became a favorite of the god Zeus, who rewarded the young man with control of the winds. Aeolus became king of the floating island of Aeolia, where he kept the winds in a cave and released them as he pleased or as the gods instructed. He is most famous for giving the Greek wanderer Odysseus a leather bag containing powerful winds intended to blow his ships home. (Unfortunately, Odysseus's men prematurely untied the bag, upsetting the plan.) Aeolus was also said to have invented the sail. **See** Alcy-

one; **also** The Wanderings of Odysseus (Chapter 6).

2. One of the three sons of Hellen, founder of the Greek race. According to legend, Aeolus received the lordship of Thessaly from his father and there gave his name to the Aeolian branch of Greeks (some of whom later migrated to the northern coastal region of Asia Minor).

Agamemnon

A king of Mycenae, the brother of Menelaus (king of Sparta), and the overall commander of the Greek expedition to Troy. As told in Homer's *Iliad,* it was Agamemnon's quarrel with the warrior Achilles that caused the latter to withdraw from the fighting, with serious consequences. Earlier, Agamemnon had sacrificed his own daughter, Iphigenia, to appease the goddess Artemis and thereby obtain favorable winds for the journey to Troy. In retaliation for this pitiless act, his wife, Clytemnestra, and her lover murdered Agamemnon when he returned from Troy. The fateful homecoming is the subject of Aeschylus's *Agamemnon,* the first play in the monumental *Oresteia* trilogy. For a more detailed account of Agamemnon's deeds and troubles, **see** Aegisthus; Clytemnestra; Iphigenia; Orestes; **also** *Agamemnon* (Chapter 5); The Curse of the House of Atreus; The Trojan War (Chapter 6).

Agapenor

The king of Tegea, located in Arcadia (in the central Peloponnesus), during the Trojan War. In that famous conflict, he led the Arcadian portion of the Greek army that besieged Troy. Agamemnon, supreme leader of the expedition, lent Agapenor sixty ships; but these were lost in a storm off the coast of Cyprus. Agapenor remained on that large eastern Mediterranean island, where he established the city of Paphos.

Ajax

(or Aias) **1.** The son of Telamon, king of the island of Salamis (off the western coast of Attica), and leader of that island's troops during the Greek siege of Troy. He was often called "Ajax the Greater" to distinguish him from another Greek by the same name (see below). Ajax was said to be a huge man with enormous strength and courage. According to Homer in the *Iliad,* he was second only to Achilles among the Greeks at Troy and frequently protected his comrades' backs when the going got tough. One of his greatest feats was hurling a great rock at—and nearly killing—Hector, the Trojan hero; and it was Ajax who carried Achilles' dead body back to the Greek camp after the famous hero had been slain by the Trojan prince, Paris.

The most famous episode involving Ajax centers on the dispute over who should receive Achilles' armor as a reward for skill and bravery. This is the subject of Sophocles' great play *Ajax.* The other Greek leaders voted to give the armor to Odysseus (king of Ithaca), which drove Ajax to plan violent revenge on his colleagues. The goddess Athena intervened, however, making Ajax temporarily insane, so that he slaughtered a flock of sheep instead. When he came to his senses, he was so ashamed that he committed suicide by falling on his sword. However, other versions of the hero's death circulated in ancient times, among them that he was slain by Paris or by Odysseus. **See** Achilles; Odysseus; **also** *Ajax* (Chapter 5); The Trojan War (Chapter 6).

2. The other well-known Ajax was called "Ajax the Lesser" to differentiate him from his larger colleague. The smaller Ajax hailed from Locris (in central Greece) and led the troops from that region at Troy. He was said to be the fastest runner in the Greek army. His most infamous deed in the war was to drag the Trojan princess Cassandra from the local altar of Athena, an act that brought down Athena's vengeance on the Greeks. As Ajax sailed for home, Athena wrecked his ship, but he managed to swim to safety;

however, he made the mistake of boasting that he had defied the gods and lived, whereupon the sea god Poseidon killed him with a thunderbolt.

Alcestis

Daughter of Pelias, king of Iolcos. Alcestis offered to die in place of her husband, Admetus, but she managed to return to the world of the living. Two ancient versions of how this came about existed, the first claiming that Persephone, queen of the Underworld, sent Alcestis back to reward her uncommon devotion to her husband. In the second version, told by the playwright Euripides in his play *Alcestis,* the famous strongman Heracles went to her tomb and wrestled Thanatos (the god of death) for her. Victorious, Heracles returned her to Admetus. **See** Admetus; Heracles; **also** Thanatos (Chapter 2); *Alcestis* (Chapter 5).

Alcinous

In Homer's *Odyssey,* the king of the Phaeacians, on whose happy island Odysseus found himself shipwrecked. It was to Alcinous and the members of his court that the Greek hero told the tale of his recent wanderings; and Alcinous gave Odysseus a ship with which to reach his homeland of Ithaca. **See** The Wanderings of Odysseus (Chapter 6).

Alcmaeon

The leader of the expedition launched against the city of Thebes by the Epigoni, the sons of the so-called Seven Against Thebes. Alcmaeon did this to avenge his father, Amphiaraus, who had died during the Seven's earlier failed attempt on the city. After Thebes's fall, Alcmaeon slew his own mother, Eriphyle, also to avenge his father (since she had forced her husband to embark on the fateful expedition). For committing matricide, Alcmaeon was hounded by the Furies (or, in another version, he was driven mad by his mother's ghost). He traveled from place to place, stopping for a while in Psophis (in southern Greece), where he married the daughter of the local king, Phegeus. But the Furies or madness drove Alcmaeon to move on. He finally found purification of his sins on an island in the Achelous River (in western Greece), where the river god gave Alcmaeon his daughter in marriage. Soon afterward, however, the sons of Phegeus caught up with Alcmaeon and killed him.

Alcmena

(or Alcmene) The wife of Amphitryon, king of Tiryns (in the northeastern Peloponnesus), and the mother of the legendary strongman Heracles. Zeus wanted to sire a heroic mortal to aid the gods in the coming fight with the giants. Therefore, he came to Alcmena in Amphitryon's form and mated with her. Later that night, Amphitryon himself slept with her, too. As a result she became pregnant with twins— Heracles, Zeus's son, and Iphicles, Amphitryon's son. After Amphitryon's death, Alcmena married Rhadamanthys, who later became one of the judges of the dead. **See** Amphitryon.

Alcyone

The wife of Ceyx, king of Trachis (in eastern-central Greece). The two were said to be very happy and carefree until Ceyx accidentally drowned in the sea. Out of pity, the gods transformed the former lovers into birds—specifically, kingfishers. And so that they could nest in peace, Aeolus, lord of the winds, sent two weeks of calm weather each winter.

Amazons

A legendary race or nation of warrior women. The location of their homeland varied from one myth to another, but most often cited were the then-wild and little-known steppes lying west and north of the Black Sea. The Amazons get their name from their supposed custom of cutting off one breast to allow for more effective use

This classical statue of an Amazon shows her with only one breast, which, according to legend, was characteristic of her race.

of bows, spears, and other weapons. The term *a-mazon* means "without breast." Their society was all-female and therefore not a matriarchy in the strict sense, since that would require a society that contained both men and women, with women dominating men. But some who argue (probably mistakenly) that Greek society was originally matriarchal suggest that the Amazon myths are distorted, oversimplified memories of a time when women were indeed in charge. The warrior women claimed descent from the war god, Ares, whom they worshiped, along with the goddess of hunting, Artemis.

Greek mythology contains numerous myths featuring fighting between these women and Greek men, a type of warfare the Greeks called Amazonomachy. For example, in one story the Athenian hero Theseus invaded part of the Amazon homeland along the Black Sea coast and captured their queen, Hippolyte (or, in another version, her sister). To rescue her, the Amazons launched a counterstrike, landing an army at Marathon, northeast of Athens, and threatening the city. The warrior women besieged the Acropolis, but Theseus and his troops defeated them. The Greek strongman Heracles also fought the Amazons in his efforts to capture Hippolyte's girdle as one of his famous twelve labors. Later, during the Trojan War, the Amazons, led by Queen Penthesilea, aided the Trojans against the Greeks. The Greek hero Achilles killed her in battle, but he subsequently fell in love with her corpse.

Such episodes of Amazonomachy became a common theme depicted in classical Greek literature, sculpture, and painting. Some of the sculptures carved into the Parthenon (the temple of the goddess Athena erected atop the Athenian Acropolis during the 430s B.C.), for example, show the battle between Theseus and the Amazons.

The classical Greeks were convinced that the Amazons had been real. The fifth-century B.C. historian Herodotus traveled through some of the supposed former Amazon lands along the Black Sea, and the local people, seminomadic horsemen called Scythians, told him tales about warrior women who had, in the past (and perhaps still), inhabited the nearby steppes. Although the Scythians called them "man killers," Herodotus called them Amazons after the female fighters of the myths. He later recorded what the Amazonian leaders supposedly told a group of Scythian men who wanted to intermarry with them:

> We and the women of your nation could never live together; our ways are too much at variance. We are riders; our business is with the bow and the spear, and we know nothing of women's work; but in your country no woman has anything to do with such things—your women stay at home in their wagons occupied with feminine tasks, and never go out to hunt or for any other purpose. We could not possibly agree [to live like that]. (*Histories* 4.114–115)

Well into modern times, most historians assumed that such stories were little more than myths and/or morality tales used by Greek men to rationalize their highly male-dominated society. Greek women, like the Scythian women Herodotus wrote about, traditionally stayed home, reared children, and left the tasks of governing and fighting exclusively to their menfolk. By utilizing a total and unflattering gender reversal—namely the savage and unfeminine Amazons—Greek men might show their wives and daughters how improper it was for women to act like men. In recent years, however, this explanation of the Amazonian tales has steadily given way to the distinct possibility that such warrior women may actually have once roamed the Russian steppes. In the 1950s archaeologists excavating burial mounds of the ancient nomadic inhabitants of the steppes began finding female grave sites containing armor, swords, spears, and arrowheads. An American-Russian excavation team discovered more such sites in the mid-1990s, including seven graves containing iron swords, bronze arrowheads, and whetstones for sharpening weapons. Nomadic tribes like these, in which women played decisive political and military roles (undoubtedly alongside their menfolk), may well have given rise to the legends of the race the Greeks called the Amazons. **See** The Adventures of Heracles; The Exploits of Theseus (Chapter 6).

Amphiaraus

A seer, he drove Adrastus, king of Argos, from his throne; the two later made amends, and Amphiaraus married Adrastus's sister, Eriphyle. They had two sons—Alcmaeon and Amphilochus. Amphiaraus was able to foresee that the expedition of the Seven Against Thebes would fail, so he refused to go. But his wife coerced him, much to his regret and anger. So later, he asked his sons to avenge him by punishing her. At Thebes, Amphiaraus disappeared into a hole in the ground created by one of Zeus's thunderbolts. **See** Alcmaeon; **also** *Seven Against Thebes* (Chapter 5).

Amphion and Zethus

The twin sons of Zeus and a mortal woman, Antiope, a princess of Thebes. When she was pregnant, she traveled to Sicyon and married its king. But her father and her uncle pursued her. Her father died, but her uncle, Lycus, killed her husband. After she gave birth to the twins, Lycus left them outside to die. However, some kindly shepherds found and reared them. When the boys were grown, Antiope escaped from her uncle's clutches in Thebes and joined them, after which they sought and achieved revenge for the wrongs they had suffered by attacking Thebes and killing Lycus. Afterward, Amphion and Zethus ruled Thebes jointly and erected high walls to protect the city, along with its famous seven gates. Later, Amphion came to a tragic end after the gods killed his wife, Niobe, and their children. He either committed suicide out of grief or was slain by Apollo after attacking the god's temple to get revenge for the death of his loved ones. As for Zethus, he, too, died tragically of grief after the death of his young son. **See** Niobe.

Amphitryon

The son of Alcaeus, king of Tiryns, and the grandson of the renowned hero Perseus. Amphitryon wanted to marry his cousin, Alcmena, daughter of his uncle, Electryon, king of Mycenae. But Electryon would not agree to the marriage until Amphitryon had punished some raiders who had killed Electryon's sons and stolen his cattle. In an attempt to expedite matters, Amphitryon recovered the cattle; but when he returned with them, he accidentally killed Electryon. Unfairly branded as a murderer, Amphitryon fled Mycenae, along with Alcmena, and took refuge in Thebes. However, Alcmena would not consummate the marriage until Amphitryon agreed to avenge her brothers. With the aid of the Theban king, Creon, Amphitryon traveled to the islands where the raiders lived and killed their leader. On returning to Thebes, Amphitryon discovered to his surprise that his wife had been seduced and impregnated by the god Zeus. (The child of this union turned out to be the great hero Heracles.) Amphitryon died in battle many years later. **See** Alcmena.

Amulius

A descendant of the Trojan hero Aeneas and the younger brother of Numitor, king of Alba Longa (on Italy's plain of Latium). Amulius stole the throne from his brother. And when Numitor's daughter, Rhea Silvia, became pregnant with twins (after being raped by the god Mars), Amulius imprisoned her. He also ordered that when the babies were born they should be drowned in the Tiber River. The servants entrusted with this gruesome task did not fulfill it, however, and left the infants, Romulus and Remus, on the riverbank. Some shepherds subsequently raised them, and they ended up meeting their grandfather, Numitor, and learning their true identities. They then slew Amulius and restored Numitor to the throne. **See** Romulus; **also** The Founding of Rome (Chapter 6).

Anchises

The father of the Trojan hero Aeneas and an important figure in the story told in Virgil's *Aeneid*. As a handsome young man, Anchises was herding sheep on Mt. Ida when the goddess Aphrodite came to him disguised as a mortal woman. Zeus had caused her to fall in love with the young man, and

she soon bore Anchises a son—Aeneas. Anchises subsequently boasted to some friends
about his relationship with the goddess, for
which Zeus punished him by making him
lame. By the time the Trojan War began,
Anchises was an old man; but he proudly
watched Aeneas become one of Troy's
greatest champions. When Troy fell to the
Greeks, Aeneas bore Anchises on his back
out of the burning city. The old man then accompanied his son on the great voyage to
find a new home far to the west. During a
rest stop on the island of Sicily, Anchises
died of old age. But he reappeared to his son
later in the Underworld, where he showed
Aeneas the marvelous future of Rome and
its great leaders. **See** Aeneas; **also** Aeneas's
Journey to Italy (Chapter 6).

Andromache

Daughter of a king of Eetion, a city in the
southern Troad (the region of northwestern
Asia Minor). Andromache married the Trojan hero Hector. She has a famous and moving scene in Homer's *Iliad,* in which she,
carrying her young son, Astyanax, bids
farewell to her husband prior to his battle to
the death with the Greek warrior Achilles.
Following Troy's fall, the child was thrown
from the city's walls and Andromache was
dragged away by Achilles' son, Neoptolemus. She later bore Neoptolemus three sons;
when Neoptolemus died, she married the
Trojan prophet Helenus, to whom Neoptolemus had granted a small kingdom in northwestern Greece. Andromache bore Helenus
one son, after which Helenus, too, died. Finally, one of her sons took her back to Asia
Minor, where she established the city of
Pergamum. **See** Neoptolemus; **also** *Andromache* (Chapter 5); The Trojan War (Chapter 6).

Andromeda

The daughter of Cepheus, king of Joppa (often referred to as Ethiopia, but located in
Palestine), and his wife, Cassiopeia. Cassiopeia made the mistake of bragging that

her daughter was more beautiful than the
Nereids (a group of sea nymphs). When the
nymphs complained to their lord, sea god
Poseidon, he sent punishment in the form of
a monster that devastated the countryside
around Joppa. An oracle claimed that the
only way to drive off the creature was to feed
it Andromeda. But when she was chained to
a rock awaiting her grisly fate, the hero
Perseus happened by, carrying the head of
the Gorgon Medusa, whom he had just slain.
Perseus held up the Gorgon's head to the
monster, who instantly turned to stone;
Cepheus then gave Andromeda in marriage
to the young hero. Many years later, so the
story goes, the goddess Athena transformed
Andromeda, Perseus, Cepheus, Cassiopeia,
and the monster into constellations in the
heavens, where they remain to this day. **See**
Perseus and Medusa (Chapter 6).

Antenor

One of the Trojan elders during the Greek
siege of Troy, who argued that it was wrong
for Troy's Prince Paris to have abducted
Sparta's Queen Helen (the deed that reportedly caused the war) and that she should be
returned to her husband, Menelaus. For this,
Menelaus and his colleague Odysseus
spared Antenor and his family during the
sacking of Troy. Later, according to one
story, Antenor traveled to Italy and established the city of Patavium (modern Padua);
in another tale, he traveled to North Africa
with Menelaus and settled there in the
Greek city of Cyrene.

Antigone

One of the daughters of Oedipus, king of
Thebes. Antigone followed her disgraced father into exile after his own sons, Polynices
and Eteocles, seized the throne and drove
him away. Later, after Oedipus's death, she
returned to Thebes. Polynices, who had been
pushed aside by Eteocles, attacked the city
(in a famous episode called "The Seven
Against Thebes"); the brothers killed each
other; and the new king, Creon (Oedipus's

brother-in-law) refused to allow Polynices a decent burial. Defying this edict, Antigone buried her brother. For this, Creon condemned her to death, but he later changed his mind, only to arrive too late to save her. The story is told in Sophocles' plays *Oedipus at Colonus* and *Antigone;* it was also the subject of a play titled *Antigone* by Sophocles' colleague Euripides, a work that has not survived. For more detailed accounts of her story, **see** *Antigone* (Chapter 5); The Theban Myth Cycle (Chapter 6).

Antilochus

The son of Nestor, king of Pylos (in the southern Peloponnesus), and one of the Greek champions who fought at Troy. Antilochus, who was a close friend of Achilles, took on the sad duty of informing Achilles of the death of another close friend, Patroclus (who had been slain by the Trojan prince Hector). During the funeral games for Patroclus, Antilochus cheated in the chariot race, gaining second place over Menelaus, king of Sparta; but he soon apologized and awarded the prize to Menelaus. Later, when a Trojan ally, the Ethiopian Memnon, attacked Nestor, Antilochus intervened but died during the effort. His comrades buried him in Achilles' grave.

Antinous

In Homer's *Odyssey,* the leader and the most arrogant of the suitors demanding the hand of Odysseus's wife, Penelope. When Odysseus unexpectedly returned from his long wanderings following the close of the Trojan War and confronted the suitors, Antinous was the first to die. **See** The Wanderings of Odysseus (Chapter 6).

Antiope

For this mother of the early Theban rulers Amphion and Zethus, **see** Amphion and Zethus.

Arachne

The daughter of a king of Lydia (in Asia Minor) and an expert weaver. Arachne was also vain and unscrupulous and challenged the goddess Athena, patron of weaving, to a contest. Athena accepted the challenge and wove a tapestry depicting presumptuous humans (like Arachne); meanwhile, Arachne chose as her own subject the scandalous affairs of several gods. Furious, Athena destroyed Arachne's tapestry and beat her severely, after which the young woman hanged herself. The goddess then turned her into a spider (later called an arachnid in Arachne's honor); and this is supposedly why spiders are so skilled at weaving webs.

Argonauts

The collective name of the band of young men who followed Jason in his famous quest for the Golden Fleece. The name *Argonauts* came from the name of Jason's ship, the *Argo,* which was built by the master shipwright Argus. **See** Argus; and, for a detailed account of the Argonauts' adventures, **see** The Quest for the Golden Fleece (Chapter 6).

Argus

1. The master shipwright who built Jason's ship, the *Argo,* with the aid of the goddess Athena. Argus became one of the Argonauts who sailed with Jason to retrieve the Golden Fleece. **See** The Quest for the Golden Fleece (Chapter 6).

2. A youth born in Colchis, on the shore of the Black Sea, who quarreled with the local king, Aeetes. Fleeing, Argus and his brother were shipwrecked on the Isle of Ares. There, Jason and the Argonauts found them and took them along on the remainder of the voyage, during which the two brothers proved helpful on a number of occasions. (Thus, there were two Argonauts named Argus.)

Ariadne

The daughter of Minos, king of Crete. Ariadne fell in love with the Athenian hero

Theseus and helped him find his way out of the labyrinth after he killed the fearsome Minotaur. She then departed with him on his homeward journey; but he left her on the island of Dia (later called Naxos). There, the god Dionysus rescued and married her. Other accounts say that Dionysus accused Ariadne of some crime or sin, after which the goddess Artemis killed her, or that Ariadne died while having Theseus's child. **See** The Exploits of Theseus (Chapter 6).

Aristaeus

The son of the god Apollo and the nymph Cyrene. The earth goddess, Gaia, reared Aristaeus, and the Muses (goddesses of the arts) taught him healing, prophecy, archery, olive growing, and beekeeping. Aristaeus is best known for his skill at the latter. (The Roman poet Virgil describes the character's adventures with bees in the fourth poem of the *Georgics*.) After an accident in which Eurydice, wife of the musician Orpheus, was fatally bitten by a snake while Aristaeus was pursuing her, some tree nymphs decided to punish Aristaeus by causing many of his bees to die. He did not know why the bees were dying, however; to find out, he consulted the sea god Proteus, who possessed the power of prophecy. Proteus explained the situation and added that, to atone for Eurydice's accident, Aristaeus must sacrifice several animals, including a black sheep, to Orpheus. After Aristaeus did as he was instructed, his bees began to flourish once more. **See** Proteus (Chapter 2).

Ascalaphus

1. The son of the god Ares and a coruler of the city of Orchomenus (in Boeotia). With his brother, Ascalaphus led a small group of ships and troops in the Greek army that besieged Troy. The Trojan prince Deiphobus killed Ascalaphus with a spear.

2. The son of the nymph Orphne and the river god Acheron. Zeus had promised the goddess Demeter that her daughter, Persephone, could return from her journey to the Underworld if Persephone refrained from eating there. However, Ascalaphus informed Hades, king of the Underworld, that Persephone had nibbled some pomegranate seeds. As a punishment for telling on her, Persephone (or, in another version, Demeter) turned Ascalaphus into an owl.

Ascanius

(also Iulus, or Julus) The son of the Trojan hero and founder of the Roman race, Aeneas. Ascanius left Troy with his father and took part in many of the adventures the expedition encountered on its way to Italy. The Roman historian Livy claims that Iulus and Ascanius were two different people: Iulus was Aeneas's son who was born in Troy, and Ascanius was born to Aeneas (and his Italian bride, Lavinia) in Italy. On the other hand, the poet Virgil held that Ascanius and Iulus were one and the same. The poet may have based this supposition on the claim made by members of the Julii clan, especially Julius Caesar, that they were descended from Iulus and therefore also from his parents, Aeneas and the love goddess, Venus. **See** Aeneas's Journey to Italy (Chapter 6).

Atalanta

Known primarily as a skilled huntress and a virgin (like the goddess Artemis), Atalanta was the daughter of Iasus of Arcadia, in the Peloponnesus (or, in another version, the daughter of Schoeneus of Boeotia, in central Greece). Whoever her father was, according to legend he left her outside to die when she was an infant. Luckily, a kindly bear found her and protected her until some hunters took her in and raised her. They taught her to hunt, and she came to display more manly than womanly traits, including considerable strength and fighting ability. When two centaurs tried to rape her, for example, she slew them; she also defeated one of Jason's Argonauts.

In one of Atalanta's more famous exploits, she joined a boar hunt at Calydon (in western-central Greece). One of her arrows was the first to hit the beast, but a prince of Calydon, Meleager (who was another of the Argonauts and a potential suitor for Atalanta) actually killed the boar. Because Atalanta had made the first wound, he gave her the creature's hide. His maternal uncles were angry about sharing the hunt with a woman, however, so they took the hide from her. Meleager promptly killed them, and his own mother in turn slew him, destroying Atalanta's hopes of marrying him.

Soon afterward, Atalanta's father heard about the brash young huntress and learned that she was actually his daughter, whom he had assumed was long since dead. He sought her out and advised her to find another potential husband, but she was reluctant. To win her hand, she said, a suitor would have to beat her in a footrace. Furthermore, she stipulated, if he lost the race he must be executed immediately. In the months that followed, many young men tried to win her hand, but they all failed and met with death. Finally, a young man named Milanion (or, in another version, Hippomenes) arrived to race for Atalanta's hand. A crafty young man, he acquired three golden apples from the goddess Aphrodite and tossed them into a field during the race. Atalanta saw the apples and stopped to examine them, which allowed Milanion to overtake her and win the race. Unfortunately, he neglected to give Aphrodite the proper worship in return for the apples, so the angry goddess turned both him and Atalanta into lions.

Athamas

The son of Aeolus (himself the son of Hellen, founder of the Greek race) and a king of Orchomenus and later of Thebes. Athamas married the nymph Nephele, who bore him two children—Phryxis and Helle. He later divorced Nephele and married Ino, daughter of Cadmus, founder of Thebes. By Ino, Athamas had two sons—Learchus and Melicertes. Ino subsequently became jealous of her husband's first two children and convinced him (through a false oracle) that he must kill Phryxis in a sacrifice or else Thebes would suffer a serious famine. Just as Athamas was about to kill Phryxis, a magical talking ram with a golden fleece appeared (having been sent by either Nephele or Zeus) and bore Phryxis away to safety. (The ram carried away Phryxis's sister, Helle, too. She soon fell to her death into the Hellespont, and the ram took Phryxis to Colchis, on the shore of the Black Sea. There, the youth made his home, and the ram's fleece later became a prize sought after by Jason and the Argonauts.)

Later, Athamas met with far worse misfortune. The goddess Hera (who was angry that Athamas had taken in the then-young god Dionysus, for whom she felt intense jealousy) drove Athamas and Ino mad. In this frenzied state, Athamas slew his son Learchus; and Ino, carrying the other boy, Melicertes, jumped off a cliff into the sea. These murders led the people of Thebes to banish Athamas, and he wandered the countryside until settling in Thessaly. When he was an old man, he received a piece of land from the new king of Orchomenus; and after Athamas died of old age, Phryxis's children, who had journeyed to Greece from Colchis, became his heirs. **See** Golden Fleece; Hellespont (Chapter 4); **also** The Quest for the Golden Fleece (Chapter 6).

Atreus

One of the sons of Pelops (for whom the Peloponnesus was named), a king of Mycenae, the father of the Greek kings Agamemnon and Menelaus, and the head of the royal house on which fell the most famous curse in Greek legend. After Pelops banished

Atreus and his brother, Thyestes, for killing their half brother, the brothers fell into a bitter feud. This culminated in Atreus murdering Thyestes' children, cutting them up, and serving them to their unknowing father at a banquet. On discovering the horrifying truth, Thyestes cursed Atreus; later, Aegisthus, son of Thyestes, avenged his father by slaying Atreus. **See** Aegisthus; Pelops; and, for a fuller account of Atreus's life, crimes, and the curse placed on him and his relatives, **see** The Curse of the House of Atreus (Chapter 6).

Autolycus

The son of the Greek messenger god, Hermes, and a well-known thief and trickster. Rumor had it that Autolycus inherited from his divine father the gift of making himself and the things he stole invisible. Another story claimed that Autolycus had a daughter named Anticlea, who became the mother of the renowned hero Odysseus.

Baucis and Philemon

A poor elderly couple known for their hospitality during a famous encounter with the gods. One day Zeus and his messenger, Hermes, dressed themselves as lowly beggars and traveled to Phrygia (in central Asia Minor) to test the hospitality of the local people. To their dismay, the gods encountered much rudeness and selfishness. As they went from house to house, rich and poor alike, asking humbly for a scrap of food and a place to sleep, one owner after another told them to go away. They tried a thousand houses and always received the same poor treatment.

Finally, Zeus and Hermes came to a small hut thatched with straw and reeds, the humblest and poorest hovel they had seen so far. The owners, Baucis and Philemon, who had lived together happily there all of their adult lives, welcomed the strangers and went out of their way to make them comfortable. Baucis carefully washed her wobbly wooden table, and she and her husband prepared a supper of cabbage, olives, radishes, eggs, and whatever else edible they could find. Then, as they and their guests ate the meal, Baucis and Philemon noticed that each time their mixing bowl was near to empty, it suddenly filled up again; the wine kept replenishing itself, too. Not realizing that this was the work of their superhuman guests, they became afraid and raised their hands high in prayer.

At this moment, Zeus and Hermes revealed themselves to the old people. They told them not to fear and led them to a mountaintop. From that vantage, Baucis and Philemon watched as a great flood drowned all of their neighbors, the ones who had treated the gods so badly. The deluge left only their own hut standing unscathed. Zeus then transformed the hut into a magnificent temple, and the two mortals thereafter resided in it as his devoted priests. The chief god later did the two aging lovers a further kindness, ensuring that neither would have to endure the sadness and loneliness of outliving the other and also that they would remain together for eternity. On the last day of their lives, Zeus changed them into trees—an oak and a linden—joined forever into a single trunk.

Bellerophon

The son of Glaucus, king of Corinth (or, in some stories, the sea god Poseidon) and a hero whose deeds were similar to those of two other renowned heroes—Theseus and Heracles. As a young man Bellerophon visited nearby Argos as a guest of its king and queen, Proteus and Anteia. Anteia tried to seduce the young visitor, but he righteously rejected her advances. The angry queen then lied to her husband, saying that Bellerophon had attempted to seduce her. Proteus sought revenge by sending Bellerophon, carrying a sealed letter, to Lycia (in southern Asia Minor), where Proteus's father-in-law, King Iobates, held court. Iobates read the letter, which requested that he kill Bellerophon. However, because it was against custom to slay a guest in one's house, the Lycian king sent the young man on a mission to slay the Chimaera, a hideous monster that had been ravaging the nearby countryside. Iobates was certain that Bellerophon would fail and die in the beast's clutches. However, the resourceful Bellerophon enlisted the aid of the magical winged horse Pegasus, whom he had earlier tamed. Riding on Pegasus, Bellerophon was able to attack the Chimaera from above and slay it.

When Bellerophon returned triumphant to Lycia, the surprised Iobates sent the young man out on other dangerous missions, always hoping he would be killed. Each time, however, Bellerophon returned very much alive and victorious. Completely frustrated, the king gave up trying to kill the young man and instead showed him the secret letter from King Proteus. Iobates also gave Bellerophon the hand of his daughter, Philonoe, in marriage. Bellerophon then returned to Argos and got his revenge on Queen Anteia by taking her on a ride with him on Pegasus and, after flying high above the ground, pushing her off.

Bellerophon's later life is somewhat uncertain. But one ancient source claims that he became so conceited from the praise he received for his heroics that he rode Pegasus toward heaven, attempting to outdo the gods; the angry Zeus caused an insect to sting the flying horse, who then threw the rider off. Bellerophon survived the fall, but he was badly crippled and limped away, never to be heard from again. **See** Chimaera; Pegasus (Chapter 3).

Belus

1. A son of the sea god Poseidon and the twin brother of Agenor, father of Cadmus (founder of the Greek city of Thebes). Belus became king of Egypt. Some ancient accounts say that he married a daughter of the Nile River, a union that produced two sons—Danaus and Aegyptus. Through these sons, Belus became the ancestor of a number of royal houses in Greece, North Africa, and Persia.

2. In Virgil's *Aeneid,* a king of the Phoenician city of Tyre and the father of Dido, who became queen of Carthage and fell in love with the Trojan prince Aeneas.

Briseis

The wife of Mynes, king of Lyrnessus, a city near Troy (in northwestern Asia Minor). In Homer's *Iliad,* the Greek warrior Achilles captures Briseis while raiding her city and keeps her as his slave and concubine (mistress). But during the Trojan War, Agamemnon, leader of the Greek expedition, takes her away from Achilles (to make up for the loss of another maiden, Chryseis, whom the god Apollo had ordered Agamemnon to return to her father). This selfish act by Agamemnon is the reason that Achilles withdraws into his tent and refuses to fight, a major theme of the *Iliad.* Later, however, Agamemnon returns Briseis to Achilles. **See** The Trojan War (Chapter 6).

Brutus, Lucius Junius

According to tradition, the pivotal figure in the establishment of the Roman Republic and one of the legendary heroes exalted by the later Romans. Brutus was probably a real person, but many (though certainly not all) of the deeds attributed to him are probably exaggerated or later fabrications. In the story accepted by later Romans, in the waning months of the Roman monarchy (about 510 or 509 B.C.), he opposed the rule of his uncle, King Tarquinius Superbus. When Lucretia, the wife of Brutus's friend L. Tarquinius Collatinus, was raped by the king's son and soon afterward killed herself, Brutus vowed to topple the monarchy. With the aid of other leading citizens, he led a revolution that ousted the royal family and founded a republican form of government. One of the Republic's first two elected consuls (the other one being Collatinus), Brutus became known for his strong sense of justice. He died while resisting an invading Etruscan army. The main source of his story is Livy's massive history of Rome, composed in the late first century B.C. **See** Tarquinius Superbus, Lucius; **also** Rome (Chapter 4).

Busiris

One of Poseidon's sons and also a king of Egypt. When a terrible drought struck that country, Busiris sought the advice of a prophet named Phrasius. The latter claimed that the drought would end if the king killed all strangers who arrived in Egypt by sacrificing them to the Greek god Zeus. Because Phrasius was himself a foreigner who had recently come to Egypt, he was the first to die. Not long afterward, the Greek hero Heracles arrived in Egypt. The king immediately ordered that he be chained and sacrificed. But the strongman easily escaped his fetters and then proceeded to kill Busiris, his son (and heir), and all of his attendants.

Cadmus

The legendary founder of the great city of Thebes. For his background and the story of his adventures and major accomplishments, **see** The Theban Myth Cycle (Chapter 6).

Calais and Zetes

The sons of Boreas, the north wind, and two of Jason's Argonauts during the search for the Golden Fleece. Calais and Zetes had human appearance at birth. As they grew, however, they sprouted golden wings (a gift from their father), which grew from their shoulders and enabled them to fly. **See** Boreas (Chapter 2); and, for their exploits on the voyage of the *Argo,* **see** The Quest for the Golden Fleece (Chapter 6).

Capaneus

One of the famous members of the group known as the Seven Against Thebes, who took part in the ill-fated attack on that city led by Polynices, son of Oedipus. Capaneus was so determined to succeed in the assault that he painted on his shield a picture of a man scaling a wall and the words, "I will destroy this city!" During the attack, however, the god Zeus struck him with a thunderbolt, killing him instantly. Later, Capaneus's grief-stricken wife, Evadne, took her own life by throwing herself on his blazing funeral pyre. **See** Polynices; **also** Thebes (Chapter 4); The Theban Myth Cycle (Chapter 6).

Cassandra

(sometimes referred to as Alexandra) The daughter of Troy's King Priam and Queen Hecuba and a gifted prophetess. In Homer's *Iliad,* Cassandra is the most beautiful of Priam's daughters and has two high-born suitors vying for her hand in marriage. But both of these men are killed in the war against the invading Greeks. Later traditions held that Apollo, god of prophecy, fell in love with Cassandra and bestowed on her the ability to see into the future. However, when she refused his advances, he punished her by ordaining that she would always deliver truthful prophecies but that no one would believe her. She foresaw and warned of the troubles that would occur as a result of her brother Paris's abduction of the Spartan queen, Helen, for example; Cassandra also warned her people not to drag the wooden horse (supposedly a gift from the departing Greeks, but which actually contained a hidden band of Greek soldiers) into the city. But none of the Trojans paid any attention to her warnings, since they thought she was insane.

When the Greeks captured Troy and began burning the city, Cassandra took refuge in the local temple of Athena. But the Greek warrior Ajax the Lesser entered, dragged the young woman away (overturning the goddess's statue in the process), and raped her. Outraged, Athena exacted punishment by killing or scattering many of the Greeks on their homeward journeys. Meanwhile, the leader of the Greek forces, Agamemnon, made Cassandra his concubine and took her to Mycenae, his stronghold in Greece. There, she foresaw the murders of Agamemnon and herself at the hands of Agamemnon's wife, Clytemnestra, part of the terrible curse of the house of Atreus; but as usual, the young woman's warnings went unheeded, and she was slain. **See** *Agamemnon* (Chapter 5); **also** The Curse of the House of Atreus; The Trojan War (Chapter 6).

Clytemnestra, jealous wife of Agamemnon, slays the Trojan princess Cassandra in this ancient carving.

Cassiopeia

The wife of Cepheus, king of Ethiopia (a region of Palestine). Cassiopeia brought down the wrath of the sea god Poseidon on her land and later became one of the constellations in the night sky. **See** Andromeda; **also** Perseus and Medusa (Chapter 6).

Castor and Polydeuces

(or Pollux) The brothers of Helen of Troy, two of the most distinguished of Jason's Argonauts, and eventually the objects of Roman religious worship. For the details of their exploits and worship, **see** their ancient collective name, the Dioscuri.

Cecrops

The legendary second king of Athens (and Attica, the large peninsula dominated by Athens). Cecrops was said to have sprung from the ground and to have been part man and part snake. Early in the Age of Heroes (the Greek Bronze Age), he inherited the throne of Attica from his father-in-law, Actaeus. Cecrops subsequently presided over the contest between Athena and Poseidon over which of them would become Athens's divine patron; the king named Athena the winner after she made an olive tree grow on the Acropolis. The classical Athenians preserved the tradition that Cecrops was the first Athenian ruler to recognize Zeus as the chief god; Cecrops was also credited with establishing Athens's aristocratic council and law court, the Areopagus. **See** Areopagus (Chapter 4).

Cephalus

The son of Deion, king of Phokis (or Phocis, in central Greece), or, in another tale, the son of the god Hermes and a mortal woman. Cephalus married Procris, daughter of Erechtheus, king of Athens, and the lovers took a vow of sexual fidelity. But one day when Cephalus was out hunting, Eos, the goddess of the dawn, fell in love with him and abducted him. He remained with her for several years, giving her a son—Phaëthon. Eventually, though, Cephalus returned to Athens. Deciding to test his wife's love and loyalty, he disguised himself as a stranger and offered her a huge sum of money if she would consent to be his mistress. At first, she refused; but he continued to tempt her until she gave in, after which he revealed himself and condemned her for being unfaithful. Upset, she fled into the mountains, where the goddess Artemis gave her a magic spear (that never missed its mark) and a magic hunting hound (that always caught its prey). Later, Cephalus and Procris reconciled, and she gave these gifts to her husband to celebrate their reunion. The couple's fate was ultimately tragic, however. Procris heard a rumor, which turned out to be false, that Cephalus was again carrying on with another woman. So one day when he was out hunting, Procris hid in some bushes to spy on him. He heard her moving and, assuming it was a wild animal, hurled the magic spear, fatally wounding her. For this deed, the Athenians banished Cephalus, who spent the rest of his life in exile.

Chryseis

In Homer's *Iliad,* the daughter of a priest of Apollo on an island near Troy (in northwestern Asia Minor). During the Trojan War, the Greeks sacked the island and Agamemnon, leader of the Greek forces, took Chryseis as his concubine. He liked her so much that he refused a large ransom offered by her father. In desperation, the father prayed to Apollo, who sent a plague to ravage the Greek camp. After nine days, Agamemnon relented and agreed to return Chryseis to her home; but to replace her,

he took Briseis, Achilles' favorite concubine. Achilles' anger over this act is a central theme of the *Iliad.* **See** Achilles; Agamemnon; Briseis; **also** The Trojan War (Chapter 6).

Cincinnatus, Lucius Quinctius

A semilegendary hero of early Rome who, if a real person, lived during the fifth century B.C. It was said that he accepted the office of dictator in 458 B.C. to deal with a threat posed by a neighboring Italian tribe, the Aequi. Having defeated the enemy army, rather than abuse his great power or use his notoriety to pursue a political career—as most Roman men of his day would have—he dutifully resigned his office after only sixteen days and returned to his farm. In the eyes of future generations, this gesture made Cincinnatus a model of old-fashioned Roman agrarian simplicity and virtue. **See** Rome (Chapter 4).

Cloelia

In Roman legend, a young Roman woman who became a heroine during the days of the founding of the Republic. After the Etruscan king (of the city-state of Clusium) Lars Porsenna failed to capture Rome, he made a deal with Rome's new republican government. In exchange for the Janiculum Hill (across the Tiber from Rome), which he had managed to capture, Porsenna received several Roman hostages, including Cloelia. Not long afterward, she hatched a plot to free herself and some of the other hostages. They managed to swim back across the river to Rome. Porsenna was so impressed with Cloelia's courage that he eventually gave up trying to get her back and even freed some of the remaining hostages in her honor. The Romans themselves later honored her with a public statue. **See** Lars Porsenna; **also** Rome (Chapter 4).

Clytemnestra

The daughter of Tyndareos, king of Sparta; the sister of Helen of Troy, Castor, and

Polydeuces; and the wife of Agamemnon, king of Mycenae. At first, Clytemnestra married Agamemnon's cousin, Tantalus; but Agamemnon killed Tantalus and took Clytemnestra as his own wife. She bore her second husband four children—Iphigenia, Chrysothemis, Electra, and Orestes. When Agamemnon sacrificed Iphigenia to the goddess Artemis to ensure favorable winds for his ships bound for Troy, Clytemnestra turned against her husband. She and her lover, Aegisthus, plotted and later carried out Agamemnon's murder. Later still, her son Orestes killed her and Aegisthus in revenge. All of these murders turned out to be part of the terrible curse visiting the generations of Agamemnon's family. For more on these events, **see** Aegisthus; Agamemnon; Electra; Iphigenia; Orestes; **also** *Agamemnon; Electra* (Chapter 5); **and** especially The Curse of the House of Atreus; The Trojan War (Chapter 6).

Codrus

An early king of Athens who saved the city and established a long-lived royal dynasty. Originally a member of the royal family of Messenia (in the Peloponnesus), Codrus left his native city after the Dorians (Greek-speaking invaders from far to the north) captured it. He went to Athens and there challenged and killed the local king, Xuthus. Codrus's ascension to the throne marked the end of the dynasty founded by the hero Theseus and the beginning of a new dynasty. Soon, however, the Dorians attacked Athens. The Delphic Oracle prophesied that the Dorians would be victorious as long as they spared Codrus's life. Hearing of this prophecy, Codrus disguised himself as a woodcutter and rushed into battle, hoping the enemy would unknowingly kill him and thereby Athens would be saved. The plan worked. Codrus was slain and the Dorians were forced to withdraw. According to legend, Codrus's descendants ruled Athens until sometime in the eighth century B.C., when

the Athenians replaced the position of king with three archons (civil administrators). **See** Dorians; **also** Athens (Chapter 4).

Coriolanus, Gnaeus Marcius

One of Rome's greatest early legendary heroes, whose exploits may have been based partly on those of a real person of the early fifth century B.C. According to Roman tradition, he received the name Coriolanus after capturing the enemy Volscian town of Corioli in 493 B.C. After he adopted an arrogant attitude toward the people during a corn shortage, many Roman leaders accused him of having tyrannical ambitions; so he fled to his old enemies, the Volscians, and marched on Rome at the head of their army. At the last moment, however, he refused to attack his native city and pulled back. For this, the Volscians executed him. Both the Roman historian Livy and the Greek biographer Plutarch tell his story, Plutarch's version being the one on which Shakespeare based his play *Coriolanus*.

Creon

1. A king of the Greek city of Corinth, who gave sanctuary to the hero Jason and the sorceress Medea after their enemy, Acastus, drove them from Iolcos (following their return to Greece with the Golden Fleece). Jason soon rejected Medea in favor of Creon's daughter, which drove Medea to exact a terrible revenge—the murder of Creon, his daughter, and Medea's own children by Jason. **See** Medea; **also** *Medea* (Chapter 5).

2. In legend and in Sophocles' Oedipus cycle of plays, the brother of Jocasta (the wife and mother of Oedipus, king of Thebes). Creon first ruled Thebes as regent after its king, Laius, had been killed by an unknown assailant (who turned out to be Oedipus). When the monstrous Sphinx began to terrorize the city, Creon offered the throne to any man who could overcome the beast. The newly arrived Oedipus did so and became king. Later, after Oedipus's fall from grace (after learning that he had killed his father and married his mother), Creon took the throne; Creon ruled Thebes still again after Oedipus's son, Eteocles, died during the assault of the Seven Against Thebes. Creon led the resistance that drove the enemy army away, then condemned Oedipus's daughter Antigone to death for burying one of the leaders of the attack, her brother Polynices. Creon later gave his daughter, Megara, in marriage to the hero Heracles. While Heracles was away, a usurper named Lycus slew Creon and seized the throne. (In another version, the Athenian hero Theseus attacked Thebes and killed Creon.) **See** Thebes (Chapter 4); **also** *Antigone; Oedipus at Colonus; Oedipus the King; Seven Against Thebes* (Chapter 5); The Theban Myth Cycle (Chapter 6).

Creusa

1. The youngest daughter of the early Athenian king Erechtheus and the wife of another Athenian king, Xuthus. Creusa was also the mother of Ion, Achaeus, and Dorus, after whom the three branches of the Greek-speaking race (Ionians, Achaeans, and Dorians) were named. **See** *Ion* (Chapter 5).

2. A daughter of Troy's King Priam and Queen Hecuba as well as the wife of the Trojan hero Aeneas. While the Greeks were sacking the city at the climax of the Trojan War, Aeneas; Creusa; their son, Ascanius; and other refugees escaped. But in the smoke and confusion, Creusa became separated from the others and disappeared. When Aeneas returned later and searched for her, he encountered her ghost, who told him that his wife was dead and also prophesied that he would find a new home far to the west. **See** Aeneas; **also** Aeneas's Journey to Italy (Chapter 6).

Curtius

The name of three legendary characters, any one of whom might have given his name to a pond, the Lacus Curtius, which existed in the Forum Romanum (Rome's principal main square) during the city's early centuries. The pond finally dried up early in the first century B.C. and the Romans paved over it. But by that time, three separate legends had grown up to explain its origins. The first involved a warrior named Mettius Curtius, one of the Sabine soldiers who battled the early Romans, led by Rome's first king, Romulus. Curtius played a key role in driving the Romans off the Capitoline Hill. But then Romulus counterattacked and pursued Curtius until the latter and his horse fell into the pond and drowned. The second legend held that the pond received its name when an early Roman administrator, Gaius Curtius Chilo, declared it a sacred spot after lightning had struck it. The third and most popular version claimed that a deep hole mysteriously appeared in the Forum in 362 B.C. An oracle said that Dis (or Pluto), lord of the Underworld, was responsible and would not be satisfied until the bravest of Rome's citizens sacrificed himself by jumping in. A Roman soldier, Marcus Curtius, immediately threw himself into the void, which then closed but left a depression that soon filled with rainwater.

Daedalus

A legendary Athenian inventor, craftsman, and sculptor thought to have lived during the Age of Heroes (Greece's Bronze Age). As a young sculptor, Daedalus created statues so realistic that they appeared to be alive. When his apprentice, Talos, who was also his nephew, began to reveal tremendous talent of his own (inventing the saw and the potter's wheel), Daedalus grew jealous and pushed the boy off the Acropolis, killing him. (Out of pity, the goddess Athena changed the dead boy into a living partridge.) The Athenians put Daedalus on trial for murder, but he fled to the island of Crete. There, he constructed the famous labyrinth (underground maze) for the Cretan king Minos. The king placed the monstrous Minotaur (which was half man and half bull) in the center of the labyrinth and fed it the boys and girls he forced the Athenians to send him each year. When the Athenian hero Theseus arrived in Crete and slew the Minotaur, Daedalus helped his countryman escape from the maze. For this affront, Minos locked the inventor and his young son, Icarus, inside the labyrinth and refused to let them out. The resourceful Daedalus then constructed wings out of wax and feathers and attached them to his and Icarus's backs. The two flew out of the labyrinth, as planned. However, Icarus ignored his father's warning not to fly too close to the sun. Just as Daedalus had feared, the wax in Icarus's wings melted and the youth fell to his death in the sea.

After burying Icarus, Daedalus traveled to the island of Sicily (off southern Italy) and took refuge at the court of Cocalus, king of the city of Camicus. But Minos, still furious with the inventor, managed to discover Daedalus's whereabouts. The Cretan king demanded that Cocalus surrender Daedalus, but Cocalus refused. So Minos besieged the city. Thanks to some inventive defenses erected by Daedalus, however, Camicus proved to be impregnable. Daedalus and Cocalus then hatched a deadly plot. Cocalus pretended to make peace with Minos and invited him into the city to attend a banquet celebrating the treaty. But first, Cocalus insisted, his noble guest must have a comfortable bath to rid himself of the dust of battle. Minos obligingly got into the tub, having no idea that Daedalus had built it. At the appropriate moment, the inventor sent a torrent of boiling water into the tub, causing Minos

to die in agony. Many other inventions and constructions were attributed to Daedalus in ancient times, among them masts and sails for ships, carpentry tools, glue, wooden puppets that could walk, Apollo's temple at Cumae (in western Italy), and a reservoir in Sicily. **See** Minos; Theseus; **also** Minotaur (Chapter 3).

Danae

The daughter of Acrisius, the king of Argos and the brother of Proetus; and the mother of the renowned hero Perseus. **See** Perseus and Medusa (Chapter 6).

Danaus

The son of the Egyptian king Belus, the twin brother of Aegytpus, and one of the most important ancestors of the Greek race. Belus gave Aegyptus the kingdom of Arabia to rule, and he awarded Libya (bordering Egypt in the west) to Danaus. The warlike Aegyptus soon invaded Egypt in an attempt to get his hands on more of his father's lands. Aegyptus had fifty sons, and he suggested that they marry Danaus's fifty daughters, the Danaids. But Danaus suspected that this was his brother's ploy to gain control of Danaus's kingdom. To avoid trouble, therefore, Danaus gathered together his daughters and a few loyal followers and sailed northward to Greece. They landed at Argos because it was the birthplace of Io, a Greek maiden who long before had traveled to Egypt and had started the family line that eventually produced Belus, Aegyptus, and Danaus. The people of Argos made Danaus their king. The inhabitants of the area were subsequently called the Danaoi in his honor.

In time, however, Aegyptus's fifty sons, feeling that they had been cheated of their promised brides, arrived in Argos to claim those maidens. Despite Danaus's and his daughters' protests, the young men forced them to agree to the marriages. Desperate to foil this plan, Danaus instructed each of his daughters to carry a dagger into her wedding bed and stab her new husband to death. All of the young women complied, except for one—the eldest, Hypermnestra. She had come to truly love her husband, Lynceus, so she revealed to him the plot and allowed him to escape. For her disobedience, her father put her on trial; but the Argive court, perhaps swayed by the influence of the love goddess, Aphrodite, acquitted her. Later, Danaus came to accept the marriage and made amends with Hypermnestra and Lynceus.

Meanwhile, the god Hermes and goddess Athena extended forgiveness to Danaus's other forty-nine daughters for the murders they had committed. Danaus wanted to find the girls suitable husbands. To this end, he contrived a contest. Potential husbands had to compete in a footrace, the winner of which could take his pick of the girls. Many footraces were held until all of the Danaids had found husbands. One ancient legend claims that Lynceus eventually avenged his dead brothers by killing Danaus and all of the Danaids, except for Hypermnestra. The Greek playwright Aeschylus told much of this story in his play *The Suppliant Women*. **See** Belus; Io; **also** *The Suppliant Women* (Chapter 5).

Daphnis

A legendary herdsman of Sicily credited with originating pastoral poetry (poems extolling the virtues of the countryside, which later became extremely popular among the Romans). Though ancient versions of Daphnis's origins vary, the most common one claims that he was the son of the god Hermes and a woodland nymph. Several such nymphs brought Daphnis up on pleasant slopes of Mt. Aetna. When he grew into a young man, he was headstrong and made the mistake of bragging that no one could ever make him fall in love. Hearing of this boast, the love deities Aphrodite and Eros made the shepherd fall madly in love with a river nymph named Nais. She agreed to marry Daphnis only if he swore eternal fidelity to her, which he did. But then a local princess named Xenia got the young man drunk, and in his stupor he made love to her. Furious, Nais punished Daphnis by blinding him. Thereafter, he wandered the countryside reciting sad poetry until he fell into a river and drowned.

Other ancient versions of Daphnis's life claimed, variously, that he actually loved Xenia and died of sorrow because she rejected him; that he fell from a cliff, rather than drowned; and that he fell in love with a nymph named Pimplea, who was abducted by pirates. Daphnis searched for Pimplea and eventually found her a slave at the court of Lityerses, king of Phrygia (in Asia Minor). There, with the help of the famous strongman Heracles, Daphnis eliminated Lityerses, saved Pimplea, and ascended the Phrygian throne. **See** Lityerses.

Dardanus

The son of Zeus and Electra (daughter of Atlas, one of the Titans) and the ancestor of the kings of Troy. According to one legend, Dardanus was born in Samothrace (a northern Aegean island) and eventually traveled to Phrygia (in Asia Minor), where he received a hearty welcome from Teucer, the local king. Teucer encouraged Dardanus to marry his daughter Batia and also gave his new son-in-law part of the kingdom. Thereafter, this portion of Phrygia became known, appropriately, as Dardania. Eventually, Dardanus inherited all of Teucer's kingdom. Dardanus's grandson, Tros, sired Ilus, who established the city of Ilium, better known as Troy. And Ilus's grandson, Priam, was king of Troy during the famous siege by the Greeks. Another ancient version, told by Virgil in his *Aeneid,* claims that Italy was Dardanus's birthplace. In Virgil's epic, Dardanus leaves Italy and travels to Asia Minor, where his descendants establish Troy; after the Trojan prince Aeneas escapes the burning Troy, the gods instruct him to search out the homeland of his noble ancestor, Dardanus. **See** Aeneas's Journey to Italy (Chapter 6).

Deiphobus

A son of Troy's King Priam and Queen Hecuba and a prominent warrior in the Trojan War. When the Trojan prince Paris died in the fighting, Deiphobus married Helen, the Greek queen whose abduction by Paris had started the war. After the Trojans dragged the wooden horse (with several Greek soldiers hiding inside) into the city, Helen, who sensed the Greek trick, removed all the weapons from Deiphobus's house. Thus, when her Greek husband, Menelaus, who had climbed out of the horse, arrived to retrieve her, Deiphobus was unable to defend himself and Menelaus slew him. The dead man's body disappeared, but, as told in Virgil's *Aeneid,* the Trojan prince Aeneas encountered Deiphobus's ghost in the Underworld.

Deucalion

A son of the Titan Prometheus and a character similar in some ways to the biblical figure Noah. Deucalion is credited with surviving a flood sent by the gods by building a large boat; he also repopulated the earth after the waters receded. For a more detailed account, **see** The Creation of the Gods and Humans (Chapter 6).

Dido

A princess of the Phoenician city of Tyre who, according to legend, journeyed to North Africa and there founded the great city of Carthage (which would later become Rome's archenemy). When the king of Tyre died, Dido's brother, Pygmalion, ascended the throne. Pygmalion murdered Dido's husband, who was a priest of the Phoenician god Melqart, but Dido, her sister, and some followers escaped. They sailed westward, landed in the North

African region now known as Tunisia, and there erected a fort, the Byrsa, which became the central citadel of the city of Carthage. In his *Aeneid,* the Roman poet Virgil describes the Trojan hero Aeneas's landing in Carthage, Dido's falling passionately in love with him, his decision to leave on his quest for Italy, and her subsequent outrage and suicide. For a detailed account of Dido and Aeneas's relationship, **see** Aeneas's Journey to Italy (Chapter 6).

Diomedes

1. The son of Tydeus (one of the Seven Against Thebes) and a famous Greek champion who helped conquer both Thebes and Troy. Both Diomedes' father and grandfather (Adrastus, king of Argos) died in the Seven's failed attempt to destroy Thebes. To avenge them, when he grew to young manhood Diomedes became one of the Epigoni (the sons of the Seven), which launched another—and this time successful—expedition against Thebes. Later, Diomedes was one of the suitors of the Spartan maiden Helen, but she ended up marrying Menelaus.

When Troy's Prince Paris abducted Helen, initiating the Trojan War, Diomedes, by now king of Argos, led the Greek troops from Argos and Tiryns (located near Argos). During the war, Diomedes distinguished himself on numerous occasions. With the aid of the goddess Athena (who favored the Greeks), he killed the Trojan prince Pandarus, wounded another prince—Aeneas— and even managed to wound the goddess Aphrodite and god Ares (who favored the Trojans). Diomedes also helped his colleague Odysseus rescue the Greek warrior Philoctetes, who had been stranded on an Aegean island.

After Troy's fall, Diomedes returned to Argos to find that his wife had been unfaithful to him (thanks to the influence of Aphrodite, who sought revenge for the wound Diomedes had given her at Troy).

Also, various local nobles contested his claim to the Argive throne. As a result, Diomedes left Argos and traveled to Italy. There, he married a princess of the city of Apulia and, according to some tales, founded the city of Argyripa. **See** Helen; **also** *Seven Against Thebes* (Chapter 5); The Theban Myth Cycle; The Trojan War (Chapter 6).

2. The son of the war god, Ares, and the nymph Cyrene and a king of the city of Bistones in Thrace (in northern Greece). Diomedes owned the four savage, flesh-eating horses that the hero Heracles captured to complete his eighth labor. **See** The Adventures of Heracles (Chapter 6).

Dioscuri

The collective name of the heroes known individually as Castor and Polydeuces to the Greeks and Castor and Pollux to the Romans. In the works of the poets Homer and Hesiod, they were the twin sons of Tyndareos, king of Sparta, and his wife, Leda, as well as the brothers of Helen of Troy and Clytemnestra (who eventually married Agamemnon, king of Mycenae). The term *Dioscuri* comes from the Greek *Dios Kouroi,* meaning "Sons of Zeus." This refers to a later legend in which Polydeuces was that god's son and, therefore, immortal. In this version of their story, Castor, the mortal son of Tyndareos, was mortally wounded and his brother saved him by sharing with him a portion of his immortality (see below). Still another account claimed that they were both Zeus's sons and had been born from an egg, like their sister Helen.

The brothers took part in several exploits. In their youth they sailed with the hero Jason to retrieve the fabulous Golden Fleece. On that voyage, Polydeuces distinguished himself by accepting the challenge of a boxing match with Amycus, king of a land on the southern shore of the Black Sea. An arrogant, violent individual who enjoyed killing his opponents in the ring, Amycus met his match in and lost to Polydeuces. At the conclusion of the voyage, Castor and Polydeuces helped Jason destroy the city of Iolcos to punish its treacherous king, Acastus. And in a later adventure, the brothers saved their sister Helen. The Athenian hero Theseus had carried her off to Attica (the peninsula dominated by Athens); but Castor and Polydeuces rescued her and retaliated by capturing Theseus's own mother, Aethra. Later still, the Dioscuri entered into a dispute with their cousins, Idas and Lynceus. Castor was seriously wounded; meanwhile, Polydeuces, with Zeus's aid, killed Idas and Lynceus, then returned to the dying Castor and conferred part of his own immortality on him, thereby saving him. Thereafter, the two brothers alternated days, staying in the Underworld one day and on Mt. Olympus, home of the gods, the next. Zeus later placed them in the sky as the constellation of Gemini, the twins.

Eventually, these minor gods inspired a popular cult of worshipers in Rome. There, the residents erected a temple to them (usually referred to as the Temple of Castor). The building commemorated the help the Romans believed the twin gods had given them at the Battle of Lake Regillus, fought against the Latins in 496 B.C. According to the popular tale, Castor and Pollux charged the enemy at the head of the Roman cavalry, and only minutes after the Romans had won the battle, the twins appeared many miles away in Rome to deliver the news of the victory. In time, the two gods became the patrons of the well-to-do social order of equestrians (or knights). **See** Helen; **also** Zeus (Chapter 2); The Quest for the Golden Fleece (Chapter 6).

Dirce

The wife of Lycus, regent of the city of Thebes for the child-king Labdacus. Before committing suicide, Nycteus, Lycus's brother, had urged Lycus to find and punish Antiope, Nycteus's daughter (who had given birth to twin boys—Amphion and Zethus—out of wedlock). Lycus tracked down the young woman and brought her back to Thebes, where he made her Dirce's slave. The selfish and cruel Dirce mistreated Antiope terribly until Amphion and Zethus arrived and rescued their mother. When she was safe, they tied Dirce to the horns of a wild bull, which dragged her to death. However, because Dirce had been a follower of Dionysus, that god avenged her death by driving Antiope mad. **See** Amphion and Zethus.

Dorians

A Greek-speaking people who originated in the remote region north of Greece and south of the Danube River and who, it is long believed, invaded Greece at the close of the Bronze Age. In legend, the Dorians were descendants of Dorus, son of Hellen, founder of the Greek race. The classical Greeks (of the fifth and fourth centuries B.C.) believed that in about 1100 B.C. (two generations after the Trojan War), the Dorians descended into southern Greece, accompanied by the sons of Heracles (the Heracleidae). Long before, according to legend, Zeus had promised Heracles that he and his family could rule much of what later came to be known as the Peloponnesus (the southern third of Greece). When other rulers (including Pelops and Agamemnon) ended up ruling the area, the Heracleidae, with Dorian aid, invaded and took over the Peloponnesus.

Beginning in the nineteenth century, modern scholars found evidence that the kingdoms of Bronze Age (or Mycenaean) Greece (with the exception of Athens) had collapsed circa 1100 B.C., initiating the Dark Age of Greece. Therfore, they theorized that the legend of the "Return of the Heracleidae" was based on a distorted but real memory of a Dorian invasion. However, more recent scholarship suggests that other factors (such as civil conflicts or the economic collapse of the Greek kingdoms) destroyed Mycenaean civilization, and that the Dorians were not invaders but opportunists, who took advantage of the power vacuum in Greece and moved in. Once settled there, the Dorians apparently attacked Athens. But they failed to take it. The most famous of the Dorians' descendants were the Spartans, who were themselves often at odds with the Athenians. **See** Aegimius; Codrus; Dorus; Hellen; Heracles; **also** Athens; Peloponnesus; Sparta (Chapter 4).

Dorus

The grandson of Deucalion (survivor of a great flood sent by Zeus); son of Hellen (founder of the Greek race); and initiator of the Dorian branch of Greeks, who were named for him. **See** Dorians; Hellen.

Electra

The daughter of King Agamemnon and Queen Clytemnestra of Mycenae and the sister of Orestes. Electra played a pivotal role in Orestes' murder of Clytemnestra, part of the terrible curse afflicting Agamemnon's family line. The Athenian playwrights Sophocles and Euripides both wrote plays titled *Electra* (which have survived); and she is a prominent character in Euripides' *Orestes* and Aeschylus's *Libation Bearers* as well. When Electra and Orestes were young, she helped him escape the clutches of Clytemnestra and her lover, Aegisthus, who had just murdered the children's father, Agamemnon, and who wanted to kill Orestes, too. Later, when Orestes returned as a young man to seek vengeance, Electra recognized him and helped him dispatch Clytemnestra and

Electra greets her brother Orestes, who has come to Mycenae to seek vengeance against those who killed his father.

Aegisthus. **See** Aegisthus; Agamemnon; Clytemnestra; Orestes; **also** *Electra; Libation Bearers* (Chapter 5); and, for a more complete account of Electra's exploits, **see** The Curse of the House of Atreus (Chapter 6).

Electryon

The son of the renowned hero Perseus and Andromeda, a princess of Joppa in Palestine. Electryon succeeded his father on the throne of Mycenae and bore a daughter, Alcmena, who subsequently gave birth to the strongman Heracles. One day six young men from the Taphian Islands (off Greece's western coast), who were distantly related to Electryon, arrived and demanded that he give them part of his kingdom. When he refused, they stole his cattle. Amphitryon, Alcmena's suitor, got the cattle back, but soon afterward he accidentally killed Electryon with a club. **See** Alcmena; Amphitryon.

Elpenor

The youngest of the warriors who sailed homeward with the hero Odysseus at the conclusion of the Trojan War. When Odysseus was visiting the sorceress Circe on her island, Elpenor got drunk and fell off the roof of Circe's palace. The fall killed the young man. Odysseus forgot to bury him before leaving the island; later, however, when Odysseus visited the Underworld, Elpenor's ghost appeared and implored Odysseus to return to the island and give his body a proper burial. Odysseus did so. **See** The Wanderings of Odysseus (Chapter 6).

Endymion

The son of Calyce (daughter of Aeolus, a mortal to whom Zeus gave control of the winds and who later came to be called the god of the winds) and the king of Elis (a region and city in the northwestern Peloponnesus). Selene, the moon goddess, fell in love with Endymion, partly because of his extreme good looks, and she bore him fifty daughters. She loved him so much, in fact, that she could not bear the thought of his growing old and dying. Thus, she made him fall into an eternal sleep in a cave inside Mt. Latmus (in Asia Minor).

Erechtheus

One of Athens's legendary early kings, whom the classical Athenians associated with a serpent that guarded the goddess Athena. In one ancient tale, Erechtheus was the son of an Athenian king, Pandion. In this version, Erechtheus had many children, including a daughter named Chthonia. When Athens went to war with its neighbor, Eleusis, the Delphic Oracle said that Erechtheus could not attain victory without sacrificing one of his daughters. Thus, he sacrificed Chthonia, whose death allowed Athens to win the war and annex Eleusis. In another ancient tradition, told by Homer, Erechtheus sprang up from the soil without human parents, after which Athena took him into her shrine on the Acropolis (in the temple that later became known as the Erechtheum, after him) as her semidivine consort. Classical sculptors frequently portrayed Erechtheus as a serpent coiled near the goddess's feet. **See** Erichthonius.

Erichthonius

An early king of Athens who was—and still is—often confused with Erechtheus. They may have originally been one person, or at least may have derived from the same early legend. Later, however, different stories grew up around each king. According to one such story, Erichthonius was born of the sperm of Hephaestos, god of the forge. The sperm fell to the ground while Hephaestos was attempting to embrace the goddess Athena, and Erichthonius, half human and half snake, grew from the spot where the sperm landed. Athena then took pity on the deformed lad and raised him in her temple (later called the Erechtheum) on the Acropolis. After Erichthonius grew up, he became the city's king and initiated the Panathenaea, Athens's primary religious festival, which paid homage to Athena. Another story claims that Erichthonius invented the chariot; and for this noteworthy achievement, the gods later placed him in the sky as the constellation Auriga, the charioteer. **See** Erechtheus.

Erigone

1. The daughter of Icarius, an Athenian peasant credited with being the first human to cultivate wine grapes. In the tale, fertil-ity god Dionysus showed Icarius how to grow the grapes. But when the man offered some of his first batch of wine to his neighbors, they thought it was some kind of poison and killed Icarius. Meanwhile, Dionysus seduced Erigone by appearing to her as a cluster of grapes, which she ate and thereby took him inside her. Afterward she searched for her father; upon finding his body, she was so stricken with grief that she hanged herself.

2. The daughter of Clytemnestra (queen of Mycenae) and Clytemnestra's lover, Aegisthus. Clytemnestra's son Orestes killed both her and Aegisthus and would have killed Erigone, too, had the goddess Artemis not saved her. Soon afterward, the young girl became a priestess of Artemis. Later, according to one story, Erigone took Orestes to court for having killed Clytemnestra, but she failed to get a conviction. Another version claims that Erigone actually slept with Orestes and bore him a son—Penthilus. For more about Orestes' murder of his mother and her lover, **see** The Curse of the House of Atreus (Chapter 6).

Eteocles

One of Oedipus's two sons, the brother of Antigone, and the king of Thebes during the attack of the Seven Against Thebes. After Oedipus's fall from the throne (after learning that he had married his mother and had killed his father), he stayed near Thebes. Out of pity (and following custom), each day Oedipus's sons, Eteocles and Polynices, brought him a portion of the best meat served in the palace. One day, though, they gave him the worst cut of meat. Furious, Oedipus pronounced a curse on the young men, predicting that they would eventually kill each other. This prediction came true. When old enough to rule, Eteocles and Polynices agreed to share the throne, each reigning in alternate years. But at the end of his first term, Eteocles refused to surrender the kingship.

Aided by Adrastus, king of Argos, and five other champions, Polynices marched on and assaulted Thebes. But the attackers suffered defeat. Eteocles and Polynices met in single combat and slew each other, fulfilling their father's curse.

Although the preceding is the most common version of Eteocles' and Polynices' story, some of the details vary in other ancient accounts. In the plays of Sophocles, for instance, Oedipus's brother-in-law, Creon (who acts as regent for Eteocles and Polynices when they are still boys), banishes Oedipus immediately after the latter's fall; and Oedipus curses the boys for failing to intervene on his behalf. **See** Adrastus; Creon 2; Oedipus; **also** *Antigone; Seven Against Thebes* (Chapter 5); and, for a more detailed account of these happenings, **see** The Theban Myth Cycle (Chapter 6).

Europa

The daughter of Agenor, king of the Phoenician city of Tyre, and mother of the Cretan king Minos. One day the god Zeus spied Europa frolicking with her friends at the beach and found himself strongly attracted to her. Changing himself into a bull, he walked up to the girls, who, thinking it an unusually handsome beast, petted it. Europa liked the bull so much that she decided to ride it. But as soon as she climbed onto its back, the beast suddenly leapt into the sea. With the startled girl still clinging to it, the bull swam all the way to Crete, where it finally revealed itself as Zeus. The two made love several times, producing three sons—Minos, Rhadamanthys, and Sarpedon. Minos later became king of the island and built the famous labyrinth (underground maze), and Europa gave her name to the continent of Europe. As for Zeus, he placed his temporary alter ego, the bull, in the sky as the constellation of Taurus. Meanwhile, Europa's distraught father sent his son, Cadmus, to Greece to find the girl; Cadmus ended up

establishing the great city of Thebes. **See** The Theban Myth Cycle (Chapter 6).

Eurydice

The wife of Creon, regent of Thebes following the fall of King Oedipus. Creon condemned Oedipus's daughter Antigone to death (for disobeying Creon's order not to bury her dead brother Polynices). Hearing this, Creon's and Eurydice's son, Haemon, who loved Antigone, loudly protested, but the king refused to listen. After Antigone's death, Haemon committed suicide in front of his father. Mad with grief, Eurydice cursed Creon for causing their son's untimely end and then took her own life. **See** The Theban Myth Cycle (Chapter 6).

Eurystheus

A descendant of the hero Perseus and a king of Tiryns and Mycenae (in the region of the eastern Peloponnesus known as the Argolid). Zeus had promised that his son, the heroic Heracles, would rule the Argolid when he grew to manhood. But Zeus's wife, Hera, jealous that her husband had conceived the boy with a mortal woman (Alcmena), contrived to have Eurystheus inherit the Argolid instead. Not surprisingly, Heracles resented this and came to hate Eurystheus. Soon afterward, in a fit of madness, Heracles slew his own wife and children; and, according to the Delphic Oracle, he had to pay a hefty price to atone for the murders. Though he hated Eurystheus, Heracles had to become his servant for twelve years and perform for him twelve seemingly impossible labors. Later, after Heracles had successfully completed the tasks and joined the gods on Mt. Olympus, Eurystheus persecuted some of the hero's sons (by a second wife); one of these young men, Hyllus, killed Eurystheus in battle. (In Euripides' play the *Children of Heracles,* Eurystheus is captured and later executed.) **See** *Children of Heracles* (Chapter 5); **also** The Adventures of Heracles (Chapter 6).

Ganymede

The son of Tros, founder of the city of Troy (or, in another version, a brother of Priam, king of the city during the Trojan War). According to Homer, Ganymede was so handsome that the gods (or Zeus himself) sent an eagle to abduct him, and he became a cupbearer on Mt. Olympus. In return for the lad, Zeus gave his father, Tros, two immortal horses and a golden vine that Hephaestos, god of the forge, had fashioned. Later, Zeus placed Ganymede in the sky as the constellation of Aquarius, the water carrier; the eagle that had taken Ganymede to Olympus became Aquilla, a constellation alongside Aquarius.

Glaucus

1. A fisherman who lived in Anthedon, near Thebes. One day Glaucus caught and killed a fish and laid it down on some unfamiliar-looking herbs growing near the shore. The fish soon came back to life. Intrigued by this, Glaucus ate some of the herbs himself and suddenly grew fish fins and a tail; he also became immortal and very wise. Thereafter, he gave advice to various sailors and travelers, reportedly including Jason's Argonauts and the Spartan king Menelaus.

2. The son of Sisyphus (founder of the city of Corinth) and a king of Corinth. Glaucus raised the hero Bellerophon without realizing that the boy had been secretly sired by the sea god Poseidon. Later, Glaucus entered his chariot, pulled by mares he had never allowed to breed, in a race in the funeral games for Pelias, former king of Iolcos. When Glaucus lost the race, the horses turned on him, killing and then eating him. After that, his ghost was said to haunt the stadium at Isthmia (near Corinth) and to frighten horses rounding the far turn in chariot races.

3. A son of the Cretan king Minos. As a small child, Glaucus accidentally fell into a large storage jar of honey and drowned. The distraught Minos heard that a magician named Polyidus was visiting Crete, so Minos summoned him, and ordered that he find a way to bring the boy back to life. Polyidus managed to do so using a magic herb similar to the one discovered by another character named Glaucus (see above).

4. In Homer's *Iliad,* one of the hero Bellerophon's grandsons and the commander of the army of Lycia (in southern Asia Minor), which fought in the Trojan War as an ally of Troy's King Priam. When Glaucus found himself in single combat with the Greek warrior Diomedes, the two men suddenly realized that their grandfathers had been friends. So Glaucus and Diomedes stopped fighting and swore to avoid each other for the rest of the war. To seal the bargain, they exchanged armor. **See** Diomedes 1.

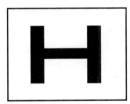

Hector

The eldest son of Priam and Hecuba, king and queen of Troy, and the mightiest of the Trojan warriors during the famous war with the Greeks. As Homer tells it in his *Iliad,* Hector played a major role in the early phases of the fighting. Later, after bidding farewell to his wife, Andromache, and small son, Astyanax (one of the most touching and memorable scenes in Western literature), Hector led several offensives against the enemy. These climaxed in his killing of Patroclus, the close friend of the great war-

The heart-rending farewell of the mighty Hector to his wife, Andromache, and infant son, Astyanax (held by a nurse).

rior Achilles. In retaliation, Achilles entered the fray, led a Greek offensive that pushed the Trojans back, and met Hector in single combat outside the city walls. Achilles managed to slay Hector, then dragged the corpse behind his chariot. (The death of Troy's greatest champion foreshadowed the city's eventual fall.) Later, Achilles released Hector's body to King Priam; the Trojans gave the fallen hero a funeral fitting his stature. **See** Achilles; Andromache; **also** *Iliad* (Chapter 5); and, for a more detailed account of Hector's exploits, **see** The Trojan War (Chapter 6).

Hecuba

(or Hacabe) The wife of Troy's King Priam and the mother of nineteen of his children, among them Hector, Paris, Cassandra, Helenus, Troilus, Creusa, and Deiphobus. In Homer's *Iliad,* Hecuba remains mostly in the background as a dutiful wife, advancing into the foreground now and then to grieve for a slain son. In Euripides' *Trojan Women,* after the Greeks sack Troy, Hecuba becomes a slave of King

Odysseus of Ithaca; and she has to watch as the Greeks sacrifice one of her daughters and Hector's young son at the tomb of the Greek hero Achilles. In another play, *Hecuba,* Euripides tells how, after the war, Hecuba's youngest son, Polydorus, was found dead, having been murdered by a Greek king named Polymestor. A later legend said that when she died, Hecuba turned into a fiery-eyed dog that wandered through Polymestor's kingdom terrorizing people. **See** Priam; **also** The Trojan War (Chapter 6).

Helen

The daughter of Zeus and the mortal Leda (wife of Tyndareos, king of Sparta); the wife of Sparta's King Menelaus; the sister of the heroes Castor and Polydeuces (the Dioscuri); and a central character in the legendary saga of the Trojan War. In the most common version of Helen's birth, Zeus visited Leda disguised as a swan. They made love, and later the young woman laid an egg, from which Helen hatched. (Another version claims that Zeus mated with the goddess Nemesis, who was disguised as a goose; she laid the egg containing Helen; and some shepherds brought the egg to Leda, who raised the child as her own.) These stories supported ancient beliefs that Helen was semidivine. And she and her brothers, the Dioscuri, were worshiped as minor gods in Sparta for centuries.

However, later literature, beginning with Homer's *Iliad,* portrayed Helen as a real person. As a young Spartan woman, she became widely known for her phenomenal beauty and, not surprisingly, became the object of many men's attentions. The Athenian hero Theseus abducted her and took her to Athens, for example; but Castor and Polydeuces soon rescued her. Helen then attracted numerous suitors of noble stature, who thronged Tyndareos's court in hopes of winning her hand. She chose a wealthy former royal prince of Mycenae, Menelaus. Not long after that, the aged Tyndareos willingly abdicated his throne, giving it to Menelaus, which elevated Helen to the position of queen.

Several years passed. Then, one day while Menelaus was away, a Trojan prince, Paris, arrived in Sparta and either persuaded or forced Helen to return with him to Troy. (One story says that the love goddess, Aphrodite, manipulated both Helen and Paris, causing them to fall in love.) Reaching Paris's home, the couple formally married, though most Trojan leaders objected to his taking a Spartan bride. Meanwhile, the enraged Menelaus and his brother, Agamemnon (king of Mycenae), rallied the leaders of Greece to retrieve Helen, initiating the Trojan War.

Years later, near the close of the conflict, the Greek warrior Philoctetes slew Paris, and Helen married Paris's brother, Deiphobus. Soon afterward, however, the Greeks won the conflict and sacked Troy, killing Deiphobus along with many other Trojan leaders. Menelaus took Helen back to Sparta, where, according to most ancient accounts, they led a relatively uneventful and happy life. **See** Leda; Deiphobus; Dioscuri; Menelaus; Paris; **also** Aphrodite (Chapter 2); *Helen; Iliad; Trojan Women* (Chapter 5); The Trojan War (Chapter 6).

Helenus

In Homer's *Iliad,* one of the sons of Troy's King Priam and Queen Hecuba. Helenus possessed the gift of prophecy (because snakes had licked his ears while he lay sleeping in one of Apollo's temples). Taking advantage of that gift, Helenus warned his brother, Paris, not to go to Sparta because it would cause trouble; and, of course, it did since Paris abducted Sparta's Queen Helen and thereby started the Trojan War. For a few years, Helenus fought bravely in the conflict. Eventually, though, the Greeks captured him, and he told their leaders that he foresaw their final victory. Nevertheless, he added, said victory would not occur unless they rescued the Greek warrior Philoctetes from an island on which he had been stranded and brought him and his special bow and arrows back to Troy. (The Greeks did this, ensuring their victory.)

After Troy's fall, Helenus became the captive of Achilles' son, Neoptolemus. Helenus and Neoptolemus became friends, and the latter allowed Helenus to marry Andromache, widow of the Trojan prince (and Helenus's brother), Hector. Helenus also built a settlement in Epirus (in northwestern Greece). It was there (as told in Virgil's *Aeneid*) that another Trojan prince, Aeneas, visited Helenus; during the visit, Helenus predicted that Aeneas's voyage west would be long and difficult. **See** Neoptolemus; **also** Aeneas's Journey to Italy (Chapter 6).

Hellen

The eldest son of Deucalion (survivor of the great flood sent by Zeus) and the traditional founder of the Greek race. The classical Greeks believed that Hellen's name was the derivation of Hellenes ("Sons of Hellen"), the term they used to describe themselves, although the word more likely came from Hellas, the ancient Greek name for mainland Greece. According to legend, Hellen married a nymph, Orseis, and by her fathered three sons—Dorus, Aeolus, and Xuthus. Dorus subsequently gave rise to the Dorian Greeks and Aeolus to the Aeolian Greeks; and Xuthus's sons, Ion and Achaeus, spawned the Ionian and Achaean Greeks, respectively.

Heracleidae

The sons and daughters of the heroic strongman Heracles. In legend, they joined the Dorians (Greek-speaking people from far to the north) in an invasion of the Peloponnesus to claim the lands that Zeus had earlier promised to their father. The Greek playwright Euripides told their story in his *Children of Heracles.* **See** Dorians; **also** Peloponnesus (Chapter 4); *Children of Heracles* (Chapter 5); The Adventures of Heracles (Chapter 6).

Heracles

The most famous of all Greek heroes and a legendary strongman whose deeds figure in dozens of Greek and Roman myths. (The Romans called him Hercules.) For a detailed synopsis of his background and exploits, **see** The Adventures of Heracles (Chapter 6).

Hero and Leander

Two star-crossed lovers who died tragically, as told by Musaeus, a fifth-century A.D. Greek poet. Hero was a priestess of the love goddess, Aphrodite, at Sestos, on the Greek shore of the Hellespont (the Dardanelles Strait); Leander was a young man who dwelled at Abydos, a town on the other side of the waterway. Hero's beauty was so striking that both Apollo, god of prophecy, and the love god, Eros, vied for her attentions; but she paid no attention to them, feeling that she was a mortal and should therefore marry a mortal man. One day Leander came to the temple in Sestos, where Hero served. The two saw each other and fell deeply in love at first sight. Hero's parents, however, would hear nothing about their daughter, an important priestess, marrying a common character like Leander, and they forbade her from seeing him.

The young lovers refused to be kept apart, though. They managed to invent a series of signals to facilitate their secret nightly meetings; whenever Hero hung a lantern in the tower of the temple, Leander would swim across the Hellespont and stay with her for a few hours before swimming back. This went on for some time without incident. One fateful night, however, a storm blew up out of the north while Leander was out swimming in the middle of the Hellespont. He tried to keep his eyes focused on the distant lantern in the temple, but the howling winds extinguished the lantern's flame and the young man lost his way. Valiantly he tried to keep his head above the waves, but the storm was too much for him and he eventually sank and drowned. The next morning his lifeless body washed ashore on the beach where Hero was standing. Grief-stricken, she climbed the temple tower one last time and threw herself off, ending her life.

Hippolyte

(or Hippolyta) Queen of the Amazons, a legendary race of warrior women. The Greek strongman Heracles acquired her girdle as part of his ninth labor. In one ancient version of the story, a battle over the girdle ended with Hippolyte's death. In another, she survived and later led the Amazons in an attack on Athens to avenge the abduction of her sister, Antiope, by the Athenian hero Theseus. (Still another version claims that, after the assault on the city failed, Hippolyte married Theseus and gave birth to the tragic Greek character Hippolytus.) **See** Amazons; Hippolytus; Theseus; **also** *Hippolytus* (Chapter 5); The Adventures of Heracles; The Exploits of Theseus (Chapter 6).

Hippolytus

The son of the Athenian hero and king Theseus and, in some ancient stories, the queen of the Amazons, Hippolyte. In his *Hippolytus,* the Greek playwright Euripides dramatized the legend in which Theseus's second wife, Phaedra, fell in love with and propositioned the grown-up Hippolytus. He refused her advances. But

Theseus suspected that it was his son who had made the advances, so he banished the young man, who died shortly afterward. In an ancient Roman version of the tale, the goddess Diana (the Greek goddess Artemis) and the god Aesculapius (the Greek god Asclepius) brought Hippolytus back to life and the young man moved to the plain of Latium (south of Rome). There, he became king of the town of Aricia. For a more detailed account of Euripides' version, **see** *Hippolytus* (Chapter 5).

Horatii

A noble Roman family that distinguished itself by its patriotism and heroism during the semilegendary wars of the Roman monarchy (the Roman realm ruled by kings before the Republic was established ca. 509 B.C.). The events of the myth were attributed to the reign of King Tullus Hostilius (673–642 B.C.). Rome was at war with the city of Alba Longa, in the Latium plain, lying south of the city. After a number of skirmishes, both the Romans and the Albans decided it would be better to conserve their manpower to fight their common enemy—the Etruscans. Thus, each side chose three champions who would fight to decide the war's outcome. The three Romans were members of the Horatii family, and the three Albans came from another noble family—the Curiatii. Two of the Horatii died in the battle; the third was ultimately victorious. "The cheering ranks of the Roman army," the Roman historian Livy recalled, "welcomed back their champion. . . . Alba was subject now to her Roman mistress." (*History of Rome from Its Foundation* 1.26)

Horatius

(Publius Horatius Cocles) A legendary Roman hero credited with saving Rome from the invading Etruscans under King Lars Porsenna, circa 508–504 B.C. In the patriotic story, which is likely fabricated or at least highly exaggerated, Horatius single-handedly held the main bridge leading into the city, keeping the enemy army at bay until his companions finished demolishing the structure. According to the Roman historian Livy, "The enemy forces came pouring down the hill. . . . Horatius acted promptly. . . . Proudly he took his stand at the outer edge of the bridge . . . [and] the advancing enemy paused in sheer astonishment at such reckless courage." (*History of Rome from Its Foundation* 2.10) Livy said that Horatius managed to swim to safety. Another ancient version claimed that he drowned. Either way, his thankful countrymen honored him with a statue in the city's main square. **See** Lars Porsenna.

Hyacinthus

An early Spartan prince who was said to be so handsome that Thamynis (a traveling minstrel), the god Apollo, and Zephyrus (the west wind) all fell in love with the young man. Hyacinthus returned such feelings only to Apollo. Jealous, Zephyrus blew a discus that Apollo had thrown off course so that it struck and killed Hyacinthus. The grief-stricken Apollo caused some drops of the dead youth's blood to grow into a flower, the hyacinth. The petals bore the inscription *ai ai,* or "alas!"

Hylas

The son of Theodamas, king of Dryopes (a pre-Greek people who inhabited Doris, northeast of Delphi in central Greece), and, for a time, the faithful companion of the hero Heracles. Heracles fought and killed Theodamas, after which the strongman took the boy in as his personal squire. The two eventually joined the Argonauts' expedition. When the *Argo* stopped briefly at Mysia (on the northern coast of Asia Minor), Heracles sent Hylas to fetch some water. Because the boy was so good-looking, some local water nymphs fell instantly in love with him and pulled him into their pond. When the *Argo* moved on, Heracles stayed to search for the lad but never found him. In historical times, the people of Mysia held an annual ritual in which they searched for Hylas in honor of Heracles' memory. **See** The Quest for the Golden Fleece (Chapter 6).

Hyperboreans

According to legend, a people who lived a happy existence in a land far to the north of Greece. The term came from the words *hyper borean,* meaning "beyond the north wind." The early Greeks believed that the god Apollo spent the winter months with the Hyperboreans. In the story of Perseus and Medusa, Perseus visited the Hyperboreans, as did the hero Heracles while chasing the Cerynthian Hind (huge deer). According to the Greek poet Pindar, the Hyperboreans lived a blessed life without any sickness or pain. And some Greeks came to believe that winning the special favor of a god might be rewarded by their spending the afterlife in Hyperborea.

Hypsipyle

A legendary queen of the Greek island of Lemnos. As a young woman, Hypsipyle, along with the island's other women, neglected to worship Aphrodite and thereby incurred that goddess's wrath. Aphrodite polluted the women with a foul odor, which drove their husbands away and into the arms of foreign women. The Lemnian women then retaliated by slaying all of the men on Lemnos; Hypsipyle, however, spared her father, King Thaos, and helped him escape. Later, Jason and his Argonauts arrived on the island and stayed for a year. They married many of the local women, in spite of the stink, and Hypsipyle bore Jason two sons.

In another version, the other Lemnian women, having discovered that Hypsipyle had let King Thaos live, punished her by selling her as a slave to King Lycurgus of Nemea (in the northeastern Peloponnesus). One day, while she was nursing the king's son, the warriors later known as the Seven

Against Thebes happened by on their way to attack that famous city. While Hypsipyle fetched some water for the thirsty men, a snake killed the child. Discovering the tiny body, the Seven buried it; and they honored the dead boy by establishing the Nemean Games, which subsequently became, along with the Olympics, one of the "big four" athletic competitions of ancient Greece. Not long afterward, Hypsipyle's sons found her living in servitude and carried her away to safety.

Icarius

1. An Athenian farmer who legend claims was the first human to grow wine grapes, thanks to knowledge given to him by the fertility god, Dionysus. For more details, **see** Erigone 1.

2. A Spartan prince and the father of Penelope, wife of the hero Odysseus. Icarius did not want his daughter to go to Ithaca (Odysseus's island kingdom), so he tried to persuade Odysseus and Penelope to stay with him. But they refused and left to make their home in Ithaca.

Icarus

The son of the renowned Athenian inventor and sculptor Daedalus. Icarus escaped from the Cretan labyrinth by flying with wings fashioned by his father, but the boy later fell to his death. **See** Daedalus.

Idomeneus

A king of Crete, a grandson of King Minos, and the commander of the Cretan forces during the Trojan War. Though one of the oldest of the Greek leaders in the conflict, Idomeneus distinguished himself in the fighting. He and his squire, Meriones, were among the select group of soldiers who hid inside the Trojan Horse and climbed out in the middle of the night to open the gates for the Greek army. Two different versions of Idomeneus's homecoming existed. In the first, he sailed safely home to Crete, where his remaining years were uneventful. The second version claims that a huge storm struck his ships on their homeward voyage; Idomeneus swore to the sea god Poseidon that he would sacrifice the first living thing that he encountered on Crete if the god would only save him and his men. When the travelers escaped with their lives and made it to Crete, the first living thing they encountered was the king's son. Reluctantly, Idomeneus kept his vow and killed the boy; but his countrymen banished him for this act. According to the Roman poet Virgil, Idomeneus subsequently settled on Italy's southern coast.

Io

The daughter of the river god Inachus (whom legend claimed was also the first king of Argos) and a mortal woman, Melia. As a young woman, Io became a priestess of the goddess Hera. However, Hera's husband, the mighty Zeus, noticed Io and decided to seduce her. Whispering to her at night in her dreams, he begged her to come lie with him in some nearby meadows. Hera soon discovered what was afoot, though, and, as she often did with other mortal women whom Zeus chased after, she sought to punish the young woman. To prevent this, Zeus turned Io into a white heifer (young cow).

However, the ruse did not fool Hera. To make sure that Io did not remain still long enough for her husband to seduce her, the goddess sent gadflies to sting the heifer and keep it moving. Hera also called in Argus, a giant with a hundred eyes, to keep watch over Io. Zeus responded by sending his messenger, Hermes, who played lullabies on his flute until all of Argus's eyes closed in sleep. Then, Hermes cut off the giant's head.

Unfortunately, this did not help either Io or Zeus very much because Hera's gadflies kept driving the heifer from place to place. She traveled hundreds of miles until finally reaching Egypt. There, Zeus changed her back into a woman. They had a son together—Epaphus, the ancestor of Danaus, who became a famous king of Argos. (This was the story as it was related by the Greek playwright Aeschylus in his *Prometheus Bound.* In the version by the Roman poet Ovid, some of the details differed; for instance, Ovid told how, after Hermes slew Argus, Hera placed the giant's many eyes on the tail of her symbol, the peacock.) **See** Argus 1 (Chapter 3).

Ion

The son of Xuthus (son of Hellen, founder of the Greek race) and the ancestor of the Ionian branch of Greeks. One version of Ion's origins says that Xuthus went to Athens and married Creusa, the daughter of King Erechtheus. They had two sons— Ion and Achaeus. Ion later settled in the northern Peloponnesus (then called Aegialus); after becoming king of the region, he renamed the inhabitants Ionians, after himself. The Athenians soon asked Ion to return to their city to help them fight a war with their neighbor, Eleusis. Ion died in the fighting. Years later, Achaeus's descendants drove the Ionians eastward, and they crossed the Aegean Sea to the coast of Asia Minor, which became known as Greek Ionia. The other version of Ion's story, which Euripides told in his play *Ion,* claims that Apollo raped Creusa, producing Ion. She left the baby to die in a cave beneath the Acropolis. However, Apollo asked Hermes to take the infant to Delphi for safekeeping; several years later, Xuthus went there, and through the oracle, Apollo declared that the man should take the boy in and raise him. **See** Creusa 1; Hellen; Xuthus; **also** *Ion* (Chapter 5).

Iphigenia

The ill-fated daughter of Agamemnon and Clytemnestra, king and queen of Mycenae. Agamemnon sacrificed the young girl to the goddess Artemis to ensure favorable winds for his ships bound for Troy. This action later had terrible consequences for the family. For more details, **see** The Curse of the House of Atreus; The Trojan War (Chapter 6).

Jason

The hero who led the famous expedition of the *Argo* and its crew (the Argonauts) to find the fabulous Golden Fleece. Jason was the son of Aeson, who should have become the king of Iolcos (in Thessaly) when the old king (Aeson's father) died. But Aeson's half brother, Pelias, usurped the throne. Fearing for the life of her infant son, Jason's mother secretly sent him to the kindly centaur Chiron to raise; meanwhile, she told Pelias and his courtiers that the child was dead. When Jason grew to young manhood, he returned to Iolcos to claim the throne, which marked the beginning of his famous adventures. Jason's childhood and his quest for the Golden Fleece were told by Apollonius of Rhodes in his *Argonautica;* the events of Jason's life after his return to Greece appear in Euripides' play *Medea.* **See** Medea; **also** Chiron (Chapter 3); Iolcos (Chapter 4); Apollonius of Rhodes, *Argonautica* 1; *Medea* (Chapter 5); and, for a full account of the voyage of the *Argo,* **see** The Quest for the Golden Fleece (Chapter 6).

Jocasta

The wife of the Theban king Laius and later the mother and the wife of another Theban ruler, Oedipus. Jocasta bore Oedipus two sons—Eteocles and Polynices—and two daughters—Antigone and Ismene. For Jocasta's tragic story, **see** Oedipus; **also** *Oedipus the King* (Chapter 5); The Theban Myth Cycle (Chapter 6).

Laius

The king of Thebes following the brief reign of Amphion and Zethus (sons of Zeus and a mortal woman, Antiope), the husband of Jocasta, and the father of Oedipus. Laius left the infant Oedipus outside to die; the child survived, however, and as a young man he ended up killing Laius (not realizing that the old man was actually his father). Both men, it turned out, attempted to subvert divine prophecies and paid heavy prices for their insolence. For more about Laius's tragic story, **see** Oedipus; **also** *Oedipus the King* (Chapter 5); The Theban Myth Cycle (Chapter 6).

Laocoön

A Trojan prince who was a priest of Poseidon (or, in some versions, Apollo) and who warned his countrymen not to accept the gift of the Trojan Horse (or Wooden Horse) left by the Greeks in the tenth year of the Trojan War. Pretending that they had given up the siege, the Greeks sailed away, leaving one of their number, Sinon, behind. He claimed he was a deserter and that the horse was an offering to the goddess Athena. If the Trojans dragged it into the city, he said, it would bring them good luck. But Laocoön warned that Sinon was lying and urged the Trojans not to touch the horse. At that moment, two huge serpents sprang up from the nearby sea and attacked and killed Laocoön and his two

Now in the Vatican Museum, this magnificent version of the death of Laocoön and his sons was carved in the first century A.D. by sculptors from the Greek island of Rhodes.

young sons. Various ancient sources gave different reasons for the attack. One said the gods punished Laocoön for disobeying them on an earlier occasion. Another claimed that Athena arranged for the death of the man and his sons to make the Trojans believe Sinon's story and drag the Wooden Horse into the city. In any case, the Trojans did just that, and it sealed their doom.

The death of Laocoön and his sons is the subject of one of the finest and most famous sculptures in history. Carved in the first century A.D. by three Greek sculptors from the island of Rhodes, it was discovered in Rome in 1506 and now rests in the Vatican Museum in that city. For the events leading up to Laocoön's death, **see** Aeneas's Journey to Italy; The Trojan War (Chapter 6).

Laomedon

An early king of Troy and the father of Priam, who sat on the city's throne during the Trojan War. At one point, the gods Poseidon and Apollo fought with Zeus, and he punished them by forcing them to work for a year in the service of a mortal man. Poseidon and Apollo went to Laomedon and offered to build strong defensive walls around Troy, which had none at the time. When the deities had finished the task, however, the king refused to pay them, which had been part of the deal. Apollo responded by sending a plague to ravage the city. Poseidon's punishment took the form of a large sea serpent. Laomedon was forced to chain his daughter, Hesione, to a rock, where she would become the creature's next meal. Luckily for the young woman, however, the renowned hero Heracles happened by and saved her in the nick of time. To repay the strongman for this noble deed, Laomedon promised to give him some special horses that Zeus had earlier bestowed on him. But once more, Laomedon unwisely went back on his word and rescinded the offer. For this, Heracles returned later with an army, besieged the city, and killed Laomedon. The strongman also slew the king's sons, except for Priam. **See** Apollo; Poseidon (Chapter 2); **also** The Adventures of Heracles (Chapter 6).

Lapiths

An early tribe of Greeks who inhabited the northern portion of Thessaly (in central Greece). When they invited their neighbors, the centaurs (creatures half man and half horse), to a royal wedding, the creatures tried to abduct the bride and other Lapith women. However, the Lapith men rescued the women and drove the centaurs away, an episode that became a frequent and popular subject in classical Greek art (including several sculpted panels on the Parthenon temple in Athens). In another episode, the Lapiths invaded the region of Doris (south of Thessaly) ruled by King Aegimius, but the hero Heracles drove them out. **See** Aegimius; **also** centaur (Chapter 3); The Adventures of Heracles (Chapter 6).

Lars Porsenna

A king of the Etruscan city of Clusium (north of Rome) and likely a real historical person, although some of the deeds attributed to him are probably distorted or fabricated. Shortly after the establishment of the Roman Republic (ca. 509 B.C.), Porsenna invaded Roman territory, but the Romans and their neighbors eventually forced him to retreat. **See** Cloelia; Horatius; **also** Rome (Chapter 4).

Latinus

An early Italian king who became the father-in-law of Aeneas, founder of the Roman race. Various versions of Latinus's origins circulated in ancient times. Some said he was the son of the Greek hero Odysseus and the sorceress Circe; others claimed that he was a son of Heracles; and the Roman epic poet Virgil said Latinus was the son of the Roman god Faunus. Accounts of Latinus's dealings with Aeneas also differed. According to Virgil, the king and his wife, Amata, wanted their daughter, Lavinia, to marry an Italian prince named Turnus. Aeneas, however, fought Latinus and Turnus, and at the conclusion of the war Latinus had no choice but to allow Lavinia to marry Aeneas. In the Roman historian Livy's version, by contrast, Latinus joined Aeneas against Turnus and died during the fighting. The plain of Latium (south of Rome), the scene of most of these events, was said to be named for Latinus. For a fuller account of Virgil's version of the story, **see** *Aeneid* (Chapter 5); **also** Aeneas's Journey to Italy (Chapter 6).

Lavinia

The daughter of Latinus and the wife of Aeneas after Aeneas had won a war against the Latin (early Italian) tribes in the region of Latium (south of the future site of Rome). **See** Latinus; **also** *Aeneid* (Chapter 5); Aeneas's Journey to Italy (Chapter 6).

Leda

The daughter of Tyndareos, king of Sparta, and the mother of Clytemnestra (later the wife of Agamemnon, king of Mycenae), Helen of Troy, and the Dioscuri (Castor and Polydeuces). Zeus was said to have been the father of some of these children; however, ancient sources differ on which ones. Some accounts claim that Leda laid an egg from which Helen hatched (but others say that a goddess named Nemesis laid the egg). **See** Dioscuri; Helen; **also** Nemesis; Zeus (Chapter 2).

Lityerses

The son of Midas, the legendary king of Phrygia (in Asia Minor). After becoming king, Lityerses required that all strangers to his kingdom (or even some of his own subjects) compete with him in harvesting grain. If they were unable to harvest as much or more than Lityerses, he had them killed. One stranger who entered this competition was the shepherd Daphnis (in one of several variations of Daphnis's story), who had come to Phrygia looking for his beloved, Pimplea. But the hero Heracles, who was visiting Phrygia at the time, offered to take Daphnis's place in the contest. Heracles won, killed Lityerses, and placed Daphnis on the Phrygian throne. **See** Daphnis.

Lotus-eaters

In Homer's *Odyssey,* the Lotus-eaters inhabit a fabulous island and live on the fruit of the lotus plant, which is said to cause forgetfulness. After landing on the island, some of Odysseus's men eat the fruit. Soon, they forget why they have come and where they are going and express the desire to remain forever in Lotus-land. Odysseus has to drag them back to their ships by force. **See** The Wanderings of Odysseus (Chapter 6).

Lucretia

In Roman legend, the wife of Lucius Tarquinius Collatinus (a Roman noble) and a key figure in the events surrounding the fall of the Roman monarchy and rise of the Roman Republic. Her rape by the king's son set in motion the revolution led by her husband and the great patriot Lucius Junius Brutus. **See** Brutus, Lucius Junius; Tarquinius Superbus, Lucius; **also** Rome (Chapter 4).

Lynceus

1. One of the fifty sons of the Egyptian prince Aegyptus. Lynceus was the only one of the fifty to survive his wedding night after he and his brothers had married the fifty daughters of Aegyptus's brother, Danaus. For the full story, **see** Danaus.

2. The son of Aphareus, king of Messenia (in the Peloponnesus), and the younger brother of another Messenian prince, Idas. For years, the brothers were inseparable. Together, they eventually joined the crew of Jason's ship, the *Argo,* and took part in the famous quest for the Golden Fleece. Lynceus proved particularly useful because he possessed unusually keen eyesight, which allowed him to see great distances. Lynceus and Idas died during a fight with their cousins, the Dioscuri (Castor and Polydeuces). **See** Dioscuri.

Marpessa

A daughter of the river god Evenus and the object of the love of both a god and a mortal. Idas, brother of Lynceus (both of them

princes of Messenia), fell in love with Marpessa and carried her away on a flying chariot (supplied by the sea god Poseidon). Apollo, who also loved Marpessa, chased down the chariot and was about to kill Idas when Zeus intervened. The king of the gods allowed the young woman to choose between the two suitors; she chose Idas, whom she married. After Idas was killed in a fight with the Dioscuri, Marpessa committed suicide. **See** Dioscuri; Lynceus 2.

Medea

The daughter of King Aeetes of Colchis (on the coast of the Black Sea), a beautiful sorceress, and a lover of the Greek hero Jason. Medea first appears in the story of Jason and the Argonauts (as told by Apollonius of Rhodes in the *Argonautica*), when she falls in love with Jason and helps him acquire the Golden Fleece. Returning to Thessaly with him, she makes it possible for him to defeat his enemies. Euripides' play *Medea* picks up the story after Jason and Medea have fled to Corinth. There, Jason decides to marry the daughter of Creon, the Corinthian king, who orders Medea and her two children by Jason to leave the city. Seeking revenge, Medea kills Creon, his daughter, and her own children, then escapes to Athens. Euripides' colleagues, Aeschylus and Sophocles, also wrote plays about Medea, but they have not survived. **See** Aeetes; Creon 1; Jason; **also** Colchis; Golden Fleece (Chapter 4); and, for fuller accounts of Medea's deeds, **see** *Medea* (Chapter 5); The Quest for the Golden Fleece (Chapter 6).

Melampus

A gifted prophet and wonder worker, and the first in a family line of famous prophets. Melampus and his brother, Bias, grew up in Pylos (in the southwestern Peloponnesus). One day, Melampus and several other local Pylians accompanied their king on a hunting trip. When a large snake suddenly bit a member of the party, the king ordered the snake killed. Afterward, Melampus sought out the snake's nest, found its young, and, out of pity and compassion, raised them with great care. Thankful, they repaid him by licking his ears, which endowed him with the ability to understand the speech of animals.

Melampus soon found occasion to put this marvelous ability to good use. His brother Bias wanted to marry the daughter of Pylos's king, but Bias had to prove himself first by stealing cattle belonging to Phylacus, king of Phylace (in Thessaly). Worried about his brother's safety, Melampus undertook the mission himself; Phylacus, however, caught him in the act and threw him in prison for a year. Melampus's sentence was almost up when one morning he overheard some woodworms conversing within the roof of his cell. They said that they planned to finish eating through the main roof beam that very evening. Melampus convinced the jailer to move him to another cell; and sure enough, late that night the roof of the first cell collapsed.

When King Phylacus heard what had happened, he was so impressed with Melampus's abilities that he asked the prophet to help cure his son, who was unable to sire children. Melampus agreed and proceeded to talk to some vultures who were dining on a dead bull. The vultures told the prophet where to find a certain knife that King Phylacus had long ago plunged into a sacred oak tree. The prophet mixed some rust from the knife with wine. And when the king's son drank the potion, it cured him. Phylacus was so grateful that he gave Melampus the cattle, which the prophet drove back to Pylos and presented to the king in exchange for Bias's right to marry the princess. In another wondrous cure, Melampus fulfilled the request of Proetus, king of Argos, to restore the sanity of a number of local women who had gone mad. For an account of this episode, **see** Proetus.

Meleager

A prince of Calydon (a city near the mouth of the Gulf of Corinth in western Greece) and one of Jason's Argonauts. At the conclusion of the quest for the Golden Fleece, Meleager married Cleopatra, daughter of Idas (a prince of Messenia) and Marpessa. Later, the goddess Artemis sent a giant wild boar to attack the people of Calydon to punish Meleager's father, King Oeneus, for neglecting her worship. Meleager took it upon himself to invite any and all Greek heroes and warriors to join him in tracking down and killing the beast. Among those who answered the call was Atalanta, a skilled female hunter. She managed to wound the boar, but Meleager delivered the fatal blow and thereby acquired the creature's hide as a prize. Having grown fond of Atalanta, Meleager gave her the hide, which raised the ire of his uncles, who objected to the idea of a woman hunting alongside men. Meleager ended up killing them, for which his mother, Althea, cursed him.

Ancient stories differed on what happened next. In one version, Althea prayed that Meleager would die in battle. But Meleager subsequently survived a war with a neighboring city, so the curse was not fulfilled. The second version claims that when Meleager was born, Althea heard a prophecy (from the three goddesses known as the Fates) that her son would die when a piece of wood then burning in her hearth was totally consumed. She quickly removed the wood, doused it with water, and put it away for safekeeping. But years later, hearing that Meleager had slain her brothers, she retrieved the wood and burned it, causing her son to collapse and die. Unable to live with this crime, Althea hanged herself. **See** Atalanta; Marpessa.

Memnon

The son of Eos (goddess of the dawn), a king of Ethiopia, and one of the more famous combatants in the Trojan War. According to legend, Memnon and his brother, Emathion, had black skin because they spent a great deal of time with Helios, the sun god, who exposed them to unusually hot climates. After Memnon became ruler of Ethiopia, he attacked Persia and captured one of its capitals, Susa. Then he led a force of his Ethiopians northward to aid his uncle, Priam, king of Troy, against the Greeks. Memnon managed to slay Achilles' friend Antilochus; however, Achilles then killed Memnon. One ancient story said that, at Eos's urging, Zeus made her fallen son immortal. Another claimed that Zeus turned the smoke rising from Memnon's funeral pyre into birds, which thereafter visited the dead man's tomb each year. **See** Antilochus; **also** Eos (Chapter 2).

Menelaus

A son of Atreus (king of Mycenae), the brother of Agamemnon, the husband of Helen of Troy, and a king of Sparta. Menelaus and Agamemnon grew up in Sicyon (in the northern Peloponnesus) while their uncle, Thyestes, ruled Mycenae. As a young man, Menelaus became one the many suitors of Helen, princess of Sparta, where Tyndareos ruled. Helen chose Menelaus over all of the others to be her husband, and later Tyndareos willed the Spartan throne to him. When the Trojan prince, Paris, ran off with Helen to Asia Minor, Menelaus and Agamemnon organized the great Greek expedition to Troy. After sacking Troy and returning to Sparta with his wife, Menelaus led a more or less uneventful life; and his nephew, Orestes, succeeded him as king of Sparta. For fuller accounts of Menelaus's life and exploits, **see** Helen; **also** The Curse of the House of Atreus; The Trojan War (Chapter 6).

Mentor

In Homer's *Odyssey,* a resident of the island kingdom of Ithaca and an old friend of Odysseus, king of that realm. On leaving to fight at Troy, Odysseus asked Mentor to watch over his wife, Penelope, and son, Telemachus, as well as the royal household. Mentor became a close older companion and adviser of Telemachus, the origin of the term *mentor* to describe such an elder adviser.

Merope

1. The faithful wife of Sisyphus, the founder of Corinth. Sisyphus told Merope that if Thanatos, the god of death, snatched his soul away, she should leave her husband's body unburied (an act the Greeks viewed as sacrilegious). Hades, god of the Underworld, was angry with Merope and allowed Sisyphus to return to the earth only long enough to force her to bury the body. **See** Sisyphus; **also** Thanatos (Chapter 2).

2. The wife of Polybus (king of Corinth) and foster mother to Oedipus, king of Thebes. Oedipus grew up thinking that Polybus and Merope were his real parents; later, however, he discovered that he had been abandoned by his real father, Laius, a Theban king, and some shepherds or servants had placed him in Merope's care. See Oedipus; **also** The Theban Myth Cycle (Chapter 6).

3. The wife of Cresphontes, king of Messenia (in the southern Peloponnesus). A usurper, Polyphontes, killed the king and two of his sons, after which Merope smuggled her third son, Aepytus, out of Messenia. Polyphontes forced Merope to marry him against her will; but eventually, Aepytus returned and rescued his mother, killing Polyphontes in the process.

Mezentius

In Virgil's *Aeneid,* king of the Etruscan city of Caere and an ally of the Rutulian prince, Turnus. Mezentius and Turnus opposed the settlement of western Italy by Aeneas and his band of Trojan refugees. Eventually, Aeneas killed both Mezentius and Turnus as well as Mezentius's son,

Lausus. **See** Aeneas's Journey to Italy (Chapter 6).

Midas

A king of Phrygia (in central Asia Minor), to whom the satyr Dionysus granted a wish. Midas chose to have everything he touched turn to gold; but he soon found that this included his food, so he begged to have the gift nullified. In a different legend, Midas judged a musical contest between the gods Apollo and Pan, and when he chose Pan the winner, Apollo gave Midas a donkey's ears to demonstrate his stupidity. The king tried to hide this deformity by wearing a cap, but he could not hide the ears from his barber. The barber swore he would never tell anyone, but he was unable to keep the hilarious secret and whispered it into a hole in the ground. Unfortunately for Midas, some reeds grew up from the hole and their rustling in the wind repeatedly sounded out the words "Midas has an ass's ears!"

Minos

A son of the god Zeus and the Phoenician princess Europa, and a famous king of Crete. Not long after Minos became ruler of that island, his wife, Pasiphae, mated with a bull (a punishment sent by the sea god Poseidon) and gave birth to the Minotaur, a creature half man and half bull. Minos had a special underground maze, the labyrinth, constructed to hide the fearsome beast. Minos subsequently became lord of the Aegean sea lanes and subjugated large portions of Greece. According to legend, he defeated both Megara and Athens and demanded that Aegeus, the Athenian king, send seven boys and seven girls each year (or in some accounts every ninth year) to Crete to be fed to the Minotaur.

Eventually, the Athenian hero Theseus came to Crete, killed the Minotaur, and departed with Minos's daughter, Ariadne. Minos found out that his court inventor, Daedalus (who had built the labyrinth), had been implicated in these events, so the king locked Daedalus inside the labyrinth. Daedalus escaped, and when Minos pursued him all the way to distant Sicily, the inventor and a local king killed the Cretan ruler by boiling him in a specially rigged bathtub. After Minos's death, Zeus made him one of the judges of the Underworld. On excavating the palace at Knossus (in northern Crete) beginning in 1900, the English archaeologist Sir Arthur Evans dubbed its builders "Minoan" after the legendary Minos. **See** Aegeus; Daedalus; Europa; Pasiphae; Theseus; **also** Minotaur (Chapter 3); labyrinth; Knossus (Chapter 4); The Exploits of Theseus (Chapter 6).

Minyans

A legendary race of heroes mentioned in Homer's *Iliad*. They dwelled in Orchomenus (in Boeotia), and perhaps Iolcos (in Thessaly) as well, and were said to be descendants of Minyas, an ancient king of Orchomenus. Because many of Jason's Argonauts hailed from these areas, they were sometimes referred to as Minyans. **See** Minyas.

Minyas

The legendary founder of the city of Orchomenus (near Thebes in Boeotia) and the ancestor of the Minyans (a mythical group of heroes). Minyas had three daughters—Alcithoe, Leucippe, and Arsippe—whose arrogance and impiety brought them to grief. When they refused to take part in local worship of the fertility god, Dionysus, he made their weaving looms sprout leaves and vines and filled their house with smoke, driving them away. Various versions of their fate circulated in ancient times. According to one, Dionysus or some other god turned them into bats. Another said that Dionysus drove them insane, after which they killed Leucippe's small son; this act so horrified the Maenids, a groups of Dionysus's fanatic devotees, that they slew the three sisters. **See** Minyans; **also** Dionysus (Chapter 2).

Mopsus

1. A prophet of Thessaly (in central Greece) who had a minor role in a number of famous myths. Among these were the quest for the Golden Fleece, in which Mopsus interpreted the flight patterns of birds, a form of divination; the Calydonian boar hunt, in which Meleager killed the boar; and the battle between the Lapiths and the centaurs.

2. The son of Manto, a Greek prophetess (who was the daughter of the seer Tiresias, who foretold that Oedipus was the criminal who had brought down the gods' wrath on Thebes). As a young man, Mopsus took charge of the oracle of Clarus, near Colophon (a Greek city on the western coast of Asia Minor). In the days following the Trojan War, another Greek prophet, Calchas, arrived at Clarus, and the two seers fell into a contest to decide who was the more far-seeing. Mopsus outdid Calchas, killing him in the process. Later, Mopsus had a dispute with his half brother, Amphilochus (not to be confused with his uncle of the same name, the son of Amphiaraus), and the two ended up killing each other.

Narcissus

The son of the Boeotian river god Cephisus and a nymph, Liriope. Narcissus was so handsome that he attracted many lovers, both male and female. But he was vain and eventually rejected them all. Then a nymph named Echo fell in love with him. The goddess Hera had earlier robbed her of speech, except for the ability to repeat the last syllables of words she heard. Narcissus callously ignored her advances, as he had those of so many others, and she was so crushed that she wasted away until only her voice was left (the origin of the phenomenon known as an echo, named after her). Appalled at Narcissus's cruelty, Aphrodite (or, in an alternate account, Nemesis) caused the young man to fall in love with his own image reflected in a pool of water. Day after day he reclined beside the pool, enamored of what he saw, until he, like Echo, wasted away and perished. Today, people who are overly impressed with themselves are called narcissists, after Narcissus.

Nausicaa

In Homer's *Odyssey,* the daughter of Alcinous, king of the Phaeacians, who inhabited an island visited by the hero Odysseus during his long journey.

Neleus

A king of Pylos (in the southwestern Peloponnesus) and the twin brother of Pelias (king of Iolcos). Neleus's and Pelias's mother abandoned them when they were young, but some horse breeders took them in and reared them. After Pelias became ruler of Iolcos, he quarreled with Neleus and banished him. Neleus went to Messenia (not far east of Pylos), where his cousin, King Aphareus, befriended him and gave him part of his kingdom. Neleus then returned to Pylos and conquered it; he also married Chloris (daughter of Niobe, a queen of Thebes) and sired thirteen children, including Pero, who married Bias (**see** Melampus), and Nestor (who later became one of the leaders of the Greek expedition to Troy). According to legend, Neleus eventually got into a dispute with the hero Heracles, who slew Neleus and his whole family, except for Nestor, who was away at the time.

Neoptolemus

The son of the Greek hero Achilles and Deidamia, a princess of the northern

Aegean island of Skyros. Neoptolemus was sometimes called Pyrrhus (meaning "Red-Haired"). After Achilles died at Troy, the captured Trojan prophet Helenus told the remaining Greek leaders that the city could not be taken unless both Neoptolemus and Philoctetes were present. (The Greeks had earlier abandoned Philoctetes on the island of Lemnos.) Odysseus and Phoenix (the tutor and friend of Achilles) traveled to Skyros and collected Neoptolemus, who then accompanied Odysseus to Lemnos to fetch Philoctetes.

When the Greeks built the Wooden Horse to trick the Trojans, Neoptolemus was among the warriors who hid inside. He also slew the Trojan king, Priam, as well as Priam's daughter, Polyxena, at Achilles' tomb. Neoptolemus then returned to Greece, taking along Andromache (widow of the Trojan hero Hector) and her brother Helenus as slaves. According to Homer, Neoptolemus went to Phthia (in southeastern Thessaly), where his grandfather, Peleus, was king. But another ancient tradition said that Neoptolemus ended up in Epirus (in northwestern Greece) instead. The later kings of Epirus claimed descent from him and often bore the name Pyrrhus in his honor. **See** Philoctetes; **also** The Trojan War (Chapter 6).

Nestor

The son of Neleus, king of Pylos (in the southwestern Peloponnesus), and one of the leaders of the famous Greek expedition to Troy. In Homer's *Iliad,* Nestor is an old man at the time of the war and plays the role of a senior statesman for the Greek rulers, often giving them advice (in the form of long, rambling speeches filled with stories about his youth). During one battle, the Ethiopian king, Memnon, almost killed Nestor; however, Nestor's son, Antilochus, intervened, saving his father but losing his own life in the process. After the conclusion of the conflict, Nestor returned safely to Pylos, where, as told in

Homer's *Odyssey,* several years later he met with Odysseus's son, Telemachus. The circumstances of Nestor's death are unknown. **See** Antilochus; Memnon; Neleus; **also** Pylos (Chapter 4); The Trojan War (Chapter 6).

Niobe

The daughter of Tantalus (king of Lydia, in Asia Minor), the wife of Amphion, and an unfortunate participant in and victim of the infamous curse on Tantalus's family line (including his grandson, Atreus, and great-grandson, Agamemnon). For insulting the goddess Leto, Niobe incurred the wrath of Leto's divine children, Apollo and Artemis, who slew all of Niobe's children. For more details, **see** The Curse of the House of Atreus (Chapter 6).

Nisus

1. An early king of the city of Megara (not far west of Athens). Nisus was a son of an Athenian king, Pandion. They quarreled, and Pandion expelled the young man, who went to Megara and in time managed to become its king. The most famous story about Nisus concerns a single lock of red hair on his head, which he needed to keep intact to sustain his life. When Minos, king of Crete, invaded Megara, Nisus's daughter, Scylla, accepted a bribe from Minos to betray her father. She cut off his precious lock of hair, thereby killing him. One ancient source says that Minos then turned on Scylla and drowned her; another claims that she could not live with her crime and drowned herself.

2. One of Aeneas's companions on the famous journey from Troy to Italy, where Aeneas founded the Roman race. Nisus and his friend, Euryalus, tried to attack the troops of Aeneas's Italian enemy, Turnus, on their own; but they died in the effort.

Numa Pompilius

The legendary successor of Rome's founder, Romulus, and the second king of

Rome. Tradition held that Numa reigned from about 715 to 673 B.C. The later Romans, including Livy in his monumental history (written in the first century B.C.), looked on this period as a sort of golden age during which many of their important religious and other institutions were established; among these were state worship of the god Janus and the state tradition of the Vestal Virgins (maidens who kept the sacred fire going in the Temple of Vesta in Rome). However, modern historians believe it is likely that Numa was not a real person and that these and the other institutions attributed to him developed more gradually. **See** Seven Kings of Rome; **also** Vesta (Chapter 2).

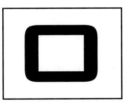

Odysseus

A king of the island kingdom of Ithaca, one of the principal leaders of the Greek expedition to Troy, and the central character of Homer's epic poem the *Odyssey.* Odysseus (whom the Romans called Ulysses) was one of the cleverest of the Greek leaders. He devised the plan for getting Greek troops into Troy by hiding them inside the hollow Wooden Horse, for example. After the city fell, Odysseus's ships were blown off course and he wandered for ten years, encountering numerous adventures and crises, until finally returning home to his wife, Penelope, and son, Telemachus. **See** Aeolus 1; Ajax 1; Alcinous; Mentor; Neoptolemus; Palamedes; Penelope; Telemachus; **also** Circe; Poseidon Chapter 2); Argus 2; Polyphemus; Sirens (Chapter 3); Ithaca (Chapter 4); *Odyssey* (Chapter 5); and, for a full account of Odysseus's exploits following the Trojan War, **see** The Wanderings of Odysseus (Chapter 6).

Oedipus

A famous king of Thebes by virtue of outwitting a monster, the Sphinx, that had been threatening the city. Later, Oedipus learned that he had unwittingly killed his father, the former Theban king Laius, and that he had married and had children by his mother, Jocasta. Horrified, Oedipus blinded himself and went into exile, attended by his loving daughter Antigone. But after he had suffered for many years, the gods finally forgave him. Oedipus's powerful and moving story is told in Sophocles' great plays *Oedipus the King* and *Oedipus at Colonus.* **See** Antigone; Creon 2; Eteocles; **also** Sphinx (Chapter 3); Delphic Oracle; Thebes (Chapter 4); *Oedipus at Colonus; Oedipus the King* (Chapter 5); and, for a full account of Oedipus's story, **see** The Theban Myth Cycle (Chapter 6).

This modern drawing depicts Oedipus, after his fall from power, comforted by his loving daughter Antigone.

Orestes

The son of Agamemnon and Clytemnestra (king and queen of Mycenae), and the last major participant in and victim of the terrible curse of the family line of Atreus (Agamemnon's father). With the help of his sister, Electra, Orestes slew their mother (and her lover, Aegisthus), who had earlier murdered their father. Then Orestes fled Mycenae, pursued by the vengeful Furies. The goddess Athena finally purified him of his crime, ending the curse. **See** Aegisthus; Agamemnon; Clytemnestra; Electra; **also** Athena (Chapter 2); Furies (Chapter 3); *Eumenides; Libation Bearers* (Chapter 5); and, for a full account of Orestes' story, **see** The Curse of the House of Atreus (Chapter 6).

Orpheus

A Greek poet and musician who, according to legend, lived during the generation before the Trojan War. He was the son (or pupil) of the god Apollo and the muse Calliope, from whom he inherited his musical talent. That talent was said to be so great that when Orpheus played his lyre (harp), all nearby people, animals, and even rocks and trees stood entranced by his sweet songs. Orpheus joined Jason's Argonauts in their search for the Golden Fleece, often singing and playing to calm the crew when they were tense; the poet's music also drowned out the songs of the deadly Sirens, allowing the Argonauts to escape them.

The most famous story associated with Orpheus began after the *Argo* returned to Greece and he married Eurydice, a beautiful nymph. He loved her so deeply that when a poisonous snake bit her and she died, he was devastated. Soon, he followed her into the Underworld and played his lyre for Hades (or Hades' wife, Persephone), who was so moved that he (or she) allowed Eurydice to leave and rejoin the living. The one condition was that Orpheus must walk ahead of his wife and never look back at her until they had reached the earth's surface. At the last moment, though, the man could no longer resist the temptation to look back, and when he did so, Eurydice was sucked back into the depths, never to return.

After that, Orpheus became a hermit, even shunning the company of the Maenids (fanatic followers of the fertility god, Dionysus), with whom he had earlier worshiped on a regular basis. Angry over his neglecting them, they tore Orpheus apart. Some inhabitants of the island of Lesbos eventually found his head floating in the sea. They gave it a proper burial and established an oracle on the spot. In classical times, a cult named after Orpheus, called Orphism, became popular in various Mediterranean lands. A central tenet of the faith was Orpheus's guilt over his failure to rescue Eurydice. The secret rites of Orphism supposedly freed worshipers from their collective or individual guilt and improved their chances for happiness in the afterlife. Not much is known about the cult, outside of references in ancient poems attributed to (but obviously not actually written by) Orpheus; and it may not have been a well-organized spiritual movement.

Palamedes

A legendary Greek whose name meant "Clever" or "Handy" and who was credited with inventing the game of checkers as well as some dice games and several letters of the Greek alphabet. When the hero Odysseus attempted to evade joining the other Greek kings in their war against Troy, the clever Palamedes pointed out his deception. Seeking revenge, Odysseus showed that he was clever, too. Once the Greeks had assembled before Troy, he hid some gold beneath Palamedes' tent, then forged a letter purporting to be from the Trojan king, Priam, to Palamedes, promising to pay him gold if he would betray his fellow Greeks. Odysseus made sure that the letter fell into the hands of the expedition's leader, Agamemnon, who ordered Palamedes stoned to death. In retaliation, Palamedes' father, Nauplius, later caused some of the Greek ships returning to Greece from Troy to crash onto some rocks. **See** The Trojan War (Chapter 6).

Pallas

The son of the early Athenian king Pandion and the younger half brother of Aegeus (the father of the great Athenian hero Theseus). Pallas at first helped Aegeus acquire the throne; but later the two opposed each other and Theseus ended up killing Pallas's fifty sons. **See** The Exploits of Theseus (Chapter 6).

Pandora

In Greek legend, the first human woman. At the order of Zeus (who wanted to punish the Titan Prometheus), Hephaestos (god of the forge) fashioned Pandora from clay, and various gods endowed her with physical and mental gifts (hence her name, meaning "All Gifts"). Zeus sent her to Prometheus's slow-witted brother, Epimetheus, who took her into his home, even though Prometheus had warned him not to accept any gifts from Zeus. Once inside, she unwittingly opened a jar (or in some accounts a box), unleashing all of the evils that still plague the human race. **See** Prometheus (Chapter 2); **also** The Creation of the Gods and Humans (Chapter 6).

Paris

The son of Priam and Hecuba, king and queen of Troy, and the instigator of the trouble that led to the Trojan War. Paris, who also bore the name of Alexander, went to Sparta (in southern Greece) as an ambassador for his father and there became involved with Helen, wife of Sparta's King Menelaus. When Paris took Helen back to Troy, it angered many of the Greek kings, who banded together to attack the city. For more details, **see** Helen; Menelaus; **also** Iliad (Chapter 5); and, for a full account of Paris's exploits relating to the great conflict, **see** The Trojan War (Chapter 6).

Pasiphae

The wife of Crete's King Minos and the mother of Ariadne and Phaedra. Minos had promised the sea god Poseidon that he would sacrifice a fine bull to him; when the king neglected to keep that promise, Poseidon punished Minos through Pasiphae. The god caused her to become inflamed with a burning passion for the bull, and she soon gave birth to the monstrous Minotaur, a creature half human and half bull. Minos put the beast in the labyrinth, a huge underground maze. Later, upset over Minos's frequent affairs with other women, Pasiphae used witchcraft to make her husband pass on a painful disease to any woman he slept with (except for her, of course). **See** Minos; **also** Minotaur (Chapter 3).

Patroclus

In Homer's Iliad, the close friend and fellow warrior of the hero Achilles. Patroclus convinced Achilles, who sat in his tent refusing to fight, to allow him to wear Achilles' armor in battle. Achilles consented. As Patroclus entered the battle, the Trojans thought he was Achilles and began to retreat. But soon the Trojan champion Hector confronted and slew Patroclus, which in turn motivated Achilles to reenter the fray. For a fuller account, **see** The Trojan War (Chapter 6).

Peleus

The son of Aeacus, an early ruler of the island kingdom of Aegina (lying southwest of Athens), and the father of the renowned Greek hero Achilles. Peleus and his brother, Telamon, killed their half brother, Phocus, for which King Aeacus banished them. Peleus journeyed to Phthia (in southern Thessaly), where the local king, Actor, welcomed him and gave him the hand of his daughter, Antigone. Soon afterward, Peleus joined Jason and the Argonauts on the quest for the Golden Fleece. Later still, Peleus took part in the Calydonian boar hunt with Meleager, Atalanta, and others. On that hunt, though, Peleus killed Actor's son, which resulted in Peleus's banishment from Phthia.

Next, Peleus went to Iolcos, where the king, Acastus, a fellow Argonaut, took him in. Once more, however, Peleus ran into trouble. This time, Acastus's wife, Astydamia, made sexual advances toward Peleus, and when he rebuffed her, she sent Peleus's wife, Antigone, a letter claiming that Peleus was about to marry another woman. Antigone believed what she read and promptly hanged herself. Astydamia also lied to Acastus, saying that Peleus had tried to seduce her, and Acastus tried to get back at his guest by abandoning him on a remote mountainside. However, the kindly centaur Chiron happened by and helped Peleus out of his predicament. Peleus now gathered together a group of the former Argonauts, entered Iolcos, and killed Acastus and Astydamia.

The great god Zeus approved of the way Peleus had handled the situation in Iolcos and rewarded him by allowing him to marry Thetis (daughter of the sea god Nereus and herself a sea goddess). The union of Peleus and Thetis produced Achilles, one of Greece's greatest early champions. According to legend, Peleus soon asked Chiron to educate the young Achilles. Eventually, when Peleus became an old man, his grandson, Neoptolemus, ended up ruling Phthia; and Peleus joined Thetis in the sea, where she allowed him to share immortality with her. **See** Aeacus;

Acastus; Achilles; Neoptolemus; **also** Thetis (Chapter 2); Chiron (Chapter 3).

Pelias
The brother of Neleus (king of Pylos), the father of Acastus (one of Jason's Argonauts), and a usurper of the throne of Iolcos (in Thessaly). Pelias's half brother, Aeson, was the true heir to the throne, but Pelias seized it from him. When Aeson and his wife had a child, Jason, they feared Pelias might kill him (since he might pose a threat to Pelias's power); so they secretly sent Jason to be reared by the centaur Chiron. As a young man, Jason returned to Iolcos to claim the throne. Pelias promised (falsely, of course) to honor the young man's claim, providing he proved himself by retrieving the fabulous Golden Fleece from faraway Colchis (on the shore of the Black Sea). Pelias paid for his treachery with his life when Jason eventually returned from Colchis. **See** Acastus; Neleus; **also** Chiron (Chapter 3); and, for the full story of Pelias and Jason, **see** The Quest for the Golden Fleece (Chapter 6).

Pelops
The son of Tantalus (king of Lydia, in Asia Minor) and the founder of the Pelopid family, for which the Peloponnesus (the southern third of Greece) was named. In one ancient story, Tantalus entertained some of the Olympian gods by throwing them a banquet, at which he served them the flesh of Pelops (whom he had ordered killed and butchered); however, the gods were not fooled. They restored Pelops to life and placed a curse on Tantalus's family line, which eventually became known as the curse of the house of Atreus (because Atreus was Tantalus's grandson). The other version of the origin of the curse held that Ilus, king of Troy, drove Pelops out of Asia Minor. Pelops then settled in Pisa (near Elis, in the western Peloponnesus) and there killed the local king, Oenomaus, with the help of the king's

charioteer, Myrtilus. Perhaps to keep Myrtilus from implicating Pelops in the murder, Pelops killed Myrtilus, too; and with his last breath, Myrtilus cursed Pelops and his descendants. However it began, the curse soon manifested itself in Pelops's sister, Niobe, and his sons, Atreus and Thyestes. For a full account of the curse and its dire effects over the generations, **see** The Curse of the House of Atreus (Chapter 6).

Penelope

In Homer's *Odyssey,* the daughter of Tyndareos (king of Sparta), and the loving, dutiful, and resourceful wife of the hero Odysseus, king of the island kingdom of Ithaca. After Odysseus left Ithaca to fight at Troy, Penelope waited for him faithfully for twenty years, managing to resist pressure from a pack of suitors to marry one of them (since they thought her husband was dead). Finally, Odysseus returned, killed the suitors, and he and Penelope were reunited. For the full story, as told by Homer, **see** The Wanderings of Odysseus (Chapter 6).

Some later Greek writers claimed that, after Odysseus died, Penelope married Telegonus, Odysseus's son by the sorceress Circe (whom Odysseus had encountered during his ten years of wandering). Penelope then bore Telegonus a son, Italus, for whom Italy was named. Eventually, Circe made Penelope and Penelope's first son by Odysseus—Telemachus—immortal. **See** Circe (Chapter 2).

Penthesilea

A queen of the Amazons, a legendary tribe of warrior women. One ancient tale claims that Penthesilea accidentally killed an ally; another says that it was her own sister, Hippolyte. Either way, Troy's King Priam purified Penthesilea of the sin, and in return, she aided him in his famous war with the Greeks. She managed to kill several Greek warriors before the formidable champion, Achilles, slew her. **See** Amazons; Hippolyte.

Perseus

The son of Zeus and a mortal woman, Danae (daughter of Acrisius, king of Argos), and the famous hero who slew the snake-headed Gorgon Medusa. After killing her and engaging in other adventures, Perseus became king of Tiryns (in the eastern Peloponnesus); according to one ancient story, he also established the nearby city of Mycenae. For the details of his exploits, **see** Perseus and Medusa (Chapter 6).

Phaeacians

In Homer's *Odyssey,* a happy maritime people inhabiting an island on which the hero Odysseus washed ashore. He told the story of his wanderings to the local king, Alcinous, and his royal court. **See** The Wanderings of Odysseus (Chapter 6).

Phaedra

One of the daughters of King Minos (of Crete) and wife to Theseus, king of Athens. Phaedra fell in love with Theseus's son, Hippolytus, and falsely accused him of seducing her, bringing about tragedy for all involved. For her story, **see** Hippolytus; **also** *Hippolytus* (Chapter 5).

Phaëthon

A son of Helios (god of the sun). Phaëthon grew up without meeting his illustrious father. Thus, when he reached young manhood, his mother, then queen of Egypt, sent him to Helios's palace, which lay far to the east, where the sun rose each morning. Helios was so thrilled to meet Phaëthon that he agreed to grant the young man any wish. Phaëthon demanded to drive the god's gleaming chariot across the sky for a day, and though reluctant, Helios complied. Unfortunately, though, Phaëthon was unable to control his father's mighty horses, and a wild ride through the heavens ensued. The blazing chariot created a bright swash across the sky, which became the Milky Way; then it scorched the earth, causing the skin of the people who lived near the equator to turn black. Finally, Zeus saw what was happening and intervened, hurling a thunderbolt at Phaëthon, whose charred body fell into a river, the legendary Eridanus. **See** Helios (Chapter 2); **also** Eridanus (Chapter 4).

Philemon

In Ovid's *Metamorphoses,* a poor old man who, with his wife, Baucis, unknowingly invited into their humble house the gods Zeus and Hermes, who had taken human form to test the hospitality of humankind. For the charming story, **see** Baucis and Philemon.

Philoctetes

The son of Poeas (a shepherd of Malis, a small area in eastern Greece, and possibly one of Jason's Argonauts) and one of the more important Greek warriors who fought at Troy. When the great hero Heracles decided that he wanted to die and lay down on his funeral pyre, he asked Poeas to light it since none of the strongman's friends would do it; in return, Heracles gave the shepherd his mighty bow and poisoned arrows. Poeas then passed these formidable weapons on to his son, Philoctetes.

Later Philoctetes became king of Malis and led seven ships carrying archers in the great Greek expedition bound for Troy. Soon after the expedition's leaders landed temporarily on an Aegean island to sacrifice to the gods, a snake bit Philoctetes, who began crying out in pain and cursing everyone in sight. He made such a scene that his fellow commanders, at Odysseus's suggestion, marooned him on the island of Lemnos. There, Philoctetes sustained himself by hunting with his special bow and arrows.

Several years passed, and the Greek leaders learned from a prophet that they could not defeat the Trojans unless they went back and retrieved Philoctetes. So Odysseus and Neoptolemus (son of Achilles) journeyed to Lemnos and brought Philoctetes to Troy. Entering the fighting, Philoctetes shot an arrow at Paris, the Trojan prince who had instigated the war, killing him. Variations of Philoctetes' story appeared in several ancient sources, including Homer's *Iliad* and Sophocles' play *Philoctetes.* **See** Neoptolemus; **also** The Trojan War (Chapter 6).

Philomela and Procne

Two daughters of an early Athenian king, Pandion. According to Ovid in his *Metamorphoses,* Procne married Tereus, king of Thrace (in northern Greece). But Tereus soon secretly raped Philomela, cut out her tongue, and locked her away in a distant fortress. Unable to call for help, the imprisoned girl wove a tapestry depicting the crime and managed to send it to Procne. The latter found her sister and smuggled her into the palace. There, Procne decided to punish her husband by slaying her own son, which robbed Tereus of an heir to the throne. The women then cooked the boy's flesh and fed it to Tereus. When the king finally realized what had happened, he drew his sword to kill the sisters. But the gods suddenly intervened, turning him into a bird (called a hoopoe). Philomela and Procne were likewise transformed into birds. (The Greeks said Philomela became a swallow and Procne a nightingale; the Romans held that it was the reverse.)

Phineus

In the tale of Jason's search for the Golden Fleece, a former king of Thrace (in northern Greece) whom the Argonauts encountered during their voyage. When they found Phineus, he was in sad shape because the hideous Harpies continually fouled his food, keeping him from nourishing himself. **See** Harpy (Chapter 3); and, for the story of how the Argonauts found and rescued poor old

Phineus, **see** The Quest for the Golden Fleece (Chapter 6).

Phoenix

The son of Amyntor (king of Ormenium, not far south of Iolcos in eastern Thessaly). When he was a young man, Phoenix and his father quarreled, so the youth left home and journeyed to Phthia (in southern Thessaly), where King Peleus (father of the Greek hero Achilles) welcomed him. Peleus gave Phoenix the prestigious job of training the young Achilles to fight. Later, when the Trojan War began, Phoenix, though by then he was quite old, accompanied Achilles to Troy. At the conclusion of the war (when Achilles met his death), Phoenix returned to Greece with Achilles' son, Neoptolemus. **See** Neoptolemus.

Polydorus

1. The youngest son of Priam, king of Troy. According to Homer in the *Iliad,* Polydorus was a fast runner, and Priam ordered him not to fight in the Trojan War (to ensure that at least one of his sons would survive the conflict). However, the Greek warrior Achilles found and killed Polydorus. In a different version, that of the playwright Euripides in *Hecuba,* Priam and Polydorus's mother, Queen Hecuba, sent the young man to safety in Thrace (in northern Greece), where the local king, Polymestor, agreed to watch over him. After Troy's fall, however, Polymestor killed Polydorus. Hecuba (now the slave of the Greek hero Odysseus) discovered her son's body lying on the Thracian shore; in revenge, she blinded Polymestor and killed his children. Still another ancient version claimed that Polydorus's sister was Polymestor's wife, who had reared Polydorus from infancy in Thrace. She switched the infant Polydorus with Polymestor's own son. Thus, when Polymestor went to kill Polydorus years later, he slew his own son instead. Polydorus then escaped; but he later came back and killed Polymestor. **See** Hecuba; **also** Aeneas's Journey to Italy (Chapter 6).

2. An early king of Thebes, said in some ancient sources to be the only son of Cadmus, founder of that city. Polydorus left the throne to his infant son, Laius, who later sired Oedipus.

3. One of the Epigoni, the sons of the Seven Against Thebes. Several years after the Seven failed to capture Thebes, Polydorus and his companions managed to take the city. **See** *Seven Against Thebes* (Chapter 5); The Theban Myth Cycle (Chapter 6).

Polynices

The son of Oedipus (king of Thebes), the brother of Eteocles, and the leader of the group of military leaders known as the Seven Against Thebes. Polynices and Eteocles agreed to share their father's throne after his fall from grace (**see** Oedipus), each ruling in alternate years. But Eteocles refused to relinquish the power when his time was up. Polynices reacted by organizing an attack on Thebes by the Seven (which included himself). The brothers ended up killing each other; and their sister Antigone got into serious trouble when she tried to give Polynices a decent burial. For more details, **see** Adrastus; Antigone; Eteocles; **also** *Seven Against Thebes* (Chapter 5); The Theban Myth Cycle (Chapter 6).

Polyxena

A daughter of Priam and Hecuba, king and queen of Troy. After the city's fall, the Greek leaders heard the ghost of their dead colleague, Achilles, demand that Polyxena be killed so that her own ghost would provide him with companionship in the Underworld. Fulfilling this request, Achilles' son, Neoptolemus, slew the young woman at his father's tomb. A later romantic tradition developed, claiming that, while he was still alive, Achilles had fallen in love with Polyxena and that this was why he demanded to have her with him in the afterlife. **See** Neoptolemus.

Priam

The king of Troy during the Trojan War. Priam was the only surviving son of Troy's King Laomedon, who had been slain, along with Priam's brothers and sisters, by the famous strongman Heracles (after Laomedon had refused to pay Heracles for rescuing his daughter). Priam inherited the Trojan throne (by default) and rebuilt the city (which Heracles had wrecked). He eventually had fifty sons, including Paris, Hector, Helenus, and Polydorus; and fifty daughters, among them Cassandra, Cruesa, and Polyxena. **See** Hecuba; Laomedon; and, for Priam's involvement in the Trojan War and his death at the conclusion of that mighty conflict, **see** The Trojan War (Chapter 6).

Proetus

The son of Abas (king of Argos); the twin brother of Acrisius, and a king of Tiryns (in the eastern Peloponnesus). As children, Proetus and Acrisius quarreled incessantly. When Abas gave them his kingdom to rule jointly, they fought each other for sole possession of the throne. Proetus lost the fight and fled. But he returned later with an army, which met that of Acrisius in a furious battle. Because the outcome was indecisive, the brothers made a deal and divided the kingdom in half, Acrisius maintaining rule in the south, dominated by Argos, while Proetus ruled the north from a new city he erected—Tiryns.

In time, Proetus had three daughters: Iphinoe, Lysippe, and Iphianassa. The god Dionysus (or, in some accounts, the goddess Hera) drove the daughters mad, and they roamed the countryside committing terrible acts. Many other women in Proetus's kingdom subsequently went mad, too; so he enlisted the aid of a seer, Melampus, to restore their sanity. Melampus succeeded in curing the women, but he demanded a high price—two-thirds of Proetus's lands. The loss of so much territory may have been the motivation for Proetus's subsequent attack on his brother in the south. Proetus drove Acrisius away and claimed Argos for himself. Eventually Acrisius's grandson, the hero Perseus, killed Proetus by turning him to stone (by showing him the severed head of the Gorgon Medusa). **See** Melampus; **also** Tiryns (Chapter 4); Perseus and Medusa (Chapter 6).

Protesilaus

A king of Phylace (a city lying west of Iolcos in eastern Thessaly) and one of the Greek leaders who took part in the Trojan War. Not long after marrying Laodamia, daughter of Acastus (king of Iolcos), Protesilaus sailed for Troy, commanding forty ships. An oracle had proclaimed that the first Greek who set foot on Trojan soil would also be the first Greek to die in the war; so the soldiers and their leaders were at first reluctant to leave their ships. But Protesilaus defied the oracle and went ashore, and his comrades, impressed by his courage, followed him. Nevertheless, the prophecy came true, for the Trojan champion Hector soon slew Protesilaus. Hearing the news of her husband's death, Laodamia was so consumed by grief that the gods took pity on her. Hermes restored Protesilaus to life for three hours, which the lovers spent together. When the man finally disappeared into the Underworld, Laodamia decided to follow him and took her own life.

Psyche

The heroine of a long romantic story told by a character in *The Golden Ass,* a novel by the second-century A.D. Roman writer Lucius Apuleius. In the tale, Psyche's beauty rivals that of the love goddess, Venus (Aphrodite to the Greeks), and Venus's son, Cupid (the Greek Eros), falls in love with the young girl, which leads to unforeseen tragedy (although Apuleius provides a happy ending). **See** Cupid; Venus (Chapter 2); Apuleius, Lucius

(Chapter 5); and, for the complete story of Psyche and her divine lover, **see** Cupid and Psyche (Chapter 6).

Pygmalion

According to Ovid in his *Metamorphoses,* a king of the island of Cyprus (lying south of Asia Minor) who fell in love with a statue of an ideal woman. The common name given to that woman—Galatea—does not appear in ancient sources and must have become part of the myth in medieval times. In the ancient story, Pygmalion had convinced himself that women were weak and deceitful; so he determined never to marry. In time, however, for reasons that are unclear, he ordered a sculptor to create a statue of a young woman. The work turned out to depict a maiden of such matchless beauty that Pygmalion fell passionately in love with it, despite his misgivings about women. He began spending more and more of his time with it, often imagining it was alive. In Ovid's words:

> He kissed, he fancied she returned; he spoke to her, held her, believed his fingers almost left an imprint in her limbs, and feared to bruise her. He paid her compliments, and brought her presents such as girls love, smooth pebbles, winding shells, little pet birds, flowers with a thousand colors. . . . He brought a necklace, and earrings, and a ribbon for her bosom . . . and took her to bed, put a soft pillow under her head, as if she felt it, [and] called her *Darling, my darling love!* *(Metamorphoses* 255–275)

This weird adoration continued until the advent of the yearly festival of the love goddess, Aphrodite. There, Pygmalion fervently beseeched the goddess to find him a wife as perfect as the one depicted in his statue. Aphrodite complied with this request in a way the man did not expect, for when he returned home he saw that the statue had been transformed into a living, breathing maiden who willingly returned his strong feelings of love. Pygmalion married the maiden, whom he named Galatea, and they had a daughter named Paphos, who gave her name to an important city in western Cyprus. Among Cyprus's buildings was Aphrodite's most famous and beautiful temple.

Pylades

The son of Strophius, king of Phokis (in central Greece); and the cousin and friend of Orestes, son of Agamemnon and Clytemnestra (king and queen of Mycenae). Worried that Clytemnestra and her lover, Aegisthus, might harm young Orestes, Orestes' sister, Electra, took the lad to King Strophius and asked him to look after her brother. There, Orestes and Pylades became close friends. Pylades eventually traveled to Mycenae with Orestes and helped him kill Clytemnestra, a deed for which Strophius banished Pylades from Phokis. Pylades later married Electra and had two sons by her. **See** Orestes.

Pyramus and Thisbe

As described in Ovid's *Metamorphoses,* two young lovers who lived with their families in the great Near Eastern city of Babylon (located in what is now Iraq). Because the families' houses shared a common wall, Pyramus and Thisbe became well acquainted. They eventually fell in love and wanted to marry; but their parents forbade the union and tried to keep them apart. Soon, however, the lovers found a small hole in the wall that separated their houses, and through this opening they communicated daily. In time, they planned to escape from their parents and run away together, agreeing to meet at night near a tall mulberry tree covered with snow-white berries.

Thisbe arrived at the appointed spot first. Suddenly, she saw a lioness approaching, its jaws covered with blood after a recent kill; fearing the beast might kill her too, she fled. But in her haste, she dropped her cloak. The curious lioness sniffed the garment, then tore it to shreds before sauntering away. Pyramis arrived only seconds later, found the blood-stained remnants of the cloak, and, completely distraught, plunged a knife into his body. As he fell, his blood spurted out over the white mulberries, staining them red. Not long afterward, as the young man lay dying, Thisbe returned. Seeing the ghastly scene and her lover's hopeless condition, she decided to die with him and used the same knife on herself.

When Pyramis's and Thisbe's parents discovered what had happened, they were filled with shame and grief. The gods' hearts were also filled with pity, and they created a lasting memorial for the unfortunate lovers by ordaining that thereafter the mulberry would bear only deep-red fruit.

A fanciful modern engraving of Romulus, whom the ancient Romans credited with founding their city-state.

ful and prosperous reign, Romulus disappeared into the sky, the common explanation being that the gods, pleased with his achievements, had welcomed him into their realm. **See** Rome (Chapter 4); and, for a full account of Romulus's life and exploits, **see** The Founding of Rome (Chapter 6).

Remus

The twin brother of Romulus, founder of the great city of Rome. **See** Romulus; and, for a more detailed account, **see** The Founding of Rome (Chapter 6).

Romulus

The legendary founder and first king of Rome. He and his twin brother, Remus, were the grandchildren of Numitor, king of Alba Longa (on the plain of Latium, south of the later site of Rome). When they reached young manhood, they set out to build a city of their own. They quarreled, however, and Romulus slew his brother. After burying Remus, Romulus went on to create the city and rule it as its first king. Forty years later, after a peace-

Sabines

An early Italian people who lived in the region directly northeast of Rome. They appear to have contributed considerably to Rome's early development. (Some of the original noble Roman families may have had Sabine roots, for instance.) The most famous myth about the Sabines and early Romans claims that Romulus, Rome's founder, invited the Sabines to a celebration, then kidnapped their women to help populate his new city. For the details of this story, **see** The Founding of Rome (Chapter 6).

Sarpedon

1. The son of Zeus and Europa and the brother of Minos (king of Crete) and Rhadamanthys. When the three brothers grew up, they all came to admire a young man named Miletus and quarreled over which of them might spend the most time with him. Because Miletus chose only Sarpedon to be his close friend, the angry Minos drove Sarpedon, Miletus, and Rhadamanthys out of Crete. Sarpedon and Miletus decided to settle in southern Asia Minor. There, Miletus established the famous Greek city that bore his name; Sarpedon journeyed farther south to Cilicia, a kingdom recently founded by Sarpedon's uncle, Cilix. They conquered a neighboring land, which Sarpedon then ruled jointly with Lycus, brother of Aegeus (king of Athens). The region later became known as Lycia, after Lycus.

2. A king of Lycia and one of the main allies of Priam, king of Troy, during the Trojan War. Very early Greek writers said that this Sarpedon was the same one who ruled Lycia with Lycus several generations before (**see** Sarpedon 1, above). However, later writers rejected this idea and asserted that the man who fought at Troy was the grandson of the original Sarpedon. During the struggle for that city, he distinguished himself by slaying Tlepolemus, son of the hero Heracles; but soon afterward, the Greek warrior Patroclus, friend of the great hero Achilles, killed Sarpedon.

Scaevola, Gaius Mucius

In Roman legend, a citizen who entered the camp of Lars Porsenna, the Etruscan king who was then besieging Rome, and tried but failed to kill Porsenna. First, Scaevola disguised himself as an Etruscan and slipped into the enemy camp. He saw an officer handing out money to a group of soldiers and, believing this to be Porsenna, slew the man. The onlookers immediately captured and arrested the Roman spy and took him to the real Porsenna, who demanded he divulge information about Roman positions. Scaevola showed his defiance and bravery by thrusting his right hand into a fire while continuing to stare calmly at the king. Porsenna was so impressed by this display of courage that he released the would-be assassin and handed him his sword. Because of the injury to his right hand, Scaevola accepted the weapon with his left, earning the name by which history came to know him (since the Latin word *scaeva* meant "left hand"). Scaevola then told Porsenna that three hundred other Romans had infiltrated the Etruscan camp and were waiting for their chance to assassinate its leader. Hearing this, the king contacted Roman leaders and asked for a truce. **See** Lars Porsenna.

Servius Tullius

According to tradition, the sixth king of Rome, said to have ruled during the late sixth century B.C. It is possible that Servius was a real ruler, though the exact dates of his reign are unknown and many of the deeds attributed to him are likely exaggerated or fictitious. In the version of his story told by the Roman historian Livy, King Tarquinius Priscus (Rome's fifth king) owned a slave who gave birth to a son. Various omens suggested the boy was special in some way, so the king and his wife brought him up as their own. Servius eventually succeeded his foster father on the Roman throne. The new king then distinguished himself by defeating the ruler of the nearby Etruscan city of Veii. Servius was also credited with dividing the Roman population into classes based on wealth, introducing worship of the Latin goddess Diana, and building a large defensive wall around the city (later called the Servian

Wall in his honor). Eventually, Servius's daughter, Tullia, and Tarquinius Priscus's son (or grandson?), Lucius Tarquinius (later called "Superbus"), murdered Servius; and the younger Tarquinius ascended the throne. **See** Tarquinius Superbus, Lucius.

Seven Against Thebes

The collective name of seven warriors, including Oedipus's son, Polynices, who took part in an attack on the city of Thebes with the goal of forcing Polynices' brother, Eteocles, from the throne. The other six captains of the expedition were Adrastus, Tydeus, Parthenopaeus, Capaneus, Hippomedon, and Amphiaraus. The Greek playwright Aeschylus told the story in his play *Seven Against Thebes.* **See** Adrastus; Amphiaraus; Antigone; Creon 2; Eteocles; and, for a full account of the story, **see** *Seven Against Thebes* (Chapter 5); The Theban Myth Cycle (Chapter 6).

Seven Kings of Rome

According to tradition, the seven monarchs who ruled Rome from its founding, in 753 B.C., to the establishment of the Roman Republic, circa 509 B.C. The first of the seven was Romulus, said to have reigned from 753 to 717 B.C. His successors were Numa Pompilius, Tullus Hostilius, Ancus Marcius, Tarquinius Priscus, Servius Tullius, and Tarquinius Superbus (or "Tarquin the Proud"). Some of these rulers, especially the first three, were likely legendary rather than real persons, although the last four may well have been real. In any case, modern scholars are uncertain about the exact length of the monarchial period as well as the number of kings and the lengths of their reigns. The consensus is that the period of the monarchy was shorter than tradition held and that there were more than seven kings, some of whose identities and deeds merged with those of the traditional seven in historical accounts fashioned centuries

later. For some of these legendary deeds, **see** Numa Pompilius; Servius Tullius; Tarquinius Superbus, Lucius; **also** Rome (Chapter 4).

Sibyl

A name, essentially meaning a gifted prophetess, assigned to several legendary priestesses of the ancient Greco-Roman world. The original Sibyl lived near Troy and dedicated herself to the service of the god Apollo. She was said to deliver oracles (prophecies) in riddles and often to write them down on leaves. The most famous of the various Sibyls who followed her was the one who resided at Cumae (in the Campania region of southwestern Italy). According to the Roman poet Virgil, she guided the Trojan prince Aeneas into the Underworld, where he learned about Rome's glorious future. Another legend told how she offered Rome's last king, Lucius Tarquinius Superbus, nine books of her prophecy for a high price; after he continually refused the deal, she burned six of the books, but he finally gave in and bought the last three (at the original price!). This was supposedly the origin of the sacred Sibylline Books, which the later Romans consulted from time to time, partly for guidance in making future plans and policies and also to find out how to appease angry gods. **See** Aeneas's Journey to Italy (Chapter 6).

Sisyphus

A son of Aeolus (himself the son of Hellen, founder of the Greek race) and the founder of the great city of Corinth. Sisyphus fortified the Acrocorinth, the massive, rocky acropolis in the city's center. He also established the Isthmian Games, one of the four most prestigious athletic competitions in the Greek world.

The most famous story about Sisyphus involves his defiance of and punishment by Zeus and the other gods. The Corinthian king happened to witness Zeus abducting Aegina, daughter of the river god Asopus, and Asopus asked Sisyphus for any information that might help him find the missing girl. Sisyphus told what he had seen. In return, Asopus created a freshwater spring on the Acrocorinth. When Zeus found out that Sisyphus had informed on him, he sent Thanatos (god of death) to escort the man to the Underworld. However, Thanatos was no intellectual match for Sisyphus, who was widely renowned for his cleverness. Somehow the man tricked the god and trapped him in a prison cell; as a result, humans no longer died, which, not surprisingly, the gods found disturbing. The god Ares rushed to release Thanatos, who immediately went looking for Sisyphus, found him, and took his soul to the Underworld.

The wily Sisyphus was not yet defeated, though. He had left instructions with his wife, Merope, that if Thanatos did manage to snatch his soul away, she should leave her husband's body unburied (a terrible, sacrilegious act in ancient Greece). Furious with the woman, Hades, god of the Underworld, allowed Sisyphus to return to the earth long enough to force Merope to bury the body. Once he had made it back to Corinth, however, Sisyphus defied Hades and lived out a long life. When the man finally died, the gods afflicted him with a cruel and unusual punishment. For eternity, he had to roll an incredibly heavy stone up a hill; just before he made it to the top, the stone would roll back down and he would have to begin the agonizing process all over again. **See** Thanatos (Chapter 2); **also** Corinth (Chapter 4).

Tantalus
A wealthy ruler of a part of Lydia (in western Asia Minor) who was best known for his betrayal of the gods and a gruesome trick he played on them. The gods had honored him by allowing him to eat at their table on several occasions, which made him immortal. But he repaid them with treachery. Tantalus had his own son, Pelops, killed and cooked and fed this awful dish to the gods. Seeing through the ruse, however, they restored Pelops to life and proceeded to punish Tantalus severely. **See** Pelops; and, for a full account of the story, **see** The Curse of the House of Atreus (Chapter 6).

Tarpeia
In Roman legend, the daughter of Spurius Tarpeius, leader of Rome's central fortress during the attack of the Sabines, which took place sometime near the beginning of Romulus's reign during the eighth century B.C. When the Sabine king, Titus Tatius, and his men approached the fortress, Tarpeia secretly arranged a meeting between herself and Tatius. What happened next is disputed, for two conflicting versions of the story have survived. In the first, the young woman gave Tatius the keys to the fortress in exchange for the gold bracelets and rings of his men, in which case she was a traitor to Rome. In the other, more popular story, Tarpeia gave Tatius the keys intending to trick him. In exchange for them, the Sabine soldiers gave her their shields; and without them, these men were unable to defend themselves properly against a counterattack led by Romulus. In this second story, therefore, Tarpeia was a heroine who saved the city. In any case, the hill on which the fortress sat was at first called the Tarpeian Hill, after her. (Later, it came to be known as the Capitoline Hill.) **See** Tarpeian Rock (Chapter 4).

Tarquinius Superbus, Lucius
The seventh and last of Rome's legendary kings. Also known as Tarquin the Proud or simply Tarquin, he was either the son or

grandson of the fifth legendary king, Tarquinius Priscus. Together with his second wife, Tullia, daughter of Servius Tullius (Rome's sixth king), Tarquin plotted and carried out the assassination of Servius and thereby gained the throne.

Wasting no time in establishing a reputation as a tyrant, Tarquin refused to give the dead king a proper burial and also murdered many of Servius's leading supporters. Indeed, the new king initiated a reign of terror and quickly earned the name *Superbus,* meaning "Arrogant." Nevertheless, legend claims that Tarquin was a talented military commander and a prodigious builder. He conquered numerous neighboring Latin towns not yet under Rome's sway; and he completed both the Temple of Jupiter on the Capitoline Hill and the Cloaca Maxima ("Great Sewer") running through the city's Forum (main square).

Tarquin's fall from power (and the collapse of the monarchy itself) began when his equally arrogant son, Sextus, raped Lucretia, wife of a Roman noble, Lucius Tarquinius Collatinus. In retaliation, Collatinus and another leading Roman, Lucius Junius Brutus, locked Tarquin and Sextus out of the city and launched the rebellion that led to the establishment of the Roman Republic. After losing his throne, Tarquin took refuge with the Etruscans, who inhabited the region north of Rome. **See** Brutus, Lucius Junius; Lucretia; Sibyl; **also** Rome (Chapter 4).

Telamon

The son of Aeacus (king of the island of Aegina, located southwest of Athens) and the brother of Peleus. Telamon and Peleus killed their half brother, Phocus, and hid the body. But their father soon uncovered the crime and banished both culprits. Telamon settled on the small island of Salamis (just off the coast of Attica, near Athens's urban center). There, he married Glauce, daughter of the island's king; and when

that ruler died, Telamon ascended the throne. Glauce soon died, too, and the new king married again, this time siring a son, Ajax, who later became a famous hero. Telamon also served as one of Jason's Argonauts and helped the renowned strongman Heracles wreck the city of Troy (to punish Troy's king, Laomedon, for refusing to pay Heracles a debt). To repay Telamon for his help, Heracles gave him Laomedon's daughter, Hesione, as a slave. She bore Telamon an illegitimate son— Teucer—who joined Telamon's legitimate son, Ajax, in fighting in the Trojan War. Various versions of Telamon's death circulated in ancient times, the most common one claiming he passed away of natural causes in Salamis. **See** Aeacus; Ajax 1; Laomedon; Peleus; Teucer 2; **also** The Adventures of Heracles (Chapter 6).

Telemachus

The son of the Greek hero Odysseus (king of Ithaca) and his faithful wife, Penelope. Nine years after his father had failed to return from the Trojan War (and nineteen years after Odysseus had left for Troy), Telemachus, by then a young man, traveled extensively seeking news of Odysseus's whereabouts. The youth visited King Nestor in Pylos as well as King Menelaus in Sparta. Neither could offer any concrete information. When Telemachus returned to Ithaca, his father had just arrived there. The two had a moving reunion in the hut of a local farmer. Telemachus and Odysseus then slew the suitors who had been demanding that Penelope marry one of them. These events appear in Homer's *Odyssey.* Later traditions offered various renditions of what happened to Telemachus after Odysseus regained his throne. One claimed that the young man married Nestor's daughter, Polycaste; another held that Telemachus wed Circe, a sorceress whom his father had encountered during his ten years of wandering. **See** Mentor; Odysseus; Penelope; **also** Circe (Chapter 2); The Wanderings of Odysseus (Chapter 6).

Telephus

The son of the famous heroic strongman Heracles. Telephus's mother, Auge, was the daughter of Aleus, king of Tegea (in the central Peloponnesus), and a local priestess of the goddess Athena. When Heracles visited the city, he seduced Auge, and she soon realized she was pregnant. Her father found out and was duly angry (because as a priestess she was supposed to be a virgin); and ordered her to be drowned. The king of the city of Nauplia (several miles east of Tegea) rescued Auge, however. Various and conflicting ancient versions of Telephus's subsequent birth and youth existed. In one, his mother reared him. A more common story claimed that the two were separated somehow when he was still an infant; Auge ended up in Teuthramia, a city in Mysia (a region of northwestern Asia Minor). When Telephus grew up, he wished to know his origins, so he consulted the Delphic Oracle. The oracle advised him to search in Mysia. There, the youth became friendly with Teuthras, the king of Teuthramia, who, because he had no son of his own, made Telephus his heir. The king wanted to give the young man the hand of his adopted daughter; however, she turned out to be none other than Auge, Telephus's mother. Luckily, Telephus and Auge discovered their real identities and relationship before the wedding night.

Not long after Telephus succeeded Teuthras as king, the Trojan War began. Initially, Telephus announced his support for Troy's King Priam. But then the Greek expedition landed in Mysia (by mistake), and Telephus, believing he was under attack, put up a fight. The renowned warrior Achilles wounded him just before the Greeks departed. (They returned to Greece to regroup and get a fresh start.) Telephus noticed that his wound would not heal; and on the advice of an oracle, he sailed to Greece and demanded that Achilles, who had caused the wound, should heal it. The Greek leaders struck a deal with Telephus, offering to heal him if he would guide them to Troy. Telephus agreed. Achilles' colleague Odysseus then took some rust from Achilles' spear and rubbed it on the wound, which quickly healed. Telephus then kept his end of the bargain by leading the Greeks to Troy, although he refused to join them in their fight against Priam. **See** The Trojan War (Chapter 6).

Teucer

1. An early legendary king of the city of Troy. One story said he was the son of a local river god. Another version (Virgil's *Aeneid*) claimed that Teucer was a Cretan who, during a famine, sailed with a third of the island's inhabitants to Asia Minor and settled at Troy.

2. The illegitimate son of Telamon (king of Salamis) and Hesione (daughter of Laomedon, a Trojan king). Teucer fought in the Trojan War alongside his half brother, the mighty Ajax. According to Homer in his *Iliad,* Teucer killed numerous Trojans before the Trojan hero Hector wounded him with a large rock. Teucer was also one of the Greek soldiers who hid inside the Wooden Horse, which the Trojans unwarily dragged into their city. Returning safely to Salamis after the war's conclusion, Teucer found to his dismay that his father, Telamon, would not allow him to come ashore. The king insisted that Teucer should somehow have prevented Ajax from committing suicide (which was unfair, since Teucer had been away in Mysia at the time of Ajax's demise). But though Teucer tried to reason with his father, Telamon still refused to let him land. So Teucer sailed away to the large island of Cyprus (lying south of Asia Minor) and there established a new city, which he named Salamis after his homeland. **See** Telamon.

Thersander

The son of Polynices (son of Oedipus, king of Thebes) and one of the Epigoni (the sons of the Seven Against Thebes). After his father, one of the famous Seven, had been killed in the failed attack on Thebes, Thersander wanted revenge and was instrumental in organizing another expedition. The other Epigoni included Alcmaeon (who led the army), Diomedes, Sthenelus, Promachus, Amphilochis, and Aegialeus. They managed to capture Thebes. However, the city was badly damaged in the attack, and Thersander, who took the throne, had to call on many of the Thebans who had fled during the fighting to return home and help him rebuild the city. Later, he sailed with Achilles, Agamemnon, Menelaus, and their colleagues to fight at Troy; but when the party landed by mistake in Mysia (in northwestern Asia Minor), the local king, Telephus, attacked them and killed Thersander with a spear. **See** Seven Against Thebes; Telephus.

Theseus

A legendary early Athenian king, ancient Athens's national hero, and one of the greatest of all Greek heroes. The son of King Aegeus (after whom the Aegean Sea was named), Theseus was said to have performed numerous heroic deeds, including traveling to Knossus (on Crete) and slaying the hideous Minotaur, to which Athenian youths had regularly been sacrificed. After succeeding his father as king, Theseus reportedly unified the scattered communities of the Attic peninsula into a single Athenian state. Many years later, rebellions drove him from Athens to the isle of Skyros, where he died. For a detailed rendition of his exciting life and deeds, **see** The Exploits of Theseus (Chapter 6).

Tiresias

(or Teiresias) A blind prophet who dwelled in the city Thebes. Of the two ancient versions of Tiresias's loss of sight, the first said that as a young man he saw Athena bathing naked in a stream. As a punishment, the goddess blinded him; but to be fair, she compensated by giving him the ability to understand the speech of birds, the gift of prophecy, and a greatly increased life span. The other version claimed that young Tiresias saw two snakes mating on a mountainside and killed the female. Suddenly Tiresias turned into a woman. He remained that way for seven years. Then he saw two more snakes mating and this time slew the male, which turned him back into a man. Soon afterward, Zeus and his wife, Hera, had an argument over who enjoys sex more—men or women? In Hera's view, men enjoy it more. To settle the argument, the deities consulted Tiresias, knowing that he had been both male and female. Tiresias replied that women enjoy sex much more than men do, an answer that angered the goddess so much that she blinded Tiresias. Though Zeus could not reverse what his wife had done, the god gave Tiresias the gift of prophecy to help make up for his loss of sight.

Aside from these myths, the most famous story about Tiresias concerns his involvement in the fall of Oedipus, king of Thebes, and the city's subsequent troubles. Tiresias revealed that Oedipus had killed his own father and had married his own mother. Oedipus, however, refused to listen and only later discovered that the prophet had spoken truly. A while later, after Polynices, Oedipus's son, had led the failed attack of the Seven Against Thebes, Tiresias warned Creon (Oedipus's brother-in-law), who then sat on the throne, to bury Polynices' body. Like Oedipus, Creon refused to listen; the result was the death of Oedipus's daughter Antigone and Creon's son, Haemon. Tiresias died after being captured by the Epigoni (the sons of the Seven), who had launched a new attack on Thebes.

Even in death, though, Tiresias continued to dispense advice. In Homer's *Odyssey,* the hero Odysseus visited Tiresias's ghost, who, thanks to Zeus or another god, still retained the gift of prophecy. The ghost revealed to Odysseus many of the adventures he would encounter during his wanderings. **See** Antigone; Creon 2; Oedipus; Polynices; also *Antigone; Oedipus the King* (Chapter 5); The Theban Myth Cycle (Chapter 6).

Tithonus

A son of Troy's King Priam and the husband of Eos, goddess of the dawn. Eos begged Zeus to make Tithonus immortal like herself, and the god granted her wish. However, she failed to stipulate that her husband should also remain young. So Tithonus grew older and older, but at the same time he could not die. Eventually he was helpless, barely able to move a finger or toe; and he prayed fervently for death to release him from his misery. At last, out of pity, Eos shut him away in a room, where thereafter he babbled endlessly, his words and sentences having little or no meaning. In one version of the story, he also shrank in size; and finally, the goddess turned him into the tiny, thin, and noisy grasshopper. **See** Eos (Chapter 2).

Triptolemus

A young native of Attica (the territory controlled by Athens), who became a favorite of the agricultural goddess Demeter. The goddess chose Triptolemus to go from city to city and land to land and teach humans how to cultivate grain and other crops. To aid in this task, she gave him a magic chariot pulled by two winged serpents. A number of kings and other humans were envious of either Triptolemus's knowledge or his chariot, and they tried to kill or imprison him; each time, though, Demeter rescued him. Later, Zeus made Triptolemus one of the judges of the dead. The Athenian playwright Sophocles wrote a play about Triptolemus; unfortunately, only a few fragments of the work have survived. **See** Demeter (Chapter 2).

Trophonius and Agamedes

The sons of Erginus, king of the city of Orchomenus (near Thebes in Boeotia).

The young men were gifted architects whose splendid works included the magnificent Temple of Apollo at Delphi (home of the famous oracle). They eventually designed a treasure house for a Greek king (whose identity varied from one version of the story to another). As usual, they did an excellent job erecting the building; but this time, they committed a despicable act: They placed a loose stone in the structure's back wall. Because they were the only ones who knew about the stone and how to remove it, they were repeatedly able to get away with stealing precious items from the king's collection.

One night, however, when the two brothers removed the stone and climbed inside the treasure house, some heavy objects fell and trapped Agamedes. Trophonius tried desperately to free his brother, but he could not. Thus, they agreed that Trophonius should cut off Agamedes' head. That way, the king's guards would find only a headless body, and no one would be able to trace it back to Trophonius. After completing the hideous deed, Trophonius escaped. However, some god must have decided to punish him, for not long afterward a hole opened in the earth and he disappeared into it. Later stories claimed that the man's ghost inhabited a cave on or near that spot and dispensed advice to those with enough nerve to enter the cavern.

Turnus

A prince of the Rutulians, an early people inhabiting western Italy. In Virgil's *Aeneid*, Turnus wanted to marry Lavinia, daughter of Latinus, king of Latium. But then the Trojan prince Aeneas arrived and also made a bid for Lavinia's hand. A war ensued in which Turnus met his death during single combat with Aeneas. For a fuller account of these legendary events, **see** *Aeneid* (Chapter 5); **also** Aeneas's Journey to Italy (Chapter 6).

72 GREEK AND ROMAN MYTHOLOGY

Tyro

The daughter of the king and queen of Elis (in the western Peloponnesus). When Tyro's mother died, her father married another woman, Sidero, who treated Tyro cruelly. Eventually the sea god Poseidon encountered and fell in love with Tyro, and they had twin sons—Pelias and Neleus. Tyro abandoned the babies, who were reared by some horse breeders. Tyro then married the king of Iolcos (in eastern Thessaly) and bore him three sons. When these sons became young men, Pelias suddenly arrived in Iolcos and usurped the throne. **See** Neleus; Pelias.

Xuthus

One of the three sons of Hellen, founder of the Greek race, or the son of Hellen's son, Aeolus. This disparity in identity reflects the fact that two different accounts of Xuthus's parentage and exploits existed in ancient times. The first said that Xuthus, son of Hellen, went to Athens and aided the local king, Erechtheus, in a number of ways. When Erechtheus died, one of his sons drove Xuthus out of the city. Xuthus then settled in the northern Peloponnesus; and his sons, Achaeus and Ion, subsequently gave rise to the Achaean and Ionian Greeks, respectively. The other ancient story was that of the Athenian playwright Euripides in his *Ion.* In this version, Xuthus, Aeolus's son, succeeded Erechtheus as king of Athens and had two sons—Achaeus and Dorus. Euripides made Ion a son of the god Apollo and had Xuthus later accept the young man as his own son. **See** Hellen; Ion; **also** *Ion* (Chapter 5).

CHAPTER 2
MAJOR AND MINOR GODS

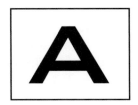

Acca Larentia

In Roman legend, the wife of the herdsman Faustulus, who found Romulus, Rome's founder, and his brother, Remus, abandoned as babies. Some Romans worshiped Acca Larentia in very ancient rituals that had become obscure and of minor importance by the third or second century B.C. Her festival was known as the Larentalia, held on December 23.

Aesculapius

The Roman name for the Greek Asclepius, god of healing. When a terrible disease struck Rome in 293 B.C., local priests consulted the Sibylline Books (sources of prophecy), which advised sending a delegation to Epidaurus (in Greece's eastern Peloponnesus), site of the most important temple of the Greek healing god. The Romans did this. Soon afterward, they imported worship of Asclepius into their capital, establishing a temple dedicated to the god, whom they called Aesculapius, on an island in the Tiber River. For the original Greek myths associated with this god, **see** Asclepius.

Anna Perenna

A Roman goddess whose festival was held on the Ides of March (March 15). Typically, celebrants picnicked on the banks of the Tiber River, and many ended the day by getting drunk. Anna Perenna's origins and attributes remain unclear; apparently, though, she had some connection with the year and its passage since she was sometimes referred to as "the year goddess." **See** Mars.

Aphrodite

The Greek goddess of love and beauty and one of the twelve Olympians. Among her many symbols were dolphins, rams, doves, and roses. According to the Greek poet Hesiod, she was born out of sea foam, an image captured in numerous artistic representations through the ages. The foam had been stirred up by the dismembered genitals of the god Uranus (**see** Uranus). The goddess first stepped onto dry land on the island of Cyprus (in the eastern Mediterranean), which thereafter became the site of her main shrines and cult. Homer, on the other hand, claimed that Aphrodite was the child of Zeus and Dione (a minor earth goddess).

Though married to the god of the forge, Hephaestos, Aphrodite secretly loved the war god, Ares (with whom she had a son— Eros, a love god often depicted in Greek art as her companion). When Hephaestos discovered their illicit affair and exposed it to the other gods, they ridiculed the lovers. In fact, Aphrodite had affairs with several other gods (including Dionysus, Poseidon, and Hermes) as well as a few mortals. For that reason, the Greeks identified her more with sexual passion than with the love and loyalty of the marriage bond. Thus, she came to be seen by most Greek men (although not necessarily most Greek women) as adulterous and irresponsible as well as hostile and even dangerous to men, a decidedly negative female role model.

Part of Aphrodite's preoccupation with love and desire came from her power to make any gods (with the exception of Athena, Artemis, and Hestia) and humans fall in love with anyone she chose. Sometimes she used this power to punish, as in the case of Pasiphae, wife of Minos (king of Crete). The goddess caused the woman to be overcome with desire for a bull, and the union of Pasiphae and the bull produced the fearsome Minotaur (a creature half man and half bull). On the other hand, the goddess often used the same power to

help people. When Jason needed an ally to help him win the Golden Fleece, for example, Aphrodite made the sorceress Medea fall in love with him; the sudden love and desire the beautiful Spartan queen Helen felt for Troy's Prince Paris was also the work of the goddess, who wanted to see the young man succeed in all of his endeavors.

The manner in which Paris became Aphrodite's favorite lies at the core of her most prominent myth—usually referred to as the Judgment of Paris. The young man was chosen to judge a contest in which the goddesses Aphrodite, Hera, and Athena competed for the title of "the fairest." The official prize was a golden apple, although, of course, a great deal of pride and prestige were involved as well. Paris chose Aphrodite, who thereafter helped him whenever she could. **See** Ares; Eros; Hephaestos; **also** Helen; Paris; Pasiphae (Chapter 1); and, for a fuller account of the Judgment of Paris and how it led to the siege of Troy by the Greeks, **see** The Trojan War (Chapter 6).

Apollo's priestess at Delphi receives gifts in the god's name in this drawing based on an ancient sculpted relief.

Apollo

The versatile Greek and Roman god of prophecy, healing, truth, poetry, music, and archery; the son of Zeus and the Titan Leto; and the twin brother of the goddess Artemis. Apollo's chief symbol was the laurel tree. Leto gave birth to him on the tiny Aegean island of Delos. There—fed on ambrosia and nectar (the magical food and drink of the gods)—he grew to adulthood in only a few days and immediately set out in search of a suitable site to establish an oracle. At Delphi, a beautiful spot in central Greece on the southern slopes of Mt. Parnassus, Apollo found what he was looking for. But the area was guarded by a female serpent named Python, who had prophetic powers not unlike his own. After slaying Python, Apollo established his oracular shrine, which became the most renowned of its kind in the known world. (He named the priestess of his temple there the Pythia, after Python.) Soon, the Greeks began to hold public games at Delphi, called the Pythian Games; at first they consisted of only musical contests, but eventually athletic competitions were added.

Although Apollo communicated with humans through the oracle, he also directly interacted with humans on a number of occasions. One of the first of these was the violent episode in which he and his sister Artemis slew the children of Niobe, who insulted Apollos and Artemis's mother, Leto. A while later, Apollo had no choice but to interact with mortals. For killing the Cyclopes, the one-eyed servants of Zeus, the leader of the gods punished Apollo by forcing him to work as a slave for a mortal man. Apollo chose to serve Admetus, a kindly king of Thessaly. Disguised as a farmhand, the god aided Admetus by making all of his cows give birth to twins and by allowing the man to escape death by substituting another mortal for himself when it was time for him to die. Apollo later served under another mortal, Laomedon, a Trojan king, when Apollo and Poseidon built the walls of Troy. (When Laomedon refused to pay for the work, Apollo unleashed a plague on Troy.)

Apollo's later dealings with the Trojans were more cordial and constructive. During the famous Trojan War, the god sided with Troy's King Priam and helped the Trojans against the besieging Greeks at every opportunity. For example, Apollo inflicted a plague on the Greek camp and also guided the arrow shot by Troy's Prince Paris to the vulnerable heel of the Greek hero Achilles. The god also figured prominently in the lives of the children of the leaders of the Greek expedition. Apollo urged Agamemnon's son, Orestes, to avenge Agamemnon's murder by Clytemnestra (Orestes' mother), for instance; and later, the god defended Orestes in an Athenian court, where the young man stood trial for killing Clytemnestra.

Another way that Apollo interacted with humans was by mating with mortal women. By Coronis (daughter of a king of Orchomenus, in Boeotia), he sired the god Asclepius (who inherited his father's powers of healing and became the chief healing god of the Greco-Roman world); and by the sea nymph Cyrene, Apollo fathered Aristaeus, who became famous as a bee-keeper.

Although he originated as a Greek god (possibly borrowed by the Greeks in very early times from somewhere north or east of Greece), Apollo became equally important to the Romans. They came to know him though the Sibyl (prophetess) at Cumae (in southwestern Italy), who was thought to be strongly influenced and supported by the god. Augustus, the first Roman emperor, chose Apollo as his patron and erected a magnificent temple dedicated to him on Rome's Palatine Hill. **See** Artemis; Asclepius; Leto; **also** Admetus; Aristaeus; Laomedon; Niobe; Sibyl (Chapter 1); Python (Chapter 3); Delphic Oracle (Chapter 4); The Trojan War (Chapter 6).

Ares

The Greek god of war (whom the Romans later equated with their god Mars) and one of the major Olympian gods. In their art and myths, the Greeks usually pictured Ares, the only son born of the marriage of the deities Zeus and Hera, as a violent and often arrogant warrior. They also typically portrayed Ares with one or more of his symbols—a burning torch, a spear, dogs, and vultures. According to these myths, although he never married, he did have lovers—the Greek love goddess, Aphrodite, the most prominent among them. With her, he had a daughter, Harmonia (who became the wife of Cadmus, founder of Thebes), and twin sons, Phobos ("Panic") and Deimos ("Fear"), who sometimes fought alongside their father in battle. Ares' affair with Aphrodite ended when her husband, Hephaestos (god of the forge), found out about it and embarrassed the lovers in front of the other gods.

Ares also had a daughter named Alcippe, born of an affair with a mortal woman—Aglaurus (daughter of an Athenian king). When one of the sea god Poseidon's sons raped Alcippe, Ares flew into a rage and killed the young man. Poseidon then called for the major gods to assemble on the site where the killing took place and try Ares for murder. Believing that Ares' act had been justified, however, the deities found the war god not guilty of murder. In any case, the site, a hill near the Athenian Acropolis, thereafter became known as the Areopagus, or "Hill of Ares," in memory of these legendary incidents.

Ares was generally at his best on the battlefield, of course. However, he was not as smart as some of the other gods and was easily outwitted by them, particularly Athena, goddess of war and wisdom. During the Trojan War, Ares backed the Trojans while Athena supported the Greeks. She helped the Greek warrior Diomedes wound Ares, who immediately lodged a complaint with Zeus, calling it foul play. Later, after Athena insulted him repeatedly, Ares hurled his spear at her; but it struck her in her magical breastplate (the

aegis) and bounced off, after which she tossed a huge stone that sent him crashing to the ground. Later, Athena also helped the hero Heracles wound Ares in the thigh. **See** Aphrodite; Athena; Hephaestos; Mars; **also** The Adventures of Heracles; The Trojan War (Chapter 6).

Artemis

One of the major Greek Olympian deities; the goddess of wild animals, hunting, and archery; and the protector of children, particularly young girls. Deer, dogs, and cypress trees were her symbols. She was a virgin and was fiercely proud of it, insisting that her attendants, usually nymphs (minor nature goddesses), also remain virgins. The daughter of Zeus and Leto, one of the Titans, Artemis was the twin sister of Apollo, god of prophecy. Leto gave birth to the twins on the island of Asteria, which later became known as Delos. Zeus's wife, Hera, was naturally jealous of any female children born to her husband by other women, so she often opposed or harassed Artemis. In Homer's *Iliad,* for example, Hera insults and even strikes the younger Artemis, who runs to Zeus in tears.

In most other myths, however, Artemis displayed considerable strength, determination, and even ferocity. When a giant named Tityus tried to rape her mother, Artemis and Apollo slew him; and when Niobe (a queen of Thebes) insulted Leto, the twins savagely and methodically used their deadly arrows to kill the woman's children. Artemis also slew Orion, a giant hunter. (The reasons varied from one ancient story to another and included, among others, his trying to rape her or one of her attendants or his threatening to kill of all the animals in the world.) In addition, during the famous battle between the gods and giants Artemis defeated and killed a giant named Gration.

Artemis was no less formidable in dealing with mortals who crossed her in some way. When, for example, Actaeon (a mortal grandson of Apollo) saw the goddess bathing naked, she turned him into a stag, which Actaeon's own dogs then attacked and killed. Artemis also punished Oeneus, king of Calydon (in western Greece). When he neglected to perform her rituals at an important religious festival, she unleashed a giant boar that terrorized the local countryside. One of the most famous incidents involving punishment by and appeasement of Artemis took place at the outset of the Trojan War. Agamemnon, leader of the Greek expedition, displeased the goddess (the reason varying from story to story), and in return she demanded that he sacrifice his daughter, Iphigenia, to obtain the fair winds needed to launch his ships toward Troy. Agamemnon did so. This dramatic story is the subject of Euripides' magnificent and moving play *Iphigenia in Aulis*. **See** Apollo; Asteria; Hera; **also** Actaeon (Chapter 1); giants; Orion (Chapter 3); *Iphigenia in Aulis* (Chapter 5); The Trojan War (Chapter 6).

Asclepius

The Greek god of healing and the son of the god Apollo and Coronis, a princess of Orchomenus (in Boeotia). Several versions of Asclepius's birth circulated in ancient times. In the most common, after the goddess Artemis (Apollo's sister) killed Coronis (for sleeping with a mortal man behind Apollo's back), the messenger god, Hermes, took the infant Asclepius to the kindly centaur Chiron, who reared the child, teaching him much about the arts and medicine. Aiding the process was the fact that the young god had inherited his father's talent for healing (since this talent was one of Apollo's many attributes). Once he was grown, Asclepius married a mortal woman, Epione, who bore him two sons—Machaon and Podalirius. They both took part in the Trojan War, often aiding wounded soldiers.

The main myth associated with Asclepius concerns his death, which was an unusual fate for a god. In addition to healing people, he dared to bring some dead individuals back to life, which angered the chief god, Zeus, who felt that once mortals had passed to the Underworld, they should stay there. Zeus hurled a thunderbolt at Asclepius, killing him. Apollo then retaliated by slaying Zeus's own servants, the Cyclopes (one-eyed giants).

Worship of Asclepius had spread to all parts of the Greek world by about 400 B.C. Many shrines were erected to him, but his main temple was at Epidaurus (in the eastern Peloponnesus). A group of Romans visited Epidaurus in 293 B.C., and thereafter the Romans worshiped him, too (calling

Asclepius, Greek god of healing. The famous statue is missing the upper part of the deity's signature staff and serpent.

him Aesculapius). Both Greeks and Romans often brought sick friends and relatives to his sanctuaries, hoping he would cure them. Asclepius's symbols were the snake and the staff (which survive as the symbol of the modern medical profession). **See** Aesculapius; Apollo; **also** Chiron (Chapter 3).

Asteria

One of the Titans (the first race of Greek gods). The daughter of the Titan Phoebe, Asteria was best known for trying to elude the amorous attentions of the Olympian god Zeus. When he pursued Asteria, she turned herself into a quail and jumped into the Aegean Sea. An island later grew up on the spot where she landed; at first it bore the name Asteria, after her, but later it became known by its more familiar name—Delos. There, Asteria's sister, Leto, gave birth to the Olympian deities Apollo and Artemis. **See** Delos (Chapter 4).

Atargatis

Also known as Dea Syria, "the Syrian Goddess," a deity of vegetation and fertility who originated in Syria and southern Asia Minor. Her main temple was at Hierapolis (in Syria), where artists pictured her on a throne flanked by lions. Both fish and doves were sacred to her, and in some regions worshipers believed that she was half woman and half fish. Besides fish and doves, her chief symbols were stalks of grain and vines. Atargatis's worship spread to Egypt in the third century B.C. and to Greece in the following century; but she became only marginally popular in Rome and its non-Greek provinces. A colorful and humorous description of a band of Atargatis's wandering priests—called Galli—taking part in a bizarre public display of self-humiliation appears in Roman novelist Lucius Apuleius's *The Golden Ass* (the only Latin novel that has survived complete). **See** Apuleius, Lucius (Chapter 5).

Athena

(also Athene) The Greek goddess of war and wisdom, as well as numerous urban arts and crafts (especially spinning and weaving), and one of the most important of the major Olympian gods. Her symbols were the owl and the olive tree. Athena (whom the Romans later came to associate with their goddess Minerva) was also the patron deity (divine protector) of many Greek cities, most famously of Athens. There, over the centuries, the Athenians raised several temples to her, including the renowned Parthenon and the Erechtheum. The goddess's cult image (statue) inside the Parthenon, known as the *Athena Parthenos,* was only one of several manifestations of the goddess. She was believed to have a number of different sides to her character, each of which personified a special talent or physical or mental attribute. In Greek homes, a room where a young woman, ideally a virgin, dwelled before her marriage was often referred to as a *parthenon.* So Athena Parthenos was "Athena the Virgin," an image emphasizing not only the fact of her perpetual virginity (like that of the goddess Artemis) but also her feminine beauty and the purity of her wisdom.

By contrast, Athena Promachos ("Athena the Warrior Champion") and Athena Nike ("Athena the Victor") were images stressing her physical strength, courage, and fearsome fighting skills. Other manifestations of Athena included Hygieia ("Goddess of Health") and Ergane ("the Worker"). She was also frequently called Pallas Athena, a term of obscure origins. Some modern scholars think that *Pallas* may have been the name of a Bronze Age war goddess whose identity merged with Athena's in later times.

Athena was so important to the Greeks that she figured in numerous myths. One of the most famous of these concerned her own birth, which was unusual in that she sprang, fully clad in her armor, from the head of her father, Zeus, leader of the Olympian gods. The seventh-century B.C.

Greek poet Hesiod recorded the details of this miraculous birth:

Zeus first took the goddess Metis [daughter of two Titans and a deity known for her great wisdom, much of which she passed on to both Zeus and Athena] as his wife, but later deceived her and swallowed her, for fate had decreed that Metis would conceive children filled with wisdom. And the first of these would be the bright-eyed maiden Athena, who would have strength and wisdom equal to her father's. Metis remained concealed inside of Zeus and eventually conceived Athena, who received from her father the *aegis* [his majestic and invincible breastplate], with which she surpassed in strength all her brother and sister gods. And Zeus brought her into the world, bearing the *aegis* and clad in battle armor, from out of his head. (*Theogony* 886–929)

Another myth described how Athena and the sea god Poseidon had a contest to decide which of them would preside over and protect Athens. Poseidon touched the Acropolis with his trident, producing a miraculous saltwater spring. Athena then countered him by causing the first olive tree to sprout from the hill's summit; seeing this, Zeus and the other gods judging the contest declared her the winner. (Other versions of the story say a mortal judged the contest.) Still another tradition held that Athena sent an olive-wood statue of herself hurtling out of the sky. The spot on which it supposedly landed, near the Acropolis's northern edge, became the site for a succession of temples that housed the sacred statue *Athena Polias* ("Athena of the City"). The name of these temples—the Erechtheum—derived from Erechtheus, a legendary Bronze Age Athenian king who came to be seen as a sort of partner to Athena or custodian of her temples. (Painters and sculptors often pictured him as a serpent guarding the goddess.)

As might be expected, a majority of the many myths in which Athena took part involved war or adventure. She was the fiercest and most active champion of the Greeks during the Trojan War, for example. (Yet the Trojans still revered her and maintained several shrines to her, one of which held a sacred cult statue, the Palladium. Believing that they could not win the war as long as the Trojans possessed this statue, the Greek warriors Odysseus and Diomedes, with the help of Helen, sneaked into Troy one night and stole the Palladium.) During the war, according to Homer in his *Iliad,* Athena often fought with the war god, Ares, who favored the Trojans. She also aided a number of heroes and adventurers, among them Perseus (to whom she gave the tools he needed to kill the dreaded Gorgon Medusa), Bellerophon, Jason, Heracles, and Odysseus.

In helping another young man, Athena demonstrated that she could wield justice as effectively as a sword and shield. After slaying his own mother, Clytemnestra, Orestes, son of Agamemnon, was pursued by the vengeful Furies. As described in the third play in Aeschylus's mighty trilogy, the *Oresteia,* when Orestes reached Athens, the goddess intervened and arranged for the young man to receive a fair trial. The jury was split, so Athena cast a tie-breaking vote that acquitted Orestes; then she transformed the Furies into the Eumenides ("the Kind Ones"), in the process ending the infamous, generations-long curse of the house of Atreus. **See** Ares; Metis; Minerva; Zeus; **also** Ajax 2; Cassandra; Diomedes 1; Erechtheus; Erichthonius (Chapter 1); Furies; Gorgons; owl (Chapter 3); Athens (Chapter 4); *Eumenides* (Chapter 5); The Adventures of Heracles; The Creation of the Gods and Humans; The Curse of the House of Atreus; Perseus and Medusa; The Quest for the Golden Fleece; The Trojan War; The Wanderings of Odysseus (Chapter 6).

Atlas

A Titan and the son of Iapetus. According to early Greek tradition, Atlas guarded the pillars of heaven, which supported the sky; later stories, however, say that he himself held up the sky or even the entire earth. The two main myths about Atlas involved the heroes Perseus and Heracles. In the tale of Perseus and Atlas, Perseus happened by, carrying the head of the Gorgon Medusa whom the hero had recently slain. Hearing that Perseus was the son of Zeus, Atlas tried to drive the young man away, since the Titan had earlier been warned that one of Zeus's sons would come to steal the golden apples that grew on a magical tree in the nearby garden of the Hesperides (minor goddesses). Angry at Atlas's lack of hospitality, Perseus showed him Medusa's face, which turned the Titan to stone. In ancient times, many people believed that this was the origin of the Atlas Mountains in northwestern Africa.

The trouble is that this incident was supposed to have happened well before Heracles' visit with Atlas (since Heracles lived two generations later than Perseus). According to the story, Heracles arrived to retrieve the golden apples to fulfill his eleventh labor for the Greek king Eurystheus. Atlas offered to go get the apples while Heracles temporarily held up the sky for him; but when Atlas returned with the treasure, he refused to relieve Heracles of the great load. Atlas would have left Heracles there forever had Heracles not tricked him. Saying that he needed to adjust the weight better on his shoulders, Heracles got Atlas to resume holding up the sky, then picked up the golden apples and headed back to Greece. **See** Hesperides; **also** The Adventures of Heracles; Perseus and Medusa (Chapter 6).

Attis

The young consort of Cybele, a goddess who originated in Phrygia (in Asia Minor). According to legend, Attis was the son of a local river god. When the younger deity decided to marry a young mortal, the goddess Cybele, who loved him and wanted to prevent the marriage, drove him mad, with the result that he castrated himself and died. Believing in this myth, in classical times the priests of Cybele castrated themselves to appease the goddess. Worship of Attis regularly accompanied that of Cybele, which spread to various Mediterranean lands during the last few centuries of the second millennium B.C. The Roman state officially accepted the two gods during the reign of the emperor Claudius (A.D. 41–54). **See** Cybele.

Bacchus

Originating perhaps in Lydia (in Asia Minor), the alternative name for the Greek fertility and wine god, Dionysus, and the name the Romans used for him. According to the Roman historian Livy, the god's wild rites, known as the Bacchanalia (or the Bacchic Mysteries or the *orgia*), originally included drunken orgies and other acts generally viewed as socially unacceptable or immoral. (Usually, such rites were led by Bacchus's most fanatical female followers, the Bacchants.) Disturbed by these revels, in 186 B.C. the Roman Senate banned the Bacchanalia from Italy, although scattered examples of it occurred in later times. For the original Greek myths in which the god took part, **see** Dionysus.

Bellona

A Roman goddess of war who, in very early times, bore the name Duellona. The Romans sometimes viewed her as the sister or the wife of Mars, their war god, and in the third century B.C. they built a temple for her in Rome's Campus Martius ("Field of Mars") and held a festival for her on June 3.

Bona Dea

("the Good Goddess") A Roman fertility deity worshiped almost exclusively by women. The Romans sometimes identified Bona Dea with another goddess of fertility, Fauna, and celebrated her festival annually on December 3. In her only myth, her father, the agricultural god Faunus, raped her after getting her drunk. This was said to be the reason that wine was banned from her ceremonies. **See** Faunus.

Boreas

Greek god of the north wind who, it was said, hailed from Thrace (in northern Greece). Boreas was often portrayed as a very forceful, even violent wind, in contrast with Zephyrus, the deity associated with the more gentle west wind. In legend, Boreas carried off one of the daughters of the Athenian king Erechtheus, and she bore him two sons, Calais and Zetes (who joined the crew of Jason's ship, the *Argo*), as well as two daughters, Chione and Cleopatra. Boreas was fond of horses, and Greek artists frequently pictured him as a horse.

Calliope

One of the nine Muses (Greek goddesses of the fine arts). She was usually represented as the Muse of epic poetry and was depicted holding a writing tablet. One legend claimed that her son was Orpheus, the famous Greek poet and musician. **See** Muses.

Calypso

A minor Greek goddess or nymph. Said to be a daughter of the Titan Atlas, she ruled a remote island, Ogygia, where the Greek hero Odysseus was stranded after a shipwreck during his perilous voyage home from Troy. Calypso fell in love with Odysseus and kept him on the island for seven years. Eventually, however, Zeus sent the god Hermes to persuade her to release her captive; she then helped Odysseus build the boat he needed to continue his trip home to Ithaca. **See** The Wanderings of Odysseus (Chapter 6).

Camenae

Some minor Italian goddesses who may have been originally associated with water but who eventually came to be identified with the Greek Muses, goddesses of the fine arts. Rome's Vestal Virgins (state priestesses who tended the temple of the goddess Vesta) drew the water they used in their rituals from a spring said to be sacred to the Camenae. **See** Muses.

Carmentis

(or Carmenta) A minor Roman goddess said to have been the mother of Evander, the first settler on the future site of Rome. (According to tradition, Carmentis mated with Mercury, the Roman version of the Greek god Hermes, to produce Evander.) Roman women came to worship Carmentis as a protector of childbirth. And the Roman state assigned a special priest to her and held a small religious festival, the Carmentalia, for her in mid-January. In addition, one of Rome's gates (at the base of the Capitoline Hill) was named for her— the Carmentalis. **See** Evander.

Castalia

A Greek nymph known for throwing herself into a spring on the slopes of Mt. Parnassus, near Delphi, while the god Apollo was chasing her. Afterward, the spring became sacred to Apollo as well as to the

Muses; and all pilgrims who came to Delphi to consult the famous oracle had to purify themselves first by dipping into Castalia's spring. **See** Delphic Oracle (Chapter 4).

Ceres

A very ancient Italian goddess of grain who also personified nature's yearly renewal and regeneration. The Romans, who came to identify Ceres with the important Greek fertility goddess, Demeter, celebrated her popular festival, the Cerialia, from April 12 to 19. People often sacrificed to her after a funeral to purify the house of the deceased. For the traditional Greek myths associated with the goddess, **see** Demeter.

Charon

The son of Erebus (Darkness) and Nyx (Night), and the boatman who ferried dead souls across the River Styx and into the Underworld. Charon demanded that each traveler pay him a fee of one obol (a common Greek coin); this may be the origin of the Greek custom of placing an obol in the mouth of a dead person just prior to burial. The ghastly boatman played a minor role in several myths. Most memorably, the hero Heracles forced Charon to take him across the Styx, and as a punishment for allowing the strongman into his realm, Hades (god of the Underworld) put the boatman in chains. **See** Underworld (Chapter 4).

Circe

A minor goddess and a sorceress who inhabited the remote island of Aeaea, best known for her encounter with the Greek hero Odysseus and his men during their wanderings following the Trojan War. Said to be the daughter of the sun god, Helios, Circe often changed humans into animals if she felt they had offended her. For example, she transformed several of Odysseus's men into pigs. And when the sea god Glaucus asked her for a love potion to woo a young woman named Scylla, Circe fell in love with Glaucus, and out of jealousy she turned Scylla into a dreadful monster that attacked unwary sailors. Many other humans whom the sorceress had transformed roamed as wolves, lions, and other beasts in the woods near her house. **See** The Wanderings of Odysseus (Chapter 6).

Consus

An ancient Italian deity associated with grain, granaries, and horses. In Rome, his festivals, the Consualiae, took place on August 21 and December 15, at which times a special underground altar and barn located under the Circus Maximus (a large facility used for chariot racing) were temporarily uncovered. On these same days, in honor of Consus, farmers gave horses and donkeys a day of rest and sometimes draped them with flower garlands.

Cronos

(or Cronus) The son of Uranus (Sky) and Gaia (Earth) and the leader of the Titans (the first race of Greek gods). When Gaia complained to Cronos that Uranus was being a tyrant by imprisoning some of her other offspring, the Hecatoncheires (hundred-handed giants) and Cyclopes (one-eyed giants), Cronos attacked his father and used a sickle to castrate him. (The Furies, giants, and nymphs sprang from the splattered blood droplets.) As the new ruler of the universe, Cronos proved just as mean and crude as Uranus. Cronos also imprisoned his half brothers, the giants. Then, after marrying his sister Rhea, he fathered the first Olympian gods—Zeus, Hestia, Hera, Poseidon, Hades, and Demeter; but because he feared that one of these children would overthrow him, Cronos swallowed them one by one after they were born. The exception was Zeus, whom Rhea hid and asked some nymphs to raise in secret. Later, Zeus returned, made Cronos vomit the other gods back up, and led the Olympians in a mighty war against Cronos and his Titans.

In an alternate ancient tradition, generally followed by the Romans, Cronos, whom the Romans identified with an Italian god, Saturn, was a kindly ruler who reigned during a legendary golden age. **See** Curetes; nymphs; Saturn; Titans; Uranus; Zeus; **also** Cyclops; Furies; Hecatoncheires (Chapter 3).

Cupid

A popular Roman god of love who was said to be the son of the deities Venus (the Greek Aphrodite) and Vulcan (the Greek Hephaestos) or of Venus and Mars (the Greek Ares). Like the Greek love god, Eros, with whom the Romans associated him, Cupid was often portrayed in art as an incredibly handsome young man and/or a comely male child with wings and a quiver of arrows. He also appeared as a symbol of life after death on coffins. Cupid played a leading role in a famous myth in which he had a love affair with a beautiful young mortal woman named Psyche, as told in the Latin novel *The Golden Ass* by the Roman writer Lucius Apuleius. **See** Eros; and, for a full telling of Cupid's and Psyche's romantic tale, **see** Cupid and Psyche (Chapter 6).

Curetes

A group of minor male Cretan gods said to live among the nymphs on the slopes of Crete's Mt. Ida. When the Titan Rhea hid her son Zeus in a cave on Crete (to keep his father, Cronos, from swallowing him), the Curetes danced around the cave's entrance, beating their spears on their shields to hide baby Zeus's cries from Cronos's ears. Ironically,

many years later the grown-up Zeus killed the Curetes for taking the side of his wife, Hera, in a dispute. **See** Cronos; Zeus.

Cybele

("the Great Mother") A goddess who originated in Phrygia (in western-central Asia Minor) and eventually became extremely popular across much of the Mediterranean world. Cybele was a fertility deity who came to be seen as a life-giving ancient

Young Cupid cavorts with his mother, Venus (the Greek Aphrodite) in this second-century B.C. sculpture.

mother. People also thought she could cure (or if angry, inflict) disease and protect people in wartime. Her male consort, Attis, was later worshiped along with her. By the fifth century B.C. she became known to the Greeks, who often identified her with the Titan Rhea, mother of Zeus (thereby fulfilling her role as a mother figure).

The Romans began worshiping Cybele in 204 B.C., near the close of the Second Punic War. At this time, a Roman ambassador journeyed to Phrygia and brought her sacred black stone (supposedly a meteorite) back to Rome, where a few years later it was installed in a temple built to honor her on the Palatine Hill. (The Romans sometimes identified Cybele with an ancient Italian fertility goddess, Bona Dea.) During the first century A.D., Cybele's festival, the Megalesia, celebrated from April 4 to 10, became popular throughout the Roman Empire.

Cybele's mythical origins were the subject of several original and conflicting Phrygian myths (some of which the Greeks and Romans no doubt altered over the years). In the most popular version, Zeus (or his Phrygian equivalent) was asleep one day on the slopes of Mt. Dindymus (in Phrygia) and his sperm fell on the ground. Soon, a unique living thing sprang from that spot, a divine being having both male and female sex organs. Disturbed at what such a deity might be capable of, the gods castrated the being, who then transformed into the fertile female goddess Cybele.

Meanwhile, the severed male organs implanted themselves in the ground and grew into a tree, which eventually shed a seed that entered the womb of Nana, the daughter of a local river god. A few months later, Nana gave birth to Attis, who grew into a handsome youth with whom Cybele fell madly in love. When he decided to marry someone else, though, she drove him mad and he died. But afterward, she was sorry for what she had done and asked Zeus to make sure that Attis's body never decayed. **See** Attis; Bona Dea; **also** Phrygia (Chapter 4).

Daphne

One of the better-known nymphs (minor Greek nature goddesses), who was said to be a virgin, like the goddess Artemis. In one ancient story, Leucippus, son of the king of Pisa (in the western Peloponnesus) fell in love with Daphne. But fearing she would reject him, he disguised himself as a woman and went hunting with her and her companions. The god Apollo, who also cared for Daphne, wanted to expose Leucippus, so the god planted in the hunters' minds the idea of bathing in a stream. When Leucippus refused to strip off his clothes, Daphne and the others tore them off and, discovering his ruse, killed him.

In another story about Daphne, Apollo argued with the love god, Eros, saying that Eros's weapons were inferior to his own. To prove this was untrue, Eros shot one of his special arrows at Apollo, striking his heart and causing him to fall madly in love with Daphne; Eros also shot an arrow at the young nymph, this shaft making her resistant to the advances of any lover, no matter how handsome. A mad chase ensued, with Apollo hot on Daphne's heels. He almost caught up to her; but in desperation, she called out to her father, a local river god, for help. He turned her into a laurel tree, depriving Apollo of his prize. But Apollo still loved Daphne; and in her memory, he ordained that thereafter a garland of laurel should decorate his lyre as well as the heads of poets and singers. **See** Apollo.

Demeter

The Greek goddess of plants, especially grain crops (as exemplified by her symbol, a sheaf of wheat); one of the major Olympian gods; a daughter of the Titans Cronos and Rhea; and the mother of Persephone, queen of the Underworld. Demeter not only oversaw agriculture, but she was also the central deity worshiped at the shrine of the Mysteries in Eleusis (not far west of Athens). The way the goddess attained this important position is the theme of her central tale and one of the most famous and enduring of all Greek myths.

The story began when Zeus (leader of the Olympians) secretly agreed to allow his brother Hades (lord of the Underworld) to have Demeter's daughter, Persephone, as his bride. One day when Persephone was out picking flowers, the ground suddenly opened up and Hades burst forth in his chariot, grabbed the surprised girl and carried her back to his subterranean realm. Hearing that Persephone had disappeared, Demeter began a frantic search for her; finally, the sun god, Helios, who had witnessed the abduction, revealed to Demeter what had transpired.

Angry and distraught, Demeter caused drought and famine to sweep across the earth. Zeus tried to reason with her, but she refused to listen to him and shunned towering Olympus, the abode of the gods, instead taking human form and wandering from one human habitation to another. One day, disguised as a sorrowful old woman, Demeter stopped to rest in the town of Eleusis, near Athens. The local people treated her kindly, and she finally revealed her true form and instructed them to build her a large and splendid temple. Once the building was finished, Demeter entered it and, still brooding over the loss of her daughter, refused to come out for a whole year.

Meanwhile, the earth was growing increasingly barren. Zeus worried that humanity would soon be extinguished, and therefore the gods would receive no more sacrifices. According to the oldest surviving version of the story, Zeus sent the rainbow goddess, Iris, to coax Demeter back to Olympus. When this failed,

> Zeus the father sent all the blessed gods to her [Demeter] in turn, and they came, one following another, summoning her. But she firmly spurned all their attempts, for she declared she would not set foot on sweet-smelling Olympus or bring forth fruit from the earth before she looked upon her fair daughter again with her own eyes. When loud-thundering Zeus . . . heard this, he sent Hermes . . . so that he might persuade Hades with gentle words to allow him to lead chaste Persephone forth from the misty land of darkness to the light . . . in order that her mother might behold her with her own eyes and cease her bitter anger. (*Homeric Hymn to Demeter* 325–350)

A deal was struck in which Hades and Zeus agreed to allow Persephone to return to the earth's surface on the condition that she ate nothing while in the Underworld. Unfortunately, the girl ate some pomegranate seeds; so Zeus decreed that thereafter she could spend only part of the year on the surface with her mother and must dwell the rest of the time with Hades in his kingdom. Demeter did not like this outcome, but she finally accepted it and restored her blessings to humanity. She sent an Athenian youth, Triptolemus, to journey from place to place teaching people the agricultural arts. And she also saw to it that her shrine at Eleusis had a proper priesthood so it would thrive and attract many worshipers.

With this myth as their basis, the Eleusinian Mysteries did indeed thrive. The classical Greeks celebrated Demeter's festival in September, in one ceremony reenacting the goddess's loss of and ultimate reunion with her daughter. Demeter's cult also required new members to undergo a secret initiation (hence the name *Mysteries*). Membership was open to all, male or female, free or slave. New initiates first purified themselves by bathing in the sea, then sacrificed a young pig. After that, they joined the other members in a great procession in which they carried the "sacred objects" (stored in the Eleusinion, a temple near the foot of the Acropolis in Athens) to Demeter's sanctuary at Eleusis, about a twelve-mile walk. The nature of these objects was as secret as the initiation itself. The festival's climax occurred in the sanctuary's initiation hall, where apparently a cult leader revealed the sacred objects. This worship of Demeter remained popular and active among generations of Greeks, and later a number of Romans (who identified her with an Italian goddess, Ceres), until the Christian Roman emperor Theodosius I suppressed the Mysteries in A.D. 393. **See** Ceres; Hades; Persephone; Zeus; **also** Triptolemus (Chapter 1); Eleusis (Chapter 4).

Diana

An ancient Italian goddess of forests and wild nature who eventually came to be identified with the Greek deity Artemis and took on her image as goddess of hunting and wild animals as well as a protector of women. The *Hymn to Diana,* written by the Roman poet Catullus, effectively describes Diana's various roles. The early Romans raised a temple to her on Rome's Aventine Hill, and her festival was held on August 13. For the original Greek myths associated with her, **see** Artemis.

Dictynna

One of the names of an early Cretan goddess (another being Britomartis). Like the Greek Artemis and Roman Diana, Dictynna was an overseer of wild things, and she eventually came to be identified with both of these goddesses. **See** Artemis; Diana; **also** Dicte, Mt. (Chapter 4).

Dionysus

The versatile Greek god of the vine, wine, and fertility; the son of Zeus; and the central deity of an important mystery cult and several prominent religious festivals across Greece and other parts of the Mediterranean world. Dionysus was the youngest of the major Greek gods. He appeared in Homer's works (probably composed in the ninth or eighth century B.C.) as only a minor deity, but his stature grew over time until, by the last three centuries B.C. (the Hellenistic Age), he was the most widely worshiped god in the Greek-speaking lands. Dionysus bore several alternate names, including Bacchus, Bromius, Lenaeus ("of the Wine-Vat"), and Dendrites ("of Trees"), and many people identified him with Iacchus, a god who aided Demeter and her own mystery cult, the Eleusinian Mysteries. (Another god associated with Dionysus—known as Dionysus Zagreus—was actually an alternate version of him that emerged during Hellenistic times; this version was killed and reborn.) Dionysus was, in addition, the patron of Athens's great dramatic festivals.

Several ancient stories purported to describe Dionysus's birth. In the most common version, Zeus took the form of a human man and seduced Semele, daughter of Cadmus (founder of Thebes). When Zeus's wife, Hera, found out that Semele was pregnant with her husband's child, the goddess tricked Zeus into revealing his true form to the young woman, which was so dazzling that it caused her to shrivel into a shrunken corpse. At the last moment, Zeus rescued the fetus from her womb and implanted it in his own thigh. Several weeks later Dionysus was born from that thigh.

At the request of Zeus and Hermes, Semele's sister, Ino, raised the young Dionysus. This proved difficult, for the jealous Hera still wanted to harm the child, and the goddess eventually drove Ino and her husband, Athamas, mad to punish them for helping Dionysus. After the young god reached manhood, he brought his real mother, Semele, back from the Underworld and made her a minor goddess on Mt. Olympus, renaming her Thyone.

A number of the myths associated with Dionysus involved kings and other humans who refused to accept the fact of his divinity or to join his cult. One of the most famous of these stories, told in Euripides' great play the *Bacchae* (first performed in 405 B.C.), involved Pentheus, the god's cousin and a Theban king. After Dionysus drove Thebes's women into a religious frenzy that made them wander and dance through the countryside, Pentheus imprisoned the young god in a dungeon. But the door to the prison miraculously flew open. And Dionysus convinced Pentheus to disguise himself as a woman and go out and watch the Theban women in their strange revels. When these revelers spied the king hiding in a tree, however, they saw him not as a woman but as a wild animal and reacted by tearing him limb from limb. Other similar stories involved the daughters of King Minyas of Orchomenus (near Thebes) and the daughters of King Proetus of Argos (in the Peloponnesus); because these young women refused to join the Maenids, Dionysus's ecstatic female followers, he drove them mad and they killed their children.

Dionysus was also famous for his wanderings and adventures in lands outside of Greece. In one ancient tale, Hera drove him mad, causing him to wander through Syria, Egypt, and Phrygia (in Asia Minor). In Phrygia, the goddess Cybele (or Rhea, with whom the Greeks identified Cybele) cured him of his madness, and he established his cult in that land. When one of his followers, Silenus (who had a horse's ears and tail and was known for his wisdom) got lost and

ended up in Crete, the local king, Midas, treated Silenus well; as a reward, Dionysus granted Midas any wish he desired. Midas asked that everything he touched turn to gold (which backfired on him since even his food became gold). Some legends claimed that Dionysus founded an oracle in Egypt and also visited Mesopotamia, where he erected a bridge made of grape vines and ivy over the Euphrates River. **See** Cybele; Dionysus Zagreus; Hera; Zeus; **also** Athamas; Erigone 1; Icarius; Midas; Minyas; Proetus (Chapter 1); satyr; Silenus (Chapter 3); *Bacchae* (Chapter 5).

Dionysus Zagreus

A later, alternate version of the traditional Greek god Dionysus. Dionysus Zagreus was the son of Zeus and Persephone (later queen of the Underworld) rather than Zeus and Semele, daughter of Cadmus, as in the traditional tales of Dionysus. In this alternate story, as the boy grew, Zeus's wife, Hera, became jealous of the constant attentions

This surviving herm (bust atop a pedestal) of the fertility god Dionysus was created during the Hellenistic Age (323–31 B.C.).

paid to the child by Zeus and other gods living on Mt. Olympus. So one day Hera grabbed Dionysus Zagreus, tore him apart, and swallowed the pieces. The heart survived, however. Athena, goddess of war and wisdom, found it and gave it to Zeus. Then the chief god placed the organ inside Semele; and she soon gave birth to a new version of Dionysus Zagreus. This tale of death and rebirth became widely popular in Greek-speaking lands during Hellenistic times (the last three centuries B.C.), when several eastern "mystery" religions associated it with their tenets of death, resurrection, and purification of sins.

Dis

The principal Roman name for Hades, Greek ruler of the Underworld. **See** Hades.

Echo

A Greek nymph who lived on the slopes of Mt. Helicon (in Boeotia). She was extremely talkative and continually chattered away while the goddess Hera was trying to spy on the affairs of her divine husband, Zeus, often alerting the god to his wife's presence. Hera eventually grew exasperated and ordained that Echo could only speak when spoken to. Also, the nymph could only repeat the last syllables of whatever words people spoke. Later, Echo fell in love with the handsome, conceited youth Narcissus, who rejected her. She was so crushed that she slowly wasted away until all that was left was her echoing voice (the supposed source of the phenomenon of echoes).

In an alternate ancient version of Echo's story, Pan, god of shepherds and flocks, fell in love with Echo, but she spurned

him. Hurt and angry, Pan struck her dumb, except for the ability to repeat people's last words. After that, the local shepherds of Mt. Helicon became so frustrated with Echo's constant repetition that they tore her apart, leaving only her voice. See Pan; **also** Narcissus (Chapter 1).

Eidothea

(or Idothea, or Ido) A nymph and the daughter of the god Proteus, known as "the Old Man of the Sea." She appears as a minor but important character in Homer's *Odyssey*. On his way home from the Trojan War, Menelaus (king of Sparta and husband of Helen of Troy) was blown off course and ended up off the coast of Egypt. Menelaus tried to contact Proteus to ask the reason for this misfortune, but the sea god avoided him. Finally, Eidothea told Menelaus how she might find Proteus and force him to explain what had happened and how the Greeks could get back home. **See** Proteus.

Eileithyia

(or Ilithyia) The Greek goddess of childbirth, who was sometimes viewed (by Homer, for example) as multiple deities (the Eileithyiae). Another early Greek poet, Hesiod, claimed that she was the daughter of Zeus and Hera. Perhaps this is why the Greeks usually pictured Eileithyia as working for and with Hera, who was herself a protector of women and childbirth. The two main myths in which Eileithyia takes a small role are those of the birth of Apollo and Artemis by Leto and the birth of the hero Heracles. In both cases, out of jealousy Hera wanted to prevent the births and tried to keep Eileithyia from aiding in the deliveries. In the case of Leto, some other goddesses gave Eileithyia a gold necklace as a bribe to allow Apollo's and Artemis's birth. In the case of Heracles' mother, Alcmena, at Hera's order Eileithyia sat outside the pregnant woman's room for several days with her arms, legs, fingers, and toes crossed (a charm to put a hex on the birth); but the scream of a servant woman distracted Eileithyia, and when she uncrossed her appendages the charm was broken, allowing the birth of Heracles and his twin brother, Iphicles. **See** The Adventures of Heracles (Chapter 6).

Electra

A daughter of the Titans Oceanus and Tethys and the mother (by the Titan Thaumus) of Iris, goddess of the rainbow, and the obnoxious flying Harpies. **See** Iris; Oceanus; Titans; **also** Harpy (Chapter 3).

Eos

The Greek goddess of the dawn (whom the Romans called Aurora). Eos was the daughter of the Titans Hyperion and Theia and the sister of the sun god, Helios, and the moon goddess, Selene. The early Greeks pictured Eos riding a chariot across the sky by day alongside her brother, Helios. And her first literary mention was in Homer's epic poems, in which he regularly refers to her as "early-rising" and "rosy-fingered."

In her myths, Eos fell in love with several attractive mortal men, but the affairs typically ended unhappily. After marrying one of them, Tithonus, she asked Zeus to make him immortal but forgot to include that he should maintain his youth eternally; and poor Tithonus eventually wasted away and became a grasshopper. Eos also fell in love with a young man named Cephalus, who was happily married to a woman named Procris. The goddess abducted the man and had a child with him (Phaëthon), but Cephalus yearned to return to his wife. He did so, but a tragic series of events led to the death of both Cephalus and Procris. **See** Cephalus; Phaëthon; Tithonus (Chapter 1).

Epimetheus

A son of the Titan Iapetus and the brother of the Titan Prometheus (champion of the early human race against hostile gods). Epimetheus's name meant "Afterthought," in contrast with his brother's, which meant "Forethought," reflecting the fact that Epimetheus was not nearly as wise and cautious as Prometheus. This became clear when Prometheus warned Epimetheus not to take in Pandora, the first woman, whom the gods had sent down to earth. Epimetheus ignored this advice, and as a result Pandora unleashed a host of troubles and misfortunes on humanity. The daughter of Epimetheus and Pandora, Pyrrha, married Deucalion, and they repopulated the earth after a great flood was sent by the gods. For a fuller account of all of these happenings, **see** The Creation of the Gods and Humans (Chapter 6).

Epona

A Celtic goddess of horses whose worship became popular in eastern Gaul (what is now France) and Germany in the last few centuries of the first millennium B.C. and the early centuries of the first millennium A.D. Because the Romans had frequent contact with and eventually intermarried Celts in that region, they adopted her and gave her an annual festival held on December 18; and her cult spread throughout the western parts of the Roman Empire. Artists usually pictured her either riding or walking alongside horses and holding various fertility symbols, such as ears of corn and baskets of fruit.

Eris

The minor Greek goddess of strife. Daughter of Nyx (Night), Eris appeared in few myths but played a prominent, important role in one of them—the Judgment of Paris, one of the key events leading up to the famous Trojan War. Eris became enraged when she realized that she had not received an invitation to the marriage of the goddess Thetis to a mortal king, Peleus. So the deity of strife flew over the gathering and tossed down a golden apple with a note attached, saying that a treasure should be awarded to the fairest goddess of them all. Just as Eris had expected, Athena, Hera, and Aphrodite all stepped forward to claim the prize; when Troy's Prince Paris, who had been chosen to judge the contest, picked Aphrodite the winner, she helped him abduct Helen, queen of Sparta, the act that caused the Greeks to declare war on Troy. **See** Aphrodite; Thetis; also Paris (Chapter 1); The Trojan War (Chapter 6).

Eros

The Greek god of love (and fertility, particularly of a sexual nature), whom the Romans called Cupid (meaning "Desire"). Two versions of Eros's origins were known in ancient times. In the first and oldest (described by the poet Hesiod), he was one of the first beings (or perhaps natural forces) born out of Chaos at the beginning of time. In this version, Eros arranged the union between Gaia (the earth) and Uranus (the sky), who subsequently gave rise to the first race of gods, the Titans.

The second and later tradition about Eros made him the son of the Greek love goddess, Aphrodite, and the war god, Ares. In this more familiar role, Eros was an extremely handsome and athletic young deity whose symbols were his bow and arrows and a torch. In the Hellenistic Age (the last three centuries B.C.), when romantic love came into fashion in Greek art and literature, the image of Eros/Cupid changed accordingly with the times; in his myths he became increasingly involved in making people fall into or out of love (by shooting his arrows at their hearts). Some artists came to portray him as a child with wings (or as multiple winged children), and he was frequently depicted as the companion of his mother, Aphrodite. As Cupid, the god played a leading role in the renowned romantic myth titled "Cupid and Psyche," which

the Roman writer Lucius Apuleius told in his Latin novel *The Golden Ass*. **See** Aphrodite; Cupid; **also** The Creation of the Gods and Humans (Chapter 6); and, for a full telling of Cupid's and Psyche's romantic tale, **see** Cupid and Psyche (also Chapter 6).

Eurydice

A nymph (minor nature goddess) loved by the famous poet Orpheus. For the tragic story of how he tried but failed to rescue her from the Underworld, **see** Orpheus (Chapter 1).

Evander

Originally an obscure Greek god identified with Pan (deity of shepherds and flocks) and worshiped mainly in Arcadia (in the central Peloponnesus), especially at a town called Pallantion. In Italy, after Greek myths began to spread though the region beginning perhaps in the seventh or sixth century B.C., the Romans identified him, as they did Pan, with their woodland god, Faunus.

Later, however, the Roman poet Virgil created a revised mythology for Evander in his great epic the *Aeneid*. In the story, Evander was a human king who emigrated from Arcadia to Italy about sixty years before the Trojan War. There, Faunus, also portrayed as a human king, welcomed Evander and his followers, who established a settlement on the Palatine Hill (naming it after Pallantion in Arcadia). They therefore became the first people to settle on the future site of Rome. When Evander was an old man, he welcomed the Trojan hero Aeneas when the latter visited the settlement on the Palatine. Evander's son, Pallas, became a follower of Aeneas in the subsequent war with the Rutulian prince Turnus; but Turnus killed Pallas, causing Aeneas to show his enemy no mercy in their later, climactic battle. **See** Faunus; **also** Aeneas's Journey to Italy (Chapter 6).

Fates

Three goddesses who probably originated as protectors of the birth process but came to be seen as somehow guiding people's destinies, although exactly how they did so eventually became obscure. Usually pictured in art and literature as old women spinning or weaving, the Greeks called them Klotho ("the Spinner"), Lachesis ("the Drawer of Lots"), and Atropos ("the Inevitable"), collectively called the Moirai; the Romans knew them as Nona, Decuma, and Morta, collectively called the Parcae or Fata. Some people thought that their fateful spinning led up to and halted at the moment of birth; others held that the spinning continued throughout life until the thread ran out.

The Fates played only minor roles in a few myths. In one of the stories about Meleager (a prince of Calydon, near Corinth), they informed his mother, Althea, that the boy would die when a piece of wood then burning in her hearth was totally consumed. Thus, Althea removed the wood, doused it with water, and stored it in a place where it was safe from fire. And in the myth of Apollo and Admetus (king of Pherae, in Thessaly), Apollo got the Fates drunk to trick them into allowing Admetus to live beyond a normal human life span (as long as he could find someone willing to die in his place). **See** Admetus; Meleager (Chapter 1).

Faunus

An early Italian pastoral deity who protected hunters and oversaw agriculture. As Roman culture increasingly felt the influence of Greek culture, the Romans identified Faunus with Pan, the Greek god of shepherds and flocks. (The Romans also came to identify Faunus with Evander, an obscure nature god worshiped in Arcadia, in the Peloponnesus). People generally thought that Faunus could reveal the future in their dreams, as well as through oracles (divine speech) delivered in sacred groves. The Romans often portrayed him as the husband of Bona Dea, a fertility goddess who was called Fauna when associated with Faunus. It also became common to picture multiples of Faunus, called Fauni (fauns), which the Romans identified with the Greek satyrs, who were half man and half goat.

Perhaps the best-known myth about Faunus involved Numa Pompilius, the legendary second king of Rome. Numa found out where Faunus and another woodland god, Picus, stopped to drink in the forest and eventually confronted the two gods and asked them to arrange an audience with Jupiter (the Roman version of Zeus). They did so, and Jupiter appeared. Numa then cleverly got the chief god to explain the items humans could sacrifice to him to keep them safe from being struck by lightning. (These turned out to be garlic, human hair, and fish.) **See** Bona Dea; Evander; Pan; **also** Numa Pompilius (Chapter 1).

Flora

An ancient Italian goddess of the spring season and the flowers that accompany it. The Romans erected a temple to her in 238 B.C. near the Circus Maximus in Rome. And from April 28 to May 3, they celebrated her festival, the Floralia, which involved considerable merriment, some of it on the vulgar side. The Roman poet Ovid told a brief story that linked Flora to Greek mythology. When Zephyrus, the west wind, was chasing a maiden named Chloris, she suddenly changed into Flora and exhaled a shower of flowers into the countryside.

Fortuna

(or Fors Fortuna) A minor Roman fertility goddess who eventually came to be identified with Tyche, the Greek deity of fate, chance, and/or luck and thereby gained a wider following. Fortuna's festival, held on June 24, was extremely popular. Large numbers of people rowed or walked to her principal shrine (which included an oracle), located about a mile downstream from Rome; and after watching the ceremonies, they held picnics and feasts. She had many other shrines in Rome as well as in other Roman cities. People addressed or worshiped her by a wide variety of names, depending on the kind of luck she brought or the kinds of people on whom she bestowed it. These names included, among others: Fortuna Augusta ("Luck of the Emperor"), Fortuna Balnearis ("of the Baths"), Fortuna Equestris ("Helper of the Equites," in reference to a class of well-to-do Roman businessmen), Fortuna Huiusce Diei ("Luck for Today"), Fortuna Muliebris ("Women's Luck"), Fortuna Privata ("Luck for the Private Individual"), Fortuna Publica ("the People's Luck"), and Fortuna Romana ("the Luck of Rome").

Gaia

A primitive goddess personifying the earth, and the first of the original group of beings, or spirits, born out of the primeval Chaos, as described by the eighth-century B.C. Greek poet Hesiod in his *Theogony.* Gaia soon gave rise to Uranus, the sky or heavens. Then these two spirits mated to produce the first race of Greek gods, the Titans, including Cronos and Rhea (who later became the parents of Zeus and some of the other Olympian gods). Gaia and Uranus also produced three one-eyed giants and three hundred-handed giants. (Later, according to legend, Gaia mated

with some of her other children, including Pontus, the sea, producing various gods, goddesses, and monsters.)

After Zeus was born and turned on his father, Cronos, a war erupted between the Titans and the Olympians, which the Olympians won. Gaia had originally supported her grandson, but when Zeus locked away most of the other Titans in the Underworld, she objected. She created a huge monster—Typhon—to fight for her, and she also won the allegiance of a race of giants (who had sprung from droplets of Uranus's blood after Cronos had attacked and castrated him). Zeus and his followers also won the new war that ensued (which the Greeks called the Gigantomachy), just as they had the one against the Titans. Still, Zeus spared Gaia again. She later attended his wedding to Hera, and as a wedding present she gave Hera the golden apples that the Hesperides (daughters of the goddess Nyx) came to guard.

The Greeks also held that Gaia had the power of prophecy and linked her to the famous oracle at Delphi. One common legend said that she was the first deity to have a shrine there; that she commanded the huge serpent, Python, that guarded it; and that when Apollo killed Python and took control of Delphi, he had to compensate Gaia by establishing the Pythian Games, consisting of poetry and later athletic contests. For more on the creation of Gaia, Uranus, and the other early gods and spirits, as well as their wars with one another and the giants, **see** Cronos; Oceanus; Titans; Uranus; **also** Briareos; Chaos; Cyclops; giants; Hecatoncheires; Typhon (Chapter 3); **and** especially The Creation of the Gods and Humans (Chapter 6). For more on the Delphic Oracle, **see** Apollo; also Delphic Oracle (Chapter 4).

Galatea

A Greek nymph who lived in the sea near an island not far from the larger island of Sicily.

The Cyclops (one-eyed giant) Polyphemus (who later had a famous run-in with the Greek hero Odysseus) fell in love with Galatea and actively pursued her. But thinking the giant repulsive, she spurned and mocked him, preferring the company of a handsome young mortal, a shepherd named Acis. Unfortunately, Polyphemus crushed Acis to death with a huge boulder. The grief-stricken Galatea then made a freshwater spring bubble up from beneath the boulder in memory of her lover.

Graces

Three minor Greek goddesses (Euphrosyne, Aglaia, and Thalia) who symbolized and personified beauty, charm, and grace. It was thought, variously, that they associated with or accompanied the Muses (goddesses of the fine arts) and/or the love deities Aphrodite and Eros, and that they enhanced the comforts and enjoyments of life. The Graces were favorites of Greek and Roman artists, who pictured them often; but the three appeared in few myths. **See** Aphrodite; Muses.

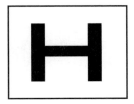

Hades

(also Plouton) God and ruler of the Underworld, the kingdom where the souls ("shades") of dead people as well as various mythological creatures, including the Titans (confined there by Zeus), dwelled. (The common later reference to the Underworld itself as Hades is incorrect; the ancients sometimes called it "the house of Hades," but the name Hades by itself designated only the god.) Hades, whom the Romans called Dis or Pluto, was also identified with precious metals since these rest underground; hence, he was thought to be

unusually wealthy or to be a bringer of wealth.

The Greeks and Romans saw Hades as cold, grim, and a punisher of evil, but not as evil or unjust himself. Therefore, Hades was not the equivalent of the Christian devil, nor was his realm equivalent to hell. Still, people feared him, so saying his name aloud was considered unlucky. Therefore, most people referred to him by descriptive names, such as Plouton (Pluto in Latin), meaning "the Rich One." Other names for him included Klymenos ("Renowned"), Pylartes ("the Gate-Locker"), Stygeros ("Hateful"), and Zeus Katachthonios ("Zeus of the Underworld"). Almost no actual worship of Hades took place, as the Greeks believed that he had no interest in the living.

Perhaps because people tended not to speak Hades' name or to worship him, he appeared in very few myths, and in those stories he was usually a relatively minor character. He had a small role in the most common story of the birth of the first Olympians, for instance, since he was one of the children of the Titans Cronos and Rhea (along with Zeus, Poseidon, Hera, Demeter, and Hestia). So Hades was among the young gods Cronos swallowed and later vomited up. In another story, Hades put the human kings Theseus and Pirithous, who had made their way down into the Underworld, in "chairs of forgetfulness," hoping to make them forget who they were and why they had come. But the famous strongman Heracles, who himself visited Hades' realm on more than one occasion, rescued Theseus. (He was unable to help Pirithous.)

The only important myth in which Hades played a major role was that dealing with his abduction of Persephone, daughter of the goddess Demeter. Hades wanted to make Persephone his bride, consort, and queen of the Underworld; and Zeus agreed to let his brother have his way. Persephone was out picking flowers one day when the earth shook and a large hole suddenly appeared. Out of the hole came Hades, riding his imposing chariot drawn by black horses. Before the young girl could turn to run, the god had snatched her; he quickly carried her back to his underground kingdom. Demeter was understandably angry and unleashed drought and famine on the earth, eventually forcing Zeus and Hades to make a deal. Namely, Persephone could spend part of each year on the surface with her mother, but the rest of the time she had to remain with Hades as his queen. **See** Demeter; Persephone; and, for a detailed description of Hades' dark realm, **see** Underworld (Chapter 4).

Hebe

A daughter of Zeus and Hera and the cup-bearer of the gods living on Mt. Olympus. Hebe's name meant "Youth," and the Greeks saw her as the personification (flesh-and-blood representation) of that state of being. The Romans eventually adopted her, calling her Juventas. In Homer's *Iliad,* Hebe dressed the wounds that her brother, war god Ares, received at the hands of the Greek warrior Diomedes. And after the gods allowed the heroic Heracles to join their number after his death, they gave him Hebe as his bride. **See** The Adventures of Heracles (Chapter 6).

Hecate

A very ancient and fairly mysterious Greek goddess sometimes confused or identified with Artemis (the Roman Diana) since both goddesses were thought to oversee the fertility of the soil and the growth of crops. According to the Greek poet Hesiod, Hecate was a Titan whom Zeus allowed to keep her powers after the Olympian gods defeated the Titans (a singular honor). "If a man prays to her and she receives that prayer, he can receive great honors, and she can bestow wealth on him, too," Hesiod writes, describing her versatile powers.

Help and success come to those humans she favors; in court, she watches over the most respected individuals; in the assembly [of the people] her favorites stand out. And when men prepare for war, the goddess helps those she chooses to help and eagerly brings them victory and fame. She is also a splendid ally of participants in the [athletic] games; there, too, she brings help and success. . . . Just as easily, though, she can take away all that she has given, if she so chooses. (*Theogony* 419–443)

In addition to bringing fertility and good fortune to humans, Hecate sometimes brought fear, both of the dead and the unknown. The Greeks associated her with ghosts and demons and often recognized her as a practitioner of sorcery and black magic. This is the role the goddess takes in Euripides' *Medea,* when the title character (a human sorceress) calls on her for aid. Accordingly, because the ancients viewed crossroads as having magical properties of various kinds, on the last day of each month Hecate's worshipers placed offerings of food for her at crossroads. Artists and sculptors usually portrayed the goddess as having three faces, carrying torches, and/or accompanied by dogs.

Helios

The Greek sun god, whom the Romans called Sol. Most often, people viewed or portrayed him as a mighty charioteer, driving his flaming chariot (or gleaming horses) from east to west across the sky each day. (At night, according to legend, he crossed back to the east by floating in a golden cup on the stream of Ocean, a mythical river thought to encircle the flat earth.) Because Helios was in the sky all day looking down on the earth, people assumed he saw and heard everything that went on in that domain; thus, both gods and humans called on him as a witness to various events or oaths sworn. For example, the goddess Demeter consulted him after her daughter, Persephone, disappeared; and he told her that Hades, ruler of the Underworld, had abducted the girl.

The most famous myth in which Helios takes part is that of his mortal son, Phaëthon. The boy demanded that the god allow him to drive his gleaming chariot across the sky for a day. However, Phaëthon was unable to control his father's horses, and the chariot ran wild through the heavens until Zeus intervened and struck the young man dead.

In another story, one day Zeus made each of the gods the patron deity of one or another earthly land or city—all except for Helios, that is, who at the time was fulfilling his daily duty of driving his chariot across the sky. To compensate for the oversight, Zeus gave Helios dominion over the newly created island of Rhodes (located off the southwestern coast of Asia Minor). There, the sun god's three grandsons—Camirus, Lindus, and Ialysus—ruled and gave their names to the three largest cities. This myth was the basis of the Rhodians' worship of Helios as their national god. They honored him as the subject of the huge bronze statue they erected circa 280 B.C. at the entrance to their main harbor. Called the Colossus of Rhodes, it later made the prestigious list of the seven wonders of the ancient world. **See** Demeter; **also** Phaëthon (Chapter 1).

Hephaestos

(or Hephaestus) The Greek god of fire, the forge, and the patron of craftsmen, whom some ancient stories claimed was the son of Zeus and Hera, others Hera by herself. In one of the most famous myths about Hephaestos, Hera was disgusted because the child was born with a lame leg, so she threw him off of Mt. Olympus into the sea. Luckily, Thetis, a sea nymph (and the mother of the Greek hero Achilles), found the discarded infant and raised him secretly in a cave. After growing up and learning the skills of the forge, Hephaestos created a golden throne and sent it to his real mother, Hera; but it was as much a booby trap as a gift, for when she sat on the throne it imprisoned her, and none of the other gods knew how to free her. So they begged Hephaestos to come to Olympus to release Hera.

Back in the abode of the gods, where he had been born, Hephaestos became their master craftsman. He erected palaces and other structures for them. He also fulfilled the requests of various deities for him to make suits of armor for their mortal champions, including the great Achilles (at the request of Thetis) and the legendary Aeneas (at Aphrodite's request). Another famous piece of craftwork credited to Hephaestos was the creation of Pandora, the first woman, whom Zeus ordered him to make so that the chief god could punish the Titan Prometheus for helping humanity. In another task for Zeus, the god of the forge made the chain that bound Prometheus to a crag on Mt. Caucasus (where a giant eagle pecked at Prometheus's insides each day). Hephaestos crafted many of these and numerous other things in a forge set up on Mt. Olympus. But the Greeks also believed that he had a forge under a volcano on the Aegean island of Lemnos, where his worship was particularly popular. (Some modern scholars think that Greek worship of the god may have begun on that island.) By contrast, the Romans, who called him Vulcan, believed that his main forge lay beneath Mt. Etna, the great volcano on the island of Sicily.

Despite his incredible usefulness to both gods and humans, Hephaestos continued to have difficulties after his return to Olympus. First, he endured much ridicule, not only because of his pronounced limp but also because his wife, love goddess Aphrodite, had affairs behind his back. The most famous of these was with the war god, Ares. Hephaestos even-

This panoramic view from the northern rim of the summit of the Athenian Acropolis shows the Temple of Hephaestos at the far side of the Agora (ancient marketplace).

tually found out and threw a huge net over the lovers as they lay naked in bed; then he humiliated them by calling for the rest of the gods to come and laugh at them. But they laughed at poor Hephaestos, too, for taking so long to find out about his wife's infidelity. Later, when Zeus and Hera had one of their vehement arguments, Hephaestos took his mother's side (having reconciled with her by that time). This angered Zeus so much that he hurled Hephaestos from Olympus; this time his landing spot was Lemnos. **See** Aphrodite; Ares; Prometheus; Zeus; **also** Achilles; Pandora (Chapter 1); Etna, Mt. (Chapter 4); and The Creation of the Gods and Humans (Chapter 6).

Hera

Both the sister and the wife of Zeus, the queen of the Greek Olympian gods, and the protector of marriage and women's life. Her symbols were the peacock, a symbol of showy pride, and the pomegranate. (In ancient Athens, people often gave pomegranates to brides in honor of Hera, and a large proportion of weddings took place in the month dedicated to the goddess—Gamelion, roughly equivalent to the modern January.) Women all over Greece worshiped Hera (whom the Romans identified with an ancient Italian protector of women—Juno), offering her regular prayers and sacrifice. Although her function of overseeing childbirth eventually passed to a minor goddess, Eileithyia (whom the Romans called Lucina), the latter was usually depicted as Hera's daughter and/or assistant.

A number of different versions of Hera's birth and later marriage to Zeus existed in ancient times. The most famous and widely accepted was that she was one of the six original children of the Titans Cronos and Rhea (the others being Hestia, Demeter, Hades, Poseidon, and Zeus). Cronos swallowed the infant Hera, along with the others, except for Zeus, who later forced Cronos to regurgitate the brood. Subsequently, Zeus had love affairs with various goddesses until deciding that Hera was the only one worthy of being his permanent mate. In a popular alternate version, Zeus saw his sister Hera walking in the woods near Argos (a city that became one of the two main centers of her worship in Greece, the other being the Aegean island of Samos). Consumed with desire for her, he caused a thunderstorm, disguised himself as a bird, and took refuge inside her dress. There, he changed back to his true form, embraced her, and promised to marry her.

Zeus was not alone in lusting after Hera. During the famous battle between the gods and the giants, a giant named Porphyrion tried to rape her, but Zeus killed him with a thunderbolt. When another giant, Ephialtes, made advances on Hera, her sister Demeter intervened and slew the interloper.

Yet Hera quite often showed that she was capable of taking care of herself, sometimes helping and other times hindering various mortals. She helped the hero Jason, for example, in his quest for the Golden Fleece, in large part to punish Pelias, king of Iolcos (who had earlier committed sacrilege by stabbing his stepmother to death at the goddess's altar). On the other hand, Hera persecuted the Trojans during their famous war with the Greeks. The goddess's anger was provoked by the Trojan prince, Paris, when he failed to award her the prize for most beautiful goddess in the famous Judgment of Paris. (For this episode, **see** The Trojan War in Chapter 6.)

In fact, Hera became so intent on helping the Greeks against the Trojans that she risked incurring her husband's wrath. He had warned her and the other gods to stop siding with one army or the other. But she sought and found a way to help the Greeks behind his back. "Hera, poised on her golden throne, looked down, stationed high at her post aloft Olympus's peak," writes Homer in the *Iliad*.

> She saw great Zeus at rest on the ridge and craggy heights of Ida [a mountain located to the southeast of Troy] . . . and her heart filled with loathing. What could she do?—Queen Hera wondered. . . . How could she outmaneuver Zeus, the mastermind . . . with his battle-shield of storm and thunder? At last one strategy struck her mind as best; she would dress in all her glory and go to Ida—perhaps the old desire would overwhelm the king to . . . make immortal love [with her] and she might drift an oblivious, soft warm sleep across his eyes and numb that seething brain. (*Iliad* 14.187–203)

Hera's plan worked. After she and Zeus made love, he fell asleep (thanks to the god of sleep, Hypnos, who helped Hera) and the sea god Poseidon, who also supported the Greeks against the Trojans, turned the tide of battle in favor of the Greek army. (Eventually Zeus woke up, ordered Poseidon to desist, and scolded Hera for her scheme.)

This was not the only time that Zeus and Hera found themselves at odds. One of the most famous of their spats was an argument over who enjoyed sex more—men or women? Hera insisted that men enjoyed sex more, and Zeus claimed it was women. To settle the argument, they asked the opinion of a mortal named Tiresias (because he was the only being they knew of who had been both male and female in his lifetime). Tiresias told them that women enjoy sex more, which made Hera so angry that she blinded the poor man.

Most of the bad feelings between Hera and her husband, however, stemmed from

Zeus's frequent extramarital affairs. Hera was renowned for her jealousy and punishment of his lovers and their relatives. Perhaps the most famous example was her hatred and persecution of the hero Heracles, provoked by Zeus's love affair with a mortal woman, Alcmena, Heracles' mother. Hera also persecuted Io, a princess of Argos, after Zeus had seduced her. Trying to save the girl from his wife's wrath, the god turned Io into a young cow. But Hera saw through the ruse and sent gadflies to sting Io. **See** Cronos; Eileithyia; Hypnos; Juno; Zeus; **also** Io; Pelias (Chapter 1); giants (Chapter 3); Argos (Chapter 4); *Madness of Heracles* (Chapter 5); The Adventures of Heracles; The Quest for the Golden Fleece; The Trojan War (Chapter 6).

Hermes

The Greek messenger god and patron of travelers, merchants, thieves, literature, and athletics. This multitalented deity also supposedly invented the alphabet, astronomy, and mathematics; brought good fortune; and also led the souls of the dead to the Underworld (in which capacity he was known as Psychopompos, "the Guide of Souls"). His symbol was a herald's staff (*kerykeion* in Greek; *caduceus* in Latin), and in art he was often pictured wearing winged sandals and a wide-brimmed winged hat. In early times, Hermes, whom the Romans called Mercury, was also a fertility god, which led to the frequent addition of a carved penis to statues of him, called Herms. A typical Herm consisted of a short pillar or other pedestal topped by a bust of the god. People set them up along roads to bring travelers good luck and also near the doorways of houses since tradition said that a Herm kept evil from entering.

Also according to tradition, Hermes was born in Arcadia (in the central Peloponnesus), the son of the union of Zeus and the nymph Maia, daughter of the Titan Atlas. The affair transpired while Zeus's wife, Hera, was asleep. And because of

Hera's reputation for bringing grief to her husband's lovers and their offspring, the young Hermes decided to get on the goddess's good side as quickly as possible. While still an infant (but a highly precocious one who could walk, reason, and so forth), Hermes, disguised as Hera's son Ares, crawled into her lap and she breastfed him; that made her Hermes' foster mother, which required that she treat him as her own child.

Hermes' extraordinary abilities as a child were also evident in his relationship with another versatile god—Apollo. The younger deity stole fifty cows from Apollo and sacrificed them to the Olympian gods, then hurried back to his crib and pretended he knew nothing about the theft. Zeus and Apollo were sure the child was guilty, and Zeus ordered Hermes to return the cattle. But then Apollo and Hermes made a deal. In exchange for the lyre (harp) that Hermes had just invented, Apollo agreed to forget about the cattle; thereafter, the two gods became fast friends.

In the years that followed, Hermes took part in many exploits, often fulfilling various tasks for Zeus or other gods. At Zeus's request, for instance, he helped save the young god Dionysus from death at the hands of Hera (who was angry that Zeus had conceived Dionysus with another woman). Hermes also helped Zeus protect Io, another woman Zeus had seduced, from Hera's wrath by killing Argus, a creature with many eyes, which Hera had sent to keep watch on Io. In another incident, Zeus sent Hermes to negotiate with Hades (god of the Underworld) for the release of Persephone (Demeter's daughter), whom Hades had abducted. In addition, Hermes accompanied Zeus in many of his travels on Earth; the two gods, disguised as mortals, paid a fateful visit to the poor peasants Baucis and Philemon, the only humans who had the decency to show the strangers hospitality. During the famous Trojan War, Hermes helped arrange for the warrior Achilles' return of the corpse of his slain enemy, Hector, to Hector's father, King Priam; and after the war, the messenger god helped the far-wandering Greek hero Odysseus escape the clutches of the sorceress Circe and the nymph Calypso. **See** Calypso; Hera; Maia; Mercury; Persephone; Zeus; **also** Baucis and Philemon; Io (Chapter 1); Argus 1; Typhon (Chapter 3); Arcadia (Chapter 4); Perseus and Medusa; The Trojan War; The Wanderings of Odysseus (Chapter 6).

Hesperides

The three (or, in some accounts, four or seven) daughters of the primeval divine forces Nyx (Night) and Erebus (Darkness); or, in some later stories, the daughters of the Titan Atlas (like the Hyades and Pleiades). In versions that mentioned seven of these Greek nymphs (minor nature goddesses), their names were Aegle, Arethusa, Erythea, Hespera, Hespereia, Hesperusa, and Hestia (not to be confused with Hestia, goddess of the hearth). According to legend, the Hesperides lived in a beautiful garden (called the Garden of the Hesperides, after them) located far to the west of human lands, near the spot where Atlas held up the sky. There, aided by a serpent named Ladon, the nymphs guarded the golden apples that Gaia, mother of the Titans, had given Hera, queen of the Olympians, as a wedding gift. In his eleventh labor, the famous hero Heracles tricked Atlas into helping him steal the apples; but later, the goddess Athena made sure that these treasures were returned to the Hesperides. **See** Atlas; Gaia; **also** The Adventures of Heracles (Chapter 6).

Hestia

The Greek goddess of the hearth (a central symbol of home and family in ancient Greece) and the eldest of the three daughters of the Titans Cronos and Rhea. Cronos swallowed Hestia, along with four of her siblings, and they remained in his belly until Zeus made him vomit them up. There-after, Hestia, whom the Romans called Vesta, remained a virgin and demanded that her priestesses be virgins, too. She became known for her kindness and purity, and people worshiped her at shrines all over the Greco-Roman world. **See** Vesta; **also** The Creation of the Gods and Humans (Chapter 6).

Horus

A very ancient Egyptian god who came to be recognized by many Greeks and Romans and became particularly popular as one of their minor gods in Hellenistic times (the last three centuries B.C.). In Egyptian mythology, Horus was the son of the god Osiris and the goddess Isis and avenged his father's death at the hands of the evil Seth (or Set), after which Osiris became lord of the afterlife. Egyptian kings (pharaohs) were considered the living manifestations of Horus until they died, after which they became one with Osiris and the next pharaoh became one with Horus. This mysterious cycle of life and death appealed to the Greeks and Romans, and they appropriately came to view Horus (whom the Greeks called Harpocrates) as a god of mystery and secret things. Artists often depicted him as child holding a finger to his lips, indicating silence and secrecy. **See** Isis.

Hours

(the Horai or Horae) In spite of this common ancient name for these minor Greek goddesses, they personified the seasons of the year rather than the hours of the day. **See** Seasons.

Hyades

"Rainers"; a group of five nymphs thought to have been the daughters of the Titans Oceanus and Tethys or, in a different version, the daughters of another Titan, Atlas. The Hyades nursed the infant god Dionysus. As a reward, Zeus placed them in the sky as a group of stars (in the constellation of Taurus, the bull). In another tale, after the Hyades' brother, Hyas, died, they cried so much that the gods put them in the sky, where they remained ever after, the moisture of their tears falling to earth as rain. **See** Titans.

Hypnos

The Greek god of sleep, whom the Romans called Somnus. According to legend, Hypnos was the brother of Thanatos (Death), and their mother was Nyx (Night). Hypnos lived in a secret cave somewhere beneath the Aegean island of Lemnos, a dark, misty place through which flowed a river called Forgetfulness; his countless sons, the Dreams, dwelled there with him. Perhaps the most famous myth in which Hypnos took part involved a favor he did for the goddess Hera during the famous Trojan War. Her husband, Zeus, king of the Olympians, had forbidden her from taking sides in the war, and she decided to try to lull him into sleep so she could help the Greeks behind his back. Hera visited Hypnos and asked for his help. At first he refused, fearing Zeus's wrath; but when Hera offered to arrange for one of the lovely Graces to be Hypnos's bride, he changed his mind. Hera made love to Zeus on Mt. Ida (near Troy), and Hypnos made him fall into a deep slumber, after which the sea god Poseidon, at Hera's bidding, led the Greeks to a victory over the Trojans. **See** Hera.

Iacchus

A minor Greek god worshiped mainly at Eleusis (in western Attica, near Athens) as part of Demeter's cult, the Eleusinian Mysteries. People thought, variously, that Iacchus was a son of Demeter, or Persephone (Demeter's daughter), or that he was actually the fertility god, Dionysus, in another form. In the grand procession from Athens to Eleusis during the Eleusinian festival (held in September), the worshipers frequently shouted Iacchus's name, either to honor him or to invoke his presence, or both. Another legend grew up around the god during the Persian Wars (490–479 B.C.), during which the Greeks beat back an invasion by the mighty Persian Empire. Shortly before the sea battle of Salamis, a stunning Greek victory, people saw a huge dust cloud moving toward Salamis from the direction of Eleusis, as if stirred up by the marching of thousands of soldiers. Some Greeks interpreted this as an omen of victory sent by Iacchus. **See** Demeter; Dionysus.

Iris

The Greek goddess of the rainbow and an important messenger between the gods and humans (since the rainbow was seen as a sort of connecting bridge between heaven and earth). Some Greek writers actually depicted Iris as sleeping beneath Hera's throne on Mt. Olympus so that she might be ready at a moment's notice to do an errand for the queen of heaven. Born the daughter of the Titans Thaumus and Electra, Iris was the sister of the hideous Harpies and protected them from Jason and his Argonauts, who attempted to kill them for fouling the food of an old man named Phineus. According to legend, Iris married Zephyrus, the west wind. **See** Electra; **also** Calais and Zetes (Chapter 1); Harpy (Chapter 3); The Quest for the Golden Fleece (Chapter 6).

Isis

An important Egyptian mother, fertility, and marriage goddess whose cult spread to Greek and Roman lands in Hellenistic times (the last few centuries B.C.). In Egyptian myths, Isis was the sister and wife of the god Osiris (whom the Romans came to call Serapis) and the mother of the god Horus (the Greek Harpocrates). The Hellenistic Greeks often identified Isis with their love goddess, Aphrodite. When the Romans imported Isis's cult during the late Republic, they viewed her as a kind and compassionate mother figure, sometimes pictured in art holding or nursing her son (which influenced later portrayals of the Virgin Mary and baby Jesus). Her cult became widely popular. The rituals and beliefs of Isis's cult, which were similar to those of the eastern mystery religions (like those of Demeter, Mithras, and also the early Christians), included initiation, baptism, and the promise of eternal salvation. **See** Demeter; Horus; Mithras.

This temple honoring the goddess Isis, one of many such shrines in the Greco-Roman world, is on the tiny Greek island of Delos.

Janus

The Roman god of beginnings as well as of gates and doorways. His familiar symbol was a head with two faces looking in opposite directions. The Romans named the first month in their calendar (January) after him. A very ancient god, he may once have been as important as Jupiter (leader of the Roman gods). Perhaps because of this former importance, in classical times Janus came to have various manifestations, such as Janus Patulcius, who opened doors; Janus Clusivus, who closed doors; and Janus the Father, a creator deity. His temple, located in the Roman Forum, was small but important; its doors were left open during wartime and were closed in times of peace.

Janus played little part in mythology, though the Roman poet Ovid provided a few minor tales. In one, a nymph named Carna continually tricked her many suitors by asking them to enter a cave, where she promised she would follow and make love to them. But when their backs were turned, she would run away. The trick did not work on Janus, however, since he had a backward-looking face and saw her preparing to run. In return for her sexual favors, he gave Carna the power to repel vampires, which plagued the area at night. Another legend claimed that Janus had a son, Tiberinus, who drowned in a river near Rome; thereafter, it was called the Tiber River in the boy's memory.

Juno

(or Iuno) Originally a prominent Italian goddess, a protector of women and the sanctity of marriage, and the wife of Jupiter, the chief god. Thanks to contact with Greek culture, the Romans came to identify her with the Greek goddess Hera, wife of Zeus, Jupiter's Greek equivalent. Juno had several manifestations, among them Juno Lucina, who oversaw childbirth; Juno Regina, who was part of the Capitoline Triad (worshiped on Rome's Capitoline Hill), which also included Jupiter and Minerva; Juno Caprotina, a fertility goddess; Juno Sispes, a protector of the state; and Juno Sororia, who protected girls during puberty. All of these and other sides of Juno's character had festivals celebrated at various times of the year. Besides the temple on the Capitoline, shrines to Juno were built on the Aventine Hill and in the Campus Martius, both in Rome, as well as in other cities. For the original Greek myths associated with the goddess, **see** Hera.

Jupiter

The supreme god of the Roman state pantheon. He was originally an Italian sky god thought to cause rain and lightning and to oversee agriculture; through ongoing cultural contact with the Greeks, however, the Romans came to identify him strongly with Zeus, leader of the Greek Olympian gods. Like Zeus, Jupiter's chief symbols were the thunderbolt and the eagle.

During the Roman monarchy (dated roughly from the mid-eighth to late sixth centuries B.C.), the Romans developed the cult of Jupiter Optimus Maximus (the "best and greatest" of all Jupiters), part of the Capitoline Triad, a group that included two other prominent deities—Juno and Minerva. (The principal temple to Jupiter and the Triad was located on Rome's Capitoline Hill, where generals deposited the spoils of war and the Senate held its first meeting each year.) Besides Optimus Maximus, Jupiter had a number of other manifestations, among them Conservator ("Savior"), Divis Pater ("Father of Heaven"), Fugurator ("Sender

of Lightning"), Invictus ("Invincible"), Lapis ("Overseer of Oaths"), Latialis ("Leader of the Latin Feast"), Prodigalialis ("Sender of Omens"), and Triumphator ("Victor"). Each had its special characteristics, cult following, and temples.

Jupiter appeared in many myths, but the vast majority of them were the original Greek ones involving Zeus. A notable exception was the important role Jupiter played in the *Aeneid,* the great epic poem composed by the Roman writer Virgil in the late first century B.C. Virgil depicted Jupiter as having a master plan for Aeneas, a Trojan prince, to journey to Italy and there establish the "master race"—the Romans—who would one day rule of all the known world. For the Romans, Virgil had Jupiter tell the love goddess, Venus, "I see no measure nor date, and I grant them dominion without end. Even Juno [who opposed Aeneas and his mission] . . . will mend her ways and vie with me in cherishing the Romans, the master race, the wearers of the toga. So it is willed!" (*Aeneid* 1.278–284) For the original Greek myths associated with Jupiter, **see** Zeus; **also** Rome (Chapter 4); *Aeneid* (Chapter 5); Aeneas's Journey to Italy (Chapter 6).

Juturna

An Italian water nymph and the Roman goddess of fountains, springs, and rivers. According to a well-known myth, Juturna was originally a mortal woman for whom Jupiter developed a passion. When he pursued her, she tried hiding in the Tiber River, but he eventually caught her and made love to her. To compensate for her loss of virginity, he made her immortal and gave her power over flowing waters. In his *Aeneid,* the Roman poet Virgil depicted Juturna as the sister of the Italian warrior Turnus, Aeneas's principal enemy. For a while, she managed to keep Turnus from fighting Aeneas, since she knew that Jupiter had ordained that Aeneas would be the victor; but Jupiter eventually sent one of the Furies to tell her to desist; and she sorrowfully sank into one of her springs. Some later Romans identified this spring with one near the Temple of Vesta in Rome's main Forum. **See** Turnus (Chapter 1); **also** Aeneas's Journey to Italy (Chapter 6).

Leto

One of the Titans and the mother of the major Greek Olympian deities Apollo and Artemis. According to legend, before marrying Hera, Zeus slept with Leto, conceiving the twin gods. When Hera found out Leto was pregnant, the jealous goddess forbade people everywhere from giving Leto a place to rest and have her babies. Zeus finally intervened, ordering Boreas (the north wind) and the sea god Poseidon to help Leto. Poseidon took her to Asteria, later called Delos, a tiny island in the middle of the Aegean, and there she had the divine children. (An alternate story claimed that only Apollo was born on Delos and that Leto gave birth to Artemis on a different island.) Thereafter, Apollo and Artemis remained close and loyal to their mother, protecting or avenging her on a number of occasions. For instance, Apollo slew Python, a serpent inhabiting Delphi (in central Greece), which had earlier, at Hera's order, driven the pregnant Leto away; and both Apollo and Artemis slaughtered most of the children of Niobe, a mortal woman who had insulted Leto. **See** Apollo; Artemis; Asteria; Hera; **also** Niobe (Chapter 1); Python (Chapter 3); Delos (Chapter 4); The Curse of the House of Atreus (Chapter 6).

Maia

The eldest of the Pleiades, the daughters of the Titan Atlas; and the mother of the Greek messenger god, Hermes. The chief Greek god, Zeus, slept with Maia while his wife, Hera, was asleep, and this illicit union produced Hermes. Luckily for Maia, Hera did not seek retribution, as she did with so many of Zeus's other extramarital lovers. This was probably because Hermes, while still an infant, got on Hera's good side by tricking her into breast-feeding him, thus forcing her to treat him thereafter as one of her own sons. **See** Hera; Hermes; Pleiades.

Mars

Originally a very ancient Italian god of agriculture who protected farmers' fields and boundaries. But in time, as the Romans had increasing contact with Greek culture, Mars came to be identified with Ares, the Greek god of war. As Mars Ultor ("Mars the Avenger"), war became his principal domain, although he continued to oversee agriculture as "Mars the Father." The Romans came to see him as second in importance only to Jupiter. March, originally the first month in the Roman year (because it witnessed the annual rebirth of agriculture), was named after Mars (as was the great parade ground in Rome—the Campus Martius, or "Field of Mars").

March also witnessed several religious festivals to honor Mars, including one that began on March 1 and lasted for over three weeks, featuring parades, dancing, hymn singing, and feasts. Another festival of Mars, the Equirria, was held on March 14 and featured horse races in the Campus

Martius. On the last day of still another of the god's celebrations, the Greater Quinquatrus, held from March 19 to 23, priests purified Rome's sacred war trumpets (*tubae*). Mars's most important altar stood, appropriately, in the Campus Martius; and he had numerous temples, including one erected by Augustus (the first Roman emperor) in the Forum of Augustus and another on the Appian Way, a major road outside the city.

Most of the myths associated with Mars were borrowed from the Greeks. But the god did have a few important Roman myths separate from those involving Ares. In one, Mars came one night to Rhea Silvia, a Vestal Virgin (one of several priestesses of Vesta, goddess of the hearth), and with her conceived the twin boys Romulus and Remus; Romulus, of course, subsequently went on to establish the city of Rome. Another famous Roman story said that in the time of Romulus's successor, Numa Pompilius, Mars dropped a shield (the ancilia) from the sky into Rome; and a special order of priests—the Salii—were created to guard the artifact, since the fate of Rome depended on its safekeeping. To confuse and thwart potential thieves, the Salii made eleven replicas and hung the twelve shields in Mars's temple in the Campus Martius. A third Roman tale about Mars involved a minor goddess named Anna Perenna. Mars fell in love with the goddess Minerva and asked Anna Perenna to convey these amorous feelings to Minerva. Anna Perenna came back with the good news that Minerva had consented to marry the war god. But when he raised the bridal veil on his wedding day, he saw, to his dismay, not Minerva but Anna Perenna, a joke the other gods enjoyed at Mars's expense. For some of the original Greek myths associated with the god, **see** Ares. In addition, **see** Anna Perenna; Minerva; **also** Numa Pompilius; Romulus (Chapter 1); ancilia; Rome (Chapter 4); The Founding of Rome (Chapter 6).

Mercury

The Roman messenger god and deity of trade and commercial success, whom the Romans identified with the versatile Greek messenger god Hermes. Like Hermes, Mercury was frequently depicted holding a herald's staff with snakes coiled around

Mars (whom the Greeks called Ares) sleeps while his lover, the goddess Venus (the Greek Aphrodite), watches.

it and wearing a winged hat and sandals. Mercury was particularly popular in Roman Gaul and Britain, where people venerated him as the inventor of the various creative arts. His festival was celebrated on May 15. In his epic poem the *Aeneid,* the Roman writer Virgil had Jupiter send Mercury to Carthage to remind the hero Aeneas of his destiny to establish a beachhead in Italy. For the original Greek myths associated with Mercury, **see** Hermes.

Merope

One of the Pleiades, the seven daughters of the Titan Atlas, who were so upset over the death of their sisters, the Hyades, that they committed suicide. According to tradition, when the Pleiades ended up as a group of stars in the night sky, Merope's star was the faintest of the seven because she had married a mortal. **See** Hyades; Pleiades.

Metis

"Thought"; daughter of the Titans Tethys and Oceanus and the first wife of the Olympian god Zeus. All of the gods considered Metis the wisest of their number. This proved to be a problem for Zeus after Metis became pregnant, for Gaia (the earth, and the mother of the Titans) warned him that if the child was a girl, she would be equal to Zeus in wisdom and strength. Feeling threatened, he swallowed Metis. But Metis gave birth to the child while inside of Zeus; subsequently, the new goddess—Athena—sprang, dressed in full armor, from Zeus's head. The chief god turned out to be happy about this series of events, especially because he inherited Metis's practical wisdom as a by-product of her temporary residence in his body. **See** Athena; Zeus.

Minerva

An ancient Italian goddess of household arts, crafts, and trade guilds, whom the Romans may have borrowed from the Etrus-

cans (a culturally advanced people who originally lived north of Rome). Over time, the increasing influence of Greek culture on Roman culture caused the Romans to identify Minerva with the Greek goddess Athena (goddess of war and wisdom), particularly in her role as Athena Promachos, the "Warrior Champion." In this guise, Minerva (along with the Roman war god, Mars) was worshiped in the Greater Quinquatrus, a Roman religious festival held in March. She had a temple on Rome's Aventine Hill and a shrine on the nearby Caelian Hill. Minerva was also one of the three deities in the Capitoline Triad (a revered group of three gods that included Jupiter and Juno). For the original Greek myths associated with Minerva, **see** Athena.

Mithras

An ancient Indo-Iranian (later Persian) god of light and truth, whom the Romans imported into their pantheon of gods during the late first century B.C. His cult, seen as an eastern mystery religion, became widespread in the Roman Empire; restricted to men, it was particularly popular among merchants and soldiers. The beliefs and rituals of Mithraism involved the miraculous birth of a baby, baptism, a sacred meal of bread and wine, the promise of resurrection after death, and other elements in common with other eastern-derived religions, including Christianity.

According to the original myths associated with Mithras, he supported Ahura-Mazda (the chief deity of the Persian pantheon) in the eternal battle between light (goodness) and darkness (evil). Ahura-Mazda sent Mithras to earth to kill a sacred bull (the chief god's first creation), and from that animal's blood sprang all living things. Because the death of the sacred bull was thought to have taken place in a cave, Mithras's worshipers constructed his temples underground.

Mnemosyne

A female Titan who coupled with Zeus and then gave birth to the Muses (goddesses of the fine arts). The Greeks recognized Mnemosyne, whose name meant "Memory," as the living embodiment of that mental attribute. **See** Muses.

Muses

The nine daughters of Zeus and the goddess Mnemosyne (Memory); the Greek deities who inspired musicians, poets, dancers, and other artists and intellectuals. The frequent mention of these relatively minor goddesses in ancient writings probably derives from the fact that poets and other writers liked them and/or attributed their talent to them. The late eighth-century B.C. Greek poet Hesiod, for example, claimed that they gave him the gift of storytelling one day when he was tending his sheep. So it is not surprising that at the beginning of his *Theogony,* which tells about the origins of the earth, gods, and humans, he calls on the divine Muses to inspire him. "Hail, daughters of Zeus!" he writes.

> Give me sweet song, to celebrate the holy race of gods who live forever. . . . Tell how the gods and earth arose at first, and rivers and the boundless swollen sea and shining stars, and the broad heaven above, and how the gods divided up their wealth and how they shared their honors, how they first captured Olympus with its many folds. Tell me these things, Olympian Muses, tell from the beginning, which first came to be? (*Theogony* 104–115)

According to tradition, the Muses had wings and lived on or near mountains, especially Mt. Helicon (in Boeotia) and Mt. Olympus (in northern Thessaly). Appropriately, therefore, their two most important shrines were located near these two peaks, although lesser shrines dedicated to them were scattered throughout the Greek lands. (The Romans came to recognize these goddesses, too, identifying them with some obscure Italian water deities, the Camenae.)

Some ancient writers said there were three Muses, and the names of these goddesses sometimes varied from place to place. But most of the ancients accepted Hesiod's claim that nine Muses existed, as well as the names he assigned them. In later centuries, each of these nine came to be associated with a specific artistic or intellectual field. Calliope oversaw epic poetry; Clio, history; Euterpe, flute playing; Melpomene, tragic drama; Thalia, comedic drama; Terpsichore, lyric poetry or dance; Erato, lyric poetry or songs; Polymnia, mime; and Urania, astronomy. The general belief was that Apollo, god of music, the arts, and prophecy, was their leader. Artists and writers often depicted them frolicking or dancing not only with Apollo, but also with the Graces (minor goddesses of beauty, charm, and grace). **See** Apollo; Calliope; Camenae; Graces; **also** Hesiod; *Theogony* (Chapter 5).

Nemesis

A daughter of Nyx (Night); in some accounts, the true mother of Helen of Troy; and a minor goddess the Greeks thought had the power to punish heartless lovers, criminals, and other human transgressors. In the fifth century B.C., the Athenians erected a beautiful temple to Nemesis at Rhamnous (on Attica's eastern coast). The principal myth in which the goddess took part involved the strange manner of Helen's conception. Zeus, leader of the Olympian gods, one day lusted after Nemesis, who turned herself into various animals trying to escape him. When she took the form of a goose, he assumed that of a swan and mated with her, after which she laid an egg. A shepherd found the egg and gave it to Leda, a Spartan queen; and after Helen hatched from it, Leda reared the girl as her own daughter. By contrast, another ancient version said that Leda herself laid the egg. **See** Helen; Leda (Chapter 1).

Neptune

A very ancient Italian god of water who, under later Greek influence, came to be identified with the Greek god Poseidon, lord of the sea. Indeed, the Romans conveniently borrowed Neptune's whole mythology from the Greeks. Because Poseidon was strongly associated with horses, Neptune was sometimes identified with the Roman god Consus, who also had an important connection with horses. Neptune's festival, the Neptunalia, was held on July 23. The Romans built a temple for him in Rome's Campus Martius ("Field of Mars"). **See** Consus; and, for the principal myths associated with Neptune, **see** Poseidon.

Nereus

A Greek sea god said to be older even than Poseidon, lord of the seas. The son of Gaia (Earth) and Pontus (Sea), Nereus was himself the father of the Nereids, a group of nymphs who lived in the sea (among them Thetis, mother of the famous Greek hero Achilles). Nereus was sometimes confused with another "Old Man of the Sea" named Proteus; like Proteus, he had the gift of prophecy and could change his shape at will. For example, when the famous strongman Heracles wanted to find the location of the Garden of the Hesperides (to complete one of his twelve labors), he consulted Nereus. Reluctant to help, the god tried to evade Heracles by changing into various creatures. But Heracles used his great strength to hold onto Nereus and eventually forced him to reveal the information. **See** nymphs; Proteus; Thetis; **also** The Adventures of Heracles (Chapter 6).

Nike

The Greek goddess of victory, whom artists usually pictured as winged. According to tradition, she was the daughter of a Titan, Pallas, but during the famous war in heaven between the Titans and the Olympians she defected to the enemy. Nike became especially popular in Greece during and immediately following the Persian Wars (490–479 B.C.). After the Greek naval victory at Salamis, in 480 B.C., the Athenians erected a beautiful statue of her at Delphi; and about a half century later, the Athenian sculptor Phidias created a six-foot-tall statue of Nike, which stood upright in the open palm of his huge and magnificent statue of the war goddess, Athena, located inside the Parthenon temple, on Athens's Acropolis. **See** Pallas; **also** Acropolis; Parthenon (Chapter 4).

nymphs

A large number of minor Greek goddesses who were thought to inhabit, personify, or in some way affect various aspects of nature. Legend held that most nymphs were immortal or extremely long-lived, and that they were either daughters of Zeus or of various Titans and other pre-Olympian gods or spirits. Among the many subgroups of nymphs, for example, the Hesperides, Hyades, and Pleiades were often said to be the offspring of the Titan Atlas (although some stories made the Hesperides daughters of Nyx and Erebus and the Hyades daughters of the Titans Oceanus and Tethys). Oceanus and Tethys also gave rise to a group of sea nymphs, the Oceanids. And the ancient sea god Nereus fathered another brood of sea nymphs, the Nereids. Some of the many other groups of nymphs were the Dryads, Hamadryads, and Meliae (tree nymphs); Oreads (mountain nymphs); and Naiads (nymphs of lakes, rivers, and springs).

Artists and writers generally depicted these goddesses as beautiful young women who accompanied and/or cavorted and had love affairs with various other gods. Nymphs were usually fun-loving and gentle, but on occasion they could be serious and formidable, as in the case of Thetis, a Nereid and the mother of the Greek hero Achilles. When Hera plotted to overthrow her divine husband, Zeus, Thetis hurried to the Underworld and rounded up a group of giants to rescue him. Another famous nymph, Calypso, was both strong and crafty, and she managed to entrap the Greek hero Odysseus on her island for seven years. A few nymphs were also cruel. Nais, a river nymph, for example, blinded her lover, the Sicilian herdsman Daphnis, when he slept with a mortal woman. **See** Atlas; Calypso; Castalia; Daphne; Echo; Eidothea; Galatea; Hesperides; Hyades; Maia; Nereus; Oenone; Pleiades; **also** Achilles; Daphnis; Narcissus; Orpheus (Chapter 1).

Nyx

"Night"; not only the Greek goddess of night but also, according to tradition, one of the first divine forces that emerged from Chaos at the beginning of time, along with Erebus (Darkness), Gaia (Earth), and others. Nyx's main function in mythology was to produce a large number of other deities/forces that profoundly affected the fundamental workings of nature and life, including humanity. Among the offspring she created on her own were Thanatos (Death), Nemesis (Vengeance), Ker (Doom), Hypnos (Sleep), the Oneiroi (Dreams), Eris (Strife), Gera (Old Age), and Oizys (Pain). Nyx also gave rise to the three Fates, thought to influence people's destinies. She also mated with her brother, Erebus, to produce Aether (Day) and, according to some stories, a large number of nymphs (minor nature goddesses). **See** nymphs; Thanatos; and, for an account of Nyx's emergence from Chaos, **see** The Creation of the Gods and Humans (Chapter 6).

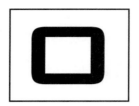

Oceanus

A son of Gaia (Earth) and Uranus (Sky) and one of the more important Titans (the first race of Greek gods). Oceanus ruled the Ocean, a wide stream that the ancients thought encircled the land portions of the earth. He and his sister (and mate), Tethys, were among the few Titans who did not take part in the great war with Zeus and his Olympians. So Zeus did not condemn these two to imprisonment in the Underworld, as he did a majority of the Titans, after the war. Oceanus and Tethys eventually gave rise to most of the gods and nymphs that dwelled in or controlled the earth's waters (including some three thousand Oceanids).

Oceanus appears in the famous story of the labors of the hero Heracles. The god lent the man a large golden cup (or bowl), borrowed from the sun god Helios, so that Heracles could ride along the waves of the Ocean and reach the island controlled by the monster Geryon and steal his cattle. **See** nymphs; Tethys; Titans; **also** Geryon (Chapter 3); The Adventures of Heracles (Chapter 6).

Oenone

A nymph who inhabited Mt. Ida, near Troy (in northwestern Asia Minor). Oenone married Paris, an important Trojan prince. And because she had the gift of prophecy, she realized that his trip to Sparta and meeting with the beautiful Spartan queen, Helen, would lead to disaster. The nymph warned her husband not to go, but he refused to listen. Later, near the close of the Trojan War, when the Greek warrior Philoctetes mortally wounded Paris, the Trojans took the fallen man to Oenone since she also possessed great healing skills. Because Paris had abandoned her years before, she refused to help. She later had a change of heart and rushed to Troy to help him, only to find that he had already died. Stricken with grief, she hanged herself. **See** Paris (Chapter 1); **also** The Trojan War (Chapter 6).

Olympians

The second and greatest race of Greek gods, who, led by Zeus, fought and succeeded the first race—the Titans—as rulers of the universe. The term *Olympian* derived from Mt. Olympus, the highest peak in Greece, which in very early times was thought to be home to Zeus and his major followers. The traditional fourteen major Olympian gods were Zeus, Hera, Poseidon, Apollo, Athena, Ares, Hestia, Aphrodite, Hades (or Pluto), Demeter, Hephaestos, Artemis, Hermes, and Dionysus. Some ancient sources list just twelve Olympians, perhaps because Hephaestos and Hestia spent little time on or eventually left Olympus. For more information, **see** the names of these gods; and, for the war between the Titans and the Olympians, **see** The Creation of the Gods and Humans (Chapter 6).

Ops

The Roman goddess of agricultural abundance. Ops was normally viewed as the consort of the agricultural god Saturn; and because the Romans identified Saturn with the Greek Titan Cronos, they also identified Ops with Cronos's wife, Rhea. The Roman festivals for Ops were the Opiconsivia, celebrated on August 25, and Opalia, held on December 19. The Romans eventually erected a temple to Ops on Rome's Capitoline Hill.

Osiris

The most widely worshiped of the Egyptian gods, who, in Hellenistic times (the last three centuries B.C.), became popular in many Greek and Roman lands. According to Egyptian tradition, Osiris had been an early pharaoh of Egypt. His brother, Seth (or Set), murdered him and cut him into pieces; but Osiris's sister and wife, Isis, collected and buried these pieces, and Osiris was reborn as the ruler of the afterlife and an important bringer of fertility. The Greeks identified Osiris with their own mysterious fertility god, Dionysus. And both the Greeks and Romans incorporated Osiris into various mystery cults that often worshiped him alongside other originally Egyptian deities, among them Isis, Horus (the Greek Harpocrates), and Serapis. **See** Horus; Isis; Serapis.

Pallas

One of the Greek Titans. Pallas mated with Styx (Abomination), the goddess who oversaw the river of the dead in the Underworld; their children were Nike (goddess of victory), Bia, Cratos, and Zelus. **See** Nike.

Pan

The Greek god of shepherds, pastures, and flocks. (The Romans identified him with an ancient Italian woodland god, Silvanus.) Like his father, the messenger god, Hermes, Pan was originally closely associated with the region of Arcadia (in the central Peloponnesus). Artists and writers usually depicted Pan with a human upper body and a goat's legs, ears, and horns. He also carried a pipe with seven reeds (the *syrinx,* or "pan-pipes"), said to be his own invention.

In mythology, Pan frequently lusted after and frolicked with various nymphs. He also took part in a music contest with the god Apollo. Because King Midas, who acted as judge, chose Pan (clearly not as good a musician as Apollo) the winner, Apollo gave Midas an ass's ears as a punishment. Though artistic and fun-loving, Pan could also be formidable, with an especially loud voice said to be frightening at times. For example, Pan's voice struck fear into the hearts of the giants during their famous battle with the Olympian gods (making them "panic," a word that appears to derive from Pan). In another myth, shortly before the Battle of Marathon (in 490 B.C.), the Athenian long-distance runner Pheidippides was on his way to Sparta to ask for aid against the invading Persians, when he encountered Pan. The god wanted to know why the Athenians did not worship him. During the subsequent battle, the Persians panicked and fled the field; and suspecting that Pan had helped them, the Athenians instituted regular sacrifices to him. **See** Silvanus; **also** Arcadia (Chapter 4).

Persephone

(also Kore) The daughter of the goddess Demeter and the chief god, Zeus, and the queen of the Underworld. Persephone became consort to Hades, ruler of the Underworld in the following manner. Zeus secretly agreed to allow Hades to take Persephone as his bride. As told in the principal ancient source about this myth, one day the girl

The lord of the Underworld, Hades, abducts Persephone, daughter of Demeter. Mother and daughter were later reunited but only for half the year.

> was playing with the . . . daughters of Oceanus [i.e., ocean nymphs] and gathering flowers over a soft meadow . . . [when] the earth open up there in the plain . . . and the lord, he who has many names [i.e., Hades], with his immortal horses, sprang out [of the ground] upon

her. . . . He grabbed the reluctant maiden on his golden chariot and bore her away as she lamented. Then she cried out with a shrill voice to her father [Zeus]. . . . But no one, either of the deathless gods or mortal men, heard her voice. (*Homeric Hymn to Demeter* 5–23)

Hades carried Persephone back to his subterranean kingdom. Meanwhile, her mother, Demeter, frantically searched for her until the sun god, Helios, who had seen the kidnapping from his vantage in the sky, told her what had happened. Furious, Demeter unleashed drought and famine on the earth. Eventually, Zeus, worried that humanity would die out, struck a deal with Hades. The latter agreed to allow Persephone to return to the earth's surface on the condition that she ate nothing while in the Underworld. Unfortunately, the girl ate some pomegranate seeds.

When mother and daughter were reunited, Demeter asked Persephone if she had eaten anything in Hades' realm. The girl claimed she had not, but then a mortal named Ascalaphus said that he had seen Persephone eat the seeds. Hearing the truth come out, Zeus decreed that thereafter the girl could spend the months from planting until harvest (basically the fall, winter, and spring) with her mother on Earth; in the hot summer months, however, she had to live with Hades in the Underworld. Eventually, both the Greeks and the Romans came to identify Persephone (whom the Romans called Proserpina) with corn planting as well as death, thereby fulfilling her roles above and below the earth. **See** Demeter; Hades.

Phoebe

According to the early Greek poet Hesiod, a daughter of Uranus and Gaia and therefore one of the Titans. Phoebe gave birth to Leto, who in turn mothered the famous Olympian god Apollo. The Greek playwright Aeschylus claimed that Phoebe was one of the three female protectors of the sacred sanctuary at Delphi. **See** Titans.

Picus

An ancient Italian nature god similar in many ways to—and also a cohort of—the Roman god of pastures and flocks, Faunus (whom the Romans identified with the Greek Pan). It was said that Picus could change his shape at will, preferring

to become a woodpecker, a bird sacred to the god Mars. Picus also had the power of prophecy and delivered oracles at one of Mars's shrines. In the best-known myth about Picus, Numa Pompilius, the legendary second king of Rome, discovered where Picus and Faunus stopped to drink in the forest; one day Numa hailed the two gods and asked them to arrange an audience for him with Jupiter, leader of the Roman gods. At first, Picus and Faunus were reluctant to help the king, but they finally summoned Jupiter for him. **See** Faunus.

Pleiades

A group of seven daughters of the Titan Atlas and the Oceanid (sea nymph) Pleione. Ancient sources usually list the names of these maidens as follows: Maia (who slept with Zeus and gave birth to Hermes, the messenger god); Electra (mother of Dardanus by Zeus); Taygete (mother of Lacedaemon, another son of Zeus); Celaeno (mother of Lycus by Poseidon); Alcyone (mother of several children by Poseidon); Sterope (mother of Oenomaus by Poseidon); and Merope (who married a mortal). When the Pleiades' sisters, the Hyades, died, the Pleiades were so upset that they killed themselves. And to honor them, Zeus placed them in the sky as a cluster of seven stars (near the spot where he had placed the Hyades). Another legend claimed that the giant hunter, Orion, had long chased after the Pleiades. So Zeus put him in the sky too, not far from them. The ancients believed that the faintest star in the Pleiades cluster was Merope, because she had mated with a mortal instead of a god. **See** Hyades; Maia; Merope; **also** Orion (Chapter 3).

Pluto

One of the Roman names, along with Dis, for the god of the Underworld, whom the Greeks called Hades. **See** Hades.

Plutus

The son of the goddess Demeter and Iasion (a mortal son of Zeus). A minor god, Plutus was mainly a protector of crops. So those who worshiped the agricultural goddess, Demeter, in her cult centered at Eleusis (in western Attica), often included her son in their prayers and sacrifices. Because his name meant "Wealth" (originally in the context of agricultural abundance), over time a common belief developed that Plutus could make people rich if he so chose. And one ancient story said that Zeus blinded Plutus to keep him from making wealthy people even wealthier. The fifth-century B.C. Athenian playwright Aristophanes wrote a comedy about Plutus in which the god's sight is restored, allowing him to tell the difference between honest and dishonest humans. **See** Demeter; **also** Aristophanes (Chapter 5).

Pomona and Vortumnus

Two minor Roman deities—Pomona a woodland goddess, Vortumnus (or Vertumnus) a god who protected fruit orchards—who played the key roles in a charming romantic myth. Ironically, the beautiful Pomona cared nothing for the woods, preferring her fruit-filled gardens and orchards. She kept them fenced off so that rustic country people could not trample her plants and vines. She also wanted to discourage the parade of young deities who regularly pursued her, and she continually managed to turn away these would-be lovers and husbands.

One day, though, Vortumnus decided to try his hand at winning the reclusive Pomona. At first he came to her in various disguises, including a reaper, an apple picker, a fisherman, and a soldier; but in each instance, to his frustration, she paid him no attention. Finally, he hit on a novel approach. He dressed himself as an old woman, gained entrance to Pomona's gardens, and pretended to admire her fruit. Then he launched into a long speech,

singing the praises of the wonderful young god Vortumnus and advising Pomona to accept his advances.

But none of this boisterous act seemed to have any effect on Pomona, so eventually Vortumnus gave up and tore off his old woman's garb. To his surprise and joy, the straightforward truth now proved the charm; for when he stood before her in all his godlike radiance, she was enchanted by his beauty, which was no less than her own. And from that day on, they tended her gardens and orchards together.

Portunus

The minor Roman god thought to protect harbors, although he appears to have originated as a protector of doors. His festival, the Portunalia, was held on August 17, and he was usually depicted in art holding a key in his hand. In his *Aeneid,* the great Roman poet Virgil depicted Portunus giving an extra advantage to one of the vessels in the boat race held during the funeral games for Aeneas's father, Anchises. **See** Aeneas's Journey to Italy (Chapter 6).

Poseidon

The principal Greek god of the seas; the brother of Zeus, Hades, and Demeter; and one of the most important and active of the Olympian gods. (The Romans identified Poseidon with Neptune, an obscure Italian water god, and adopted all of Poseidon's myths.) Poseidon became known as "the Earthshaker" because he supposedly caused earthquakes. (Hades, ruler of the Underworld, often feared that his brother's tremblers would cause the earth to cave in and bury his underground realm.) The chief sea god was also identified as Poseidon Hippios ("Poseidon of the Horses") because of his skill as a horse tamer. His symbols were the trident (three-pronged spear), dolphins, and horses.

According to the Greek poet Hesiod in his *Theogony,* like Hades and the other early Olympians, Poseidon was the son of the Titans Cronos and Rhea; and Cronos swallowed Poseidon along with the others (except for Zeus, for whom Rhea substituted a stone), only to vomit them up later. Then Poseidon aided Zeus in defeating the Titans and imprisoning them in the bowels of the Underworld.

Poseidon had numerous children. His wife, Amphitrite (daughter of the sea god Nereus or possibly another sea god, Oceanus), bore him Triton, Rhode, and Benthesicyme. By other goddesses, Poseidon sired several giants, including Antaeus, Otus, and Ephialtes. (The latter two tried but failed to scale Mt. Olympus and capture the goddesses Hera and Artemis.) Another of Poseidon's huge sons was the Cyclops Polyphemus, whom the Greek hero Odysseus outwitted and blinded (acts that angered Poseidon and caused the god to punish Odysseus by sinking the raft on which he sailed from Calypso's island). The Athenian hero Theseus slew two other unsavory sons of Poseidon—Sciron and Cercyon—who had long amused themselves by murdering innocent travelers on roadsides. Poseidon also had many mortal sons, among them the Greek kings Pelias and Neleus, and, in some accounts, the great Theseus himself (who was also said to be the son of the Athenian king Aegeus).

Poseidon figures prominently in Homer's *Iliad,* mainly because the god came to hate the Trojans and often punished or obstructed them during their famous war with the Greeks. The trouble began when Poseidon and Apollo agreed to erect Troy's mighty walls for an early Trojan king, Laomedon, in exchange for a certain sum. But when the work was finished, Laomedon refused to pay. Furious, Poseidon unleashed a hideous sea monster, which would have devoured Laomedon's daughter, Hesione, had the hero Heracles not appeared and saved her. Later, during the Trojan War, Poseidon frequently aided the Greeks, often against the orders of his

brother Zeus. At the conclusion of the war, however, the sea god vented his anger no less on the Greeks, primarily because a Greek warrior, Ajax the Lesser, committed sacrilege by raping the Trojan princess Cassandra inside Athena's temple. Poseidon killed Ajax and also shipwrecked many other Greek leaders for failing to punish Ajax.

Poseidon had frequent disputes with gods as well as mortals, most often over various lands that he wanted to control or become patron of. Perhaps the most famous of these disputes was over Attica (the territory ruled by Athens), in which Poseidon and Athena engaged in a contest. He struck the Acropolis with his trident, creating a saltwater spring; she caused an olive tree to grow on the hill's summit. When the Athenians judged the goddess the winner, Poseidon flooded much of Attica to punish them. Later, Poseidon and Zeus's wife, Hera, struggled for possession of Argos (in the eastern Peloponnesus), and again Poseidon lost and punished the locals by sending a flood. Eventually, though, the sea god managed to win patronage of an important Greek city—Corinth (in the northern Peloponnesus).

Another famous myth in which Poseidon played an important role was the creation of the Minotaur, a fearsome monster that was half man and half bull. Minos, king of Crete, asked the sea god to send him a fine bull to sacrifice to him; Poseidon did so. But Minos failed to sacrifice the beast, for which the god punished him through his wife, Pasiphae, by instilling in her a consuming passion for the bull. She mated with it, producing the Minotaur, which Minos consigned to a labyrinth (maze) beneath his palace. **See** Athena; Cronos; Neptune; Zeus; **also** Ajax 2; Laomedon; Minos; Neleus; Pasiphae; Pelias (Chapter 1); Otus and Ephialtes; Minotaur; Polyphemus (Chapter 3); Corinth (Chapter 4); The Adventures of Heracles; The Creation of the Gods and Humans; The Exploits of Theseus; The Trojan War; The Wanderings of Odysseus (Chapter 6).

Priapus

A minor Greek god of gardens, who may have originated in Phrygia (in Asia Minor). His mother was said to be the love goddess, Aphrodite, and his father was either Dionysus or Hermes. According to legend, Aphrodite rejected Priapus shortly after he was born when she saw that he was deformed. As depicted in Greek art, his body was small and twisted and featured grotesquely oversized genitals. A common myth associated with Priapus purported to explain why he hated donkeys. One day he crept up on a nymph named Lotis, who was fast asleep, and was about to embrace her when a donkey brayed and woke her up, after which she ran away. Thereafter, Priapus felt that the best kind of donkey was a dead one, and he encouraged humans to kill donkeys in his honor.

Prometheus

One of the most important and wisest Titans (the first race of Greek gods), the creator and champion of the human race, and a character of uncommon courage and compassion who refused to compromise his principles. Prometheus, whose name meant "Forethought," was the son of the Titans Iapetus and Themis. According to the poet Hesiod in his *Theogony,* Prometheus fought on Zeus's side during the war between the Titans and the Olympians; thus, Zeus did not condemn him to eternal captivity in the Underworld.

Prometheus was most renowned for fashioning the first humans out of clay (after which the goddess Athena breathed life into them). Later, Zeus asked him to decide how the humans should go about making sacrifices to the gods. Partial to his creations, the wily Prometheus tricked Zeus by arranging for the gods to receive the bones and fat of the animals sacrificed

and for the humans to keep and eat the meat. In retaliation, Zeus denied the humans knowledge of fire; but Prometheus took pity on the humans he had created and, openly defying Zeus, gave them some fire he had stolen from heaven. The angry Zeus then punished the Titan by having Hephaestos (god of the forge) chain him to a mountaintop, where a vulture (in some versions an eagle) daily devoured his liver (which grew back at night). Eventually, the hero Heracles set Prometheus free. The Athenian dramatist Aeschylus portrayed the Titan's punishment and how he bore it with an extraordinarily noble heart and spirit in the monumental play *Prometheus Bound.* **See** Epimetheus; Zeus; **also** Pandora (Chapter 1); and, for more detailed accounts of Prometheus's epic deeds and struggles, **see** *Prometheus Bound* (Chapter 5); The Creation of the Gods and Humans (Chapter 6).

Proteus

A very ancient Greek sea god, one of a few often referred to as "Old Men of the Sea." In classical times, Greek sources sometimes referred to Proteus as a son of the principal sea god, Poseidon; however, Proteus likely preceded Poseidon in the Greek pantheon. Nevertheless, once worship of Poseidon spread, Proteus remained subservient to him, often herding fish, seals, and other ocean-dwelling creatures for him. Proteus was most famous for his skill at prophecy and his reluctance to use it to aid either gods or humans. To avoid questioners, he usually transformed himself into animals and on occasion even inanimate things, including water and fire. But these efforts were not always successful. In one well-known myth, for example, Aristaeus (a son of Apollo and an expert beekeeper) managed to corner Proteus while he was resting and convinced the god to tell him how he might save his bees, many of which had been dying. Proteus explained that the bees were perishing because Aristaeus had offended the noted musician Orpheus and some nymphs; after Proteus had told Aristaeus how to appease the nymphs, the bees stopped dying. **See** Poseidon; **also** Aristaeus (Chapter 1).

Saturn

A very ancient Italian god whose original functions are somewhat obscure. He may have been the overseer of seed sowing or a bringer of blight, or both. In any case, the Romans came to see him as an agricultural god, who oversaw the sowing of crops. They also often identified him with Cronos, leader of the Titans, the earliest race of Greek gods. In one popular legend, Jupiter (the Roman version of the Greek Zeus), expelled his father, Saturn, from Mt. Olympus (corresponding somewhat with Zeus overthrowing Cronos in a famous Greek myth). Afterward, Saturn journeyed to Italy and reigned over the plain of Latium (directly south of Rome), ushering in a legendary golden age (before the advent of the later, progressively inferior ages of silver, bronze, and iron; the Greeks and Romans believed that they lived in the age of iron).

Saturn's festival, the Saturnalia (lasting from December 17 to 23), was one of the most important of the year for Romans of all walks of life, a time of goodwill and merrymaking. (Many of the customs celebrated in the Christian holiday of Christmas, including feasting, lighting candles, and exchanging presents, were borrowed directly from the Saturnalia.) Saturn's temple, located at the foot of the Capitoline Hill, served as Rome's treasury and also housed the tablets bearing the state's law codes. **See** Cronos; **also** Latium (Chapter 4).

Seasons

(Horai or Horae, meaning "Hours") The daughters of Zeus and the Titan Themis, and minor Greek goddesses who personified the seasons of the year (not the hours of the day, despite their common ancient name, the Horae). In most ancient myths, the Seasons were three in number, usually standing for Spring, Summer, and Winter; or Spring, Summer, and Harvest (Autumn). Their personal names varied. In Athens, for instance, people called them Thallo (Spring), Carpo (Harvest), and Auxo (Summer), but the Greek poet Hesiod gave them names denoting ethical concepts: Eunomia ("Law and Order"), Dike ("Justice"), and Eirene ("Peace"). Artists and writers usually pictured the Seasons hanging around the gates of the palace on Mt. Olympus, ready to see off or welcome back some major god, or as attendants to the love goddess, Aphrodite, or to the Graces.

Serapis

As ancient Egyptian gods went, a relatively new one introduced by the founder of Egypt's Greek Ptolemaic dynasty, Ptolemy I (reigned 323–283 B.C.), probably in an attempt to unite his Egyptian and Greek subjects in worshiping a god that had qualities they all could appreciate. The native Egyptians, for instance, viewed Serapis essentially as a version of their traditional god Osiris, who both ruled the kingdom of the dead and symbolized fertility and new life. At the same time, Serapis assumed some roles usually associated with Greek gods. One important one was that of healer; so many Greeks identified him with their god of healing—Asclepius. Ptolemy III (reigned 246–221 B.C.) erected a large temple to Serapis—the Serapeum—in Alexandria. And in the first century B.C. and the first century A.D., the god's cult spread to the Roman world. Because Serapis was also seen as a sky god, the Romans sometimes identified him with Jupiter. **See** Asclepius; Horus; Isis; Osiris.

Silvanus

A minor Roman god of uncultivated or wild lands who was sometimes identified with the Greek god Pan. As Rome conquered and absorbed various European regions, local peoples came to associate Silvanus with their own gods; for example, in southern Gaul he was identified with a Celtic hammer god; and the natives of northern Britain associated him with a local hunting god. Romans and many of their subject peoples who planned to cut down trees in the forest often sacrificed to Silvanus first to gain his favor. Not surprisingly, therefore, small shrines to the god became extremely numerous in the Roman world in the first three centuries A.D. **See** Pan.

Tethys

One of the Titans (the first race of Greek gods) and the wife of another important Titan, Oceanus. The two gods ruled over the distant realm of the Ocean, the wide river thought to encircle the land portions of the earth. They were able to retain this position under Zeus because during the famous war between the Titans and the Olympians (led by Zeus), Tethys and Oceanus fought on the side of the Olympians. Tethys's most important role in mythology was bearing Oceanus's huge numbers of minor gods and goddesses, among them some three thousand ocean nymphs (the Oceanids) and numerous

river deities as well as Zeus's first wife, Metis, and Electra, mother of Iris (goddess of the rainbow) and the Harpies. **See** Metis; nymphs; Oceanus; Titans.

Thanatos

The Greek god or personification of death, who legend claimed was the son of the early deities (or forces) Nyx (Night) and Hypnos (Sleep). The Greeks viewed Thanatos as a sort of angel of death who arrived to claim a person when he or she died. Most of the time he successfully performed this duty, but an occasional human outwitted or outmaneuvered him. One of the most famous of these stories is that of a young woman, Alcestis, the title character of one of Euripides' greatest plays. The playwright depicted Thanatos as a menacing figure dressed in a black robe and carrying a sword. The god came to carry away the young woman, who had agreed to die in place of her husband, Admetus, whose allotted time on earth was up. At the last moment, however, the magnificent hero Heracles appeared. The strongman wrestled and defeated Thanatos, forcing him to abandon his attempt to take Alcestis. Here are some of the powerful words Euripides had Heracles say just prior to his encounter with Thanatos:

> The woman's dead; and I must rescue her, and pay the debt of kindness I owe Admetus by returning Alcestis to her own home once more—alive! The black-robed king of the dead will come to drink the blood of victims offered at her tomb. That's where I'll find him. I'll hide there, watch for him, leap out and spring on him; and once I have my arms locked round his bruised ribs, there's no power on earth that will be able to wrench him free, till he gives her up to me! (*Alcestis* 840–850)

In another famous myth, the wily Sisyphus (founder of the city of Corinth) somehow tricked Thanatos and trapped him in a prison cell; this caused humans to stop dying, until the god Ares released the embarrassed deity of death. Thanatos quickly found Sisyphus and took his soul to the Underworld, but the clever man managed to escape and return to the earth to live out his life. (In the end, though, the gods punished Sisyphus severely for this offense.) **See** Admetus; Alcestis; Sisyphus (Chapter 1); **also** *Alcestis* (Chapter 5); The Adventures of Heracles (Chapter 6).

Themis

One of the most important female Titans (the first race of Greek gods) and, like many other Titans, a child of Gaia (Earth) and Uranus (Sky). Themis's first husband was the Titan Iapetus, by whom she bore perhaps the most famous Titan of all—Prometheus, creator of the human race. To her son, Themis passed on her gifts of wisdom and prophecy, and thereby Prometheus's name came to mean "Forethought." Themis's gift of prophecy made her the ideal candidate to take over the Delphic Oracle from its first overseer, Gaia. (Apollo subsequently became the third and most famous guardian of the oracle.) Themis also gave Deucalion (the Greek Noah) the secret knowledge he needed to repopulate the earth after the great flood, and she warned the Titan Atlas that a son of Zeus would someday come to steal the golden apples from the Garden of the Hesperides. Later, Themis became the second consort (after Metis) to Zeus, ruler of the Olympian gods; and by Zeus she gave birth to the Fates and Hours (or Seasons). **See** Atlas; Prometheus; Seasons; Zeus; **also** Delphic Oracle (Chapter 4); The Creation of the Gods and Humans (Chapter 6).

Thetis

A Greek sea nymph and the mother of the Greek hero Achilles. Thetis, who was the daughter of the sea god Nereus and there-fore one of the Nereids, grew up on Mt. Olympus as a faithful attendant of the goddess Hera. However, the nymph left the home of the gods to rescue and look after Hephaestos, god of the forge, after Hera threw him off the mountain because of his lameness. Later, when Hera plotted to overthrow Zeus, Thetis turned on her mentor. The nymph hurried down to Tartarus and enlisted Briareos, one of the hundred-handed giants, to aid Zeus, who managed to foil the plot.

Later still, Thetis found herself part of an intrigue involving Zeus and the Titan Prometheus, the champion of the early human race. Prometheus knew a secret he refused to reveal to Zeus—namely, that Thetis was destined to bear a son who would be greater than his own father. Eventually, Zeus found out, luckily before mating with Thetis and thereby fulfilling the prophecy. To make sure that Thetis married someone relatively insignificant, which would ensure that the prediction would never come true, the chief god ordained that the nymph should marry a mortal—Peleus, king of Phthia (in southern Thessaly). She did not want to marry Peleus, however. So when he chased after her, she continually changed her shape in an attempt to elude him; he held on as tight as he could, though, and refused to let her go until she consented to the marriage.

Despite her initial reluctance, Thetis became a dutiful wife to Peleus and bore him seven sons. One of these was the hero Achilles, whom as an infant she dipped into the River Styx (in the Underworld); this made his body invulnerable to wounds, except for his heel, which she held while dipping him. Later, when the child had matured into a young man, Thetis tried to keep him from entering the Trojan War after hearing a prophecy that he would die in the conflict. But the Greek hero Odysseus found Achilles dressed as a girl and hiding in his uncle's palace, where Thetis had taken him for safekeeping.

During the war, after Achilles' close companion Patroclus was slain by the Trojan champion Hector, Thetis rushed to Hephaestos and had him create a magnificent new suit of armor for her son. In this outfit, Achilles proceeded to kill Hector. Later, after Troy's Prince Paris slew Achilles with an arrow that struck his heel, the only place he could be wounded, Thetis and the other Nereids wailed so loudly that the Greek soldiers were terrified and ran back to their camp. One legend claimed that Thetis eventually conferred immortality on her husband, Peleus, and dwelled with him in the Black Sea for eternity. **See** Nereus; Prometheus; **also** Achilles; Peleus (Chapter 1); The Trojan War (Chapter 6).

Titans

The first race of Greek gods, the initial members of which sprang from the union of Uranus (Sky) and Gaia (Earth). The Greeks pictured the Titans as huge, extremely powerful beings who had human form and controlled the universe in the primeval age before the rise of Zeus, his Olympians, and the human race. The major male Titans included Oceanus, Coeus, Crius, Hyperion, Iapetus, and Cronos (who overthrew his father, Uranus, and became ruler of the earth and sky); the main female Titans were Thea, Rhea, Themis, Mnemosyne, Phoebe, and Tethys. Some of the important Titanic children of these beings were Helios (the sun god), Prometheus (Forethought), Epimetheus (Afterthought), and Atlas, who later came to hold up the sky.

By contrast, Cronos and Rhea gave birth to children who were not Titans but were rather members of a new race of gods that became known as the Olympians. Just as Cronos had overthrown his father, Uranus, the leader of the Olympians, Zeus, challenged his own father, Cronos; a huge conflict (which the Greeks called the Titanomachy) ensued between the two races of gods. After a ten-year struggle, Zeus and his allies (who included a number of Titans who fought against their own kind) won. Zeus then threw his defeated enemies down into Tartarus, the lowest and most dismal region of the Underworld. There, they remained imprisoned for eternity, with the Hecatoncheires (hundred-handed giants) as their guards. After the war, some of the Titans, including Helios, Oceanus, and Tethys, continued to serve Zeus. **See** Cronus; Gaia; Olympians; Prometheus; Zeus; and the individual names of other Titans mentioned; and, for a more detailed account of the rise and fall of the Titans, **see** The Creation of the Gods and Humans (Chapter 6).

Triton

A minor Greek sea god whose parents were Poseidon and Amphitrite (daughter of Nereus and herself a minor sea goddess). But though minor in the pantheon of gods, Triton was quite popular with Greek artists, who depicted him with a human upper torso and a fish's tail (making him a sort of merman). Artists also depicted him with a conch shell, which he blew to calm stormy seas, and a trident (three-pronged spear), like that of his father, Poseidon.

Triton played a prominent role in a few myths, including the famous tale of the Argonauts and their search for the Golden Fleece. When a monstrous wave carried the *Argo* inland past the coast of Libya (in North Africa), the god greeted Jason and his men in the form of a human named Euryphylus. The disguised Triton told the Argonauts how to make their way back to the sea and also gave them a small clod of earth as a gift. Later, one of the Argonauts dropped the clod in the sea north of Crete, and it became the island of Thera (modern Santorini). In another myth, Triton was a villain. Each time the women of Tanagra (near Thebes in Boeotia) bathed in the sea in preparation for their worship of the fertility god, Dionysus, Triton would spring from the water and harass them. Eventually, Dionysus challenged Triton to a fight. The sea god lost. **See** Poseidon.

Tyche

A minor Greek deity of fate, chance, and/or luck, whom people tended to view more as an abstraction, an integral element of life, than as a flesh-and-blood goddess. For this reason, over time each city or region came to have its own *tyche,* or lucky spirit, thought to be watching over it. The fifth-century B.C. Greek poet Pindar called Tyche one of the Fates, though this was not a universally accepted view. Tyche, or at least her concept, gained a much wider following after the Romans identified her with a minor Italian goddess, Fortuna. **See** Fates; Fortuna.

Uranus

(or Uranos) In Greek mythology, an early god or natural force who manifested himself as the sky or heavens. After Gaia (the earth) emerged from Chaos, she gave birth to Uranus (without the aid of a male seed), after which he became her mate. They subsequently gave rise to the first race of Greek gods, known as the Titans. Unfortunately, Uranus was jealous of his children and attempted to stop their births by pushing them back inside Gaia. Finally, Gaia could bear this agony no longer; she helped one of her sons, Cronos, to overpower Uranus. Cronos used a sickle to castrate Uranus. The severed genitals fell into the sea and were transformed into the love goddess, Aphrodite (who rose from the sea foam); meanwhile, numerous blood droplets from the castration became

the giants, the Furies, and various nymphs. After this episode, Uranus played no further role in mythology, and the Greeks offered him no worship. **See** Cronos; Gaia; Titans; **also** The Creation of the Gods and Humans (Chapter 6).

Venus

Originally an obscure Italian goddess, perhaps having something to do with vegetable or other gardens. Under the influence of Greek culture and religion, however, the Romans came to associate Venus with the important Greek love goddess, Aphrodite. Venus had a temple on Rome's Capitoline Hill as well as at other locations in Italy. She was often pictured as the escort of the war god, Mars, and her symbols were roses, doves, and dolphins.

Venus's roles in myths tended to mirror those of Aphrodite, with the major exception of the crucial part she played in Virgil's monumental poem the *Aeneid,* which became Rome's national epic. Venus aided

Italian artist Sandro Botticelli's famous oil painting, The Birth of Venus, *depicts the goddess as she rises from the sea foam.*

Aeneas in his escape from Troy after the Greeks sacked it. Subsequently, she protected him from the goddess Juno, who frequently tried to thwart him; Venus made Dido (queen of Carthage) fall in love with him; and she supported him in his climactic fight with the Italian warrior Turnus. **See** Aphrodite; **also** Aeneas; Dido (Chapter 1); *Aeneid* (Chapter 5); Aeneas's Journey to Italy (Chapter 6).

Vesta

The Roman goddess of the hearth, whom the Romans identified with the Greek goddess of the hearth—Hestia. Vesta was widely worshiped in Roman homes as well as by the state. In her temple in the Roman Forum, her priestesses, known as the Vestal Virgins (since they were expected to remain chaste, like the goddess herself), constantly maintained a sacred fire and restarted it each year on March 1 (Rome's New Year's Day). In Vesta's public festival, the Vestalia, celebrated on June 9, women marched barefoot carrying food offerings for her. **See** Hestia.

Vulcan

(or Vulcanus) An early Italian or Roman fire god who, over time, became identified with the Greek Hephaestos, god of the forge. In his capacity as a smelter of metals, the Romans called him Vulcan Mulciber, and he was often seen as a more destructive counterpart of Vesta (goddess of the hearth), who represented a more positive force of fire. Both the Greeks and Romans pictured the god of the forge as living and working beneath volcanoes, assisted by giants called Cyclopes. In the case of the Romans, that forge lay beneath Mt. Etna in Sicily. Vulcan's most famous shrines were in Rome's main Forum and at Rome's port city of Ostia. His festivals were held on May 23 and August 23. For the original Greek myths associated with the god, **see** Hephaestos.

Zeus

The supreme ruler of the Greek gods, known for his control of thunder, lightning, and rain as well as for maintaining justice, law, and morality. He was often referred to as Zeus Polieus, meaning "Zeus of the City," in which role he was seen as a protector of local Greek city-states. Another common name for him was Zeus Xenios, or "Zeus the Protector of Strangers"; this title reflected the belief that he oversaw the laws of hospitality and punished those who broke them. Others who felt Zeus's wrath were humans who denied others the right of religious sanctuary at religious altars, in which guise he was called Zeus Hikesios, "Zeus the Protector of Suppliants," or Zeus Soter, "Zeus the Savior."

Given his importance, the Greeks dedicated numerous religious festivals and shrines to Zeus throughout Greece and Greek-speaking lands. The most famous of these was the Temple of Olympian Zeus at Olympia (the site of the ancient Olympic Games, in the northwestern Peloponnesus); inside that structure the great Athenian sculptor Phidias created a huge and magnificent statue of the god seated on a golden throne, a work that later came to be listed among the seven wonders of the ancient world. Like other Greek artists, Phidias depicted Zeus as bearded. Often the god was also shown with one or more of his major symbols—the thunderbolt, eagle, and oak tree. The latter was a reference to his sacred oak located at his oracle at Dodona (in northwestern Greece), the second-most famous oracle in the Greek world (next to Apollo's oracle at Delphi). Through the priestesses of Dodona, Zeus was thought to dispense prophecy and advice.

Befitting his prominence in the Greek religious pantheon, Zeus played roles, both large and small, in dozens of myths. Among the more renowned of these were stories involving his birth and the crucial events that followed it. According to the early Greek poet Hesiod in his *Theogony,* Zeus was the youngest of the six children of the Titans Cronos and Rhea (the other five being Hestia, Hera, Poseidon, Hades, and Demeter). Cronos, ruler of the Titans, feared that one of these children would overthrow him, so he swallowed them one by one after they were born. The exception was Zeus. Rhea substituted a rock for the baby, the dim-witted Cronos swallowed the rock, and then Rhea secretly asked some nymphs to raise Zeus. Later, Zeus came back and forced Cronos to vomit up the other gods.

Zeus himself soon swallowed his first wife, Metis, after she became pregnant. Gaia (Earth) had told Zeus that if the child were a girl, she would be equal to Zeus in wisdom and strength, and so he felt threatened. But swallowing Metis accomplished nothing since she gave birth to the child while Metis was inside of Zeus; and Metis's and Zeus's new daughter, Athena, emerged, fully clothed in armor, from Zeus's head.

Zeus eventually led a rebellion against Cronos, and the two races of gods—the Titans and the Olympians—engaged in a mighty war (which the Greeks called the Titanomachy). The war lasted ten years; finally Zeus and his Olympians (and other allies, who included some of the Titans, notably Prometheus, Helios, Oceanus, and Tethys) won, and Zeus locked his defeated enemies away in the darkest reaches of the Underworld.

Another famous myth involving Zeus tells about the exploits of the Titan Prometheus in the years following the Titanomachy. Prometheus created the human race out of clay. Afterward, Zeus asked him to decide the manner in which humans would offer sacrifices to the gods, obviously expecting that the gods would receive the best parts of sacrificed animals. But Prometheus wanted his mortal creations to get the meat, and he tricked Zeus by arranging for the gods to receive the bones and fat of the sacrificed animals. Angry, Zeus retaliated by denying the "creatures of Prometheus" knowledge of fire; however, Prometheus took pity on the humans, stole some fire from heaven, and gave it to them. This time Zeus vented his wrath directly on Prometheus, ordering Hephaestos (god of the forge) to chain the disobedient Titan to a mountaintop, where a vulture daily devoured his liver (which grew back at night).

Zeus later punished the humans again, both as a group and individually. He sent a number of floods against them, one of which ravaged the region of Phrygia (in Asia Minor), after Zeus, disguised as a human, had been refused hospitality at every house in the region. (The exception was the poor hovel of a kind couple, Baucis and Philemon, who welcomed the stranger and fed him what little food they had; for this, the god allowed them to live.) Zeus also banished Tantalus, a later king of Lydia (also in Asia Minor), to the Underworld for killing and cooking his own son, Pelops, and trying to feed the young man's flesh to the gods. (The deities saw through the ruse, refused to eat the repulsive meal, and restored Pelops to life.)

When he was not involved in judging others and meting out punishment of one sort or another, Zeus spent much of his time having affairs with both goddesses and mortal women and begetting children by them. After his first consort, Metis, and he had produced Athena, he chose as his next consort the Titan Themis, who bore him the Hours (Seasons) and the Fates. Then Zeus had relations with a nymph named Eurynome, by whom he sired the

Graces and some other daughters; the agricultural goddess Demeter, who bore him Persephone (who became queen of the Underworld); the Titan Mnemosyne, who made Zeus the father of the nine Muses (goddesses of the fine arts); and Leto, another Titan, who bore the famous deities Apollo and Artemis.

After Leto, Zeus finally settled on his sister, the goddess Hera, as his permanent wife. Even before their marriage, however, Hera displayed her renowned jealousy for any female who caught Zeus's fancy by forbidding humans in many lands from giving the pregnant Leto a place to rest and have her babies. (Finally, Zeus intervened, and Leto gave birth to Apollo and Artemis on Delos, a tiny island in the middle of the Aegean.) Several versions of Zeus's and Hera's first meeting existed in ancient times; the commonest one held that he spied her strolling through the woods near Argos and became filled with desire for her. Zeus mustered up a thunderstorm on the spot, disguised himself as a bird, and flew inside her dress to get out of the rain. Then he changed back to his true form and asked her marry him. She eagerly agreed.

But at times Hera lived to regret her decision to marry Zeus, mainly because he continued to have affairs. And she made a point of harassing or punishing his mistresses and/or their offspring. Among the mortal women Zeus seduced were the following: Niobe (from Argos), Io (also from Argos), Europa (from the coast of Palestine, whom he approached disguised as a bull and bore away to Crete), Antiope (from Boeotia), Leda (queen of Sparta, who bore him Helen of Troy and the Dioscuri), Alcmena (from Tiryns and mother of the famous Greek hero Heracles), Danae (from Argos, whose son by Zeus—Perseus—became another renowned hero), and Semele (from Thebes, who bore the fertility god Dionysus).

The case of Semele illustrates how formidable, relentless, and cruel Hera's wrath

could be against such women and their children. After Zeus impregnated Semele, Hera tricked him into revealing to the young woman his true form, which was so radiant that she immediately shriveled up into a burnt-out husk. Thinking quickly, Zeus rescued the fetus from Semele's womb and placed it under the skin of his thigh; not long afterward, Dionysus was born from that thigh. To keep the infant god safe, the ruler of Olympus had to keep a watchful eye on his wife, for the jealous Hera was intent on harming the child any way she could. The only exception to Hera's usual retaliation against Zeus's mistresses and their offspring was the case of Maia, one of the Titan Atlas's daughters, who bore Zeus the messenger god, Hermes. Hermes tricked Hera into breastfeeding him, which made them close; so she did not seek vengeance against either Maia or Hermes.

Hera was not the only goddess who disliked Zeus's constant extramarital affairs. His grandmother, Gaia, disapproved in general with the way Zeus was running things, so she became determined to overthrow him. First, she sent a race of giants to attack Zeus atop Mt. Olympus—a stupendous battle (which the Greeks called the Gigantomachy) often portrayed by sculptors and other Greek artists. With the help of his incredibly strong and courageous son, Heracles, Zeus managed to defeat the giants. Then Gaia unleashed a large and formidable monster, Typhon, which almost defeated Zeus; the victorious god ended up burying the creature beneath the island of Sicily.

Zeus took part in numerous other battles, adventures, intrigues, and other mythological incidents. Of these, perhaps the most famous was the part he played in Homer's epics—the *Iliad* and the *Odyssey.* Here, the ruler of the gods appeared mainly as an impartial judge of human affairs, often cautioning other gods not to take sides in the Trojan War

In this rendition of the Gigantomachy, the battle between the giants and Olympian gods, the figures in the chariot may be Zeus and Hera.

(although several of them disobeyed him). Homer refers to Zeus as holding golden scales and allowing them to tip in the manner fate decreed, even when it meant that a person he favored would die. A prominent example was the episode in which the Trojan prince, Hector, fought and lost to the Greek warrior Achilles; though Zeus loved Hector, he allowed Achilles to slay him be-cause fate had decreed that it was Hector's time to die. For more on Zeus, **see** Jupiter, his Roman counterpart; Cronos; Dionysus; Hades; Hera; Olympians; Prometheus; **also** Antiope; Baucis and Philemon; Europa (Chapter 1); giants; Otus and Ephialtes; Typhon (Chapter 3); The Creation of the Gods and Humans; The Trojan War; The Wanderings of Odysseus (Chapter 6).

Chapter 3
Animals, Monsters, Spirits, and Forces

Amalthea

The goat that suckled the god Zeus when he was an infant on the island of Crete. According to the legend, Amalthea's horns contained nectar and ambrosia (the magical food of the gods); when one of them broke off, some nymphs filled it with fruit. This is the derivation of the familiar image of the "horn of plenty." Eventually, the gods transformed Amalthea into the constellation Capricorn, the goat.

Antaeus

A formidable giant said to be the son of the Greek sea god Poseidon and Gaia (the earth). Antaeus dwelled in Libya (in North Africa) and challenged anyone who entered the region to wrestle with him. What those who accepted the challenge did not know was that contact with the earth constantly renewed the giant's strength, making him practically invincible. This was not enough to stop the great hero Heracles, however. On his way to get the golden apples of the Hesperides (one of his famous twelve labors), he passed through Libya; Antaeus chal-lenged him, and Heracles accepted. After a terrific struggle, Heracles lifted his opponent off the ground, cutting off his contact with the earth, then simply squeezed the giant to death. **See** The Adventures of Heracles (Chapter 6).

Argus

1. A large, many-eyed giant (or monster) that killed a bull that was terrorizing Arcadia (in the central Peloponnesus). Zeus sent the god Hermes to slay Argus, after which Zeus's wife, Hera, placed the creature's eyes on the tail of her symbol, the peacock. For more details, **see** Io (Chapter 1).

2. Odysseus's faithful dog. In a touching scene in the seventh book of Homer's *Odyssey,* Argus recognizes and happily greets his master, who has just returned home after an absence of twenty years, and then the dog dies of old age.

Arion

An unusually swift horse that legend claimed was the son of the Greek sea god Poseidon and the agricultural goddess Demeter. Arion belonged to Adrastus, king of Argos (in the eastern Peloponnesus). After the failure of the attack Adrastus led against the city of Thebes (an episode known as the Seven Against Thebes), Arion's fabulous speed allowed the man to escape with his life. **See** Adrastus (Chapter 1); **also** *Seven Against Thebes* (Chapter 5).

Briareos

(also Aegaeon) A huge monster having a hundred arms, one of three such creatures the Greeks called the Hecatoncheires ("Hundred-handers"). The son of Gaia (Earth) and Uranus (Sky), Briareos and his brothers fought alongside Zeus during the war between the Titans and the Olympians; and after Zeus won, he had the Hecatoncheires guard the defeated Titans, whom he had locked away in Tartarus. Later, when Hera, Poseidon, and Athena plotted to overthrow Zeus, the nymph Thetis (mother of the Greek hero Achilles) hurried down to Tartarus and enlisted the aid of Briareos. The monster rushed back to Zeus's side and helped him fend off the assault by the rebellious gods. In another myth, Briareos acted as a judge in a dispute between Poseidon and Helios over which of them should control the city of Corinth. Briareos gave Helios the Acrocorinth (the city's acropolis), and he awarded the rest of the city-state to Poseidon. **See** Hecatoncheires; **also** The Creation of the Gods and Humans (Chapter 6).

Cacus

According to Roman legend, a son of Vulcan and a fire-breathing creature that inhabited a cave beneath the Palatine Hill, on the future site of Rome. Cacus consumed human flesh and kept the skulls and bones of his victims in piles inside his cave. When the famous strongman Hercules (Heracles to the Greeks) was driving Geryon's cattle back to Greece (to complete one of his twelve labors), he stopped to rest on the riverbank near the Palatine. Cacus saw the cattle and managed to steal four bulls and four heifers while Hercules was sleeping. Finally, the strongman woke up, searched in vain for the missing cattle, and was about to depart when he heard one of the lost heifers cry out from a nearby cave, which, of course, was Cacus's lair. A tremendous battle ensued between man and monster. Hercules tore the top of the hill away to get at Cacus, who used fire and smoke against him. In the end, however, the beast was no match for Hercules, who leapt into the cave and strangled his opponent to death. Recovering his cattle, Hercules then continued his journey. **See** The Adventures of Heracles (Chapter 6).

centaur

In Greek mythology, a member of a famous race of creatures who had the upper bodies of men and the lower bodies of horses. Legend claimed that they were the offspring of Apollo and a water nymph named Stilbe and that they dwelled on and around Mt. Pelion in Thessaly (in central Greece). Most of the centaurs were crude, slovenly, inhospitable beasts; the exception was Chiron, a kind, wise centaur who tutored a number of important Greek heroes and statesmen.

The principal myth about the centaurs involved their war with the Lapiths, an early group of Greeks who inhabited a nearby area of Thessaly. The Lapith king, Pirithous, made the mistake of inviting his neighbors, the centaurs, to his wedding. The horse-men proceeded to get drunk on wine and then, claiming that the Lapiths' land really belonged to the centaurs, they tried to carry off the Lapith women. One centaur, Eurytion, had the gall to try abducting the bride, Hippodamia. The male Lapiths responded swiftly and harshly, rescuing the women and killing many centaurs. This battle, which the Greeks called

A Renaissance painting shows a centaur (horse-man), a favorite mythical figure of Greco-Roman legend and art.

the Centauromachy, was a frequent subject of art; several of the sculptures on the Parthenon temple in Athens showed centaurs fighting Lapiths.

In another myth, the hero Heracles was passing through Arcadia (in the Peloponnesus, where the surviving centaurs had fled the angry Lapiths) and one of the centaurs, Pholus, invited him to dinner. The creature's hospitality proved poor, however, since he refused to give his guest any wine. When Heracles protested, a fight broke out, and he ended up killing several of the horse-men, including Pholus, with his mighty bow and deadly poisoned arrows. Unfortunately, Chiron, the kindly centaur, was killed by accident when he tried to remove an arrow

from a wounded centaur and the poisoned tip scratched him. One of the surviving centaurs, Nessus, eventually avenged the strongman's slaughter of his fellow horsemen. Nessus gave Heracles' wife, Deianira, some of his own blood before he died, instructing her to keep it and later, if she ever doubted her husband's love for her, to smear it on a tunic and give the garment to Heracles to wear. She eventually had occasion to do this; and when the strongman put the tunic on, it severely burned his flesh. **See** Chiron; **also** Lapiths (Chapter 1); The Adventures of Heracles (Chapter 6).

Cerberus

The monstrous dog said in Greek legend to guard the entrance to the Underworld. Cerberus was the offspring of the monsters Typhon and Echidna and the brother of two other monsters, the Hydra and Chimaera. Most Greek artists and writers depicted Cerberus with three heads, though the poet Hesiod claimed the creature had fifty heads. The great dog allowed the shades (souls) of the dead to walk by it on their way into the Underworld, but if they tried to get out, it devoured them. He also attacked living humans who tried to enter the realm of the dead. To get by Cerberus, therefore, the poet Orpheus (who wanted to retrieve his lover, Eurydice) calmed the monster with music; and when the Sibyl of Cumae led Aeneas into the Underworld (to see his dead father), she threw Cerberus a piece of drugged cake, which made him fall asleep. The famous hero Heracles actually managed to capture the hideous dog to fulfill one of his twelve labors. **See** Underworld (Chapter 4); **also** The Adventures of Heracles (Chapter 6).

Cercopes

Two mischievous dwarves, born the sons of the Titans Oceanus and Theia. According to Greek tradition, the Cercopes committed thefts and other minor crimes in the region of Ephesus (a Greek city on the western coast of Asia Minor) or, in other accounts,

Thessaly (in central Greece). The Greek hero Heracles encountered the Cercopes one day when they attempted to steal his armor. He hung them upside down from a pole he carried over his shoulder, thus, as he walked along, they saw only his rear end. Eventually, Heracles let the little knaves go; but later, the ruler of the gods, Zeus, who had grown tired of hearing people complain about the Cercopes, turned them into monkeys.

Chaos

In Greek mythology, the original void (region of nothingness) from which the first primitive deities/forces sprang, among them Gaia (Earth), Uranus (Sky), Tartarus (the deepest region of the Underworld), Nyx (Night), and Erebus (Darkness). For a detailed account of the Greek creation, **see** The Creation of the Gods and Humans (Chapter 6).

Charybdis

A female monster who took the shape of a large whirlpool, whom the Greeks and Romans usually located at the northern end of Sicily's Strait of Messina. Charybdis sucked in and destroyed any ships that happened to go near her. During his famous wanderings after the Trojan War, the Greek hero Odysseus sailed through the strait and had the choice of facing Charybdis or Scylla, a six-headed monster who dwelled on the opposite bank. (This is the origin of the common ancient saying "caught between Scylla and Charybdis," equivalent to the modern "caught between a rock and a hard place.") Odysseus chose Scylla and made it through. Later, however, after his men had been killed, his ship was drawn into Charybdis; at the last moment, he luckily escaped by catching hold of the branch of a fig tree that hung over the great whirlpool. **See** Scylla; **also** The Wanderings of Odysseus (Chapter 6).

Chimaera

One of the hideous creatures produced by the union of the monsters Typhon and Echidna. The Chimaera was said to have the head of a lion, the body of a goat, and the tail of a snake. The beast terrorized the region of Lycia (in southern Asia Minor) until the Greek hero Bellerophon came along and, riding the flying horse Pegasus, slew the monster. **See** Pegasus; **also** Bellerophon (Chapter 1).

Chiron

The friendliest, wisest, and most civilized of the centaurs, creatures half man and half horse who originally inhabited Thessaly (in central Greece). The son of the Titan Cronos and a nymph, Philyra, Chiron was a friend of the god Apollo and, like that god, was skilled in healing, the arts, music, and archery. Various deities, kings, and queens sent their offspring to Chiron to tutor and/or rear them; and his illustrious protégés included Asclepius, Greek god of healing; Asclepius's own sons; Actaeon, a hunter whom the goddess Artemis punished after he saw her bathing naked; and the renowned heroes Jason and Achilles. Chiron also aided the hero Achilles' son, Peleus, when Acastus, king of Iolcos (in Thessaly) abandoned Peleus on the slopes of Mt. Pelion (where Chiron lived). The kindly centaur advised Peleus on how to woo the sea nymph Thetis; and Peleus and Thetis later produced the hero Achilles. Though Chiron was immortal, he could feel pain. And when he was accidentally scratched by one of the poisoned arrows belonging to the famous strongman Heracles, the centaur's agony was so great that he transferred his immortality to someone else (in some accounts the Titan Prometheus) and thereby died. **See** centaur; **also** Achilles, Peleus (Chapter 1).

Cyclops

In Greek mythology, a giant usually depicted as having one eye. A number of conflicting traditions grew up around these creatures. According to the Greek poet Hesiod, the original three Cyclopes—

Odysseus and his crewmates blind the one-eyed giant Polyphemus on this Greek black-figure hydria (container for carrying water).

Arges (Shiner), Brontes (Thunderer), and Steropes (Lightning-Maker)—were the sons of Uranus (Sky) and Gaia (Earth). Fearing these monstrous offspring, Uranus imprisoned them in Tartarus. Later, the Titan Cronos released the three, but soon afterward he, too, became afraid and consigned them to the bowels of the Underworld. Only after Zeus defeated the Titans did the Cyclopes gain permanent release from Tartarus, after which they served him as thunderbolt makers. (They also made the sea god Poseidon's trident.) Eventually, the versatile god Apollo slew the Cyclopes in revenge for Zeus's killing of Apollo's son, Asclepius.

A different tradition, created or passed on by Homer in his epic poem the *Odyssey,* held that the Cyclopes were a race of uncivilized, uncouth one-eyed giants living in caves on a remote island. When Odysseus and some of his men went ashore to gather provisions, they encountered a Cyclops named Polyphemus and blinded him after he trapped them in his cave. Unfortunately, the giant turned

out to be a son of Poseidon; thereafter, the god sought to avenge his son's injury by thwarting Odysseus's attempts to sail home.

Still another Greek tradition claimed that a group of more civilized Cyclopes built the walls of a number of ancient citadels in mainland Greece. Among these were the walls of Tiryns and Mycenae (in the eastern Peloponnesus), which modern scholars know were constructed by a Bronze Age Greek-speaking people, the Mycenaeans. Hundreds of years after the collapse of the Bronze Age kingdoms, later ancient Greeks looked on the ruins of these walls and concluded that the huge stones could only have been moved by giants. **See** The Creation of the Gods and Humans; The Wanderings of Odysseus (Chapter 6).

daimons

("divine spirits") Spirits whose nature the Greeks viewed as lying somewhere between that of a mortal person and a god. In general, they saw daimons more like ill-defined elemental forces than flesh-and-blood divine beings like the traditional gods. No one worshiped daimons, nor did artists usually try to depict them; instead, people identified them in a loose way with the power to bring good fortune. It was common, for example, for those drinking wine to dedicate their first drink to the "Good Daimon." The eighth-century B.C. Greek poet Hesiod claimed that daimons were the spirits of people who had lived during the Age of Heroes (what the later Greeks called the Bronze Age), something akin to the later Christian concept of angels. Later, the fourth-century B.C. Athenian philosopher Socrates introduced the idea of a *daimonion,* his "divine sign," a kind of inner voice or conscience guiding him toward right behavior. Plato, Socrates' pupil, who recorded Socrates' beliefs (since Socrates left behind no writings of his own) was the first Greek writer to describe daimons this way; later Greek and Roman writers extended this idea of a good daimon inhabiting someone to include a bad daimon (or "demon") doing so.

Dirae

One of the Latin (Roman) names for the Greek Erinyes, vengeful female spirits who chased after and punished murders and other criminals. The other Latin name for them was Furiae, from which their modern name—Furies—derived. **See** Furies.

Echidna

A repulsive monster born of the union of the misshapen creature Chrysaor (who sprang from the blood of his mother, Medusa, after Perseus had decapitated her) and one of Oceanus's daughters, Callirrhoe. (In other ancient accounts, Echidna was the daughter of Gaia [Earth] and Tartarus [the darkest part of the Underworld]; or of the sea deities/creatures Ceto and Phorcys.) Echidna had the upper body of a beautiful woman, but the rest of her torso was that of a serpent. Her main role in Greek mythology was giving birth to numerous monsters that plagued humans and their habitations. Among these dreaded creatures were the Chimaera, the Hydra, and Cerberus (all by the monster Typhon); the Sphinx, the Nemean Lion, and the Crommyonian Sow (all by the two-headed

dog Orthus); as well as Orthus itself, the serpent Ladon, and the giant vulture (or eagle) that tormented Prometheus. Eventually, Argus, a many-eyed giant, slew Echidna while she was sleeping. For more information about the various monsters mentioned, **see** under their names; for Orthus, **see** Geryon; **also** The Adventures of Heracles (Chapter 6), since that famous hero met and killed several of these monsters.

Erebus

("Darkness") In Greek mythology, one of the basic, elemental deities/forces that emerged from the primeval Chaos (the void) at the beginning of time. Erebus mated with his sister, Nyx (Night) to produce Aether (Atmosphere), Hemera (Day), and Charon (the ghastly boatman who ferried dead souls across the River Styx). The Greeks did not worship Erebus, nor did he appear in any myths other than the story of the creation. **See** The Creation of the Gods and Humans (Chapter 6).

Eumenides

("the Kindly Ones") The name given to the former spirits of vengeance, the Furies, after the goddess Athena transformed them into beneficent spirits following the trial of Orestes (son of Agamemnon and Clytemnestra) at Athens. **See** Furies.

Furies

In a number of Greek and Roman myths and literary works, frightening female spirits who avenged crimes, most often murder, by hunting down and punishing the guilty. The name *Furies* derives from a Latin name for them—Furiae. The Greeks called them the Erinyes and believed that they sprang from the blood droplets that fell to earth after the Titan Cronos castrated his father, Uranus (Sky). Another ancient tradition said that the Furies were the daughters of Nyx (Night); and still another that they were the offspring of Hades, lord of the Underworld, and that they lived in that dark abode. Artists and writers usually depicted the Furies as flying creatures, sometimes carrying whips and torches with which to punish their victims.

Though the Furies chased after all murderers, they paid special attention to those who broke kinship ties by killing a father, mother, brother, or other relative. In one of the most famous myths about these creatures, they haunted Orestes, who had murdered his mother, Clytemnestra, in revenge for her killing of his father, Agamemnon. As depicted in Aeschylus's *Eumenides* (the third play in his monumental trilogy, the *Oresteia*), no matter where Orestes went, the Furies followed; they even pursued him to Delphi, where the god Apollo had offered the man protection. Only when the goddess Athena intervened and helped acquit Orestes in an Athenian court did the Furies relent. (Athena then changed them into the Eumenides, "the Kindly Ones.") **See** Alcmaeon; Dirae; Orestes (Chapter 1); **also** *Eumenides* (Chapter 5); The Curse of the House of Atreus (Chapter 6).

Geryon

(or Geryoneus) A three-headed monster (sometimes pictured with three bodies as well) that lived on the legendary island of Erythea, which lay beyond the Pillars of Heracles (the Strait of Gibraltar) on the western edge of the Mediterranean Sea.

Geryon possessed large, valuable herds of cattle, guarded by a herdsman, Eurytion, and a two-headed dog, Orthus. The tenth labor of the hero Heracles was to steal Geryon's cattle and transport them to Mycenae for King Eurystheus. The strongman succeeded, killing Geryon, Eurytion, and Orthus in the process. **See** Echidna; **also** The Adventures of Heracles (Chapter 6).

giants

(or Gigantes) A term that usually applied to a specific race of human-shaped giants who sprang from the blood droplets that fell to the earth after the Titan Cronos castrated his father, Uranus (the sky). The giants' sisters were the Erinyes (or Furies) and a group of nymphs who inhabited ash trees. Gaia (the earth) had long harbored a grudge against Zeus, leader of the Olympian gods, for imprisoning her offspring, the Titans, in Tartarus; moreover, she had grown tired of Zeus's rule and disapproved of his many illicit love affairs. So finally Gaia decided to overthrow Zeus, and to that end, she enlisted the aid of the giants. The later Greeks often depicted the giants' attack on the gods in art and literature, a great battle they called the Gigantomachy.

As the day of the battle neared, Zeus realized that one problem he and his followers faced was that the giants were immune to death at the hands of the gods. In order to win the war, therefore, Zeus had to call on the aid of a mortal hero. He chose his own son, the tremendously strong and valiant Heracles. Gaia then countered this move by concocting an herb that would make the giants immune to attack by any mortal. However, Zeus foiled her scheme by ordering Helios (the sun), Selene (the moon), and Eos (the dawn) not to appear each day until he had had time to find and destroy the herb, which he did.

Finally, the great battle began. With their leader, Eurymedon, in the forefront, the giants advanced on the gods, throwing rocks the size of mountaintops and torches fashioned from the trunks of giant oaks. Heracles immediately slew Alcyoneus, one of the more formidable of the giants; another giant, Porphyrion, tried to rape Hera, but Zeus zapped him with a huge thunderbolt and Heracles finished him off with a poisoned arrow. Heracles and Apollo then killed the giant Ephialtes, each of them hitting him in an eye with an arrow. Next, Athena slew Pallas and skinned him, planning to use his hide to make some new armor. Seeing this carnage, another giant, Enceladus, lost heart and tried to run away; however, Athena chased him down and tossed the island of Sicily on top of him (beneath which he still lives, his smoky breath emerging periodically from Mt. Etna, the famous volcano). Then Hephaestos entombed the giant Mimas in similar fashion under Mt. Vesuvius (near the Bay of Naples in western Italy). As the slaughter continued, Poseidon killed Polybotes; Hermes slew Hippolytus; Artemis laid low Gration with a shower of arrows; Dionysus used his staff to beat Eurytus to death; and the Fates used clubs to dispatch Agrius and Thoas. In the end, those few giants who survived the massacre fled in terror, and Zeus and his Olympians celebrated a great victory. For other kinds of mythological giants, **see** Cyclops; Hecatoncheires; and, for more about the gods' early battles for supremacy, **see** The Creation of the Gods and Humans (Chapter 6).

Gorgons

Three hideous female beings born of the union of the sea deities/creatures Phorcys and Ceto. (Phorcys and Ceto also bore another batch of three weird sisters—the Graiae, who shared only one eye among themselves.) The Gorgons' names were Stheno (Strength), Euryale (Wide-Jumping), and Medusa (Ruler). Ancient traditions differed on their appearance. Early accounts claimed they were beautiful, or at least that they started off as attractive nymphlike beings. Over time, however, various accounts gave them grotesque faces with wide, leering grins as well as tusks, beards, animals' legs, and/or snakes for hair; and these were usually the traits depicted by Greek artists. According to tradition, simply looking at the Gorgons caused a person to turn to stone, although many accounts imply that only Medusa possessed this singular ability. It is Medusa who played a major role in the most famous myth about the Gorgons. In the story, the hero Perseus (with the help of the deities Hermes and Athena) slew her and used her severed head to turn some of his human enemies to stone. **See** Medusa; and, for a detailed account of Medusa's death, **see** Perseus and Medusa (Chapter 6).

Graiae

(or Graeae) Three weird daughters of the sea deities/creatures Phorcys and Ceto and the sisters of the hideous Gorgons. The Graiae (Pemphredo, Enyo, and Deino) were born as old hags and shared a single eye (by passing it back and forth among themselves). They played a pivotal role in the story of the hero Perseus's search for the Gorgons so that he might slay Medusa, whose appearance turned humans to stone. **See** Gorgons; Medusa; **also** Perseus and Medusa (Chapter 6).

griffin

(or gryphon) A fabulous mythological creature having the body of a lion and the head and wings of an eagle. According to ancient Greek tradition, the griffins dwelled far to the north of the Mediterranean world, near the land of the legendary Hyperboreans, and guarded a vast treasury of gold. The image of griffins, which likely entered Greece from the Near East sometime in the second millennium B.C., was a favorite of Greek artists and sculptors. Sometimes they showed griffins accompanying sphinxlike monsters; other times griffins appeared by themselves, as on the walls of the throne room of the palace at Knossus (in Crete), a Bronze Age structure. Later, classical Greek artists rendered griffins in metal, ivory, stone, and in vase paintings. Unfortunately, no surviving ancient texts provide a clear understanding of the beasts' purpose or role, if any, in mythology.

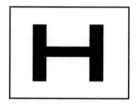

Harpy

("Snatcher") One of three (or possibly more) hideous birdlike creatures with female faces, who swooped down and either stole people's food or covered it with a vile stench, making it too disgusting to eat. According to the early Greek poet Hesiod, the Harpies were the offspring of Thaumus (an ancient Greek sea god) and the sea nymph Electra, making them the sisters of Iris, goddess of the rainbow.

The ancients sometimes called the monstrous Harpies "Zeus's Hounds" because he could send them to harass or punish someone if he saw fit. This was the case in the most famous myth about these creatures—the episode in which Jason and his Argonauts encountered them on their way to Colchis in search of the Golden Fleece. The Argonauts found a starving old man named Phineus, whose food the Harpies stole or fouled every day. Zeus was punishing him, Phineus explained, because Apollo had granted him the gift of prophecy; and the ruler of the gods resented the idea of humans possessing such powers. Hoping to help poor Phineus, Jason and his men set a trap for the Harpies. When the creatures appeared, two of the Argonauts, Zetes and Calais, who could fly (because they were sons of Boreas, the

north wind) chased after them. The two men would have killed the Harpies, but at the last moment their sister, Iris, rushed to protect them. Iris made a deal with Zetes and Calais, promising to keep them away from Phineus if the men would spare her sisters. Aeneas, father of the Roman race, also encountered the Harpies on his way to Italy. For more detailed accounts of these myths, **see** Aeneas's Journey to Italy; The Quest for the Golden Fleece (Chapter 6).

Hecatoncheires

("Hundred-handers") Three giants, each having fifty heads and a hundred arms. Named Cottus, Briareos, and Gyes, they were the sons of Gaia (Earth) and Uranus (Sky). Uranus feared them so much that he tried to push them back into Gaia's womb after they were born; when this failed, he imprisoned them in Tartarus. But Gaia gained revenge on Uranus for these acts by helping her son Cronos overthrow his father. Unfortunately, Cronos also feared the Hundred-handers and he, too, locked them away in Tartarus. Later, Zeus released the Hundred-handers, who helped him overthrow Cronos and the Titans, after which these giants became the jailors for the defeated Titans, whom Zeus banished to Tartarus. Later still, Briareos rushed again to defend Zeus, this time against a group of Olympians who were plotting to overthrow the chief god. **See** Briareos; **also** Titans; Zeus (Chapter 2); The Creation of the Gods and Humans (Chapter 6).

Hydra

A huge poisonous water snake with numerous heads, each of which grew back when someone cut one off. The Hydra, which lived in the marshes of Lerna, near Argos (in the eastern Peloponnesus), was the offspring of the monsters Echidna and Typhon. The Greek hero Heracles slew the creature, completing his second labor for King Eurystheus. For a more detailed account, **see** The Adventures of Heracles (Chapter 6).

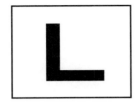

Ladon

Another monstrous child of the hideous creatures Echidna and Typhon, this one a dragon or serpent with numerous heads that guarded the golden apples in the Garden of the Hesperides. In some ancient accounts, the famous strongman Heracles killed Ladon when he arrived in the garden to retrieve the apples (to complete his eleventh labor for King Eurystheus). **See** Hesperides (Chapter 2); **also** The Adventures of Heracles (Chapter 6).

lemures

(or larvae) Spirits of the dead or ghosts, whom the Romans believed haunted people's houses during the appointed days of the religious festival called the Lemuria— May 9, 11, and 13. The spirits of children were widely seen as the scariest of the lot because people thought they bore a grudge against those who had outlived them. People performed various superstitious rituals designed to ward off the lemures, as described by the Roman poet Ovid:

> When midnight has come and lends silence to sleep, and dogs and all the birds are hushed, the worshiper . . . arises . . . makes a sign with his thumb in the middle of his closed fingers. . . [and] after washing his hands clean in spring water, he turns, and first he takes black beans and throws them away with [his] face averted [turned away from the direction he throws them]; but while he throws them away, he says; "These I throw; with these beans I redeem me and mine." This he says nine

times, without looking back. The ghost is thought to gather the beans and to follow, unseen, behind. . . . When [the person] has said nine times: "Ghosts of my fathers, go away!". . . he has duly performed the sacred rites. (*Fasti* 5.29–44)

Marsyas

A Greek satyr (half-man and half-goat) after whom, legend claimed, a river in Phrygia (in Asia Minor) was named. Marsyas found a flute that the goddess Athena had constructed and then thrown away (because she felt it distorted her face when she played it). When the satyr began playing the flute, Athena thrashed him. But after she went away, he continued to practice the instrument and soon became quite proficient as a musician. Eventually Marsyas made the mistake of challenging Apollo, god of music, to a contest (the satyr and his flute against the god and his lyre); the rule agreed to was that the winner could do whatever he pleased to the loser. The Muses (goddesses of the fine arts), who judged the competition, picked Apollo the victor. He hung Marsyas from a pine tree and skinned him alive, after which the tears of the satyr's woodland companions formed the Marsyas River. **See** satyr.

Medusa

One of the three Gorgons, the hideous daughters of the sea deities/creatures Phorcys and Ceto. According to one ancient myth, Medusa was originally a beautiful woman. But then she and the sea god Poseidon had an affair and made love inside one of the goddess Athena's temples. Furious, Athena transformed Medusa into a grotesque creature with snakes for hair and

This bronze sculpture of Perseus holding the head of Medusa is one of hundreds of artistic versions of the famous hero and monster.

a gaze that turned animals and humans to stone. Eventually the Greek hero Perseus, aided by Athena, killed Medusa by severing her head. The Gorgon was at that moment carrying two of Poseidon's offspring (Pegasus, the winged horse, and Chrysaor, a misshapen creature), which soon sprang from her headless body. **See** Gorgons; and, for a detailed account of Perseus's mission to slay Medusa, **see** Perseus and Medusa (Chapter 6).

Minotaur

A horrifying creature with a bull's head and a man's body, born of the bizarre union of a bull and Pasiphae, wife of Minos, king of Crete. Minos placed the Minotaur in the labyrinth—the maze he had built under his palace. There, the Athenian hero Theseus eventually arrived and slew the creature. For more details, **see** Minos; Pasiphae (Chapter 1); **also** The Exploits of Theseus (Chapter 6).

Nemean Lion

A monstrous lion with an invulnerable hide (which no weapons could pierce); the offspring of the monster Echidna and the two-headed dog Orthus. The goddess

Hera sent the lion to Nemea (in the eastern Peloponnesus) to thwart the famous strongman Heracles. But Heracles managed to kill it. For a detailed account, **see** The Adventures of Heracles (Chapter 6).

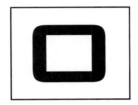

Orion

In Greek legend, a giant hunter after whom one of the most famous constellations in the night sky was named. Two traditions existed about Orion's origins. In one, his father, a king of Hyria (in Boeotia), could not sire children and begged the gods to help him. They told him to pour water on the hide of a bull and bury it, and nine months later Orion grew from that spot. The other version claimed that Orion was the son of the sea god Poseidon and Euryale, daughter of Minos (king of Crete).

Either way, Orion grew to huge proportions—so tall that he could walk on the sea bottom and still keep his head above the water's surface. In one myth about the great hunter, he raped the daughter of the king of Chios (an Aegean island). The king retaliated by blinding Orion, but the giant regained his eyesight by walking eastward into the sun's rays. Another legend claimed that the giant hunter long pursued the Pleiades, seven daughters of the Titan Atlas; and Zeus placed all of them in the sky as stars (reputedly to keep Orion from catching the maidens).

Numerous alternate versions of Orion's end existed, though. In one, Eos, goddess of the dawn, fell in love with him, but Artemis, the divine huntress, was angry that Eos had chosen a mortal lover, so she slew Orion. Other accounts claimed that Artemis killed Orion because he tried to rape her or because he threatened to kill all of the world's animals. Still another version said that Artemis herself loved Orion. Her brother, Apollo, disapproved and tricked her into shooting an arrow at a faraway object to test her skill at archery. The target turned out to be Orion, and the arrow killed him, after which, in her grief, Artemis placed him in the sky as a constellation. **See** Pleiades (Chapter 2).

Otus and Ephialtes

Two giants who legend claimed were sons of the sea god Poseidon and the god's own granddaughter, Iphimedia. Otus and Ephialtes grew so quickly that by the age of nine they were already more than fifty feet tall. To amuse themselves, they captured the war god, Ares, and put him in a jar. There he stayed for many months, until Hermes, the messenger god, discovered his whereabouts and released him. The two mischievous giants then fell in love with the goddesses Hera and Artemis and planned to capture them, too. Imprudently, they chose to storm Mt. Olympus (or, in some accounts, tried to reach the heavens by piling up mountains on top of Olympus). The twin gods Apollo and Artemis rushed to defend the gods' abode and let loose a rain of arrows that killed Otus and Ephialtes. For their impudence, the slain giants were condemned to be bound, back to back, to a pole in Tartarus (the deepest reaches of the Underworld).

owl

An important symbol with which the ancient Greeks identified Athena, goddess of war and wisdom, probably because the owl, like the goddess, was early seen as a wise being. Greek artists often portrayed the bird sitting on Athena's shoulder. One of the goddess's standard descriptive names was *glaukopis,* which may have meant "owl-eyed" or "having a penetrating glance" (though some scholars think it meant "green-eyed" or "gray-eyed"). In the fifth century B.C.,

Athens (which recognized Athena as its patron) issued a silver drachma bearing the image of an owl; these coins, which became the standard unit of currency in the eastern Mediterranean for a time, were appropriately nicknamed "owls." **See** Athena (Chapter 2); **also** Athens (Chapter 4).

Pallas

A giant whom the goddess Athena slew during the Gigantomachy (the battle between the gods and the giants). This was one of several explanations for how she acquired the title Pallas Athena, which the classical Greeks often called her. **See** giants.

Pegasus

A famous flying horse that sprang (along with its brother, the misshapen creature Chrysaor) from the body of the Gorgon Medusa after the hero Perseus cut off her head. Legend said that Medusa was pregnant with Pegasus by the sea god Poseidon at the time of her death. Later, the Greek hero Bellerophon set his sights on capturing Pegasus, which had earned a reputation for not allowing any mortal to mount it. Bellerophon received advice from a seer that he should sacrifice to the goddess Athena, who would help him. That night, the youth dreamed that the goddess came to him and gave him a special bridle for Pegasus; and when Bellerophon awoke, the bridle was lying beside him. He approached the flying horse while it was drinking from a fountain in the city of Corinth, and it allowed him to bridle it. Riding the magical steed, Bellerophon then attacked and killed the Chimaera, a dreadful monster that was ravaging the region of Lycia (in southern Asia Minor).

See Chimaera; Medusa; **also** Bellerophon (Chapter 1).

Polyphemus

A Cyclops (one-eyed giant) said to be the son of Poseidon, lord of the seas. The main myth in which Polyphemus appeared was that in which he encountered the Greek hero Odysseus and some of his men when they came ashore to find supplies on the island of the Cyclopes. The giant came home to his cave one evening to find the Greeks inside. Polyphemus barred the door with a great rock and proceeded to eat some of the men for supper as well as more of them for breakfast the next morning. Eventually, though, Odysseus outwitted the Cyclops and put out his eye, which allowed the surviving Greeks to make it back to their ships and escape the island. In his agony, Polyphemus called on his father, Poseidon, to avenge him; the god did so by harassing Odysseus during the remainder of his wanderings. **See** Cyclops; and, for a more detailed account of the episode involving Polyphemus and Odysseus, **see** The Wanderings of Odysseus (Chapter 6).

Pygmy

According to Greek mythology, a member of a race of dwarves who inhabited Africa (and, in some accounts, India and other remotes lands, too). Several Greek and Roman writers, including Homer, Aristotle, Ovid, and Pliny the Elder, mention the legends of Pygmies. Pliny provided this summary description:

> In height they do not exceed three spans—
> that is, about 2 ½ feet. . . . Homer has written
> that the Pygmies were attacked by cranes
> [large birds]. The story is that in the spring
> the Pygmies, armed with arrows and riding
> on the backs of rams and she-goats, go down
> to the sea and eat the cranes' eggs and their
> young. . . . If they did not do this, they could
> not protect themselves against the flocks of
> cranes that would result. The Pygmies'
> houses are built of mud, feathers, and

eggshell. Aristotle [by contrast] states that they live in caves. (*Natural History* 7.26–27)

These legends about Pygmies may well have been loosely based on occasional sightings by Egyptian, Greek, or Roman explorers who wandered into equatorial Africa, where groups of people of small stature (four to five feet tall on average) actually existed. These groups still exist, in fact, and outside of Africa are still referred to as Pygmies.

Python

A huge serpent that dwelled at Delphi (in central Greece) and protected the area in its earliest days while the famous Delphic Oracle was still controlled by Gaia (Earth). When the goddess Leto was pregnant with Apollo and Artemis, Zeus's wife, Hera, sent Python to harass Leto; so later, one legend claims, Apollo went to Delphi and slew Python, after which he took control of the oracle. Apollo made sure to appease Gaia by giving Python a proper burial and also by establishing the Pythian Games in its honor (which became one of the "big four" athletic competitions of ancient Greece). Python's name was preserved not only in the name of the games but also in the title of the priestess (actually a succession of priestesses) who tended the oracle: She became known as the Pythia. **See** Apollo; Gaia (Chapter 2); **also** Delphic Oracle (Chapter 4).

satyr

In Greek mythology, a creature half-man and half-goat (or half-horse) who attended the fertility god, Dionysus, and, like him, was mischievous, lustful, and fond of revelry. Greek artists often pictured the satyrs, who personified nature in its wild, fertile state, chasing after nymphs in hope of making love to them. Eventually, the satyrs became comic figures in Greek plays; at the famous dramatic festivals presented in Athens, a series of tragedies was often followed by a "satyr play," a lighthearted spoof in which the actors dressed in satyr costumes and poked fun at serious subjects. The most famous of the satyrs was Silenus, an elderly character known for his practical wisdom and powers of prophecy. **See** Marsyas; Silenus; **also** Dionysus (Chapter 2).

Scylla

A horrible sea monster that dwelled on one side of the Strait of Messina (between Sicily and southern Italy) and attacked ships. (Another monster, Charybdis, guarded the other side of the strait.) According to legend, Scylla was at first a beautiful young nymph, a daughter of the sea deity/creature Phorcys. Then a young man named Glaucus fell in love with her. He asked the mysterious sorceress Circe for a love potion to woo Scylla, but Circe herself fell in love with Glaucus. Out of jealousy, Circe transformed Scylla into a dreadful monster with six heads and twelve feet. One ancient account claimed that Scylla wore a belt made of the heads of live dogs, which howled incessantly. During his wanderings, the Greek hero Odysseus encountered Scylla, who snatched up and devoured six of his crewmen before he and the rest managed to escape. **See** Charybdis; and, for a more detailed account of Odysseus's encounter with this monster, **see** The Wanderings of Odysseus (Chapter 6).

Silenus

The most renowned of the satyrs (woodland creatures who were half man and half goat or horse). The son of Pan (or Hermes) and a nymph, Silenus usually appeared in Greek art with the tail and ears of a horse, a pot belly, and a bald head, riding a donkey. Legend said he was the tutor of the young Dionysus, the fertility god with whom he and other satyrs were often associated. Tradition also held that Silenus had lived long and acquired much practical wisdom, and that he possessed the gift of prophecy. In one myth, Midas, an imprudent king of Phrygia (in Asia Minor), wanted to learn Silenus's unique knowledge; so he drugged and captured the old satyr and demanded that he reveal the secret of human life. The wily Silenus replied that the secret was not to be born at all, or once born to die as soon as possible. Silenus had numerous sons, satyrs called the Sileni, who became, along with him, favorite characters in the comedic "satyr plays" presented in Athens's dramatic festivals. **See** satyr; **also** Midas (Chapter 1).

Siren

One of three (or, in some accounts, four) grotesque women who inhabited the small island of Anthemoessa, lying near the Strait of Messina (between Sicily and southern Italy). Accounts of the Sirens' origins varied. One version claimed that they were the daughters of a Muse and Phorcys, a sea deity; another story said they were once the companions of Persephone (Demeter's daughter), and that because they failed to stop Hades (lord of the Underworld) from abducting Persephone, some deity (perhaps Demeter) changed them into monsters.

Along with the monsters Scylla and Charybdis, who dwelled nearby, the Sirens constituted a major danger to sailors, for legend held that these women sang songs so beautiful that men were compelled to go to their island and listen, transfixed, until they died. Hence, the shores of the island were littered with the bleached bones of unfortunate seamen. The Greek hero Odysseus and his men encountered the Sirens and managed to get by them, thanks to the advice of the sorceress Circe. She suggested that, as the Greeks neared the is-

land, Odysseus should stuff his men's ears with beeswax (so they could not hear the Sirens' song) and have the crew tie him to one of the ship's masts (to restrain him from going to the island). **See** The Wanderings of Odysseus (Chapter 6).

Sphinx

(or Phix) A large winged monster having the body of a lion and the head of a woman. A daughter of the monsters Echidna and Orthus, the Sphinx terrorized the region around the city of Thebes (having been sent by the goddess Hera to punish the Theban king for offending the gods, or by the god Dionysus, who was angry that the Thebans had neglected his worship). The creature would jump out at a person and pose a riddle; if the person could not solve it, the Sphinx would devour him or her. Finally, a young man named Oedipus arrived and solved the riddle, causing the Sphinx to commit suicide. **See** *Oedipus the King* (Chapter 5); and, for a more detailed account of Oedipus and

This rendering of Oedipus confronting the winged Sphinx was painted on an Athenian red-figure wine cup by the so-called Oedipus Painter.

the Sphinx, **see** The Theban Myth Cycle (Chapter 6).

Stymphalian Birds

A swarm of dangerous birds that infested the forests along the shore of Lake Stymphalus, in Arcadia (in the central Peloponnesus). For a time, both humans and animals became victims of these creatures, which had metal-tipped feathers they shot through the air like arrows. In his sixth (or, in some accounts, fifth) labor, the great hero Heracles rid the area of these deadly pests. Using a bronze rattle created by Hephaestos (god of the forge), the strongman frightened the birds out of the trees and then shot them with his poison-tipped arrows. **See** The Adventures of Heracles (Chapter 6).

Symplegades

The so-called Clashing Rocks, located at the northern end of the Bosphorus Strait (on the southern edge of the Black Sea). According to legend, many of the ships that tried to pass through the strait were crushed by these giant rocks, which periodically clashed together violently when people or animals tried to pass between them. In the story of Jason and the search for the Golden Fleece, he and his men received advice from an old prophet named Phineus about how to make it through the Symplegades. They released a dove ahead of them, which flew between the rocks, inducing them to smash together. (Only the bird's tail feathers got caught in the crush.) Then the *Argo* pressed forward, trying to make it through while the Symplegades were moving apart. With an extra boost from the goddess Athena (who had helped build the ship), the vessel squeaked through, losing only the tip of the rear steering oar. After that, the Symplegades remained always open and no longer posed a threat to sailors. **See** The Quest for the Golden Fleece (Chapter 6).

Talos

A giant bronze man who guarded the island of Crete. In some accounts, Zeus gave Talos to Europa after the god (disguised as a bull) brought Europa to Crete; in another version, Hephaestos, god of the forge, made Talos for Minos, the noted Cretan king. Talos ran around Crete's coastline three times each day watching for would-be invaders, whom he repelled either by throwing huge rocks at them or by making himself red hot and burning up their ships. When Jason and his Argonauts approached Crete on their way back from Colchis, the sorceress Medea helped them defeat Talos. She chanted a spell that put the giant to sleep (or, in an alternate story, drugged him); then she pierced a membrane of skin at his ankle, which allowed his ichor (the blood of the gods) to drain out, thereby killing him. In the most famous literary work about Jason and his men—the *Argonautica* of Apollonius of Rhodes—Talos accidentally grazes his ankle on a sharp rock, releasing his ichor. **See** The Quest for the Golden Fleece (Chapter 6).

Telchines

In Greek mythology, a group or race of magicians who inhabited the island of Rhodes (off the southwestern coast of Asia Minor) in early Greek times. The first-century B.C. Greek historian Diodorus Siculus claimed the Telchines were Rhodes's original inhabitants. According to legend, they had the ability to change the weather, cure disease, and forge fabulous metal objects. Poseidon's famous trident was one such artifact credited to them (although another story said the Cyclopes created it). The surviving names attributed to the Telchines attest to their skill in metalworking: Chalcon ("Bronze-Worker"), Chryson ("Gold-Worker"), and Argyron ("Silver-Worker"). Some ancient accounts held that the Telchines were evil and tried to poison the soil so that farmers could not grow crops. Perhaps this was the reason that Zeus, ruler of the gods, finally drowned the Rhodian magicians in one of the floods he unleashed on humankind. **See** Rhodes (Chapter 4).

Typhon

(or Typhoeus) A terrifying monster having a hundred snakelike heads, each of either which bellowed like a bull, barked like a dog, or spoke in voices that sounded like those of the gods. Typhon was the son of Gaia (the earth) and Tartarus (the lowest region of the Underworld). When the monster was fully grown, Gaia ordered it to attack and dethrone Zeus, king of the Olympian gods. Zeus wasted no time in striking the first blow; he hurled one thunderbolt after another at the beast and managed to drive it back to a mountain in Syria. But then Typhon counterattacked and cut out the tendons of the god's arms and legs, leaving him helpless. Another monster, Delphyne, helped Typhon by hiding the tendons in a cave; however, Zeus's fellow Olympian Hermes managed to retrieve the tendons and restored them to Zeus's body. Zeus now hurried back to Mt. Olympus, gathered a new supply of mighty thunderbolts, and renewed his attack on Typhon. Eventually, the god drove the creature all the way to Italy. There, Zeus uprooted the island of Sicily and flung it on top of Typhon, imprisoning the monster.

Other myths about Typhon circulated in ancient times. In the account by the Greek poet Hesiod, Zeus's thunderbolts set the monster on fire, after which the god hurled Typhon down into Tartarus, where it thereafter remained imprisoned with Zeus's other enemies, the Titans. "The earth melted in the glow of the blazing fire," Hesiod wrote. "And in the bitterness of his anger, Zeus cast Typhon into wide Tartarus." (*Theogony* 867–869) In a last gasp of defiance, Typhon let out some mighty breaths, which became the typhoons (hurricanes) that periodically "rush upon the misty sea and create great havoc among humans with their evil, raging blasts . . . scattering ships and destroying sailors." (873–877) Another Greek legend held that during Zeus's fight with Typhon, most of the other gods fled in fear southward into Egypt and disguised themselves as animals; and this was supposedly why so many of the Egyptian gods had animals' heads and/or bodies. (In reality, of course, most of the Egyptian gods were much older than those of the Greeks.) Some ancient stories also said that, before attacking Zeus, Typhon mated with the monster Echidna, producing many monstrous children, among them the Chimaera, the Hydra, and the three-headed dog Cerberus. **See** Echidna; **also** Gaia; Zeus (Chapter 2); The Creation of the Gods and Humans (Chapter 6).

Chapter 4
Important Places and Things

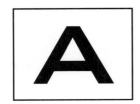

Achaea

The northern region of the Peloponnesus, lying to the east of Elis and bordering the southern shore of the Gulf of Corinth.

Acheron

Sometimes called the "River of Woe," one of the rivers flowing through the Underworld, the Greco-Roman realm of the dead. The Acheron was sometimes confused with another river in that realm, the Styx ("River of Unbreakable Oaths"). In Hellenistic times (the last three centuries B.C.), Acheron became a common name for the Underworld in general. **See** Styx; Underworld.

Acropolis

"The city's high place"; when lowercased (i.e., acropolis), the central hill of any Greek city or city-state; when uppercased (Acropolis), the most famous of all acropoli—the rocky plateau rising in the center of ancient (and modern) Athens. Like other acropoli, this hill, which is about a thousand feet long and roughly 165 feet high, was, in early times, often used as a fortress, to which the city's residents retreated in time of danger.

Athens's Acropolis also became the site of a series of religious temples and shrines, some dating back to the eighth century B.C. or perhaps earlier. The most magnificent complex of shrines was erected there during the fifth century B.C., during what modern scholars call Athens's cultural golden age. Among them were the Parthenon, Erechtheum, and Temple of Athena Nike, all dedicated to the city's patron deity, Athena, goddess of war and wisdom. The Acropolis also featured shrines to Zeus, ruler of the gods, and Artemis, goddess of wildlife. More than five centuries later, the Greek biographer Plutarch described the special, timeless quality of these structures:

> It is this, above all, which makes [these] works an object of wonder to us—the fact that they were created in so short a span, and yet for all time. Each one possessed a beauty which seemed venerable [impressive in old age] the moment it was born, and at the same time a youthful vigor which makes them appear to this day as if they were newly built. A bloom of eternal freshness hovers over these works of his and preserves them from the touch of time. (*Life of Pericles* 13)

Not surprisingly, these religious shrines were highly decorated with paintings and sculptures depicting episodes from Greek mythology, especially those dealing with Athena. Many classical Athenians believed that the sacred ground of the Acropolis had been the site of several important events in the bygone Age of Heroes (now known to be Greece's Bronze Age), a time when legendary heroes and kings supposedly walked the earth and interacted with the gods. It was on the Acropolis, for example, that the mythical Athenian king Cecrops judged the contest between Athena and Poseidon for control of Attica (the territory ruled by Athens). Here, too, Athena took another Athenian king, Erechtheus, into her sacred shrine and made him her consort (after which the shrine became known as the Erechtheum in his honor). These and other early kings of the city, real and legendary, may actually have lived on the Acropolis; scholars believe that the hill was also the site of one or more Bronze Age royal palaces. **See** Athens; Parthenon; **also** Cecrops; Erechtheus (Chapter 1); Athena (Chapter 2).

Aeaea
(or Aiaie) A remote island located in the Ocean, the wide river the ancient Greeks believed encircled the earth's land portions. Aeaea was the home of the divine sorceress Circe, who often changed humans into animals. Several of the Greek hero Odysseus's men suffered this fate when they landed there during their wanderings following the Trojan War. **See** Circe (Chapter 2); **also** The Wanderings of Odysseus (Chapter 6).

Aegean Sea
The wide inlet of the Mediterranean Sea lying between mainland Greece and Asia Minor. According to legend, the waterway received its name as a memorial to the Athenian king, Aegeus, who killed himself when he thought, mistakenly, that his son, the hero Theseus, had been killed on a mission to Crete. **See** Aegeus (Chapter 1).

Aegina
A small, mountainous island (covering about thirty-five square miles) lying in the Saronic Gulf, midway between Athens and the Peloponnesus. In Greek mythology, the island was renowned as the realm of Aeacus, grandfather of the heroes Achilles and Ajax. In classical times, Aegina owned powerful merchant fleets and became a commercial rival of Athens.

aegis
The invincible breastplate (or, in some accounts, a shield) of the goddess Athena. The aegis was at first an attribute of Zeus, but he later entrusted it to Athena, who adorned it with the image of a Gorgon's head to frighten her enemies. **See** Athena (Chapter 2).

Aetolia
The region of central Greece lying just north of the Gulf of Corinth and west of Locris and the Mt. Parnassus range. Aetolia's principal town was Calydon, site of the famous mythical boar hunt involving Atalanta and Meleager. **See** Calydon; **also** Atalanta (Chapter 1).

Alba Longa
Before and during the period of the Roman monarchy (the eighth through sixth centuries B.C.), the principal town of the plain of Latium (lying south of Rome) and the seat of the league of Latin cities. In Roman mythology, Alba Longa was established by Ascanius, son of the hero Aeneas, founder of the Roman race. **See** Latium.

ambrosia
A mythical, sweet-smelling food consumed by the Greek gods. According to tradition, ambrosia (along with nectar, a liquid) maintained these deities' immortality; and when a human ate it, he or she became immortal, too. **See** nectar.

ancilia
In Roman legend, a special shield the war god, Mars, dropped from heaven during the

reign of Numa Pompilius (Rome's second king). The shield was kept in Mars's temple in the Campus Martius ("Field of Mars"), along with several replicas, and was guarded by a group of priests called the Salii. When Rome declared war, a general temporarily removed the shields and called on Mars to awake and aid the Roman army. **See** Numa Pompilius (Chapter 1); **also** Mars (Chapter 2).

Arcadia

The central, quite mountainous region of the Peloponnesus, lying north of Laconia and south of Achaea. Arcadia's principal cities were Tegea and Mantinea. Pastoral and picturesque, the region was long associated with the gods Hermes and Pan, who legend claimed originated there. Arcadia was also connected with Roman mythology since it was the homeland of Evander, who journeyed to Italy and settled on the future site of Rome. Recalling this connection, the great Roman poet Virgil set many of his pastoral verses in Arcadia's rolling hills. In historical times, the region was long dominated by Sparta (in nearby Laconia). **See** Evander; Hermes; Pan (Chapter 2).

Areopagus

A low hill lying a few hundred feet west of the Acropolis in Athens. According to legend, the name *Areopagus,* meaning "Hill of Ares," derived from the episode in which the Greek war god, Ares, underwent a trial there for killing Poseidon's son (who had raped Ares' daughter). Later, the Areopagus hosted another famous mythical trial, that of Orestes, son of Agamemnon, who had murdered his mother, Clytemnestra. The goddess Athena intervened and helped to acquit Orestes, and she also transformed the vengeful Furies, who had been chasing him, into the kindly Eumenides. True to these traditions, in historical times the Athenians made the Areopagus a special law court. **See** Ares; Athena (Chapter 2); *Eumenides* (Chapter 5); The Curse of the House of Atreus (Chapter 6).

Arethusa

A freshwater spring on the island of Ortygia, in the harbor of the Greek city of Syracuse (on the island of Sicily). An ancient myth claimed that a river god named Alpheus, who dwelled in Arcadia (in the Peloponnesus), fell in love with a nymph, but she fled to Ortygia. Undaunted, he flowed under the Mediterranean Sea until he emerged in the spring in Sicily. Many ancient Greeks and Romans believed that the connection between the two places was real, and that if someone threw an object in the Alpheus River it might emerge in the Arethusa spring.

Argo

The ship that carried Jason and his Argonauts on their quest to find the fabulous Golden Fleece. According to the story, Argus, a master shipwright, built the ship with Athena's aid. **See** Argus 1 (Chapter 1); **also** The Quest for the Golden Fleece (Chapter 6).

Argos

A major Greek city located in the northeastern Peloponnesus near the neck of the peninsula commonly called the Argolid. (The general region was often referred to as Argolis.) That region was the site of the Bronze Age citadels of Mycenae and Tiryns (situated a few miles to the north and southeast of Argos, respectively). In Homer's *Iliad,* Argos was ruled by the Greek hero Diomedes, who gave his allegiance to Agamemnon, king of Mycenae. Perhaps because Agamemnon led the Greek army that besieged Troy, Homer sometimes referred to the Greeks in general as Argives (the name usually denoting a resident of Argos). (Mycenae and Argos are often used interchangeably in Greek mythology, so it is likely that after Mycenae was destroyed at the end of the Bronze

Age, the focus of power in the region switched to Argos.) In the Greek Dark Age, perhaps about 1000 B.C., Argos began its rise to the status of the most powerful and influential city in the Peloponnesus, reaching its height under King Pheidon in the mid–seventh century B.C. Very soon afterward Sparta and Corinth rose to prominence, however, and Argos quickly became a third-rate power.

Asia Minor

(also Anatolia) A large peninsula (today occupied by the nation of Turkey) bordered in the north by the Black Sea, in the west by the Aegean Sea, and the in south by the Mediterranean Sea. Consisting of a series of rugged mountain ranges, plateaus, and fertile valleys, Asia Minor was customarily divided into various general regions by the ancients. These included, among others, Mysia and the Troad (where Troy was located) in the northwest; Lydia, the area lying south of Mysia; Caria, south of Lydia and bordering the Mediterranean coast; Cilicia, lying east of Caria on the same coast; Phrygia, the central portion of the peninsula; and Pontus, on the northern coast bordering the Black Sea.

In the early centuries of the first millennium B.C., numerous Greek towns grew along the western coastal region of Asia Minor (including several nearby islands). The middle part of that region became known as Greek Ionia. According to legend, a number of these settlements were established by Greeks fleeing the Dorian invasion of southern Greece. Among these Greek cities (and islands) along Asia Minor's Aegean coast, the most famous, commercially prosperous, and/or culturally advanced were Miletus, Ephesus, Halicarnassus, Priene, Teos, Elaea, Chios, Cos, Lesbos, Samos, and Rhodes.

In historical times, the populous, prosperous, and well-traveled peninsula of Asia Minor was strategically important as a corridor from Greece to Persia and other Near Eastern lands. The Persians conquered the peninsula in the sixth century B.C.; later, the Greek conqueror Alexander the Great seized it; and later still, the Romans made inroads into the area, which eventually became divided into several Roman provinces. **See** Cilicia; Ephesus; Phrygia; Rhodes; **also** Dorians (Chapter 1).

Asphodel, Plain of

In Greek mythology, a vast, dismal, monotonous region of the Underworld, lying just beyond the Styx, the river that people's shades (souls) crossed to enter the realm of the dead. The common belief was that the shades of most humans dwelled for eternity on the Plain of Asphodel, wandering around more or less aimlessly or mechanically, with little or no talking or other social intercourse. They endured no torture or other mistreatment, however, so the plain, like most parts of the Underworld, was not a place of punishment like the Christian hell. **See** Underworld.

Athens

The foremost city-state of Greece in the Classic Age (ca. 500–323 B.C.), located in the southern section of the Attic peninsula about four miles from Phaleron Bay. Athens was continually inhabited from at least the early Bronze Age (ca. 3000 B.C.). The urban center grew up around the Acropolis, a large and imposing rocky outcrop on which a series of temples and other public buildings were constructed over the course of many centuries. In the late Bronze Age (ca. 1400–1100 B.C.), which the later Greeks remembered as the Age of Heroes and a source of many of their myths, Athens was largely overshadowed by other mainland cities, including Mycenae and Thebes.

Numerous important myths from the Age of Heroes were centered in or around Athens or involved Athenians. Among the most famous was the story of King

A modern restoration of the Athenian Acropolis as it likely appeared at the height of its glory in the late fifth century B.C.

Aegeus, who was forced to send young Athenian men and women to Crete to be fed to the monstrous Minotaur; Aegeus's heroic son, Theseus, who traveled to Crete, slew the creature and released the hostages. Later, Theseus became king of Athens and unified the far-flung Attic communities into one city-state, the largest in Greece. Athens was also the site where the deities Athena and Poseidon competed to see which one of them would become the city's divine patron; where the gods put one of their number, Ares, on trial for killing Poseidon's son; where Athena ended the long, bloody curse on the house of Atreus; where she also deposited a wooden image of herself, which the Athenians thereafter kept in her sacred temple, the Erechtheum; and where the local residents managed to resist an attack by the Amazons (warrior women from the far

north) as well as the invasion of the Dorians, who had already overrun the Peloponnesus.

In historical times, beginning in the latter part of the Archaic Age (ca. 800–500 B.C.), Athens began its rise to prominence. A major milestone occurred in about 508 B.C. when the Athenian political reformer Cleisthenes established the world's first democracy. In the years that followed, Athens reached its zenith of power and achievement, assuming a leading role in the repulse of the Persians (who attacked Greece in 490 B.C. and again in 480 B.C.); forming a naval empire; and becoming Greece's premiere artistic and cultural center, home of the splendid Parthenon temple (on which artists depicted famous mythological scenes) and the master playwrights Aeschylus, Sophocles, and Euripides (who recorded numerous Greek myths in their works). **See** Acropolis; Attica; Parthenon; **also** Aegeus; Amazons; Cecrops; Dorians; Erechtheus; Hippolytus (Chapter 1); Ares; Athena (Chapter 2); Minotaur (Chapter 3); Aeschylus; Aristophanes; Aristotle; Euripides; Plato; Sophocles (Chapter 5); The Exploits of Theseus (Chapter 6).

Atlantis

In Greek legend, a once powerful kingdom, island, or small continent that sank into the sea long before historical times. The first Greek documents mentioning the Atlantis were Plato's dialogues, the *Timaeus* and *Critias* (written in the mid–fourth century B.C.). According to

Plato, his predecessor, the famous sixth-century B.C. Athenian lawgiver Solon, paid a visit to Egypt. There, Solon heard from some Egyptian priests that in the distant past the Athenians had overcome the mighty maritime empire of Atlantis, after which the island had been destroyed by a natural catastrophe. Plato believed that Atlantis was much larger than Greece. And, reasoning that it could not have fit in the Mediterranean Sea, he located it in the vast, mysterious sea lying beyond the Pillars of Heracles (i.e., the Atlantic Ocean, which took its name from Atlantis).

Modern scholars long assumed that Plato had fabricated the tale of Atlantis as a parable. But archaeological evidence suggests that the story is a garbled memory of real events. The Atlanteans were likely the Minoans, an advanced maritime people who built huge multistoried palaces on Crete during the middle of the Bronze Age (the Age of Heroes). And the catastrophe that sank Atlantis was probably the now documented destruction of the island of Thera (north of Crete) by a devastating volcanic eruption circa 1600

This collapsed staircase (above) and row of ruined houses at Akrotiri, on Thera, were completely buried by the great eruption of the Theran volcano during the Bronze Age.

B.C. (or perhaps a century or so later). During this upheaval, the entire central portion of Thera collapsed into the sea, generating huge seismic sea waves that pounded the Minoan settlements of northern Crete. Athens's triumph over the Atlanteans likely recalls the takeover of the Minoan sphere by mainland Greeks (whom scholars call the Mycenaeans) in the century or so following the disaster. **See** Plato (Chapter 5).

Attica

A roughly thousand-square-mile triangular peninsula projecting southeastward into the Aegean Sea from central Greece; the homeland of Athens and the largest city-state in ancient Greece. Besides the urban center of Athens (located a few miles from Attica's western coast), the peninsula included the plain of Marathon in the northeast (where the Athenians defeated the Persians in 490 B.C.), Mt. Pentelicon in the northern-central region (the source of much of the fine marble used in building the temples on the Acropolis), Cape Sunium on the southern coast, and several dozen villages distributed more or less evenly over the territory. According to Athenian tradition, the great hero and king Theseus united these scattered villages into a single state during the fabled Age of Heroes (what modern scholars call the Bronze Age, ending about 1100 B.C.). **See** Athens; **also** The Exploits of Theseus (Chapter 6).

Augean Stables

Fabled stables belonging to King Augeas of Elis (in the northwestern Peloponnesus). The Greek hero Heracles cleaned them to fulfill one of his famous labors for King Eurystheus of Tiryns. **See** The Adventures of Heracles (Chapter 6).

Avernus

A lake located near Cumae (just north of the Bay of Naples on Italy's southwestern coast). According to ancient tradition, a cave near the lake was one of the few existing entrances to the Underworld; and some Romans came to call the Underworld itself Avernus. It was through this cave that the Sibyl of Cumae led Aeneas into the infernal region to meet with his dead father, Anchises. **See** Underworld; **also** Sibyl (Chapter 1); Aeneas's Journey to Italy (Chapter 6).

Black Sea

The large (168,500 square miles) body of water lying north of Asia Minor. The Greeks, who called it the Euxine ("Friendly") Sea, accessed it via two straits, the Hellespont (today called the Dardenelles) and the Bosphorus (with the small Propontis, or Sea of Marmara, lying between them). A number of Greek cities grew up along the sea's fertile shores during the early centuries of the first millennium B.C., some of which produced grain for Greek cities on the shores of the Aegean Sea (especially Athens, which eventually imported up to half of its grain from the Black Sea region). In mythology, the Black Sea was most famous for the voyage of Jason and his Argonauts to Colchis (on the sea's eastern shore) in search of the Golden Fleece. **See** The Quest for the Golden Fleece (Chapter 6).

Boeotia

(pronounced bee-OH-shya) The region of central Greece located to the north and northwest of Attica. Boeotia was the homeland of Thebes and the Boeotian League, an alliance of about a dozen local cities; besides Thebes, the most important of these towns was Orchomenus, in northern

Boeotia. Both towns—but especially Thebes—produced rich collections of myths. In historical times, the Boeotians were frequently at war with Athens, although they allied themselves temporarily with the Athenians in 338 B.C. in an attempt to repel the Macedonians, led by Philip II and his son, Alexander (later called "the Great"). Philip won, and Boeotia went into a decline from which it never recovered. **See** Thebes; **also** The Theban Myth Cycle (Chapter 6).

Bosphorus
(or Bosporus) The narrow strait linking the Black Sea to the Propontis (Sea of Marmara). **See** Black Sea.

Calydon
A town located in southwestern Aetolia (a region of eastern mainland Greece) and famous for a large-scale hunt to find and kill a giant boar sent by the goddess Artemis to ravage the region. Meleager, son of the Calydonian king, was eventually credited with the kill. **See** Atalanta; Meleager (Chapter 1); **also** Artemis (Chapter 2).

Carthage
An important city, and for several centuries a prosperous nation, located on a peninsula projecting into the Mediterranean Sea at the tip of what is now Tunisia in North Africa. In Greek and Roman mythology, Dido, a princess of the Phoenician city of Tyre, fled her homeland and founded Carthage. There, as told in Virgil's great epic poem the *Aeneid,* she met the Trojan hero Aeneas, who was on his way to find his destiny in Italy. After she fell in love with him, he left her to

continue his quest. Before killing herself, she pronounced a curse that her city and the one that would spring from his lineage would forever be at odds. Later, in historical times, many Romans held that this curse was the root cause of the three disastrous Punic Wars fought between Rome and Carthage (all of which Rome won).

The myths about early Carthage aside, modern scholars believe that the city was established by traders from Tyre perhaps in the ninth century B.C. Sometime in the 600s B.C., Carthage became independent of Tyre and rapidly began expanding its power, wealth, and influence in the western Mediterranean sphere. It came to control the major sea routes in that region as well as most of the islands and parts of Spain. But the Carthaginians managed to gain only partial control of Sicily, where they long competed with Greek cities on the island. Carthage's interests in the Sicilian region also ended up bringing it into conflict with the Romans, resulting in the Punic Wars (spanning the period from 264 to 146 B.C.). At the conclusion of the third war, the Romans destroyed Carthage and turned the heart of its North African territory into the Roman province of Africa. **See** Dido (Chapter 1); **also** *Aeneid* (Chapter 5); Aeneas's Journey to Italy (Chapter 6).

Chairs of Forgetfulness
Special chairs belonging to the Greek god Hades, lord of the Underworld. When the Greek adventurers Theseus and Pirithous crept down into Hades' realm in hopes of carrying off Persephone (whom Hades had abducted), the god put the two men in the Chairs of Forgetfulness, which made them forget who they were and why they had come. The famous strongman Heracles rescued Theseus from this predicament, but he was unable to help poor Pirithous, who remained in his chair forever. **See** Underworld; **also** The Exploits of Theseus (Chapter 6).

Chios

A thirty-mile-long Aegean island off the coast of Ionia (western Asia Minor) thought by many to be the birthplace of the famous epic poet Homer, author of the *Iliad* and the *Odyssey*. **See** Homer (Chapter 5).

Cilicia

The southeastern region of Asia Minor facing the island of Cyprus. According to one legend, the area was named for Cilix, brother of Europa, who settled there after fruitlessly searching for her (following her abduction by Zeus, disguised as a bull). In another ancient account, after the Trojan War a group of Greeks known as the Cilicies, who had been living in the region of Troy (in northwestern Asia Minor), migrated into Cilicia, giving it their name. In historical times, the region became the base of operations for numerous pirate bands. **See** Asia Minor.

Colchis

A city and kingdom located along the eastern shore of the Black Sea, which became famous for harboring the fabulous Golden Fleece, the skin of a magical ram. After an arduous, dangerous journey, Jason and his Argonauts arrived in Colchis to trade for the fleece. However, the local king, Aeetes, wanted to keep the object and tried to kill Jason. With the aid of Aeetes' daughter, the sorceress Medea, Jason managed to obtain the fleece and take it back to Greece. **See** Black Sea; **also** Aeetes; Medea (Chapter 1); The Quest for the Golden Fleece (Chapter 6).

Corinth

For many centuries, one of the most important and powerful cities in the Greek world. Located in the northern Peloponnesus near the isthmus bearing its name, Corinth was dominated by its lofty acropolis, the Acrocorinth. The city often controlled communications and travel to and from central and southern Greece across the strategic isthmus. Inhabited in the Bronze Age or earlier, Corinth rose to prominence in the eighth and seventh centuries B.C., when its ceramics became popular throughout much of the Greek sphere and it established colonies on the islands of Corcyra (Corfu), Ithaca, Sicily, and elsewhere. After the mid–sixth century B.C., however, Athens steadily overshadowed Corinth commercially.

In Greek mythology, Corinth was famous as the home city of its founder, Sisyphus, who cheated death (and paid a heavy price for it later), and the hero Bellerophon, who rode the flying horse Pegasus to slay the fearsome Chimaera. In another famous myth, a Corinthian king named Creon welcomed Jason and Medea after they fled Iolcos (following the death of that city's king, Pelias, which Medea had arranged). One of Corinth's most famous local legends told how the sea god Poseidon and sun god Helios competed for divine patronage of the city. **See** Bellerophon; Creon 1; Medea; Pelias; Sisyphus (Chapter 1); **also** Poseidon; Thanatos (Chapter 2); Briareos; Chimaera; Pegasus (Chapter 3).

Corycian Cave

1. A famous cavern located within Mt. Parnassus, near Delphi. The cave was sacred to the woodland god, Pan, and the local nymphs. During the Persian invasion of Greece in 480 B.C., many of the local inhabitants of Delphi fled and hid in the cave. A fabulous story later spread that they had witnessed a miracle, as Athena, goddess of war, vigorously defended her local shrine against the invaders. According to the fifth-century B.C. Greek historian Herodotus,

> Just as the Persians came to the shrine of Athena Pronaea, thunderbolts fell on them from the sky, and two pinnacles of rock, torn from Mt. Parnassus, came crashing and rumbling down amongst

them, killing a large number, while at the same time there was a battle-cry [by the goddess] from inside the shrine. All these things happening together caused a panic amongst the Persian troops. They fled; and the Delphians [in the cave], seeing them on the run, came down upon them and attacked them with great slaughter. (*Histories* 8.36)

2. A cave located at Corycus in Cilicia (in southeastern Asia Minor), where legend claimed the huge monster Typhon dwelled until Zeus drove the creature away into Syria. **See** Zeus (Chapter 2); **also** Typhon (Chapter 3).

Crete

The largest Greek island (150 miles by between 7 and 34 miles), lying about 70 miles southeast of the southern Peloponnesus and directly south of the Cyclades islands. Crete was the main site of the Bronze Age Minoan civilization, which interacted with the Greek-speaking Mycenaean strongholds on the Greek mainland. From the exaggerated or distorted memories of these two early peoples, the historical Greeks drew a large proportion of their myths about gods and heroes, since they looked back on the Bronze Age as the Age of Heroes. For example, it was to the Cretan city of Knossus, ruled by King Minos, that the Athenian hero Theseus traveled and slew the Minotaur, a monster Minos kept locked away in a maze (the labyrinth) beneath his palace. Later, the inventor Daedalus, who had built the labyrinth, and his son Icarus were imprisoned in the labyrinth for having aided Theseus. They escaped by donning artificial wings constructed by Daedalus and flying away. Jason and his Argonauts later visited Crete, where they had to confront a bronze giant, Talos, who guarded the island against outsiders. And later still, the Trojan prince Aeneas and his followers stopped at Crete on their way to Italy. **See** Knossus; **also** Daedalus; Minos (Chapter 1); Minotaur; Talos (Chapter 3); Aeneas's Journey to Italy; The Exploits of Theseus (Chapter 6).

Cumae

A town located just north of the Gulf of Cumae (today called the Bay of Naples), home of the most famous Sibyl (prophetess) in Roman legend. When the Trojan prince Aeneas arrived in Italy to fulfill his destiny, he visited the Sibyl of Cumae, who led him into a cave near Lake Avernus and down into the Underworld to visit with the shade (soul) of Aeneas's father, Anchises. **See** Avernus; Underworld; **also** Anchises; Sibyl (Chapter 1); Aeneas's Journey to Italy (Chapter 6).

Cyclades

The Aegean island group lying north of Crete and southeast of Attica, comprising Andros, Tenos, Delos, Ceos, Paros, Naxos, Thera, and others. The name *Cyclades* came from the term *kuklos,* meaning "circle," since the group is roughly circular in shape. In the late Bronze Age (ca. 1400–1100 B.C.) some of these islands, especially Thera, came under the influence of the Minoans, who controlled the large island of Crete. Various myths emerged from these islands. One said that Thera had grown from a clod of earth dropped off the *Argo* by one of Jason's men (who had received the clod as a gift from a man they had encountered in North Africa, a fellow that turned out to be the sea god Triton in disguise). Other stories said that Delos formed on the spot where the goddess Asteria leapt into the sea, and that the island later became the birthplace of the deities Apollo and Artemis. **See** Delos; Thera; **also** Asteria; Leto (Chapter 2).

Cyprus

The large island lying about fifty miles south of Asia Minor in the extreme eastern sector of the Mediterranean Sea. In Greek mythology, Cyprus is most famous as the place that Aphrodite, goddess of love, stepped ashore as she emerged from the sea foam. The island remained closely associated with her after that; in historical times, her most famous shrines were located there. **See** Aphrodite (Chapter 2).

Delos

A small (3 miles by 1.5 miles), rather barren island in the Cyclades island group and situated roughly in the center of the Aegean Sea. According to legend, the island formed on the spot where Asteria, sister of the goddess Leto, jumped into the sea. Soon afterward, Leto went there and gave birth to the twin gods Apollo and Artemis. Ever afterward, the place re-

mained associated closely with Apollo; as a result, Delos became known as the Sacred Isle. A festival held there each year drew worshipers from across the Greek world, and numerous shrines to Apollo and other gods spread across the island. When Athens formed a confederacy of more than a hundred Greek states (the Delian League) in 478 B.C., the organization kept its vast treasury on Delos. **See** Apollo; Leto (Chapter 2).

Delphi

An important Greek town located in the state of Phokis (in central Greece), on the southern slope of Mt. Parnassus just north of the Gulf of Corinth. Delphi was the site of the famous oracle of the god Apollo. Throughout most of antiquity (beginning perhaps in the seventh century B.C.), religious pilgrims journeyed there from around the known world to ask Apollo's priestess (the Pythia) questions about future events. The temple also contained a hearth in which burned the god's "eternal fire," and

The surviving columns of the Temple of Apollo blend with the stunning vista visible from the magnificent hillside site of Delphi.

the *omphalos,* the navel-stone widely thought to mark the earth's geographic center. Near the temple were numerous other splendid structures, including those related to the Pythian Games, one of Greece's "big four" panhellenic (all-Greek) athletic competitions. The sanctuary of Delphi was administered and protected by the Delphic Amphictyony, a religious organization made up of representatives from several neighboring states. **See** Corycian Cave 1; Delphic Oracle; **also** Apollo (Chapter 2).

Delphic Oracle

The most famous oracle in the Greco-Roman world, located in a breathtakingly beautiful hillside setting near the town of Delphi on the southern slope of Mt. Parnassus (in central Greece). The oracle was important in numerous myths about the Greek gods as well as to religious pilgrims who traveled to Delphi to seek divine advice. According to various ancient myths, the first divine guardian of the oracle was Gaia (Earth), who ordered a huge female serpent—Python—to guard the sacred spot. The second and third deities who watched over the oracle were Themis (Zeus's second consort) and her sister, Phoebe. Finally, Apollo (god of prophecy and music) arrived at Delphi, slew Python, and took possession of the oracle, which remained associated with him thereafter.

Out of respect for the three goddesses who had controlled the shrine before him, Apollo appointed only priestesses to his temple. Each of these women was called an oracle, as well as the Pythia (after Python); and people viewed each as a medium between the gods and humans, believing she could relay divine answers from Apollo to the questions asked by the religious pilgrims. (The messages the priestesses delivered were also referred to as oracles.) Modern scholars are uncertain about many aspects of these priestesses and their activities. But ancient sources reveal that, in historical times, a Pythia was typically older than fifty when she began delivering prophecy (although in very ancient times she may have been a young maiden). It was not required that the Pythia be a virgin before undertaking service to Apollo; but once that service began, she had to abandon her husband and children, move into a special house on the temple grounds, and remain thereafter chaste. The exact way the Pythia was selected is unknown. But it is likely that she could come from any social class and did not require any special training and education. At first, a single Pythia delivered the god's words; as the number of pilgrims arriving at the shrine grew, however, two more Pythias were added so that three were on duty simultaneously.

As for the actual delivery of prophecy, a Pythia sat on Apollo's throne, the "sacred tripod," in the *adyton,* or inner shrine, so that she could make closer contact with the god. She then fell into a trance and uttered a series of strange, usually inarticulate cries. Her assistants, the *prophetai,* stood nearby to interpret her cries, and the pilgrim who had asked a question sat quietly in a corner several feet away. The pilgrim could not actually see the Pythia since she was hidden by a curtain or other kind of barrier, helping to maintain the air of mystery. The answers given to pilgrims by the Delphic Oracle were invariably ambiguous, obscure, and/or open to various interpretations. When her message pertained to the possible fate of a city or kingdom, therefore, both religious and civil authorities argued heatedly over its meaning and if and how they should react to it. **See** Delphi; **also** Apollo; Gaia (Chapter 2); Python (Chapter 3).

Dicte, Mt.

A mountain in eastern Crete on the slopes of which existed an important religious sanctuary dedicated to Zeus, which dated back perhaps to the late Bronze Age. Zeus may at first have been associated with an earlier Cretan god, whose place he eventually took. Another ancient Cretan deity, Dictynna, had a sanctuary on Mt. Dicte, too; she endured into classical times, becoming associated with Artemis. **See** Dictynna (Chapter 2).

Dodona

A town in Epirus (in northwestern Greece) containing the second-most famous oracle in the Greek world (next to Apollo's oracle at Delphi), dedicated to Zeus, ruler of the Greek gods. The oracle at Dodona was probably very old since in the *Iliad* (parts of which may date back to 1000 B.C. or more) Homer mentions the hero Achilles visiting the shrine to pray to Zeus. Zeus was thought to dispense prophecy and advice through the oracles who lived at the shrine. At first they were priests, known as Selli; but by the fifth century B.C. (according to the Greek historian Herodotus) they had been replaced by three priestesses called "Doves." **See** Delphic Oracle; **also** Zeus (Chapter 2).

Eleusis

After Athens and Piraeus (Athens's port city), the most important town in Attica and the home of the famed religious cult known as the Eleusinian Mysteries. The classical Greeks believed that Eleusis was the site where Persephone (queen of the Underworld) was first reunited with her mother, the goddess Demeter, after being abducted by Hades, ruler of the Underworld. In legend, Demeter initiated the Mysteries herself. However these rites began, in historical times people from all parts of Greece visited Eleusis during Demeter's festival, held in September. The cult required new members to undergo a

secret initiation (hence the name *Mysteries*). But anyone—male or female, free or slave—could join. New members first purified themselves by bathing in the sea. Then they sacrificed a young pig and marched in a stately procession. The parade began at the Eleusinion, a temple near the foot of the Acropolis in Athens, where the cult's "sacred objects" were stored, and wound its way for twelve miles, ending at Demeter's sanctuary at Eleusis. The nature of the sacred objects was a secret, like the initiation. Apparently the climax of the festival came when a cult leader revealed the sacred objects to the worshipers in the initiation hall. **See** Athens; **also** Demeter; Persephone (Chapter 2).

Elis

A region and also a city-state in the northwestern Peloponnesus. Its claim to fame was its hosting of the renowned religious festival and athletic games held every four years at Olympia, a site in Elis. There stood the Altis, the most renowned sacred sanctuary of Zeus in the ancient world. The Greeks erected a magnificent temple to Zeus at Olympia in the fifth century B.C., a structure that housed the Athenian sculptor Phidias's huge seated statute of the god, later called one of the seven wonders of the ancient world. **See** Olympia; **also** Zeus (Chapter 2).

Elysium

(Islands of the Blessed) A beautiful mythical land or realm lying beyond the waters of the Ocean (the wide river thought to encircle the earth's land portions). Early Greek writers such as Homer and Hesiod said that the gods sent a chosen few heroes, who had distinguished themselves in various ways during their lives, to Elysium; there, they enjoyed sunlight, comfortable homes, good food, and pleasant company for eternity. Not all heroes made it to Elysium, however; in Homer's *Odyssey,* the main character, Odysseus, visits the Underworld and finds the shade of the great Achilles languishing with the souls of countless ordinary mortals. Achilles tells Odysseus, "I would rather be a serf in the house of some landless man . . . than king of all these dead men that have done with life." (*Odyssey* 11.466–468) Over time, other myths placed Elysium in the Underworld but set it apart from the more dismal Tartarus and Plain of Asphodel. Although scholars remain uncertain, they think that Demeter's cult at Eleusis, along with some other ancient mystery cults, may have promised worshipers eternal salvation in Elysium. **See** Eleusis; Underworld.

Ephesus

(or Ephesos) An important Ionian Greek city located on the coast of Asia Minor northeast of the isle of Samos. Two mythological stories of the city's founding existed. The first claimed that Amazons (legendary warrior women from a region far north of Greece) established Ephesus; the other tale said that Androclus, son of the Athenian king Codrus, brought colonists to the area during the legendary Age of Heroes. Ephesus was the site of the enormous Temple of Artemis (erected in the sixth century B.C. and rebuilt after a great fire in 356 B.C.), dubbed one of the seven wonders of the ancient world. **See** Artemis (Chapter 2).

Eridanus

A legendary river said to be a major source of amber (yellow- or orange-colored fossilized tree resin, often viewed as a semiprecious stone). The myth of Phaëthon, son of the sun god Helios, attempted to explain the source of the amber. After Zeus ended the youth's wild ride in Helios's chariot by zapping him with a thunderbolt, Phaëthon fell into the Eridanus. Subsequently, his sisters turned into poplar trees and cried amber tears, which dropped into the river. The Greeks held that the Eridanus was located far to the north of Greece; eventually, though, a number of Greek and Roman writers came

to identify it with the Po River in northern Italy. **See** Phaëthon (Chapter 1).

Etna, Mt.

(or Aetna) A large volcano (slightly under 11,000 feet) situated in northeastern Sicily. According to early Roman tradition, it was the location of the forge operated by the god Vulcan (the Greek Hephaestos). Various other ancient myths also claimed that Etna's periodic eruptions and emissions of smoke were the breath of giants or monsters imprisoned under Sicily by Zeus or other gods. Numerous eruptions were recorded in classical times, including one in 479 B.C., which the Athenian playwright Aeschylus described. An anonymous first-century A.D. poem, the *Aetna*, described the volcano's outbursts and attempted to explain their cause. Also, the first-century B.C. Greek geographer Strabo recorded that lookout points and huts with sleeping accommodations were established along its slopes for use by mountain-climbing enthusiasts.

Golden Fleece

The hide of a magical ram; it became the object of one of the greatest quests in Greco-Roman mythology—that of Jason and the Argonauts. The origin of the Golden Fleece was as follows: A false oracle persuaded Athamas, an early king of Orchomenus and Thebes (in Boeotia), that he must kill his son, Phryxis, to avoid a serious famine. But at the last moment, Zeus sent a fabulous talking and flying ram to save Phryxis. The ram carried the youth and his sister, Helle, to safety in Colchis, a city on the eastern shore of the Black Sea, where the animal's fleece eventually came into the possession of Aeetes, a powerful local king. When

Jason and his Argonauts arrived in Colchis to bargain for the fleece, Aeetes did not want to give it up. **See** Athamas; Aeetes (Chapter 1); and, for a detailed account of the Argonauts' voyage, **see** The Quest for the Golden Fleece (Chapter 6).

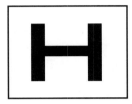

Helicon, Mt.

The highest mountain (actually a range of peaks) in Boeotia, the region of central Greece dominated by Thebes. The Greeks believed that Mt. Helicon was a principal abode of the Muses (goddesses of the fine arts); and the eighth-century B.C. poet Hes-

iod had a farm on the mountain's lower slopes, where he claimed the Muses inspired his writings. **See** Hippocrene; **also** Muses (Chapter 1); Hesiod (Chapter 5).

Hellespont

(today called the Dardanelles) The narrow, highly strategic strait connecting the Aegean Sea to the Sea of Marmara and separating Europe from Asia (more specifically, Greek Thrace from northwestern Asia Minor). The name Hellespont supposedly derived from the myth of Phryxis and his sister, Helle. As the magical ram sent by Zeus carried them from Thebes toward the Black Sea, Helle accidentally fell to her death in the strait, which thereafter bore her name. In historical times, the Hellespont was part of a vital trade route between mainland Greece and the cities along the shores of the Black Sea; in 480

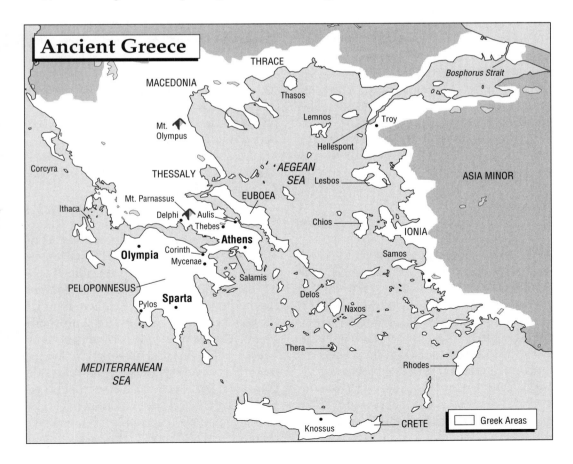

B.C. a Persian king, Xerxes, built a bridge of boats across it during his massive invasion of Greece. **See** Golden Fleece.

Hippocrene

A famous spring or small lake located on the slopes of Mt. Helicon (in Boeotia). According to legend, the spring was created by the tread of the flying horse Pegasus and became sacred to the Muses (goddesses of the fine arts); people drank from Hippocrene believing it would inspire them to creative endeavors. **See** Helicon, Mt.

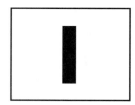

ichor

The blood of the gods, said to be thinner than that of humans and almost colorless. The most famous story involving ichor was that of Talos, the bronze giant who guarded the coastline of Crete; when the hero Jason and the sorceress Medea approached the island, Medea drugged Talos, then pierced a membrane near his ankle, allowing his ichor to flow out and thereby killing him. **See** Talos (Chapter 3).

Ida, Mt.

1. A range of peaks in Mysia (in northwestern Asia Minor) not far from the famous city of Troy. On Ida's slopes, shepherds raised Troy's Prince Paris; and there also he judged a contest among the goddesses Athena, Hera, and Aphrodite— the so-called Judgment of Paris, which turned out to be one of the more important events leading up to the Trojan War. During that famous conflict (according to Homer in his *Iliad*), Zeus, ruler of the gods, often sat on Mt. Ida's summit to watch the fighting. **See** The Trojan War (Chapter 6).

2. The highest range of peaks on the large Greek island of Crete. In a cave beneath the mountain, legend claimed, the god Zeus was nursed and grew up, unbeknownst to his father, the Titan Cronos. **See** Zeus (Chapter 2).

Ilium

(or Ilion) One of the ancient names of the city of Troy, which legend said the Greeks sacked after an eventful ten-year siege. **See** Troy; **also** The Trojan War (Chapter 6).

Iolcos

(or Jolcos) An important early Greek city located along the coast of eastern Thessaly (in central Greece) near the head of the Gulf of Pagasae (or Bay of Volos). Iolcos was most famous as the home of the hero Jason (son of Aeson), who led the quest for the Golden Fleece. Aeson's half brother, Pelias, usurped the throne and sent Jason looking for the fleece, hoping he would never come back. Jason did return, but he did not become king of Iolcos. The sorceress Medea (whom Jason brought back with him from distant Colchis) arranged the death of Pelias, and Pelias's son, Acastus, drove Jason and Medea out of the city. Acastus then ruled Iolcos until he was deposed by Peleus, king of Phthia. **See** Acastus; Medea; Pelias; Peleus (Chapter 1); **also** *Medea* (Chapter 5); The Quest for the Golden Fleece (Chapter 6).

Ionia

The central section of the western coast of Asia Minor, said to have been settled by mainland Greeks fleeing the invading Dorians during the legendary Age of Heroes. In legend, Ion, a grandson of Hellen, founder of the Greek race, settled in the northern Peloponnesus, where his followers became known as Ionians. Later, war drove the Ionians eastward across the Aegean Sea to the coasts and islands of Asia Minor. In historical times, the Greek cities of Ionia fell under Persian domination in the sixth century B.C.; became free in 479 B.C. at the conclusion of the Persian Wars (in which the Greeks defeated the Persians); and, in the late second century B.C., became part of the expanding Roman realm. **See** Asia Minor; **also** Ion (Chapter 1).

Islands of the Blessed

An alternative name for Elysium, the section of the Underworld in which the shades (souls) of a chosen few mortals lived comfortable, happy lives. **See** Elysium; Underworld.

Isthmus of Corinth

The narrow and highly strategic land bridge connecting central Greece to the Peloponnesus. **See** Corinth.

Ithaca

A small island in the Ionian group, located off the western coast of Greece. In Greek mythology, especially in Homer's epics the *Iliad* and the *Odyssey,* Ithaca was the site of the kingdom ruled by the hero Odysseus. **See** Odysseus (Chapter 1); **also** The Trojan War; The Wanderings of Odysseus (Chapter 6).

Knossus

(also Knossos, Cnossos, or Cnossus) In Greek legend, the capital of King Minos's kingdom in Crete. There, he ordered the famous inventor Daedalus to construct the labyrinth, a maze beneath the royal palace. When Minos's wife mated with a bull and produced the frightening Minotaur (a creature half man and half bull), Minos placed it in the labyrinth and fed sacrificial victims to it. Eventually the Athenian hero Theseus arrived at Knossus and killed the Minotaur.

Modern archaeologists and other scholars have revealed that the real Knossus was an important city of the Minoan culture that inhabited Crete during the Bronze Age (ca. 3000–ca. 1100 B.C.) and long controlled the nearby sea lanes. Located about four miles from the island's northern coast, the site was dominated by a huge, splendid multileveled structure that appears to have served as both a palace and an administrative center for the villages and farms surrounding Knossus. With its hundreds of rooms, corridors, stairwells, and courtyards, the building was certainly complex enough to have inspired the legend of the labyrinth. Some scholars have also suggested that the garbled memory of Minoan priests, who wore bull masks during religious rituals, may have given rise to the story of the Minotaur. **See** Crete; **also** Daedalus; Minos (Chapter 1); Minotaur (Chapter 3); The Exploits of Theseus (Chapter 6).

labyrinth

The maze built by the legendary inventor Daedalus for Minos, king of Crete. **See** Knossus.

Latium

A well-watered plain of western Italy bordered by the Mediterranean Sea in the west, the Apennine Mountains in the east, Rome and the Tiber River in the north, and the volcanic region of Campania in the south. Latium was central to Roman mythology because it was the region settled by the Trojan prince Aeneas, father of the Roman race. Aeneas married Lavinia, daughter of Latium's king, Latinus; later, Aeneas's son, Ascanius, established one of

Latium's chief towns, Alba Longa, the royal house of which eventually produced Romulus, Rome's founder.

These myths aside, historians have determined that the original Latin tribes who settled the plain of Latium formed a religious confederation and later some kind of political alliance—the Latin League—to fend off incursions by the Etruscans (who lived north of Rome) and eventually the Romans. By 338 B.C. Rome had reduced all of Latium to subject status. In the centuries that followed, when Latium was firmly a part of the Roman heartland, most of the original Latin towns in the region fell into ruin and local agriculture was replaced by pasture for goats and sheep. **See** Rome; **also** Latinus; Romulus (Chapter 1); Aeneas's Journey to Italy (Chapter 6).

Lerna

A small town lying about six miles south of Argos in the eastern Peloponnesus. In Greek mythology, the Halcyonian (or Alcyonian) Lake in Lerna contained one of the few entrances to the Underworld. Lerna was also the scene of the hero Heracles' second labor for King Eurystheus, in which the famous strongman rid the marshes near Lerna of a monster called the Hydra. **See** Hydra (Chapter 3); **also** The Adventures of Heracles (Chapter 6).

Lesbos

A large Greek island lying off the western coast of Asia Minor, several miles north of Chios. The principal city of Lesbos was Mytilene, a port on the southeastern coast. An ancient myth held that the original inhabitants were descendants of Lesbos, a grandson of Aeolus (a mortal who became god of the winds). In historical times, Lesbos gained prominence as the birthplace of a noted Greek poetess, Sappho.

Lydia

The region roughly encompassing the inland portion of western Asia Minor. During the sixth century B.C. Lydia was a non-Greek kingdom ruled by the legendary King Croesus. He greatly admired the Greeks and eagerly followed many Greek customs, including consulting the famous oracle of the god Apollo at Delphi in time of crisis or indecision. The oracle was central to the most famous myth about Croesus. He sent a messenger to ask Apollo whether it would be wise to fight Cyrus, king of the Persians, whose army was threatening Lydia. The oracle's answer was that if Croesus crossed the Halys River (in central Asia Minor) and attacked the Persians, he would destroy a great empire. This filled Croesus with confidence, and he crossed the Halys and attacked. But to his surprise, he lost the battle and had to retreat, and the Persians soon besieged and took over the Lydian capital, Sardis. According to the Greek historian Herodotus, Croesus could not blame Apollo for his misfortune because

> the god had declared that if he attacked the Persians he would bring down a mighty empire. After an answer like that, the wise thing would have been to send again to inquire which empire was meant, Cyrus's or his own. But as he [Croesus] misinterpreted what was said and made no second inquiry, he must admit the fault to have been his own. (*Histories* 1.92–93)

After Croesus's defeat, the Lydian kingdom ceased to exist.

Marathon

A village and plain in northeastern Attica, where the famous Athenian victory over the Persians took place in 490 B.C. In Greek mythology Marathon was the place where the hero Theseus killed a wild bull that had terrorized the area for some twenty years. There was also a legend that, after the Greeks defeated the Persians at Marathon, the Greek runner sent to Athens to announce the victory encountered the god Pan, who asked him why his countrymen had neglected his worship. **See** Pan (Chapter 2); **also** The Exploits of Theseus (Chapter 6).

Messenia

The southwestern region of the Peloponnesus. In Greek mythology, Messenia's king, Aphareus, welcomed his cousin, Neleus, and gave him part of his kingdom. Neleus then conquered Pylos, on the western coast, which became the stronghold of Neleus's son, Nestor, one of the Greek commanders in the Trojan War. (Archaeologists have shown that Pylos had a Mycenaean palace-citadel during the Bronze Age.) In historical times, Messenia was the homeland of the helots, serfs who did forced labor for the Spartans. **See** Mycenae; Peloponnesus; **also** Neleus; Nestor (Chapter 1).

Messina, Strait of

The strait separating southern Italy from the island of Sicily. The place was famous in Greco-Roman mythology for the dangers posed to sailors by two monsters that dwelled on the strait's opposite shores—Charybdis, a whirlpool, and Scylla, a six-headed creature. **See** Charybdis; Scylla (Chapter 3).

Miletus

The leading city of Greek Ionia, situated on the western coast of Asia Minor, southeast of the isle of Samos and northwest of Caria. The myth of the city's founding involved three brothers—Sarpedon, Minos, and Rhadamanthys,

all mortal sons of Zeus. When the three reached manhood, each wanted to become the best friend of an admirable young man named Miletus, and they quarreled over him. Miletus chose Sarpedon, and the angry Minos drove Sarpedon, Miletus, and Rhadamanthys out of Crete. Miletus went to southern Asia Minor and there established the city that bore his name. **See** Sarpedon 1 (Chapter 1).

Mycenae

An early Greek town in the northeastern Peloponnesus, near Argos and Tiryns. Dominated by an imposing stone palace-citadel erected on a hill overlooking the plain of Argos, Mycenae was the hub of one of the principal mythological kingdoms of the fabled Age of Heroes. The renowned hero Perseus (who slew the Gorgon Medusa) was credited with establishing Mycenae. Among its later kings were Atreus (son of Pelops, for whom the Peloponnesus was named) and Agamemnon (leader of the Greek expedition to Troy). Their palace was frequently tainted with the blood of the famous curse of the

A nineteenth-century drawing attempts to reconstruct the walls and acropolis of the Bronze Age citadel of Mycenae.

house of Atreus, which included the murder of Agamemnon (after his return from the Trojan War) by his queen, Clytemnestra, and her own death at the hands of her vengeful son, Orestes. By classical times (some seven to ten centuries later), these happenings were a mere mythical memory. Mycenae's citadel stood ruined and deserted. And the Greeks of that later age thought the huge stones making up its walls and its famous "Lion Gate" (named for two stone lions above this entranceway) had been erected by mythical giants—the Cyclopes.

Not until modern times did the true nature of Mycenae's original builders begin to come to light. In the 1870s German archaeologist Heinrich Schliemann initiated excavation of the ruined fortress and discovered elaborate graves containing golden masks, finely wrought weapons, and other valuables, suggesting that they belonged to the members of a royal family. This prompted his claim to have found the remains of the legendary King Agamemnon (a claim that remains unproven). Subsequent excavations at Mycenae and other Bronze Age stone citadels (at Tiryns, Pylos, Thebes, Orchomenus, and elsewhere in southern Greece) revealed that these towns were indeed Greece's major power centers during the late Bronze Age. Their builders, whom scholars dubbed the Mycenaeans, after Mycenae, controlled the Aegean sphere for over two centuries; their civilization then collapsed, for reasons still uncertain, in the twelfth century B.C.

The consensus of scholarly opinion is that various kings and other prominent figures of Mycenaean civilization (as well as members of the Minoan civilization on Crete, which the Mycenaeans supplanted) were the basis for many of the characters in later Greek mythology. There may have been a real Agamemnon who ruled Mycenae, for instance. Obviously, though, over time the deeds of such rulers became exaggerated, distorted, and sometimes completely fabricated. Of particular interest to many scholars is the possible connection between the Mycenaeans and the most important of all Greek myths—the Trojan War. Evidence suggests that in their heyday these early Greeks often raided neighboring coasts, including those of Asia Minor. So it is quite possible that the independent trading city of Troy may have been one of their targets, which would mean that the renowned siege of Troy may have been based, at least to some degree, on fact. **See** Agamemnon; Orestes (Chapter 1); **also** Cyclops (Chapter 3); The Curse of the House of Atreus; The Trojan War (Chapter 6).

nectar

A sweet-smelling liquid that ancient myths claimed the Greek gods drank. According to tradition, nectar (along with ambrosia, a solid food) helped these deities maintain their immortality. **See** ambrosia.

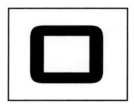

Ocean

The wide river or stream the Greeks and Romans conceived as encircling the land portions of the earth. The common belief was that all of the earth's rivers had the Ocean as their source, flowing from it either above or below the ground. Also, various remote islands in the Ocean were thought to be the abodes of fabulous creatures, peoples, or divinities, such as the Gorgons, Cimmerians, and Hesperides. The Titans Oceanus and Tethys ruled the Ocean for Zeus. **See** Oceanus (Chapter 2).

Ogygia

As described by Homer in his *Odyssey,* a remote island ruled by the nymph Calypso. She kept the hero Odysseus on Ogygia for seven years, hoping to marry him, until Zeus finally sent his messenger, Hermes, to arrange for the man's release. **See** Calypso (Chapter 2); **also** The Wanderings of Odysseus (Chapter 6).

Olympia

The site of the renowned panhellenic ("all-Greek") Olympic Games (which, according to tradition, began in 776 B.C.) and the principal religious sanctuary of Zeus, ruler of the Greek gods. Olympia, located in an idyllic country setting in the northwestern Peloponnesus, was at first administered by a small town or district called Pisa; by the beginning of the fifth century B.C., however, nearby Elis had become the host of the great festival, held every four years. **See** Elis; **also** Zeus (Chapter 2).

Olympus, Mt.

At 9,570 feet, the highest mountain (actually a range of peaks) in mainland Greece, situated in northern Thessaly not far from the Aegean coast. In early Greek tradition, Olympus was thought to be the home of the principal Greek gods (who became prototypes for several major Roman gods). The Greeks and Romans often referred to these deities as the Olympians, after the name of the mountain. By classical times, most Greeks had come to believe that the gods, if they did indeed exist, dwelled in the heavens or in some faraway land rather than on Olympus's summit. Today, that summit, often snowcapped, remains an awe-inspiring sight visible for up to seventy or more miles from either the north or the south. **See** Olympians (Chapter 2).

oracle

A message thought to come from the gods; also the sacred site where such a message was given, and the name given to the priestess who delivered the message. **See** Delphic Oracle; Dodona; **also** Apollo; Zeus (Chapter 2).

Orchomenus

A city lying northwest of Thebes in Boeotia (in eastern-central Greece), near the western shore of Lake Copais (now drained). In very early Greek times, according to legend, Orchomenus was the principal city of Boeotia until Thebes eclipsed it in importance. The legendary founder of Orchomenus, Minyas, gave rise to an equally mythical band of heroes—the Minyans—under whom the city became renowned for its wealth. Orchomenus also became famous for its splendid buildings, many of which were attributed to the mythical architects Trophonius and Agamedes, sons of Erginus, an Orchomenian king. Erginus conquered Thebes and forced the Thebans to give him tribute (payment acknowledging submission). This turned out to be a grave mistake; Thebes was the native city of the famous hero Heracles, who soon retaliated by defeating Erginus in battle, burning down his palace, and flooding the city's farmland. Thereafter, Orchomenus's importance was greatly diminished and Thebes maintained supremacy in Boeotia. **See** Thebes; **also** Minyans; Minyas; Trophonius and Agamades (Chapter 1); The Adventures of Heracles (Chapter 6).

Palatine

One of the famous seven hills of Rome and, according to tradition, the site of the first human settlement in the area. About sixty years before the Trojan War, as told in Virgil's *Aeneid,* Evander, a king of Arcadia, in southern Greece, migrated with his followers to Italy and colonized the Palatine. Later, when Evander was an old man, he welcomed the hero Aeneas (father of the Roman race), who visited the future site of Rome shortly after making landfall in Italy. In historical times, the Palatine became the site of the houses of many rich and famous Romans, including the great orator Cicero and the noted military general Mark Antony. Augustus, the first Roman emperor, acquired a house on the Palatine, which later became the site of numerous palaces erected by his successors. **See** Rome; **also** Evander (Chapter 2).

Parnassus, Mt.

A range of peaks (the tallest rising to 8,061 feet) in Phokis, in central Greece just north of the Gulf of Corinth. The whole range was sacred ground, at first associated with the worship of Dionysus and later with that of Pan and Apollo. On the slopes were the Corycian Cave, which was sacred to the local nymphs; a spring sacred to both Apollo and the Muses; and Delphi, home of Apollo's renowned oracle, lodged in a spectacular setting between two cliffs (the Phaedriades, or "Shining Ones"). **See** Corycian Cave 1; Delphi; Delphic Oracle; **also** Apollo; Muses; Pan (Chapter 2).

Parthenon

A magnificent temple erected in honor of the goddess Athena on Athens's Acropolis in the 440s and 430s B.C., at the height of the city's cultural golden age. The huge and ornately decorated building dominated the entire summit of the Acropolis, which featured numerous temples, altars, and statues. Conceived by Pericles (the leading Greek statesman of the age) and designed by the architect Ictinus and master sculptor Phidias, the Parthenon was 237 feet long, 110 feet wide, some 65 feet high. It incorporated over 22,000 tons of exquisite marble (mostly quarried at Mt.

Pentelicon, about ten miles northeast of Athens's urban center). Inside the temple stood Phidias's splendid 38-foot-high statue of Athena, with garments fashioned of beaten gold. Simultaneously simple and ornate, and seemingly possessing both serene reserve and bursting energy, the Parthenon was a visual expression of Athens's special spirit.

The Parthenon was also important for its artistic representations of numerous mythological characters and scenes. The ninety-two metopes (rectangular panels bearing relief sculptures) running along the building's four sides, just above the columns, displayed scenes illustrating the theme of Greece's triumph over the forces of barbarism and disorder. The metopes on the structure's east end, for example, depicted episodes from the primeval war between the giants and Olympian gods (the Gigantomachy). Along the north side, the metopes showed famous scenes from the Trojan War (in which the "superior European" Greeks defeated the "inferior Asiatic" Trojans). The metopes on the west end depicted the Athenians fighting the Amazons (a battle called the Amazonomachy). And finally, the temple's south-facing metopes bore reliefs showing warfare between the Lapiths and the centaurs (the Centauromachy). Phidias also carved (or painted) scenes from the Gigantomachy and the Amazonomachy on the inside and outside of the huge shield held by the statue of Athena inside the temple.

Perhaps the most impressive of all of the Parthenon's mythological sculptures were the larger-than-life statues in the pediments (the triangular spaces beneath the roof on the building's two ends). Each scene contained about twenty-two major figures and depicted one of the central myths associated with Athena. The west pediment, the one facing the Acropolis's entranceway, showed the famous contest between the goddess and Poseidon for control of Attica; the east pediment portrayed the moment following Athena's dramatic birth from her father's head, witnessed by a bevy of astonished deities. The surviving remnants of these splendid sculptures are on display in various modern museums, most notably the Acropolis Museum and National Archaeological Museum, both in Athens, and the British Museum in London. **See** Acropolis; Athens; **also** Amazons; Lapiths (Chapter 1); Athena (Chapter 2); centaur; giants (Chapter 3); The Creation of the Gods and Humans (Chapter 6).

Peloponnesus

(or Peloponnese) The large, mountainous peninsula that is separated from central Greece by the Isthmus of Corinth and makes up roughly the southern third of the Greek mainland. The name came from *Pelopos nesos,* meaning "Isle of Pelops," a reference to the mythological character Pelops, son of Tantalus, who cut up Pelops and tried to feed the pieces to the Greek gods. Legend claimed that Pelops (whom the gods restored to life) founded the Pelopid family, also referred to as the house of Atreus, since Atreus was one of Pelops's sons. The famous curse on the family manifested itself not only in Atreus but also in his son, Agamemnon, and in Agamemnon's own son, Orestes. In ancient times, the major regions of the Peloponnesus were Elis (in the northwest), Achaea (north), Arcadia (center), the Argolid (the large peninsula in the northeast), Laconia (south, homeland of the Spartans), and Messenia (southwest). **See** Arcadia; Argos; Elis; Messenia; Sparta; **also** The Curse of the House of Atreus (Chapter 6).

Phoenicia

A narrow strip of territory along the coast of Syria (southeast of Asia Minor) inhabited by a prosperous ancient maritime people—the Phoenicians. The Greeks traded with the Phoenicians for centuries; and Phoenician colonies, including Carthage (in North Africa), grew up across the Mediterranean sphere. So it was perhaps inevitable that some Phoenician characters would make their way into Greek and Roman mythology. The most famous Greek examples were Europa and Cadmus, daughter and son of Agenor, king of the Phoenician city of Tyre. Disguised as a bull, Zeus abducted Europa and took her to the Greek island of Crete; then Cadmus went looking for her and ended up founding the great Greek city of Thebes. In Roman mythology, the most-renowned Phoenician was Dido, also a princess of Tyre. She migrated to North Africa and established the city of Carthage, which later became Rome's greatest rival. She and Aeneas, father of the Roman race, fell in love; but he left her and she committed suicide. **See** Carthage; **also** Cadmus; Dido; Europa (Chapter 1); Aeneas's Journey to Italy; The Theban Myth Cycle (Chapter 6).

Phrygia

The central region of Asia Minor, occupying a large plateau lying west of Mysia and Lydia. According to the fifth-century B.C. Greek historian Herodotus, the area was first settled by an obscure people from Macedonia, the Briges, who subsequently called themselves Phrygians. A number of Greek myths took place wholly or partly in Phrygia. Among the more famous were the story of Midas, a Phrygian king whom the god Apollo gave a donkey's ears for choosing the god Pan over Apollo in a musical contest; and the tale of Baucis and Philemon, a kindly old couple who welcomed the god Zeus, disguised as a human, into their poor hovel. Phrygia was also the original home of "the Great Mother" goddess, Cybele, whose worship spread to Greece and Rome in the last few centuries B.C. **See** Asia Minor; **also** Midas;

Baucis and Philemon (Chapter 1); Cybele (Chapter 2).

Phthia

A very ancient region, city, and/or kingdom mentioned in the Homeric poems and some other early Greek writings. Its exact location remains uncertain, but the best guess is that it lay in southeastern Thessaly in the region of Mt. Othrys (east of the city of Lamia). One of Phthia's most famous rulers was Peleus, father of Achilles, champion of the Trojan War. **See** Peleus.

Pillars of Heracles

(or Pillars of Hercules) The mountains rising on either side of the Straits of Gibraltar, at the western extremity of the Mediterranean Sea. According to legend, when the famous hero Heracles set out to steal the cattle of Geryon, to fulfill his tenth labor, the strongman erected the pillars (known as Calpe and Abyla) to mark the place where Europe and Africa face each other across the strait. **See** The Adventures of Heracles (Chapter 6).

Pontus

In early Greek times, the region encompassing much of northern Asia Minor, along the southern shores of the Black Sea. Jason and his Argonauts stopped at Sinope (a city established in Pontus by Miletus) on their way to Colchis to acquire the Golden Fleece.

Pylos

A town near the southwestern coast of the Peloponnesus; the site of a Bronze Age palace said to be that of the legendary hero Nestor, one of the Greek leaders during the Trojan War. **See** Messenia; Mycenae; **also** Neleus; Nestor (Chapter 1).

Pythia

The title given to each of the oracles (priestesses) of the god Apollo at his fa-

mous temple at Delphi. **See** Delphic Oracle; **also** Apollo (Chapter 2).

Rhodes

A large Greek island lying off the southwestern coast of Asia Minor. Some ancient writers claimed that Rhodes's original inhabitants were a race of magicians known as the Telchines, who had the ability to change the weather, cure disease, and forge fabulous metal objects. In historical times, Rhodes was famous as the site of the famous Colossus, a giant statue listed among the seven wonders of the ancient world. The Colossus was an artistic representation of the sun god Helios, the island's patron deity. **See** Telchines (Chapter 3).

Rome

The Italian city-state whose empire eventually conquered and absorbed the Greek kingdoms and cities in the second and first centuries B.C. The famed seven hills of Rome were occupied by Latin tribes as early as 1000 B.C. (during Greece's Dark Age), and a central town emerged at least by the mid-700s (an event that may have inspired the city's traditional founding date, later fixed at 753 B.C.). Rome was at first ruled by kings, but in 509 B.C. the monarchy was overthrown and was replaced by the Republic, ruled largely by the Senate (made up of well-to-do aristocrats).

All of these real events were reflected, in large or small degree, in Roman mythology. The Romans believed that the first settlement in the area, on the Palatine Hill, was built by Evander, a king of Arcadia (in southern Greece). Later Evander met Aeneas, the Trojan prince who sailed to Italy and established the noble lineage

The splendid Temple of Jupiter crowns the Capitoline Hill in this modern reconstruction drawing of Rome as it appeared in late republican times.

that led to the Roman race. Aeneas's son, Ascanius, established the city of Alba Longa in the Latium plain; and Alba's royal house eventually produced Romulus, who founded the city of Rome. Romulus served as Rome's first king, and legend held that six more kings ruled the city until the leading citizens, led by the hero Lucius Junius Brutus, set up the Roman Republic. Rome's kings, along with Brutus and several other early military or political figures, became some of the chief figures of Roman myths. (Some of them were probably real people whose deeds were later magnified or fabricated.)

Most of the remainder of Roman mythology was borrowed from the Greeks since the Romans were mightily impressed by Greek culture, even if they saw themselves as politically and morally superior to the Greeks. Almost every Greek god had its Roman counterpart, often an ancient Italian god whom the Romans came to identify with a Greek deity. As a rule, most or all of the myths associated with a Greek god were adopted by the Romans along with the god.

The Romans also attempted to establish connections between their own early legendary history and important characters and incidents from Greek mythology. In the most prominent example, the Romans tried to raise the stature of their own history by creating a link between themselves and the Trojan War, widely seen in the ancient Mediterranean world as an event of unparalleled heroic and historic importance. At least by the sixth century B.C., it appears, Roman legends had incorporated the tale of the Trojan prince Aeneas's escape from the burning Troy and his fateful journey to Italy, where he became the founder of the Roman race. The longest and most magnificent telling of his story is Virgil's epic poem the *Aeneid.* As for how this blatant adoption of a Greek tradition squared with Roman pride, noted classical scholar T.J. Cornell comments (from *The Beginnings of Rome*),

In general it is not surprising that the Romans were willing to embrace a story that flattered their pride by associating them with the legendary traditions of the Greeks, whose cultural superiority they were forced to acknowledge—albeit sometimes grudgingly. More specifically, in Greek myth Aeneas possessed qualities which the Romans liked to see in themselves, such as reverence for the gods and love of his fatherland. The Trojan legend was also useful to the Romans in that it gave them a respectable identity in the eyes of a wider world, and one that could be used to advantage in their dealings with the Greeks. . . . Finally, we should note that by claiming to be Trojans the Romans were saying that they were not Greeks, and in a sense defining themselves in opposition to the Greeks. . . . In the hands of Virgil and other writers of the first century B.C., it became a means to reconcile them, and make Roman rule acceptable in the Greek world.

For the stories of legendary early Roman heroes, **see** Aeneas; Ascanius; Brutus; Cincinnatus; Cloelia; Coriolanus; Curtius; Horatii; Horatius; Romulus; Tarpeia (Chapter 1); and, for detailed accounts of the founding of the Roman race and of Rome itself, **see** Aeneas's Journey to Italy; The Founding of Rome (Chapter 6).

Salamis
A small island in the northeastern Saronic Gulf, near the coast of Attica. In Greek mythology, Salamis was ruled by Telamon (son of Aeacus, king of the island of Aegina), who sired Ajax the Greater and Teucer, both of whom became heroes in the Trojan War. Later, in historical times, the waters near Salamis were the site of the famous Greek naval victory over the Persians in 480 B.C. **See** Ajax 1; Telamon; Teucer (Chapter 1).

Saronic Gulf
An inlet of the Aegean Sea bordered by Attica in the east and the Peloponnesus in the west, with the island of Aegina roughly in the center.

Scythia
The name the Greeks used loosely to describe the large, sparsely inhabited region north of Thrace and bordering the Black Sea in the west and north. Scythia was often cited as the homeland of the Amazons, a legendary race of warrior women who launched a failed attack on Athens. **See** Amazons.

shade
Existing after death, the soul-like shadow of a mortal's once-living body. People's shades almost always inhabited the Underworld. In his *Odyssey,* Homer provides the following vivid description of the hero Odysseus's encounter with the shade of his dead mother:

> As my mother spoke, there came to me out of the confusion in my heart the one desire to embrace her spirit, dead though she was. Three times, in my eagerness to embrace her, I started forward with my hands outstretched. And three times, like a shadow or a dream, she slipped through my arms. . . . "Mother!" I cried in my despair, "why do you avoid me when I try to reach you?" . . . "My child, my child!" came her reply. . . . "You are only witnessing here the law of our mortal nature, when we come to die. We no longer have muscles and tendons keeping the bones and flesh together; but once the life-force has departed from our white bones . . . the soul slips away like a dream and flutters on the air." (*Odyssey* 11.199–225)

See Underworld.

Sicily
A large island (covering 9,830 square miles) lying off the southwestern coast of

Italy and separated from it by the narrow Strait of Messina. Sicily was one of Rome's most important territories. The island's eastern section was heavily colonized by Greeks beginning in the eighth century B.C., the most important Greek city being Syracuse. Meanwhile, the Phoenicians (a maritime people from the Palestinian coast) settled in the island's eastern section, which eventually came under the control of Carthage (in North Africa).

Sicily and its surrounding waters played a significant role in Greek and Roman mythology. In the stories about the early battles among the gods and various giants and monsters, for instance, gods sometimes uprooted the whole island and tossed it on top of an enemy (as Zeus did to Typhon). Other monsters and dangers—Scylla, Charybdis, and the Sirens—lurked in the waters in or near Sicily's Strait of Messina. The Greek hero Odysseus encountered all of these menaces during his wanderings (as told in Homer's *Odyssey*). The Trojan prince Aeneas (who became the founder of the Roman race) stopped for a while in Sicily during his own voyage of epic adventure. Sicily was also famous for its huge volcano, Mt. Etna, said to be the site of the forge operated by the god Vulcan. **See** Etna, Mt.; Messina, Strait of; **also** Vulcan (Chapter 2); Typhon (Chapter 3); Aeneas's Journey to Italy; The Wanderings of Odysseus (Chapter 6).

Sparta

(or Lacedaemon) The principal city of Laconia (in the southeastern Peloponnesus), renowned in historical times (beginning in the sixth century B.C.) for its efficient and widely feared land army. In Greek mythology, Sparta was perhaps most famous as the home of King Menelaus (brother of Agamemnon, king of Mycenae), one of the leaders of the Greek expedition to Troy, and his queen, Helen, whose affair with Troy's

Young Spartan athletes train in the Dromos (race or running course) in the heart of Spartra, which was known for its formidable army.

Prince Paris instigated the Trojan War. Sparta was also known for its connections to the Dorians, whom legend claimed invaded the Peloponnesus and introduced their war-like customs to the Spartans. In addition, a cave on Cape Taenarum (near Sparta) was said to be one of the few existing entrances to the Underworld. **See** Helen; Menelaus (Chapter 1).

Styx

One of the legendary rivers that flowed through the Underworld. According to tradition, a ghastly boatman, Charon, ferried the souls of the dead across the Styx and into the subterranean realm ruled by Hades. **See** Underworld; **also** Charon; Hades (Chapter 2).

Tarpeian Rock

A crag located at the southwest corner of Rome's Capitoline Hill. Criminals were sometimes thrown off the rock to their deaths. According to legend, the rock was named for Tarpeia, daughter of Spurius Tarpeius, leader of Rome's central fortress during the attack of the Sabines (which occurred near the beginning of Romulus's reign in the eighth century B.C.). Some stories said she betrayed Rome to the Sabines; others claimed she was a patriot who took away the Sabines' shields so that they could not defend themselves against the Roman counterattack. **See** Tarpeia (Chapter 1).

Tartarus

A part of the Underworld where Zeus imprisoned the Titans and other enemies of the Olympians; also, according to early Greek writers, where the shades (souls) of wicked people suffered punishment. **See** Underworld; **also** Titans; Zeus (Chapter 2).

Thebes

The principal city of Boeotia, the region of the Greek mainland lying just north of Attica. Thebes played a pivotal role in Greek mythology and history. According to legend, Cadmus, a prince of the Phoenician city of Tyre, established Thebes while searching for his sister Europa (whom Zeus had abducted and taken to Crete). Cadmus may be the name of an actual early king of Thebes since archaeology confirms the existence of a Mycenaean settlement on the site during the Bronze Age. Thebes was also the site of other important myths, among them Oedipus's defeat of the monstrous Sphinx and his assumption of the city's throne; his subsequent fall from power and grace after discovering that he had murdered his father, the former king; the attack on the city by seven champions known as the Seven Against Thebes; and the heroism and tragic death of Oedipus's daughter, Antigone. Thebes was also the birthplace of the great mythical hero Heracles. Various myths and legends about early Thebes were collected into three epic poems (the *Oedipodia, Thebaïd,* and *Epigoni*). Now lost, these provided inspiration for many of the plays of Aeschylus, Sophocles, and other fifth-century B.C. Athenian dramatists.

The historical Thebes rose to prominence in the sixth century B.C. when it gained dominance over Orchomenus and the other Boeotian cities, forming and leading a loose confederation of local towns (the Boeotian League). In the fifth century B.C., Thebes and neighboring Athens were usually enemies; however, in the early fourth century Sparta became Thebes's chief rival, a situation that climaxed with Sparta's defeat by a Theban army in 371 B.C. Soon afterward, Thebes enjoyed a brief period of supremacy in Greece. But the city's influence quickly waned, and in 338 B.C. Thebes and many other cities in southern Greece fell under the domination of Macedonia's King Philip II and his son Alexander (later called "the Great"). **See** Boeotia; Mycenae; Orchomenus; **also** Adrastus; Antigone; Cadmus; Eteocles; Oedipus (Chapter 1); Sphinx (Chapter 3); *Antigone;* Epic Cycle; *Oedipus the King; Seven Against Thebes* (Chapter 5); The Theban Myth Cycle (Chapter 6).

Thera

(modern Santorini) A small crescent-shaped island lying just north of central Crete. Thera, the southernmost island in the Cyclades group, was the site of a massive volcanic eruption that occurred circa 1600 B.C. and may have given rise to the famous myth of Atlantis. **See** Atlantis; Crete; Cyclades; and, for the myth of how the Argonauts, aided by the sea god Triton, created Thera from a clod of earth, **see** Triton (Chapter 2).

Thessaly

The large region of north-central Greece lying south of Macedonia and north of Boeotia, Phokis, and Aetolia. Thessaly was known for its fertile plain, the largest in Greece; its fine horses; and for the imposing Mt. Olympus range of peaks dominating its northeastern section. Besides Olympus, the traditional home of the gods, several Thessalian sites played important roles in Greek mythology. The city of Iolcos (in the region of Magnesia, near the Aegean coast), for example, was the home of the hero Jason, who led the voyage to find the fabulous Golden Fleece. And Phthia, southwest of Iolcos, was the kingdom of Peleus and his son, Achilles, central character of Homer's great epic poem the *Iliad.* **See** Iolcos; Phthia; Olympus, Mt.

Thrace

The Greek region lying directly north of the Aegean Sea, east of Macedonia, and west of the Hellespont. The area was long inhabited by native Thracians, whom the powerful city-states of the southern Greek mainland looked on as culturally backward and warlike. The city-states colonized the area off and on until Macedonia's Philip II directly annexed it in the 340s B.C. Thrace was known for its gold mines and agricultural products, and also as the birthplace of Spartacus, the gladiator who led the largest slave rebellion in Roman history. In mythology, Thrace was the homeland of the poetmusician Orpheus, who tried but failed to rescue his beloved Eurydice from the Underworld. **See** Orpheus (Chapter 1).

Tiber River

At roughly 250 miles in length, the longest river on the Italian peninsula. The Tiber was (and remains) most famous for its proximity to the city of Rome, which grew up along a bend of the waterway located about 16 miles from the sea. The Tiber's southern reaches traditionally marked the boundary between Etruria (land of the Etruscans) and the Latium plain. The river was navigable for most of the year up to Narnia, about 80 miles north of Rome.

Tiryns

In Greek mythology, an important city situated a few miles southeast of Argos (in the northeastern Peloponnesus), about a mile from the Aegean coast. According to legend, Tiryns was built by Proetus, brother of Acrisius, a king of nearby Mycenae. Proetus was said to have hired a group of Cyclopes (one-eyed giants) to lift the enormous stones making up the citadel's imposing walls. The hero Perseus (who slew the Gorgon Medusa) was one of Tiryns's later kings, as was Eurystheus, who sent the renowned strongman Heracles out to perform twelve superhuman labors. The real Tiryns was the site of an important Bronze Age fortress erected by Mycenaean warlords. **See** Mycenae; **also** Eurystheus; Proetus (Chapter 1); Cyclops (Chapter 3); The Adventures of Heracles; Perseus and Medusa (Chapter 6).

Troad

(or Troas) The region encompassing northwestern Asia Minor and bordering the southern shore of the Hellespont strait. The main town of the Troad was Troy, lying just a few miles south of the Hellespont. **See** Asia Minor; Troy.

Trojan Horse

(or Wooden Horse) A huge hollow horse constructed by the Greeks in the tenth year of their siege of Troy at the suggestion of the wily Odysseus (king of Ithaca). The Greek army sailed away, leaving the horse standing on the plain in front of the city. Subsequently, the Trojans, who thought that the Greeks had given up the siege and left the object as a gift for the goddess Athena, dragged it into the city, not realizing that a band of Greek soldiers was hiding inside. Later that night, the men climbed out of the horse and opened the city's gates for the rest of their army, which had returned under cover of darkness. This incident is the origin of the famous saying: "Beware of Greeks bearing gifts." **See** Laocoön (Chapter 1); **also** Aeneas's Journey to Italy; The Trojan War (Chapter 6).

Trojan War

The renowned ten-year-long siege of the city of Troy (in northwestern Asia Minor) by a group of Greek kings led by Agamemnon, ruler of Mycenae. The ancient Greeks looked on the Trojan War as the single-most-important event in their history. **See** Troy; **also** Achilles; Aeneas; Agamemnon; Hector; Helen; Menelaus; Paris; Priam (Chapter 1); Athena (Chapter 2); Homer; *Iliad* (Chapter 5); and, for a complete account of the events of the fateful conflict, **see** The Trojan War (Chapter 6).

Troy

(or Ilium) The famous city besieged by the Greeks in the legendary Trojan War; Troy was located on the coast of northwestern Asia Minor near the Hellespont. The siege,

conducted by the kings of many Greek states, lasted ten years and ended with the city's destruction. A number of ancient epic poems described different aspects of the war, the most famous (and the only surviving one) being Homer's *Iliad,* about the wrath of the Greek warrior Achilles during the last year of the fighting.

Until the mid–nineteenth century, most modern scholars assumed that Homer's Troy and the war he described were purely fanciful. But beginning in the 1870s, German archaeologist Heinrich Schliemann unearthed Troy, showing that it was indeed a real city in the Bronze Age. He uncovered a series of cities built on top of one another and came to believe that the sixth city from the bottom was Homer's Troy. Since Schliemann's time, however, the consensus of archaeologists has shifted. More recent evidence shows that the city now labeled Troy VIIa underwent a siege about 1220 B.C., the approximate period the mythical Trojan War supposedly occurred. Scholars are still not certain, however, that this siege was the one Homer described. For a detailed account of the siege and the events leading up to it, **see** The Trojan War (Chapter 6).

Underworld

In Greco-Roman religion and mythology, the realm of the dead, thought to lie deep under the earth's surface. The ruler of the Underworld was Zeus's brother Hades (whom the Romans called Dis or Pluto), a deity seen as grim and strict, though not evil or unjust. According to tradition, after people died the god Hermes (or, in some stories, Thanatos, god of death) led their souls (called shades) to the outer edge of the Underworld. Marking the boundary was the Styx, "the Appalling River," or "River of Unbreakable Oaths." (Some ancient accounts said that the boundary was marked by a different river, the Acheron, "the River of Woe," and that the Styx lay somewhere else in the Underworld. Other rivers flowing through Hades' realm included the Coctys, or "River of Lamentation"; the Phlegethon, or "River of Fire"; and the Lethe, or "River of Forgetfulness.")

Having reached the Styx (or Acheron), the shades encountered the ghastly boatman Charon, who ferried them across the dark waters. Along the way, they passed the hideous three-headed dog Cerberus, who prevented anyone from trying to escape. On the far side of the river, the shades came before the three judges of the dead—Minos, Rhadamanthys, and Aeacus. Their powers and the exact nature of their judgments are uncertain; apparently they carried little weight, since the vast majority of shades went on to share the same fate—to dwell for eternity on the Plain of Asphodel. As described by ancient writers, this was a dreary, monotonous region where the shades wandered aimlessly.

A few more fortunate individuals—usually famous heroes or kings—ended up in Elysium (or the Islands of the Blessed), a comfortable, happy place featuring sunlight, good food, and companionship. At the same time, a small number of wicked individuals, along with various human and monstrous enemies of the gods, spent eternity in Tartarus, the Underworld's lowest region. Tartarus was dark, gloomy, and filled with despair. There, the hundred-handed giants guarded the Titans, whom Zeus had hurled down into the depths. There, too, a few shades whose deeds the gods viewed as particularly bad suffered endless tortures. When the hero Odysseus visited the Underworld, he saw the pitiful fate of one such fellow, Sisyphus, who had managed to cheat Thanatos and gain some extra years of life. "I witnessed the tortures of Sisyphus," Odysseus recalled (according to Homer),

as he tackled his huge rock with both hands. Leaning against it with his arms and thrusting with his legs, he would attempt to push the boulder up-hill to the top. But every time, as he was going to send it toppling over the crest [of the hill], its sheer weight turned it back, and the misbegotten rock came bounding down again to level ground. So once more he had to wrestle with the thing and push it up, while the sweat poured from his limbs and the dust rose high above his head. (*Odyssey* 11.564–571)

See Elysium; shade; **also** Sisyphus (Chapter 1); Charon; Hades; Persephone; Thanatos (Chapter 2); Cerberus.

CHAPTER 5
MAJOR MYTH TELLERS AND THEIR WORKS

Aeneid

The greatest Roman epic poem, composed in Latin between 29 and 19 B.C. by the poet Virgil. In twelve books, the *Aeneid* tells the story of the Trojan prince Aeneas, Rome's national hero and the founder of the Roman race, who escaped the burning Troy and journeyed across the Mediterranean Sea to Italy. The author intended for the work to celebrate Rome's origins and achievements as well as to glorify the person and accomplishments of his friend, Augustus, the first Roman emperor. Virgil had not quite finished the poem when he died in 19 B.C., and his colleagues, Varius Rufus and Plotius Tucca, edited it on his behalf.

The work is notable not only for the skill and nobility of the writing but also for its unapologetic conception of the Romans as having a divine destiny to rule the world. Virgil portrays all of Roman history as a continuous narrative leading up to a preordained and inevitable outcome: the accession of Augustus, the "child of the Divine," and the advent of the Roman Empire, which will lead the world into a golden age of peace and prosperity. As historian R.H. Barrow puts it (in *The Romans*),

> The most significant movement of history . . . according to Virgil, is the march of the Roman along the road of his destiny to a high civilization; for in that destiny is to be found the valid and permanent interpretation of all [human] movement and all development. . . . The stately *Aeneid* progresses throughout its length to this theme, the universal and the ultimate triumph of the Roman spirit as the highest manifestation of man's powers.

Virgil begins Aeneas's epic story seven years after the sacking of Troy by the Greeks. Aeneas and his followers are in Sicily (off the coast of Italy) and are about to leave when the goddess Juno, who supported the Greeks during the Trojan War, causes a huge storm to blow up. Some of Aeneas's ships sink, and the rest beach in North Africa. The goddess Venus, Aeneas's mother, appears and informs her son that he is in the land of Carthage, ruled by Queen Dido, who was born in the Phoenician city of Tyre. Aeneas meets Dido, and Venus makes the queen fall in love with him.

After a banquet in the palace, Dido asks Aeneas to tell of his adventures during the preceding seven years. He begins by describing how the Greeks built a huge wooden horse and left it on the plain in front of Troy. Thinking it was an offering for the goddess Minerva (the Greek Athena), the Trojans dragged the horse into their city; but in the middle of the night, some Greeks who had been hiding in the horse crawled out and opened the city's gates for their army. Aeneas awoke to see the city in flames. He gathered his father, Anchises; wife, Creusa; and son, Ascanius; and fled. Unfortunately, in the confusion Creusa got separated from the others and was killed.

Aeneas led a group of Trojan survivors to Thrace (in northern Greece); but that land proved to be too dangerous, so they sailed on to the tiny Aegean island of Delos. There, they prayed at the shrine of the god Apollo, who told them to seek out their motherland, where Aeneas would become the founder of a great race of people. The group sailed to Crete, thinking that it might be the motherland of which Apollo had spoken. But some gods appeared to Aeneas in a dream and informed him that the land he sought was Italy, far to the west.

Next, Aeneas and his followers landed in Epirus (in northwestern Greece), where they were glad to find another Trojan prince, Helenus, ruling the local people. Helenus, who had the gift of prophecy, told Aeneas to establish a city on Italy's western coast. From Epirus, the Trojan band sailed westward, passing the large, ominous volcano Mt. Etna in Sicily. Then, looking for supplies, they landed on an island that turned out to be inhabited by Cyclopes (one-eyed giants), who attacked them. Barely escaping with their lives, the refugees made it to a bay in northern Sicily. Aeneas's father, old Anchises, died there; and it was when Aeneas had given the order for the journey to resume that Juno's storm had struck and blown the party to Carthage.

Having heard Aeneas's story, Dido resolves to marry the handsome young Trojan. The two spend many weeks together, during which time Dido confesses her love for him and he returns her feelings. But Jupiter, ruler of the gods, does not want Aeneas to spend the rest of his life in Carthage, so he sends his messenger, Mercury, to remind Aeneas of his duty to reach Italy and fulfill his destiny. Dido begs Aeneas to stay. However, he decides to leave and she is so crushed that she takes her own life.

After another stop in Sicily, where a fire almost destroys his ships, Aeneas at last makes it to Italy, landing at Cumae, on the southwestern coast. There, the Trojan seeks out the Sibyl, a local prophetess. She tells him that he will not be able to fulfill his destiny and establish a kingdom until he has fought a destructive war and faced a warrior as formidable as the Greek Achilles. The Sibyl then leads Aeneas into the Underworld, where he visits with the shade of his dead father, Anchises. After greeting his son, Anchises reveals to him the long line of illustrious descendants he will sire.

Moving on, Aeneas and his followers land at the mouth of the Tiber River. They soon meet Latinus, king of Latium, the region south of the river; and the old man offers Aeneas an alliance and the hand of his daughter, Lavinia, in marriage. Unfortunately, the young woman has already been promised to Turnus, prince of another Italian people, the Rutulians. Seeing an opportunity to thwart Aeneas again, Juno fills Turnus's heart with jealousy, and the result is war. Turnus attacks the Trojan camp and also tries to burn Aeneas's ships. More battles ensue. Eventually Aeneas enlists the aid of Evander, ruler of a settlement on the future site of Rome and an Etruscan king; these combined forces rout Turnus's army, forcing him to flee.

Hoping to end the war without further unneeded bloodshed, Aeneas challenges Turnus to single combat. At first, Turnus chooses to resume full-scale war; but when it becomes certain that his forces will lose, he accepts Aeneas's challenge. The two men fight, and Aeneas, wearing magnificent armor made for him by the god Vulcan, is victorious. Thus ends Virgil's *Aeneid*. Other ancient writers told how Aeneas went on to marry Lavinia and establish a new city named after her—Lavinium; and how his son, Ascanius, founded his own city, Alba Longa, which would later give rise to Romulus, founder of Rome. For a more detailed overview of the story told in the *Aeneid,* **see** Aeneas's Journey to Italy (Chapter 6).

Aeschylus

(ca. 525–456 B.C.) One of the four masters of fifth-century B.C. Athenian drama and the world's first great playwright. Aeschylus was born at Eleusis (twelve miles west of Athens) to a well-to-do family. He fought in the Battle of Marathon in 490 B.C., where his brother, Cynegirus, was one of the 192 Athenian casualties. He also fought in the great naval battle at Salamis a decade later, which he describes vividly in his play *The Persians,* produced in 472 B.C. This is the only one of his seven surviving plays (out of the eighty to ninety he is said to have written) that deals with nonmythological events.

An engraving of a bust of Aeschylus, the first great dramatist of the Western world.

Of the other six extant works, of special note is the *Oresteia* (458 B.C.), a trilogy comprising *Agamemnon,* the *Libation Bearers* (*Choephoroe*), and the *Eumenides,* dealing with the terrible curse of the house of Atreus. Aeschylus's other surviving plays are *Seven Against Thebes* (467 B.C.), *The Suppliant Women* (ca. 463 B.C.), and *Prometheus Bound* (ca. 460 B.C.). Besides the innovation of the trilogy, Aeschylus introduced the convention of a second actor, thereby expanding the storytelling possibilities of drama. (Before his time, a single actor played all of the main roles, using a different mask for each character.) His writing, rich in metaphors and striking imagery, has frequently been cited for its grandeur. **See** *Agamemnon; Eumenides; Libation Bearers; Prometheus Bound; Seven Against Thebes; The Suppliant Women.*

Agamemnon

A play by Aeschylus, the first in his monumental trilogy the *Oresteia* (written in 458 B.C.). The play opens on an optimistic note, as the watchman atop Agamemnon's palace at Argos (used interchangeably with Mycenae in various myths) watches for a signal beacon announcing that the Greeks have been victorious over the Trojans. When the signal comes, Agamemnon's queen, Clytemnestra, is glad; but then the local elders (who make up the chorus in the play) remind her that her husband sacrificed their daughter, Iphigenia, ten years before in order to acquire a favorable wind for his ships to sail for Troy. Clytemnestra now decides that her husband must die.

When Agamemnon arrives at his palace after an absence of ten years, he is accompanied by the Trojan princess Cassandra, whom he has made his concubine. Because Cassandra has the gift of prophecy, she foresees the king's murder, as well as her own, at the hands of Clytemnestra and the queen's lover, Aegisthus. These murders take place. When the elders of the city see what has happened, the queen justifies her act by citing her slain daughter, Iphigenia, and Aegisthus keeps the elders at bay with threats of violence. The play ends with the elders hoping that Agamemnon's son, Orestes, will manage to avenge the murders. **See** Aeschylus; **also** Aegisthus; Agamemnon; Cassandra; Clytemnestra (Chapter 1); The Curse of the House of Atreus (Chapter 6).

Ajax

The first of Sophocles' seven surviving tragedies, first presented circa 447 B.C. In this play, Sophocles explores the changes in personal and ethical codes that had occurred in the transition from the primitive society of the legendary Trojan War era to his own society. The title character, along with Achilles, Odysseus, and the other Greek generals who laid siege to Troy, are larger-than-life, heroic, yet aristocratic, arrogant, and self-serving figures who totally dominate their respective communities. They would have been very out of place in the more democratic city-states of Sophocles' time, in which each citizen, no matter how poor his origins, was viewed as worthy.

The legendary events leading up to the beginning of the play took place near the end of the long siege of Troy and shortly after the death of Achilles, the mightiest of the Greek leaders. The other generals vied for his weapons and armor, and Ajax (son of Telamon), recognized as the second mightiest of their number, laid the strongest claim. But the shrewd Odysseus was awarded the prizes instead, after which the enraged Ajax vowed to get revenge on all concerned.

In the play's opening scene, the goddess Athena tells Odysseus how she thwarted Ajax from killing the other Greek leaders by afflicting him with temporary madness; in this state, he mistook a herd of cows for his enemies and slaughtered the beasts. Now the mighty hero, having realized his mistake, sits mortified and contemplating suicide in his tent. In the course of the play, he recog-

nizes that his world is changing, that soon there will no longer be room for heroic but vain, ignorant, and ultimately destructive men like himself. And so, bemoaning the ravages of time and fate, he eventually falls on his sword. Menelaus, king of Sparta, says that Ajax's body should be left unburied (a fate the ancient Greeks viewed as extreme and barbaric); and Agamemnon, leader of the Greek expedition to Troy, agrees. However, Odysseus persuades his comrades to give Ajax a proper funeral, and the play ends with the Greeks bearing the great warrior's body toward his grave. **See** Agamemnon; Ajax 1; Odysseus (Chapter 1); **also** The Trojan War (Chapter 6).

Alcestis

The earliest surviving play of Euripides, composed in 438 B.C. In the events leading up to the play's opening, the god Apollo helped Admetus, king of Pherae (in Thessaly), win the hand of Alcestis, a princess of a neighboring city. The god also granted Admetus the privilege of escaping death as long as he could find another mortal who would willingly take his place when it was time for him to die. When that time came, Admetus's loving wife, Alcestis, offered to die in her husband's place.

The play opens with Apollo and Thanatos (god of death) discussing Alcestis's impending death. Apollo implores Thanatos to allow the faithful and loving young woman to live, but Thanatos insists that nothing can stop him from executing his grim and necessary duty. Then Apollo, who is able to see into the future, warns the other deity that someone is on the way to Pherae who can and will stop Thanatos from taking Alcestis. The confident god of death merely laughs at this suggestion, after which Alcestis dies.

A few hours later the renowned hero Heracles arrives in Pherae on his way northward toward Thrace to perform one of his twelve labors. The strongman is surprised to see the outside of the palace deserted and to hear loud lamentations coming from inside. Soon, a servant reveals the sad circumstances of Alcestis's death. Meanwhile, Admetus, though deeply mourning his wife, insists on extending the visitor hospitality. All this is too much for the big-hearted Heracles, who takes it upon himself to stop Thanatos from taking Alcestis to the Underworld. The hero lies in wait near Alcestis's body, and soon the god of death appears, wearing a black robe and carrying a sword. Heracles leaps out, seizes the ghastly figure, and a terrific struggle ensues. Eventually the man is victorious and Thanatos withdraws.

Not long afterward, Admetus is surprised to see Heracles approaching, followed by a woman whose face is veiled. Heracles says that Admetus should accept into his home the woman he has brought. But Admetus refuses, saying that no woman, no matter how beautiful or wonderful, could take the place of his beloved Alcestis. Then the strongman reveals that the woman is none other than Alcestis herself, restored to life. Thus, an otherwise sad and serious story ends on a happy note, thanks to the generosity and courage of Greece's greatest hero. **See** Euripides; **also** Admetus; Alcestis (Chapter 1); Thanatos (Chapter 2); The Adventures of Heracles (Chapter 6).

Andromache

A play by Euripides, written and first performed in about 426 B.C. Andromache had been the wife of the Trojan hero Hector, whom the Greek hero Achilles had slain in the Trojan War. After Troy's fall, Andromache's young son, Astyanax, was thrown from the city's walls and Achilles' son, Neoptolemus, took Andromache back to Thessaly as his concubine (mistress).

The play begins in Thessaly ten years after Andromache bore Neoptolemus a son—Molossus. The king has grown tired of his concubine and decides to marry Hermione, daughter of Sparta's King Menelaus. Hermione is childless and mis-

takenly suspects that Andromache, of whom she is jealous, has caused this condition by using some kind of black magic. While Neoptolemus is away visiting Delphi, Andromache, fearing for her life, seeks sanctuary at the shrine of the goddess Thetis (Achilles' mother); but Hermione and her father seize and threaten to kill Molossus in an attempt to force Andromache to leave the shrine (fully intending to kill both mother and son at the same time).

But this murderous scheme is foiled by the aged Peleus (father of Achilles and the grandson of Neoptolemus). Moreover, Orestes (who has succeeded his dead father, Agamemnon, as king of Mycenae and Argos) arrives from Delphi and announces that he has just slain Neoptolemus. Orestes had originally been betrothed to Hermione, and now, with Neoptolemus out of the way, he reclaims her. To make sure that all is in order, the goddess Thetis suddenly appears. She ordains that Andromache and Molossus will be properly cared for as the wife and son of the Trojan prince Helenus, whom Neoptolemus had granted a small kingdom in northwestern Greece. **See** Euripides; **also** Andromache; Helenus; Neoptolemus (Chapter 1); Thetis (Chapter 2).

Antigone

A play by Sophocles (written ca. 441 B.C.), one of his three plays dealing with the Oedipus cycle of myths (although the events depicted in *Antigone* occur, chronologically speaking, well after those of the other two works—*Oedipus the King* and *Oedipus at Colonus*). In the background events of *Antigone,* Oedipus abdicated the throne of Thebes after discovering that he had killed his father and married his mother. His sons, Polynices and Eteocles, later agreed to share power, each to rule in alternate years. But at the end of his first term, Eteocles refused to surrender the throne. Polynices retaliated by enlisting the aid of Adrastus, king of Argos, and five other champions, and attacking Thebes. But the so-called Seven Against Thebes failed to take the city. Eteocles and Polynices engaged in single combat and killed each other, and Creon (Eteocles and Polynices' uncle), having succeeded to the throne, forbade anyone from burying Polynices' body. (The ancient Greeks, who were extremely concerned with proper burial rites, considered such a decree to be cruel and barbaric.)

As the play begins, Polynices' sister Antigone feels she should defy Creon and try to bury her brother's body. She attempts to get her sister, Ismene, to help. But Ismene is too afraid, so Antigone decides to complete the task alone. Later, a guard informs Creon that he has found Polynices' body covered with dust and dry earth (a symbolic burial), which means that someone has disobeyed the king's order to leave the body unburied. The angry Creon has his guards remove the dust from the body; Antigone returns to perform the burial rites again, only to be caught in the act and brought before Creon. He condemns her, and Ismene, too, to be executed.

Having heard what has transpired, Haemon, Creon's son and Antigone's betrothed, pleads with his father to be a flexible, reasonable, and just ruler and let the sisters go. But Creon refuses to listen to this entreaty, and the father and son have violent words before Haemon storms out. The Theban elders (who make up the play's chorus) ask Creon if he intends to kill Ismene as well as Antigone. Admitting that he may have gone too far in condemning Antigone's sister, Creon says that he will spare Ismene. But he will see that Antigone is shut up in a cave until she dies.

Creon soon encounters Tiresias, the blind Theban seer who had earlier foreseen that Oedipus was guilty of terrible crimes. Tiresias warns Creon that the gods are angry with Thebes and its ruler for leaving bodies unburied and that Creon will end up paying a heavy price for mis-

treating Polynices' corpse. Considering the old man's words, Creon has a change of heart and decides both to give Polynices a proper funeral and to release Antigone. But the king is too late. Reaching the cave, he finds his son, Haemon, with Antigone's dead body. The young woman has hanged herself and now, before Creon's horrified eyes, Haemon also commits suicide. The king's grief is further compounded when, carrying his son's body, he returns to the palace and there, the queen, Eurydice, having heard the tragic news of Antigone's and Haemon's deaths, takes her own life.

Here, Sophocles touched a nerve that fascinated and moved his audiences. The core of the play was the dramatic confrontation between the laws enacted by state and society and those larger and more eternal natural laws that are the birthright of all human beings. Through the spectacle of Antigone's courage and sacrifice, the playwright seemed to be saying that even though Creon was king, he had no right to deny another person certain fundamental elements of human dignity. Indeed, *Antigone* stands as one of Western literature's greatest hymns to human worth and dignity, as well as a call for governments to honor these qualities with justice. "Wonders there are many," sings the play's chorus,

> but none more wonderful than human beings. . . . Speech and wind-swift thought, and all the moods that create a community, they have taught themselves. . . . Cunning beyond the wildest of dreams is the skill that leads them, sometimes to evil, other times to good. As long as they honor the laws of the land and revere the justice of the gods, proudly their community will stand. (*Antigone* 368–406)

See Sophocles; *Seven Against Thebes;* **also** Antigone; Creon 2; Polynices; Tiresias (Chapter 1); The Theban Myth Cycle (Chapter 6).

Apollodorus of Athens

(born ca. 180 B.C.) A noted Greek scholar who studied at the Museum, the famous Greek university in Alexandria, before settling permanently in Athens in 146 B.C. Apollodorus is best known for the *Chronicle,* a historical work covering important events from the fall of Troy (thought by the Greeks to have occurred in 1184 B.C.) to 144 B.C.; and for a treatise titled *On the Gods,* describing the various deities and their worship. Unfortunately, only fragments of these works have survived.

Apollodorus was also credited with composing *The Library,* an encyclopedia-like compendium of Greek mythology. Modern scholars believe that the version of the work that has survived (about half in the original, the rest in a summary by a later writer) is not the one written by Apollodorus; still, whomever the real author may have been, the work remains a valuable supplement to the writings of Homer, Hesiod, Ovid, and other Greek and Roman writers who recorded myths.

Apollonius of Rhodes

(ca. 295–215 B.C.) A Greek poet and scholar who served as director of the great library at Alexandria before retiring to the island of Rhodes (off the southwestern coast of Asia Minor). The date and place of the poet's death are unknown. Apollonius is most famous for his epic poem the *Argonautica* (*Voyage of the Argo*). His production of such a large-scale work supposedly caused, or at least worsened, a feud he reportedly had with his older colleague, Callimachus. The latter wrote over eight hundred volumes himself; however, all of these were likely very short compared to Apollonius's epic since Callimachus was famous for his remark, "A big book is a big evil." Callimachus evidently deemed epic poetry, along with Apollonius and others who wrote it, to be outdated. **See** *Argonautica* 1.

Apuleius, Lucius

(mid–second century A.D.) The Roman author of *The Golden Ass* (or *Metamorphoses*), the only complete surviving Latin novel. Apuleius was born in North Africa. After he married, his wife's relatives sued him, charging that he had used magic to seduce her. In his *Apologia* (which has survived), a speech in his own defense, he insisted that he was innocent and was duly acquitted. Thereafter, he traveled around North Africa lecturing and writing about philosophy. His most famous and enduring work, however, was *The Golden Ass,* a fantastic romance about a man who is transformed into a donkey. **See** *The Golden Ass.*

Argonautica

1. Apollonius of Rhodes's epic poem about Jason's quest for the fabulous Golden Fleece and his love affair with the sorceress Medea, the only complete account of the story that has survived. The work had a strong influence on later poets, most notably the Roman Virgil, in part because it was the first classical work to portray romantic love from a woman's point of view. In book 3 of the *Argonautica,* Medea has such strong feelings for Jason that she is willing to turn against her own father; and Apollonius presents her predicament in a sympathetic manner. Similarly, in book 4 of the *Aeneid,* Virgil sensitively and beautifully captures the anguish suffered by Dido (queen of Carthage) when her lover, Aeneas, decides to leave her.

Apollonius's *Argonautica* consists of four books, the first of which describes the Argonauts' preparations for the voyage to faraway Colchis and departure from the Aegean coast of Thessaly. The second book tells about the various adventures Jason and his men encounter on their way to Colchis, including their meeting with Phineus, a starving old man plagued by the Harpies, and a harrowing passage through the Symplegades (Clashing Rocks) at the north end of the Bosphorus Strait. The third book of the *Argonautica* takes place in Colchis, where Jason meets Medea; outmaneuvers her father, King Aeetes; and captures the Golden Fleece. Finally, the fourth book tells of the homeward voyage, during which the travelers encounter Talos, the bronze giant who guards the coastline of Crete. **See** *Aeneid;* Apollonius of Rhodes; Virgil; **also** Harpy; Symplegades; Talos (Chapter 3); and, for a detailed account of the story told in Apollonius's epic, **see** The Quest for the Golden Fleece (Chapter 6).

2. A Latin epic poem, composed sometime in the late first century A.D. by the Roman writer Gaius Valerius Flaccus. The author dedicated the work to the emperor Vespasian (reigned A.D. 69–79) and borrowed a great deal of the material from the epic of the same title written by the Greek poet Apollonius of Rhodes more than two centuries before. In style and tone, Valerius's *Argonautica* is clearly modeled on Virgil's *Aeneid,* another epic containing a prominent female character (Dido), although Valerius's Medea is not as strong and passionate as Virgil's Dido. Nevertheless, Valerius develops Medea's character well and, like both Apollonius and Virgil, succeeds in creating considerable sympathy for his female lead. Unlike Virgil's great masterwork, Valerius's epic was lost and forgotten until 1417, when the first half of the work came to light in an Italian monastery.

Though well written, Valerius's *Argonautica* is not nearly as comprehensive as that of Apollonius. The Latin epic consists of eight books, the first four of which deal with the voyage to Colchis to find the Golden Fleece. Valerius includes many, though not all, of the episodes Apollonius does, including the loss of Hercules' (Heracles') friend Hylas and the famous strongman's decision to depart the expedition to search for him. Most of the remaining books take place in Colchis and deal with Jason's relationship with Medea

and their acquisition of the fleece. Then the narrative suddenly breaks off, leaving Jason wondering if Medea, who has betrayed her own father for him, can be trusted. **See** *Aeneid;* Apollonius of Rhodes; Valerius Flaccus, Gaius; Virgil; and, for a detailed account of the story told in Valerius's epic, **see** The Quest for the Golden Fleece (Chapter 6).

Aristophanes

(ca. 445–ca. 385 B.C.) One of the four masters of fifth-century B.C. Athenian drama and the greatest comic playwright of the age. Almost nothing is known about his personal life. Of the thirty-two plays attributed to him, eleven survive complete and some fragments of a few others exist. The eleven complete plays are *Acharnians* (425 B.C.), *Knights* (424), *Clouds* (423), *Wasps* (422), *Peace* (421), *Birds* (414), *Lysistrata* (411), *Women Celebrating the Thesmophoria* (411), *Frogs* (405), *Women in the Assembly* (392), and *Plutus* (382). Aristophanes' plays, which mark the height of the Athenian Old Comedy

One of the many fanciful depictions of the comic playwright Aristophanes, whose works poked fun at society and politicians.

(roughly encompassing the second half of the fifth century B.C.), are fanciful, witty, bitingly satiric, and frequently poke fun at the government and leading politicians and military leaders. One of the most admired and widely performed today is *Lysistrata*, an antiwar statement in which the Athenian women stage a sex strike to persuade their husbands to make peace.

Though many of Aristophanes' themes and characters were current and topical, as in *Lysistrata,* a good many were borrowed from mythology, almost always with the intention of poking fun at serious subjects or current politics. The messenger god, Hermes, is a character in *Peace,* for instance; and Poseidon (ruler of the seas), Iris (goddess of the rainbow), and the famous strongman Heracles appear in *Birds.*

The way Aristophanes used such mythological characters is well illustrated in his *Frogs,* which contains many such characters, including Heracles, Dionysus (god of fertility, wine, and ecstasy as well as patron god of tragedy), Aeacus (one of the three judges of the dead in the Underworld), Charon (the boatman who ferried the dead across the River Styx), and Pluto (or Hades, ruler of the Underworld). Dionysus, portrayed as a weak, arrogant, foolish individual (as the playwright felt many Athenians had become), wants to go to the Underworld and resurrect the playwright Euripides, who recently died. Only a poet of his stature (Dionysus says) has the wisdom to advise the Athenians how to end the long war they have been fighting (the devastating Peloponnesian War against Sparta) and save their city.

Disguised as the strongman Heracles, Dionysus descends into the Underworld and climbs into Charon's boat; Charon calls him "fatso" (a reference to common ancient depictions of Dionysus as loving to eat and drink) and makes him row the boat himself. A chorus of frogs (from which the play takes its title) provides a steady beat for Dionysus to row to "Brekekekex ko-ax ko-ax, Brekekekex ko-ax ko-ax," and so forth. The rower quickly tires, complains that "my rear end is aching," and hurls insults at the frogs; but soon he picks up their chant and threatens "to croak away if it takes all day" to make them go away (which they do). (*Frogs* 304–372) Then Dionysus meets Aeacus, who mistakes him for Heracles (because of his attire) and abuses and threatens him (because Aeacus is angry with Heracles for making off with Cerberus, watchdog of the Underworld, to fulfill one of his twelve labors).

Eventually Dionysus encounters the spirits of Euripides and Aeschylus, who have a contest to decide which one of them is the better poet. (Sophocles does not get involved because he is too much of a gentleman.) Finally, Dionysus, who is judging the contest, chooses Aeschylus the winner and prepares to escort him out of the Underworld. Pluto sadly says farewell to the poet, wishing him good luck in saving Athens.

Through such humorous, often silly episodes, set in the usually serious and solemn mythological realm of the dead, Aristophanes made the members of his audience laugh; but he also forced them to think about how desperate for direction and sound leadership the once great city of Athens had become after more than twenty-five years of war. **See** Aeschylus; *Birds;* Euripides; **also** Aeacus (Chapter 1); Charon; Dionysus (Chapter 2).

Aristotle

(384–322 B.C.) One of the greatest scholars and philosophers of the ancient world, who had a tremendous impact on the subsequent development of philosophy, science, and knowledge in general. Aristotle's interests and research were phenomenally wide-ranging; he made detailed, logical, and sometimes profound written observations in every major branch of learning; and his ideas, as well as his efforts to collect and systematize knowledge, had a profound influence on scholars in the Renaissance and early modern era.

Aristotle was born in 384 B.C. at Stagira (on the Chalcidic peninsula on the northern Aegean coast), the son of Nicomachus, physician to King Amyntas II of Macedonia. In 367 B.C., at age seventeen, Aristotle journeyed to Athens and enrolled in Plato's Academy, where the young man lived and studied for the next twenty years. When Plato died in 347, Aristotle left Athens, settled for a time in northwestern Asia Minor, and then moved to the island of Lesbos. In 343 King Philip II asked Aristotle to come to Macedonia to tutor the crown prince, Alexander. The philosopher took the job and stayed there until 336, when Philip was assassinated and Alexander ascended the throne. Aristotle then returned to Athens, where he soon established his own school, the Lyceum.

Regularly utilizing the Lyceum's steadily growing library and zoo, during the next twelve years Aristotle produced the bulk of his important writings. Of these, almost all that were published for public consumption are lost. The large corpus of Aristotle's surviving works consists mainly of his notes, rough drafts of his lectures, and notations made of his lectures by his students. Though dry and formal, these works have served the vital function of transmitting his main ideas to later ages.

When Alexander died in faraway Babylon in 323 B.C., a wave of anti-Macedonian feeling swept through Greece; and because Aristotle had been Alexander's friend and tutor, the Athenians now looked on the philosopher as an enemy of the state. They brought him to trial, forcing him to flee northward to the island of Euboea. There, a few months later (November 322), he died at the age of sixty-two. His old friend and colleague Theophrastus succeeded him as director of the Lyceum.

Along with his huge contributions in the areas of philosophy, ethics, biology, cosmology, and logic, Aristotle provided some information about early Greek history and mythology (which at the time were more or less inseparable). Small snippets about various mythological characters and events appear in many of his surviving works, notably in his *Athenian Constitution,* composed between 328 and 325 B.C. Here, he mentions the early, legendary Athenian kings Erechtheus, Pandion, and Codrus, and tells about Theseus's reorganization of the districts of Attica into a single state. Aristotle also provides information about the semilegendary Athenian lawgivers Draco and Solon.

In addition, Aristotle discusses various mythological characters and stories in his *Poetics,* a fascinating and highly influential treatise about the origins and nature of epic poetry and Greek tragedy and comedy. Epic poetry, exemplified by Homer's *Iliad* and *Odyssey,* and tragedy, as developed by the three great early masters—Aeschylus, Sophocles, and Euripides— were important sources of Greek (and later Roman) myths; and Aristotle illuminates the probable manner in which human poets began to record these myths. Tragedy, he says,

> certainly began in improvisations [spontaneous creations] . . . originating with the authors of the dithyramb [verse stories told during religious ceremonies] . . . which still survive . . . in many of our cities. And its advance [evolution into the art of drama] after that was little by little, through their improving on whatever they had before them at each stage. It was, in fact, only after a long series of changes that the development of tragedy stopped on attaining its natural [best] form [i.e., the form it had in the years just prior to and during Aristotle's lifetime]. (*Poetics* 4.10–15)

Aristotle also asserts that myth tellers, in this case tragic playwrights and other poets, need to concentrate on making their

still physically and morally superior to average men]. (*Poetics* 15.9–15)

See Aeschylus; Euripides; Sophocles; **also** The Exploits of Theseus (Chapter 6).

The Bacchae

A play by Euripides, likely first performed in 405 B.C., about a year after the playwright's death. Before the play begins, Zeus, ruler of the gods, had impregnated Semele, daughter of Thebes's founder, Cadmus. The baby in her womb would later become the fertility god, Dionysus. Due to the intervention of Zeus's jealous wife, Hera, Zeus accidentally burned Semele to death; but he managed to rescue her child, who had become immortal.

The play begins several years later, when Dionysus, now a young man, arrives in Thebes to find that Pentheus, son of Semele's sister, Agave, is now king of Thebes (having succeeded his grandfather, Cadmus, who still lives). Disguising himself as an ordinary mortal, Dionysus observes, to his dismay, that Pentheus has banned worship of the god in the region of Thebes.

Disturbed and angry, Dionysus retaliates by causing an earthquake to destroy Pentheus's palace; the god also makes the city's women, including his aunt, Agave, go mad and wander through the countryside in a frenzied trance. When Pentheus learns what has happened to the Theban women, he is distraught. Pretending to help him, Dionysus, still in disguise, suggests that the king dress up like a woman and go out into the countryside to observe the phenomenon firsthand. Pentheus does

In his works, the Athenian scholar-philosopher Aristotle explored the origins of mythology and tragedy.

characters larger-than-life and morally superior to ordinary humans, for that is the inherent nature of these mythical characters and their deeds. "As tragedy is an imitation of people better than the ordinary man," he says,

> we in our way should follow the example of good portrait-painters, who reproduce the distinctive features of a man, and at the same time, without losing the likeness, make him handsomer than he is. The poet, in a like manner, in portraying men quick or slow to anger . . . must know how to represent them as such, and at the same time as good men, as . . . Homer has represented Achilles [who, despite the faults he displays in the *Iliad*, is

so; but just as the god had hoped, the crazed women perceive the king as some kind of wild beast, and they hunt him down and tear him to pieces. When Agave recovers from her madness, she discovers that she has killed her own son. She, Cadmus, and the other remaining members of Cadmus's family are banned from Thebes.

The author expresses the moral of the story—the formidable power of Dionysus and heavy penalty for obstructing him—in the following exchange from the last scene, in which the god finally reveals his true identity:

> DIONYSUS: If you all had chosen wisdom . . . you would have found the son of Zeus your friend, and you would now be happy.
>
> CADMUS: Dionysus have mercy on us; we have sinned.
>
> DIONYSUS: You recognize me too late; when you should have known me, you did not.
>
> CADMUS: All this we have realized; but your vengeance is too heavy.
>
> DIONYSUS: I am a god; and you insulted me.
>
> CADMUS: Gods should not be like men, keeping anger forever.
>
> DIONYSUS: Zeus, my father, ordained this from the beginning. (*Bacchae* 1341–1348)

See Euripides; **also** Cadmus (Chapter 1); Dionysus (Chapter 2); The Theban Myth Cycle (Chapter 6).

Bacchylides

(early fifth century B.C.) A noted lyric poet and the nephew of the poet Simonides. Bacchylides hailed from the Aegean island of Ceos, but he also worked in Thessaly, Macedonia, Sicily, and the Peloponnesus. His poetry survived only in fragments until the late 1800s, when some papyrus rolls bearing twenty-one complete poems were discovered. These include fifteen odes honoring victorious athletes, most using myths as background themes to add liter-

ary substance to the material. (The poet appears to have been a major rival of his contemporary Pindar, the master in this genre.) Bacchylides also wrote dithyrambs, hymns, patriotic songs, and other kinds of lyrics, several of which cite mythological characters and tales. **See** Pindar.

Birds

A comedic play by Aristophanes, first performed in 414 B.C., less than a year after Athens had dispatched a huge expedition to conquer Syracuse (in Sicily); the fate of the thousands of men taking part in the adventure was still uncertain and the mood of the Athenian people was anxious. So Aristophanes wrote *Birds* as purely escapist entertainment to lighten the people's dark mood.

In the opening of the play, two Athenians—Peisetairos and Euelpides—decide that they have had enough of the complexities of city life and its many binding laws. They seek out the mythical character Tereus, a cruel king noted for his terrible mistreatment of the Greek maiden Philomela and for paying for his crimes by being turned into a bird. The two young men assume that, because Tereus flies high in the sky, he can see the various lands below and can therefore tell them where to find a simple, comfortable place to live.

When no such place becomes obvious, Peisetairos hatches the idea of uniting all of the birds and building a city floating in the sky, to be called "Cloud Cuckoo Land." For food, he suggests, the birds can intercept the smoke from sacrifices (intended to float up to and nourish the gods). At first, the birds (who make up the play's chorus) are reluctant, but they soon come around; and the two Athenians grow wings and help them erect the city.

The gods immediately notice that their sacrifices are being tampered with, of course, and they send Iris (goddess of the rainbow) to Cloud Cuckoo Land to investigate. The birds treat her rudely, arrogantly telling her that they have taken the place of the gods, and she leaves in tears to tell Zeus. Soon, various humans sprout wings and join the birds in their city, and the god Prometheus (who can fly without wings) also joins them and offers Peisetairos advice on how to negotiate with Zeus. The negotiations are made. Peisetairos is betrothed to Zeus's daughter, Basileia, and becomes leader of the gods. **See** Aristophanes; **also** Philomela and Procne (Chapter 1); Iris; Zeus (Chapter 2).

Catullus, Gaius Valerius

(ca. 84–ca. 54 B.C.) A distinguished and popular Roman poet born in Verona (in northern Italy) into a wealthy family. In about 62 B.C., Catullus journeyed to Rome and joined a circle of poets known as the *neoterics* ("moderns" or "young ones"). Eventually he fell in love with a married woman whose name was likely Clodia, but whom he referred to in twenty-five of his poems as Lesbia. They trace his relationship with her from the ardor of first infatuation to the pain of final parting, a literary model that influenced many of his successors, including the Roman poets Ovid, Propertius, and Tibullus.

Catullus's other poems cover a wide range of subjects and genres, among them friendship, political satire, and wedding songs. A number deal also with mythological subjects and characters, including the Muses (goddesses of the fine arts), Venus (goddess of love), Hymen (a divine personification of marriage), Cybele (the Phrygian mother goddess), Thetis (mother of Achilles), Theseus (the famous Athenian hero), and various nymphs. **See** Ovid.

Children of Heracles

A tragedy written by Euripides in about 430 B.C. Eurystheus, king of Argos and Tiryns, has been persecuting the Heracleidae, the children of the famous strongman Heracles, who had recently died and ascended into the realm of the gods. The Heracleidae at first sought the protection of Ceyx, king of Trachis (in southern Thessaly). But Eurystheus made war on Ceyx, forcing him to give up the young people.

As the play begins, the Heracleidae have taken refuge in Athens, where they occupy the sanctuary of Zeus. A messenger sent by Eurystheus demands that they surrender; but they refuse. Moreover, Demophon, son of the great Athenian hero Theseus and the present king of Athens, takes their side and declares war on Eurystheus.

However, after performing divination the Athenian priests say that the Heracleidae and Athenians will not be able to win the fight unless the Athenians sacrifice a high-born maiden. To spare the Athenians this burden, Macaria, one of Heracles' daughters, steps forward and volunteers to die. The sacrifice takes place, after which Eurystheus's army moves on the city. In the battle that follows, Hyllus, Heracles' eldest son, fights alongside the Athenians, as does Iolaus, a friend of the Heracleidae, who is miraculously transformed from an old man into a vigorous youth. Iolaus captures Eurystheus and brings him before Alcmena, Heracles' mother; she curses him and orders his execution. **See** Euripides; **also** Alcmena; Dorians; Eurystheus; Heracleidae (Chapter 1); The Adventures of Heracles (Chapter 6).

Cypria

An epic poem, now lost, which was part of a group of works known as the Epic Cycle, dealing with the Trojan War. The *Cypria*, credited to a poet called Stasinus of Cyprus (who probably lived in the early

600s B.C.), dealt with the events leading up to the war, including the Judgment of Paris, Paris's abduction of Helen, and the gathering of the Greek chiefs; and the war itself up to the ninth year, where Homer's *Iliad* begins. **See** Epic Cycle; *Iliad*.

Eclogues

(also *Bucolica*) Ten poems composed by the noted first-century B.C. Roman writer Virgil, mostly between 42 and 39 B.C., although two or three may have been written later. The *Eclogues,* which are usually described as pastoral (taking place in the countryside), were an immediate public success and won the author widespread critical acclaim. Virgil was the first writer to use pastoral poetry not only to entertain but also to level moral criticism at the society of his day. The first and ninth poems in the series, for example, deal with shepherds who lose their farms when the government gives the land to retiring soldiers; here, the poet expertly contrasts the beauty and innocence of the countryside with the suffering caused by war and the greed and ambition of powerful men. Later Roman poets, as well as European writers of the Renaissance (including Petrarch and Boccaccio), were strongly influenced by the *Eclogues.*

Virgil frequently referred to mythological characters and stories in the *Eclogues.* In the fifth poem, for example, two shepherds sing the praises of Daphnis, the legendary founder of pastoral poetry, who died a tragic death after being blinded by a nymph. (The eighth poem, called "The Enchantress," also deals with Daphnis.) The sixth poem consists of a song sung by the famous satyr (half man, half goat or horse) Silenus; he tells about the creation of the world and then makes passing references to numerous myths, including Prometheus's theft of fire from heaven and Zeus's punishment of the Titan, the sadness of the Argonauts at losing Hylas (Heracles' friend) during their voyage in search of the Golden Fleece, and the transformation of Scylla from a lovely maiden into a hideous monster. **See** Virgil; **also** Daphnis (Chapter 1); Scylla; Silenus (Chapter 3).

Electra

1. A tragedy by Sophocles, composed about 415 B.C., dealing with an important episode in the famous curse affecting the house of Atreus. As the play opens, Orestes (son of Agamemnon and Clytemnestra, king and queen of Mycenae) arrives in Mycenae accompanied by his best friend, Pylades, and an old man. Orestes plans to avenge the recent murder of his father by his mother; he sends the old man into the palace to tell Clytemnestra that Orestes has died in a chariot accident. The old man finds the queen yelling at Electra, Orestes' sister, whom Clytemnestra and her lover, Aegisthus, have been verbally abusing since they killed Agamemnon. Hearing the false message that Orestes is dead, Clytemnestra is happy.

But Electra is deeply stung by the news. She had hoped that he would come and avenge her father's murder; now, thinking Orestes is dead, she decides she must slay Clytemnestra and Aegisthus herself. However, she soon meets up with Orestes and Pylades and is overjoyed to find her brother alive. Orestes and Pylades then enter the queen's chambers and kill her, after which they slay Aegisthus, too. The play's chorus, made up of Mycenaean women, rejoices that Agamemnon has been avenged. **See** Sophocles; **also** Aegisthus; Clytemnestra; Electra; Orestes; Pylades (Chapter 1); Mycenae (Chapter 4); The Curse of the House of Atreus (Chapter 6).

2. A tragic play written by Euripides and first performed sometime between 417 and

413 B.C. The plot is similar to that of Sophocles' *Electra* (see above), but it differs in some details. In Euripides' version, Aegisthus forces Electra to marry a poor farmer so that she will not produce a noble son who might later claim the kingdom. Also, Electra actually helps Orestes and Pylades kill Clytemnestra (a grisly scene that takes place offstage). In the finale, the divine Dioscuri (Castor and Polydeuces) appear and say that, for slaying Clytemnestra, Orestes and Electra must be exiled from their home city; but the gods soften the blow by ordaining that Electra will marry Pylades, who will care for her; and suggesting that Orestes go to Athens to escape the wrath of the Furies, who will hound him for killing his mother. **See** Euripides; **also** Aegisthus; Clytemnestra; Dioscuri; Electra; Orestes; Pylades (Chapter 1); Furies (Chapter 3); Mycenae (Chapter 4); The Curse of the House of Atreus (Chapter 6).

Epic Cycle

A group of early Greek epic poems (excluding Homer's *Iliad* and *Odyssey*), composed in the seventh and sixth centuries B.C. and tracing mythological events from the beginning of the world until the close of the Age of Heroes (i.e., the end of the Greek Bronze Age). Of all of these works, only about 120 lines have survived; and most of what is known about their contents comes from summaries compiled by later ancient writers.

Six of the epics dealt with the events surrounding the Trojan War—more specifically, with those events Homer had not addressed in his two great epics. (Homer's *Iliad* covered only part of the ninth year of the siege of Troy, and the *Odyssey* dealt only with Odysseus's homecoming, not the homeward voyages of the other Greek leaders.) Indeed, these six works were designed to fill in the blanks, so to speak, Homer had left. The six were the *Cypria,* covering the events leading up to the opening of the *Iliad;* the *Aethiopis, Sack of*

Troy, and *Little Iliad,* which chronicled what happened at Troy after Hector's death (where the *Iliad* breaks off); the *Nostoi (Homecomings),* telling about the return voyages of the Greek kings (excluding Odysseus); and the *Telegony,* about the adventures of Telegonus, Odysseus's son by the sorceress Circe. Together with the *Iliad* and the *Odyssey,* these six poems were often referred to as the Trojan Cycle.

The other poems of the Epic Cycle attempted to cover the main events leading up to the Trojan War. The first work, chronologically speaking, was the *Titanomachy,* which resembled Hesiod's *Theogony* in that it told about the emergence of the early gods from Chaos, the rise of the Titans, and the war between the Titans and the Olympian gods. The other three epics in the cycle—the *Oedipodea (Story of Oedipus), Thebaïs,* and *Epigoni*—formed the nucleus of the Theban Myth Cycle, including the rise and fall of Oedipus, the failed expedition of the Seven Against Thebes, and the successful attack on Thebes by the sons of the Seven, the Epigoni. Scholars believe that the playwright Sophocles drew much of the material for his three Theban plays (*Oedipus the King, Oedipus at Colonus,* and *Antigone*) from these epics. **See** *Cypria;* Hesiod; Homer; *Iliad; Odyssey; Oedipus the King; Seven Against Thebes; Theogony;* **also** Titans; Zeus (Chapter 2); The Theban Myth Cycle; The Trojan War (Chapter 6).

Eumenides

A play by Aeschylus, the third in his *Oresteia* trilogy, written in 458 B.C. In the second play, *Libation Bearers,* Orestes, son of Agamemnon (king of Argos and Mycenae), kills his mother, Clytemnestra, to avenge her murder of Agamemnon. The play ends with the Furies (hateful spirits who pursue murderers) arriving in Argos and the youth fleeing from them.

The *Eumenides* opens at Apollo's shrine at Delphi, where Orestes has come seeking sanctuary. The Furies lie sleeping around him, having been lulled to sleep by Apollo, who is protecting the young man. The god tells Orestes that he must continue fleeing the Furies; he should go to Athens, where that city's protector—Athena—will find a way to help him. Orestes leaves. Suddenly Clytemnestra's ghost rises from the ground and wakes up the Furies, urging them to chase after her murderer. "Breathe on him with that butchery breath of yours!" she shouts. "Shrivel him to ash from your smoking, burning bowels! Go after him again! Pursue him to bone!" (*Eumenides* 136–138)

A few weeks later Orestes enters the temple of Athena on the Athenian Acropolis and beseeches the goddess to help him. Then the Furies (who form the play's chorus) arrive, hot on his heels, in time to witness Athena's arrival. She listens to both sides of the story and declares that the issue is too weighty for her to decide on her own. So she ordains that Orestes will undergo a trial on the nearby Areopagus hill, where a jury of Athenian citizens will judge him and decide his fate. The Furies make their case, and Orestes defends himself, calling on the god Apollo to testify on his behalf. The Furies try to discredit Apollo, but he remains firm in his conviction that Clytemnestra deserved to die for her treacherous slaying of a great man.

Finally, Athena calls on the jury to vote. The results are an even split between those calling for conviction and those demanding acquittal. The goddess declares that in the case of an equal vote, the defendant must be acquitted (which was the custom in historical Athenian courts). Orestes heartily thanks the goddess for saving his royal house (the house of Atreus, which has long been cursed by a terrible cycle of murder and betrayal).

The Furies are livid over losing. But in a series of magnificent speeches, Athena wins them over, convincing them that it would be better for them to shed their anger and vengeful pursuits. The cycle of hatred and violence must be broken for them, just as it has been for Orestes' long-plagued house. If they would become beneficent goddesses, Athena promises, the Athenians would worship and glorify them. Moved by the goddess's words, little by little the Furies feel their anger subsiding, until Athena's miracle—their transformation into the Eumenides, "the Kindly Ones"—is complete. "Oh, you are wise to discover more kindly ways," Athena tells them.

> And now, as I gaze on these formidable faces, great is the gain I foresee for these people [the Athenians, whom the Eumenides will help Athena watch over and protect]. Blessed by the blessed and worshiped always, while steering the city and its people to do right and good things, you shall receive high honors forever. (*Eumenides* 987–995)

A large group of Athenian women escorts the Eumenides, led by Athena, toward their new shrine. **See** Aeschylus; *Agamemnon; Libation Bearers;* **also** Athena (Chapter 2); Furies (Chapter 3); The Curse of the House of Atreus (Chapter 6).

Euripides

(ca. 485–406 B.C.) One of the four masters of fifth-century B.C. Athenian drama. The youngest of the three great tragedians, Euripides was not as popular in his own time as the other two (Aeschylus and Sophocles), mainly because his works often questioned traditional religious and social values and portrayed humans in a more realistic than heroic manner. Euripides frequently emphasized nontraditional views and gave prominent voice to socially insignificant characters, such as women and slaves; likewise he showed kings and heroes dressed in rags if it was appropriate

In this life-sized statue, the playwright Euripides holds a mask of tragedy, the theatrical genre in which he excelled.

for the scene (after a shipwreck, for instance). Sophocles was quoted as saying that he showed people as they should be while Euripides showed people as they are. Although many of Euripides' countrymen viewed such informal and unconventional approaches to drama as undignified, modern scholars see him as the first playwright to deal with human problems in a modern way.

Euripides wrote perhaps eighty-eight or more plays, all or nearly all dealing with mythological tales and characters. Only nineteen of these works have survived complete: *Alcestis* (438 B.C.), *Medea* (431), *Children of Heracles* (ca. 430), *Hippolytus* (428), *Andromache* (ca. 426), *Hecuba* (ca. 424), *The Suppliant Women* (ca. 422), *Madness of Heracles* (ca. 420–417), *Electra* (ca. 417–413), *The Trojan Women* (415), *Iphigenia in Taurus* (ca. 414), *The Phoenician Women* (ca. 412–408), *Helen* (412), *Ion* (ca. 412), *Orestes* (408), *The Bacchae* (405), *Iphigenia*

in Aulis (ca. 405), *The Cyclops* (date unknown), and *Rhesus* (date unknown).

Of the nineteen plays, eleven end with the intervention of a deus ex machina ("god from the machine," referring to a crane that "flew in" the actor or actress portraying the deity). Over time, many critics accused him of overusing this device, in which the divinity neatly resolved the characters' problems. Nonetheless, Aristotle, in his *Poetics,* calls Euripides the most skilled of the tragic poets at arousing emotions like pity and fear.

However his effectiveness as a playwright may be evaluated, there can be no doubt that Euripides' collected works constitute a rich treasure trove of mythological characters and stories. **See** *Alcestis; The Bacchae; Electra; Hecuba; Helen; Hippolytus; Madness of Heracles; Medea; The Phoenician Women.*

Frogs
A play written by the Athenian comedic playwright Aristophanes in 405 B.C., depicting the god Dionysus journeying to the Underworld to bring the dead playwright Euripides back to Athens so that the city can partake of his wisdom. For a synopsis of the play, **see** Aristophanes.

The Golden Ass
The only Latin novel that has survived in its entirety, written by Lucius Apuleius (who

flourished in the mid–second century A.D.). It may have been based on a story of the prolific Greek writer Lucian; but more likely both works are based on a lost earlier work by an unknown Greek. Apuleius's expanded, embellished version is a narrative told in the first person by a young Greek man, Lucius.

Lucius's first adventure takes place in Thessaly (in central Greece) where, supposedly, practitioners of black magic can be found. Through such black arts he is transformed into an ass, after which a gang of thieves forces him to become their accomplice in a crime spree. The most famous episode in this section of the book consists of an old woman telling a story to a young girl whom the robbers have abducted. This tale, the haunting Greek myth of Cupid and Psyche, has survived only in this telling by Apuleius.

Later, Lucius has other adventures, including some temporary service to a band of wandering priests of the goddess Cybele and a stint performing tricks at public gatherings. Eventually the goddess Isis takes pity on him and turns him back into a person. He then undergoes initiation rites in the cult of Isis and Osiris. The novel is fast-paced, often quite humorous, and richly detailed, revealing many customs, beliefs, and other aspects of daily life in Apuleius's time. **See** Apuleius, Lucius; **also** Cupid and Psyche (Chapter 6).

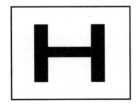

Hecuba

A tragedy by Euripides, written and first performed in about 424 B.C. After Troy's fall to the Greeks, the women of the city became slaves and concubines of the various Greek leaders; Hecuba, the Trojan queen (wife of King Priam) is now the slave of King Odysseus of Ithaca. As the play opens, Odysseus informs Hecuba that the council of Greek leaders has decided to sacrifice one of her daughters, Polyxena, at the tomb of the Greek hero Achilles in order to obtain favorable winds for the return voyage to Greece. Preferring death to slavery, Polyxena willingly and bravely undergoes the sacrifice.

Hecuba's grief at losing Polyxena is now compounded by more bad news. Before Troy's fall, to safeguard her youngest son, Polydorus, she had sent the boy to live with Polymestor, king of the Thracian Chersonese (the peninsula making up the western bank of the Hellespont, not far from Troy). After the city's fall, Hecuba discovers, Polymestor murdered Polydorus and threw the body into the sea. Some servants now bring the boy's body to the former Trojan queen, and she appeals to Agamemnon (leader of the Greek army) to avenge the murder. However, Agamemnon does not wish to anger the other Greeks, who look on Polymestor as an ally.

Hecuba decides to avenge her son's murder herself. She lures Polymestor and his two young sons to her tent; there, she and her serving women blind the man and kill the boys. The bitter Polymestor predicts that Hecuba will eventually be transformed into a fiery-eyed dog and die in misery. He also tells Agamemnon that his wife, Clytemnestra, will slay him when he returns to Greece. Insulted by what he views as a false prophecy (which, however, turns out to be an accurate one), Agamemnon orders his guards to gag Polymestor and leave him on a deserted island. **See** Euripides; **also** Hecuba; Polydorus 1; Polyxena (Chapter 1).

Helen

A tragedy with a happy ending by Euripides, first performed in 412 B.C. The author based the plot on an alternate legend about

Helen, one that claimed a phantom version of her went to Troy with Prince Paris. Meanwhile, the god Hermes magically transported the real Helen to the court of Proteus, king of Egypt, where she spent the ten years of the Trojan War waiting for her husband, Menelaus, to come for her.

The play begins after Proteus's death. His son, Theoclymenus, has been pestering the Spartan queen to marry him, and to avoid him she has taken refuge at Proteus's tomb. Unexpectedly, Teucer, one of the Greek heroes of the Trojan War, arrives and tells Helen that the war has been over for some time. Believing Menelaus to be dead, she begins to grieve; but then Menelaus shows up and explains how he was blown off course by a huge storm and was shipwrecked off the Egyptian coast. Menelaus is puzzled when he sees Helen in the local palace because, he says, he rescued his wife and took her with him after sacking Troy. Soon, however, he realizes that the Helen he rescued is merely a phantom, who now vanishes suddenly into thin air.

The real Helen warns her husband that the Egyptian king is demanding that she marry him; moreover, Theoclymenus has vowed to kill any Greek who arrives in the country to rescue her. Helen devises an escape plan. With the help of the king's sister, she fools Theoclymenus into providing a ship. Ostensibly, the vessel will be used to carry Helen and the king to a funeral to be held at sea for Menelaus, who, Helen claims, has washed up dead on the beach. At the last moment, Helen and Menelaus manage to sail away together on the ship.

Euripides' injection of a happy ending, as well as a certain amount of humor in his presentation of the escape from Egypt, makes *Helen* an unconventional (and quite innovative) tragedy, especially for its time. The author also raised a good many eyebrows with the bitterly ironic suggestion that all the years and lives lost at Troy had been for nothing—a mere phantom. Euripides brings home this idea in an almost farcical exchange between Menelaus and his messenger:

> MESSENGER: Then, is not this lady Helen, the prize of all we went through at Troy?
>
> MENELAUS: This lady was never in Troy. We were tricked by the gods. The Helen we captured was a phantom to make fools of us.
>
> MESSENGER: What? All our sweat and blood—spent for a mere ghost?
>
> MENELAUS: Yes. Hera was in a rage because of the Judgment of Paris. (*Helen* 767–773)

See Euripides; **also** Helen; Menelaus (Chapter 1); The Trojan War (Chapter 6).

Herodotus

(ca. 485–ca. 425 B.C.) A Greek historian who, in later ages, became known as the "father" of history. Born at Halicarnassus (in southwestern Asia Minor), Herodotus became famous for his *Histories,* a detailed account of the Persian Wars (490–479 B.C.). The book, which also includes numerous long digressions on various people and places involved in the conflicts, is the oldest surviving conventional historical work. (Previous writers apparently turned out only geographical works or compilations of mostly legendary figures and events.)

Not all of what Herodotus recorded as history was accurate, for he often simply repeated what he heard; however, he created a huge and often intricate portrait of the ancient world of his own era and the century immediately preceding it. Fortunately for later generations, he was an endlessly curious individual who wrote in a clear, graceful style that makes his masterwork highly entertaining reading. He gathered his information mostly by traveling for years throughout the eastern Mediterranean world (before settling in the Athenian colony of Thurii [in Italy] in 443 B.C.).

One fortunate result of Herodotus's extensive travels, curiosity, and prolific writing was that he recorded numerous stories and facts about the local gods and myths of the Egyptians, Persians, Phoenicians, and other ancient peoples contemporary with the Greeks of his era. And he discovered that many of these peoples had gods and legendary heroes in common with Greek ones. In the second of the nine books making up the *Histories,* for example, he goes into considerable detail trying to trace the origins of the various and widespread tales about Heracles, the renowned hero, strongman, and later a god. "To get the best information I possibly could on this subject," he writes,

> I made a voyage to Tyre, in Phoenicia, because I had heard there was a temple there, of great sanctity, dedicated to Heracles. I visited the temple and found that the offerings which adorned it were numerous and valuable. . . . I also saw another temple there dedicated to the Thasian Heracles; and I have also been to Thasos (in the northern Aegean), where I found a temple of Heracles built by the Phoenicians who settled there after they had sailed in search of Europa [a princess of Tyre whom Zeus, disguised as a bull, abducted]. . . . The result of these searches is a plain proof that the worship of Heracles is very ancient. (*Histories* 2.45)

See Europa (Chapter 1); **also** The Adventures of Heracles (Chapter 6).

Hesiod

(flourished ca. 700 B.C.) One of the earliest and greatest of the Greek poets, he hailed from the small town of Ascra in Boeotia. Most of what little information we have about him he provides himself in snippets imbedded in his works. In his epic poem the *Theogony,* for example, he claims that as a young man the divine Muses appeared to him while he was tending his sheep and gave him the gift of song (i.e., poetic expression). On his father's

death, the estate was divided between him and his brother; but the brother took more than his fair share, which provoked a legal battle. Hesiod's poem *Works and Days,* which among other things describes planting crops according to the calendar, was intended in part to instruct his errant brother, as well as others, in the honest, conservative, old-fashioned values of Greek farming. The *Theogony* is a sprawling, detailed rendition of the creation of the world and the gods. Along with Homer's epics, it provided the later Greeks with their most vivid picture of these beings. **See** *Theogony; Works and Days.*

Hippolytus

A tragedy written by Euripides, first performed in 429 or 428 B.C. Hippolytus's father was the Athenian hero and king Theseus, and his mother was Hippolyte, queen of the Amazons. Later, Theseus married again, this time choosing Phaedra, daughter of King Minos of Crete.

As the play opens, Hippolytus is an adult. Phaedra has fallen in love with him; but being a virtuous person, she resists her feelings. In other versions, she is less virtuous. She has told neither her husband nor Hippolytus, confiding her unsettling secret only to her nurse. However, the nurse tells Hippolytus, who reacts angrily and denounces Phaedra. Crushed, the young woman hangs herself, but not before retaliating by writing a note to Theseus, falsely claiming that Hippolytus had made advances toward her.

On reading the note, Theseus flies into a rage. He both banishes and curses Hippolytus, who steadfastly maintains his innocence. (The curse is one of three given to Theseus by the sea god Poseidon.) Leaving the palace, the young man rides his chariot near the sea, where Poseidon sends a huge wave rushing inland and a giant bull to scare Hippolytus's horses. The chariot crashes, fulfilling the curse. Meanwhile, Theseus learns the truth of his son's innocence from the goddess Artemis. But it is too late; some hunters bear the mortally wounded Hippolytus into the palace, where he absolves his father of responsibility for the tragedy and dies.

Euripides' treatment of this myth is consistent with his tendency to portray women and their personal struggles in a sympathetic manner. His Phaedra, unlike the morally tainted one of the original myth, is a good woman trapped in a bad situation, and she resorts to underhanded methods only after Hippolytus mistreats her. The playwright depicts Hippolytus, too, as a victim of events beyond his control and a victim of his own temper. **See** Euripides; **also** Hippolytus; Phaedra (Chapter 1); The Exploits of Theseus (Chapter 6).

History of Rome from Its Foundation

(*Ab urbe condita libri*) The massive and popular history of Rome composed by the great Roman prose writer Livy (Titus Livius) in the late first century B.C. Of the original 142 volumes, only about thirty-five have survived—books 1 through 10, 21 through 45 (books 41 and 43 being incomplete), and a fragment of book 91. The content of the original work was as follows: Books 1 through 5 described Rome's legendary founding, the monarchy, and the Republic's establishment and early years. Included were fairly detailed accounts of important early Roman mythological or semilegendary characters, including Evander, Romulus, Tarquin the Proud, the Horatii, Horatius, Brutus, Lucretia, Cloelia, Coriolanus, and Cincinnatus. Then, with somewhat firmer footing in historical reality, books 6 through 15 covered Rome's conquest of Italy; books 16 through 30 covered the first two Punic Wars with Carthage; books 31 through 45 dealt with the subjugation of Greece and other events from about 200 to 167 B.C.; and books 46 through 142 (all now lost) covered sub-

sequent events down to 9 B.C., about halfway through Augustus's reign.

Measured by any standard, ancient or modern, Livy's achievement was monumental. Noted modern scholar J. Wight Duff states (in his *Literary History of Rome*): "No Augustan prose writer is for a moment comparable with Livy. His prose-epic is . . . sister to the *Aeneid.* Not even in Virgil has the greatness of the Roman character found a more dignified or more lasting monument than in the colossal ruins of Livy's history." Indeed, Livy's writing style is eloquent, well organized, often dramatic, and very readable.

On the negative side, however, Livy did not set out to write an impartial historical record; rather, his aim was to illuminate the old traditions and character traits that had made Rome great in hopes of teaching a moral lesson and thereby helping to reverse what he and many other prominent figures of his day viewed as society's recent moral decay. As he himself summed up his purpose in the introduction to the work: "In history, fortunately, you can find a record of the ample range of human experience clearly set up for everyone to see; in that record, you may discover for yourself and for your country, examples and warnings." (*History of Rome from Its Foundation* 1.1)

Another of Livy's faults was that the sources he relied on were mainly written histories of varying quality and accuracy; he consulted few original documents and records; nor was he very critical of his sources. And the result was that his facts were often inaccurate or muddled. Also, like most other ancient historians, he paid little attention to economic and social history (to the frustration of modern scholars); and his narrative was riddled with references to omens and fate directing the course of historical events (though, to his credit, he personally tended to be skeptical about such supernatural forces). **See** Livy.

Homer

(late ninth or late eighth century B.C.?) A poet credited with authoring the *Iliad* and the *Odyssey,* the most famous and arguably the greatest epic poems ever written. Homer's birthplace is disputed; several cities in Greek Ionia (western Asia Minor) claim him, though Smyrna and Chios are the most plausible candidates. The later classical Greeks had no doubts that Homer was a real person, and throughout antiquity people referred to him simply and reverently as "the Poet."

However, as early as Hellenistic times (the last three centuries B.C.), some Greek scholars suggested that the two epics might not have been composed by the same person. This became part of a tradition, still ongoing, of Homeric criticism, aimed at answering the so-called Homeric question. It actually comprises several questions: Was he indeed a real person? If so, did he write both epics? Are the works as they exist today substantially his, or did later writers contribute various portions? Are the characters and events described in the epics real, imaginary, or a mixture of the two?

Though debates on these questions continue, the consensus of modern scholarship is that Homer was a real bard who was part of a long tradition of reciting poetry that had been transmitted orally from preceding generations. Thus, the epics were likely composed little by little over time, each generation of bards refining and elaborating on them. Homer's contribution may have been the greatest because the Greeks had rediscovered writing during (or perhaps just preceding) his lifetime; and committing the poems to writing (perhaps by dictating them to a scribe) would have allowed for the addition of more complex de-

A fanciful drawing of the Greek poet Homer, author of the Iliad *and the* Odyssey. *No one knows what he really looked like.*

tail and imagery than was customarily transmitted by oral means. (Still, solid evidence that the poems were committed to writing this early is lacking; tradition holds that the first written editions were those commissioned by the Athenian leader Pisistratus in the mid–sixth century B.C.)

However the Homeric epics were composed, they came to exert a profound influence on Greek culture and thought. The *Iliad,* describing a series of incidents near the end of the Trojan War (1250–1200 B.C.?), and the *Odyssey,* chronicling the adventures of Odysseus, one of the Greek chieftains who fought at Troy, were two of the most famous myths (or collections of myths) of antiquity. They were also major sources of information about the Greek gods, their powers, habits, affairs, wrath, and so forth. In addition, Homer's epics provided the Greeks with a blueprint for a heroic, noble code of conduct; contained numerous examples of practical wisdom; became the primary literary texts studied by Greek schoolchildren; and were endlessly quoted by Greek and Roman writers of all kinds for at least twelve centuries. These works, the first and among the greatest examples of Western literature, are no less highly regarded today. They remain staples of university courses in classical history, literature, and poetry, and new translations appear on a regular basis. **See** Epic Cycle; *Iliad; Odyssey.*

Homeric Hymns

A collection of Greek poems of varying lengths, each addressed to a major or minor god, and all dating from the eighth to sixth centuries B.C. The poems derived their name from the fact that for a long time they were attributed to Homer; but in the Hellenistic Age (the last three centuries B.C.), Greek scholars working in Alexandria concluded that most or all of the *Homeric Hymns* were composed by various rhapsodes (poets and/or performers who recited epic poetry at religious festivals and other public venues).

Of the thirty-three *Homeric Hymns,* most are short and likely originally intended as preludes to recitations of longer poems, such as the *Iliad,* the *Odyssey,* or selections from the Epic Cycle. Such recitations were routinely given at festivals dedicated to various gods. Typical of these are Hymns 8 through 11, addressed to Ares, Artemis, Aphrodite, and Athena, respectively. The one to Athena reads,

> Of Pallas Athena, guardian of the city, I begin to sing. Dread is she, and with Ares she loves deeds of war, the sack of cities, and shouting, and the battle. It is she who saves the people as they go out to war and come back. Hail, goddess, and give us good fortune with happiness! (*Homeric Hymn 11*)

A few of the hymns are longer and provide considerable detail about the deity involved and one or two of his or her principal myths. Of particular note are the *Hymn to Demeter,* which tells how Demeter's daughter, Persephone, was abducted by Hades (lord of the Underworld); the *Hymn to Apollo,* which chronicles the god's birth on the island of Delos and how he took charge of the oracle at Delphi; the *Hymn to Hermes,* recounting that deity's unusual and amusing feats as an infant; and the *Hymn to Dionysus,* which tells how that god performed miracles after being captured by pirates.

Horace

(Quintus Horatius Flaccus, 65–8 B.C.) One of Rome's greatest poets, born the son of a financially successful former slave. Horace studied in the best schools in Athens and Rome, then entered the republican army raised in Greece by Brutus and Cassius (leaders of the conspiracy against Julius Caesar). At the Battle of Philippi (42 B.C.), the poet, who later admitted that he was not soldier material, was so afraid that he fled the field in terror. Soon afterward he went to Rome and there had the good fortune to meet the great poet Virgil, who recognized his talents and introduced him to the literary patron Maecenas and rising political star Octavian. In about the year 37 B.C., Horace achieved financial independence and all the leisure time he needed for writing when Maecenas provided him with a country estate staffed by an overseer, five tenant farmers, and eight slaves.

In contrast to the lofty, heroic, and generally serious tone of Virgil's works, Horace's poetry explored and commented on everyday situations, feelings, and emotions, usually in an easy-going or humorous way. Horace's general view of life was that it was short and uncertain, that death was inevitable, and that a person could only achieve immortality by creating or achieving something of lasting value. Therefore, it made sense to enjoy life and its pleasures, including love and wine, although not to gross and unseemly excess. His philosophy of living and enjoying one day at a time is evident in this excerpt from one of the poems collected in his masterpiece, the *Odes* (published 23–13 B.C.): "Happy the man, and happy he alone, he who can call today his own; he who, secure within, can say: 'Tomorrow do your worst, for I have lived today.'" (3.29.8)

Horace's other works, all of which have survived, include the *Epodes* (ca. 30 B.C.), *Satires* (ca. 30 B.C.), *Art of Poetry* (ca. 19 B.C.), and *Carmen Saeculare* (a long poem commissioned by Augustus for the Secular Games in 17 B.C.). These works, particularly the *Odes* and *Art of Poetry,* achieved widespread popularity and literary influence during Europe's Renaissance and again in the eighteenth century. Horace did not deal primarily with mythological themes, but his poems are filled with references to myths and mythical characters. **See** Virgil.

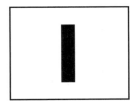

Iliad

An epic poem about the Trojan War attributed to the Greek poet Homer (based to some degree on material handed down by earlier poets and probably more or less finalized by the late eighth century B.C.). The title derives from Ilium or Ilion, alternate names for Troy. The story is set in the tenth year of the war and deals with a series of events set in motion by the wrath of the Greek hero Achilles, who has quarreled with his colleague Agamemnon, leader of the Greek expedition to Troy.

As the story begins, the god Apollo has inflicted the Greek camp with a plague to punish Agamemnon for taking as his concubine Chryseis, daughter of one of the god's priests. To stop the plague, Agamemnon reluctantly surrenders the girl; but in her place he seizes Briseis, a concubine belonging to Achilles. Incensed by this arrogant act, Achilles retires to his tent and refuses to come out. Lacking his formidable fighting and leadership skills, the Greeks suffer a series of defeats, and the Trojans drive them back to their beach encampment. Eventually the hero Hector, son of Priam, Troy's king, leads an attack that breaks through the Greek stockade, and the Trojans set fire to some of the Greek ships.

Even at this critical juncture, Achilles, who is still angry at Agamemnon, refuses to leave his tent. But Patroclus, Achilles' closest friend, feels that he must do something to stop the Trojan advance and asks Achilles for permission to enter the fray. Furthermore, Patroclus wants to borrow his friend's armor so that the enemy will be fooled into thinking that Achilles has reentered the fighting. Achilles consents, and the plan works. Believing that Achilles is leading the Greeks against them, the Trojans retreat in disarray. During this battle, however, Hector slays Patroclus.

When Achilles hears that his friend has been killed, he becomes a changed man. He patches up his quarrel with Agamemnon, receives new armor forged for him by the god Hephaestos, and charges back into battle at the forefront of the Greek army. In single combat, Achilles manages to kill the mighty Hector and humiliates and horrifies the Trojans by tying the dead man's corpse to the back of his chariot and dragging it through the dust.

The Greeks proceed to hold funeral games in honor of the slain Patroclus. Afterward, King Priam comes to see Achilles and pleads for the body of his son, Hector. Feeling genuine pity for the Trojan king, Achilles returns Hector's body, and the Trojans hold a solemn funeral for their fallen champion. **See** Homer; **also** Achilles; Agamemnon; Ajax 1 and 2; Chryseis; Hector; Helen; Nestor; Odysseus; Paris; Patroclus; Priam (Chapter 1); Trojan Horse; Troy (Chapter 4); and for a more detailed account of the plot of the *Iliad,* as well as the events before and after it, **see** The Trojan War (Chapter 6).

Ion

A tragedy with a happy ending by Euripides, probably written in 412 B.C. Apollo, god of prophecy, had seduced Creusa, the daughter of King Erechtheus of Athens, and she gave birth to Ion. Fearing that her father would disapprove of the child, Creusa reluctantly left Ion in a cave beneath the Acropolis. However, the infant survived because Apollo asked Hermes to take it to Delphi for safekeeping.

The play begins several years later. Ion has grown into a young man and Creusa, who assumes he is long dead, has married Xuthus, son of Hellen (founder of the Greek race). After repeated attempts to have children, Creusa and Xuthus remain childless, so Xuthus journeys to Delphi to ask Apollo to grant the couple offspring. The god ordains that Xuthus must accept as his son the first person he meets as he exits the shrine. This turns out to be none other than Ion.

When Xuthus and Ion return to Athens, Creusa is angry that Apollo, who caused her so much trouble before, has not seen fit to grant her an infant. Moreover, she starts to suspect that Ion is some bastard son of Xuthus who does not deserve to be her husband's heir, so she tries to poison the young man. Luckily for all concerned, the attempt fails. Fearful of Ion's retaliation, Creusa takes refuge at Apollo's shrine.

While Creusa is at Apollo's temple, the priestess shows her the swaddling clothes the infant Ion had worn. Creusa recognizes them, realizes that Ion is her own son, and,

in a moving scene, reveals this truth to him. Athena, patron deity of Athens, suddenly appears to reassure all concerned that the gods have blessed this family. Ion was a gift from Apollo to Xuthus, Athena says; in addition, as the grandson of Erechtheus, the young man is now the rightful heir to the Athenian throne. Furthermore, the goddess reveals, Ion will give rise to an important branch of the Greek race, which will be called the Ionians, after him. **See** Euripides; **also** Creusa 1; Ion; Xuthus (Chapter 1).

Iphigenia in Aulis

A tragic play by Euripides, produced in 405 B.C., shortly after the author's death. The Greek fleet, having been assembled for the attack on Troy, is moored at Aulis (on the eastern shore of Boeotia) waiting for a favorable wind. Agamemnon (king of Mycenae and Argos), leader of the Greek expedition, has been informed by a seer (who consulted an oracle) that the needed wind will not come unless the king sacrifices his daughter, Iphigenia, to the goddess Artemis. Though reluctant to carry out this terrible act, Agamemnon has given in to pressure from his brother, Menelaus (king of Sparta), on whose behalf the war is about to be fought. A message has been sent to Iphigenia, summoning her to Aulis on the pretext that she will marry the Greek warrior Achilles.

Soon, Iphigenia, accompanied by her mother, Clytemnestra, and Agamemnon's young son, Orestes, arrives in Aulis. Seeing Agamemnon's despair, Menelaus has a change of heart and offers to spare Iphigenia. But Agamemnon points out that the seer, and also Odysseus (king of Ithaca), know about the oracle and will likely tell the other Greek leaders; they have gone to great trouble to raise armies and build ships and will insist on the sacrifice.

Agamemnon tries to convince Clytemnestra, who knows nothing about the sacrifice, to go back to Argos, but she refuses. Then she has a conversation with Achilles, who professes ignorance about the supposed impending marriage to her daughter. A servant reveals the truth to them, and Achilles is outraged, both by the idea of the sacrifice and by the way he has been used to facilitate it. He decides that he will not allow the girl to die and prepares to fight for her as Odysseus leads a large contingent of soldiers against him.

At the last moment, bloodshed is averted by Iphigenia herself. She believes the war is a just one and does not want to see the Greeks fight one another when they should be facing a common enemy. Thus, she goes willingly to the altar to be sacrificed. When the dreaded moment comes and the priest swings the ax, however, the onlookers are astonished to see that Iphigenia has disappeared; in her place on the altar a deer lies dying. It is clear to all that Artemis has seen fit to take the girl to her bosom. The long-awaited wind comes up, and the fleet prepares to sail for Troy. **See** Euripides; **also** Achilles; Agamemnon; Clytemnestra; Iphigenia; Menelaus (Chapter 1).

Libation Bearers

A tragedy by Aeschylus, the second play in his *Oresteia* trilogy, first performed in 458 B.C. In the trilogy's first play, *Agamemnon,* the title character, king of Argos and Mycenae, was murdered by his wife, Clytemnestra, and her lover, Aegisthus. Meanwhile, Clytemnestra's daughter, Electra, fearing for the safety of her younger brother, Orestes, had secretly sent the boy to live with the king of a distant city.

The *Libation Bearers* begins seven years later. Clytemnestra and Aegisthus rule Ar-

gos with a heavy hand; and they have come to treat Electra, who makes no secret of her disapproval of them, little better than a slave. Electra waits patiently for the day when her brother will return and exact vengeance for Agamemnon's murder.

That day has finally come. Orestes, accompanied by his close friend, Pylades, arrives in Argos and immediately visits Agamemnon's grave. There, he sees some women approaching with some libations (sacrificial wine) to offer to the dead king's spirit, and he recognizes his sister in their number. Orestes and Electra are reunited; along with Pylades and Electra's servants, they plot the death of Clytemnestra and Aegisthus.

Later that day, Orestes and Pylades gain an audience with the queen and pretend to be messengers bringing her news of Orestes' death. Meanwhile, the nurse of the royal children summons Aegisthus to the palace and he enters. Those servants standing in the courtyard hear blood-curdling screams from inside and conclude that Aegisthus has been slain. Clytemnestra rushes into the courtyard and, upon learning of her lover's death, realizes that the man who killed him is her son, Orestes. Mother and son have a heated exchange, after which he drags her into the palace and kills her.

A few minutes later the palace doors open, revealing to the servants and other people gathered in the courtyard the dead bodies of Aegisthus and Clytemnestra. Orestes has no time to gloat, however. Already he senses the vengeful Furies (frightful spirits that pursue murderers) approaching, and he flees in terror. **See** Aeschylus; *Agamemnon; Eumenides;* **also** Aegisthus; Clytemnestra; Electra; Orestes; Pylades (Chapter 1); The Curse of the House of Atreus (Chapter 6).

Livy

(Titus Livius) The outstanding prose writer of the Augustan age of literature (ca. 43

B.C.–ca. A.D. 17) and one of the most popular of all Roman historians. Born in 59 B.C. in Patavium (now Padua), in northern Italy, he lived most of his life in Rome, where he witnessed firsthand the fall of the Republic and the rise of Augustus, the first Roman emperor. At the urging of Augustus, who became his friend, he devoted much of his life to writing the massive and detailed *History of Rome from Its Foundation* (*Ab urbe condita libri*), begun in about 29 B.C. and subsequently published in installments. Livy died, a famous and widely respected author, in A.D. 17 in his home town of Patavium. **See** *History of Rome from Its Foundation.*

Lucian

(ca. A.D.115–ca.181) A Greek born in Samosata in Syria and the prolific author of over eighty speeches, essays, stories, and dialogues. Little for certain is known about Lucian's life since none of his contemporaries mention him; however, statements he made in his own works indicate that he traveled extensively throughout the Mediterranean world and eventually settled in Athens. He became most famous for his dialogues and fantastic tales, most of which were humorous, often biting satires that poked fun at serious literary works and characters.

Several of Lucian's satires dealt with mythology. Perhaps the most famous was the *True History,* the contents of which were anything but true. The work is a parody of traveler's tales, like Homer's *Odyssey,* which were widely popular in ancient times. Lucian's travelers visit the Islands of the Blessed (a mythical place where it was thought that a few fortunate heroes went after they died), where they meet Homer himself. The renowned poet claims that the *Iliad* (thought in ancient times to be the pinnacle of great literature) was thrown together with little thought to plan or organization.

Another of Lucian's satires, *Dialogues of the Gods,* humorously satirizes noted myths such as Athena's birth from Zeus's head and the Judgment of Paris (in which three goddesses competed to see which one of them was the most fair). *Dialogues of the Dead* is set in the Underworld, where such mythical characters as Hermes, Heracles, and Achilles comment on and roundly criticize earthly life in Lucian's day. Still another work set in the Underworld—*Charon*—has the title character (the grim boatman who ferried dead souls across the River Styx) pay a visit to the earth's surface; seeing the squalor and pettiness of humanity, Charon has no pity for those whom he will someday meet in his boat.

Lucretius

(Titus Lucretius Carus, ca. 99–ca. 55 B.C.) A Roman poet and philosopher of great stature about whose life almost nothing is known. His only known work, *On the Nature of Things,* beautifully extols the virtues of the Greek thinker Epicurus and his philosophy (including the concept put forth by two earlier Greek thinkers—Leucippus and Democritus—that the physical world is made of up of microscopic building blocks called atoms).

Unlike Homer, Hesiod, Ovid, and other ancient myth tellers, Lucretius did not repeat traditional tales about mythical characters, including the gods. Indeed, the thrust of his treatise is that the world is *not* ruled by divine or magical deities and forces, but rather by atoms, matter, and natural laws. He suggests that the gods may exist, but if so, they dwell in some remote, unreachable place and have no interest in humanity. "You must not suppose," Lucretius writes,

that the holy dwelling places of the gods are anywhere within the limits of the world. For the flimsy nature of the gods, far removed from our senses, is scarcely visible even to the perception of the mind. Since it eludes the touch and pressure of our hands, it can have no contact with anything that is tangible to us. For what cannot be touched cannot touch. Therefore, their dwelling places also must be unlike ours, of the same flimsy texture as their bodies. (*On the Nature of Things* 5.146–155)

Lucretius was one of the few ancient writers known to reject all traditional mythological stories and characters as pure fable and to describe religious worship as mere superstition.

Madness of Heracles

(or *Heracles*) A tragedy by Euripides, written sometime between 420 and 417 B.C. The great hero Heracles has been gone from his native city of Thebes for a long time. Eurystheus, king of Tiryns, sent him on his twelfth labor, to fetch Cerberus, the dreaded three-headed dog that guards the border of the Underworld. In Heracles' absence, Lycus, a usurper, has killed the Theban king, Creon, and seized the throne. The new king has threatened to kill Amphitryon (the man who raised Heracles) as well as the strongman's wife, Megara (daughter of the slain Creon), and their children. The fearful family has taken refuge in the local temple of Zeus, but Lycus is preparing to burn down the temple to eradicate them.

Luckily, Heracles returns in the nick of time, kills Lycus, and rescues his family. But the happy ending everyone expects does not materialize. The goddess Hera, who hates Heracles because Zeus conceived him with a mortal woman (Alcmena, wife of Amphitryon), sends Lyssa, goddess of madness, to Thebes. Lyssa inflicts Heracles with madness, and in a frenzy he slays Megara and their children.

When Heracles recovers from his madness and discovers what he has done, he is filled with despair. "What shame, what misery!" he exclaims.

To become the murderer of my most dear sons! Why do I not take my life? Leap from some bare cliff, aim a sword at my own heart, become myself the avenger of my children's blood? Or burn my flesh with fire, to avert the infamy [reputation as a murderer] that now awaits me? (*Madness of Heracles* 1149–1154)

But before the strongman can do away with himself, he sees his friend Theseus, the famous Athenian hero, approaching at the head of an army. Theseus had heard about Lycus's seizure of the Theban throne and the threats to Heracles' family and has come to help. The Athenian convinces Heracles that this terrible act was not his fault, that Hera is to blame, and urges him to be strong. As the play ends, Theseus escorts Heracles away toward Athens, there to be purified of his sin. **See** Euripides; **also** Alcmena; Amphitryon (Chapter 1); Hera (Chapter 2); The Adventures of Heracles (Chapter 6).

Medea

A tragedy by Euripides, written and first performed in 431 B.C. *Medea* has been the most often performed of Euripides' plays in modern times. This popularity is due to certain qualities, features, and themes the work possesses that make it extremely appealing to readers and theater audiences alike. Indeed, it deals with themes universal to every society and age, among them failed marriage, men's mistreatment of women, betrayal, jealousy, deceit, revenge, and murder.

The main events leading up to action of play are as follows: To give thanks to the gods for his safe return from the voyage to

Colchis (on the far shore of the Black Sea) to get the Golden Fleece, the hero Jason dedicated his ship, the *Argo,* to the sea god Poseidon. Jason also dutifully presented the fleece to Pelias (king of Iolcos, who had sent Jason to fetch the fleece), expecting that the old man would keep his end of the bargain and abdicate his throne in favor of Jason. But Pelias refused to fulfill his earlier promise to abdicate. Instead, he continued to cheat Jason out of his rights as the true heir to the throne. While the dispute dragged on and on, Jason and the sorceress Medea (whom Jason brought back with him from Colchis) had two children together in Iolcos.

Finally, quite fed up with Pelias's deceit, Medea decided to help Jason attain both the throne and revenge on Pelias. She took the king's three daughters aside and told them a fantastic tale. Their father was an old man who would, no doubt, die in the near future, she said. Would they not like to see Pelias recapture his youth and reign for many more decades? The princesses quickly agreed that they would eagerly welcome such a turn of events, although they could scarcely believe that such a thing were possible. Medea assured them that it was indeed possible. She then proceeded to convince the gullible young women that if they killed Pelias, cut him into pieces, and treated the pieces with magic herbs and spells (which Medea would supply), he would suddenly be rejuvenated as a young man. Believing this lie, the princesses followed Medea's instructions and slaughtered their father. The result, as Medea had planned, was Pelias's grisly and very permanent death, not his resurrection.

Medea's devious plan succeeded in accomplishing only one of its intended aims, however. Jason had indeed achieved revenge on Pelias, but the young hero did not attain the throne of Iolcos, as he had desired. Pelias's son, Acastus, branded both Jason and Medea murderers and drove them and their young children from the city. The exiled family journeyed southward to the prosperous city of Corinth. Here, to Medea's surprise and dismay, Jason turned on her. He rejected her as his wife and married the daughter of Creon, king of Corinth, perhaps, as he claimed, to put himself in a better economic and political position and thereby to have a chance to inherit the city's throne someday.

It is at this fateful juncture, with Medea fuming with rage over Jason's betrayal, that the action of Euripides' great play about her begins. The scorned Medea plots her revenge. Meanwhile, fearing that the sorceress is up to something sinister and dangerous, Creon orders her to take her children and leave Corinth. But she insists that her reputation for evil doings is undeserved and that she is no threat to anyone. Medea begs to be allowed just one more day in the city, and Creon reluctantly agrees.

Jason arrives and tells Medea that she brought her banishment on herself. He also offers her money to take care of the children on her journey. Medea answers him with a furious tirade, reminding him that it was she who betrayed her own father to help him get the fleece; but he insists that his decision to marry Creon's daughter, Glauce, was best for all concerned.

In the next few hours Medea goes through with her deadly plans, which include the painful death of Glauce. The sorceress sends the young woman a beautiful crown and a dress spun of golden threads, pretending that these are wedding gifts. In reality, though, the objects are laced with an acidlike poison. Later, a servant rushes into Medea's chamber to tell her the horrendous news of two royal deaths. Medea smiles as she hears how Glauce, excited by the lovely gifts, put on the crown and dress only to have them burn away her flesh; and when her father, Creon, attempted to help her, the poison spread to his own skin and killed him, too.

A painting on a Greek vase shows Glauce (also known as Creusa) receiving deadly wedding presents from the scheming Medea.

Having accomplished this terrible deed, Medea turns next on her own children. Her desire for revenge is so great that it overpowers her normal maternal instincts, and she destroys her own flesh and blood believing that it will be the ultimate way to hurt Jason. Before Jason or anyone else can bring her to justice, Medea escapes to Athens, where the local king, Aegeus, who had earlier promised to give her refuge when she left Corinth, takes her in.

These horrifying events unfold rapidly and relentlessly. From Medea's own words, as she plots the murders, the audience knows well in advance that the princess and children are in mortal danger. And as the danger mounts, the hope that she will change her mind or that somehow the victims—especially the children—will somehow escape, causes tensions to rise in a terrible crescendo. This gives the play a highly theatrical, dramatic, and compelling tone and feeling. Another compelling aspect of the play is that it deals with a woman who says and does things that women traditionally do not say and do. As in his plays *Hippolytus, Hecuba,* and *Andromache,* in *Medea* Euripides depicts a woman driven to

or caught up in violence and tragedy by extreme circumstances. This sympathetic vision of women, which was revolutionary in Euripides' time, became one of the playwright's hallmarks. **See** Euripides; **also** Creon 1; Medea; Pelias (Chapter 1); Corinth; Iolcos (Chapter 4); The Quest for the Golden Fleece (Chapter 6).

Metamorphoses

1. A long Latin narrative poem (in fifteen books) written by the Augustan poet Ovid over several years beginning in about A.D. 2. It contains more than two hundred stories derived from Greek, Roman, and Near Eastern mythology, all supposedly involving some kind of miraculous transformation, hence the title, which means "Transformations." Often, however, the transformation has little to do with the tale, and Ovid's intention seems primarily to entertain.

Included in Ovid's *Metamorphoses,* among many others, are legends about the creation; the flood and Deucalion's repopulating of the earth; Apollo's slaying of the serpent Python and seizure of the Delphic Oracle; the founding of Thebes by Cadmus; the tale of Echo and Narcissus; the story of the tragic lovers Pyramus and Thisbe; Jason and the quest for the Golden Fleece; Juno's blinding of the prophet Tiresias; Theseus's voyage to Crete and killing of the monstrous Minotaur; the tragic tale of Orpheus and Eurydice; the wedding of the hero Perseus and princess Andromeda; the transformation of the maiden Scylla into a monster; the huntress Atalanta and the Calydonian boar hunt; the death and deification of the famous strongman Heracles; Venus and Adonis; King Midas and his golden touch; episodes from the renowned Trojan War; and the love between Aeneas and Dido.

The *Metamorphoses* turned out to be even more than a priceless repository of ancient myths; of all of the classical literary works, it also had the most influence on later European artists. The Flemish painter Peter Paul Rubens, for example, illustrated 112 of the stories for King Philip IV of Spain (in the late 1630s); in 1931 the Spanish artist Pablo Picasso published thirty illustrations based on tales from Ovid's masterwork. **See** Ovid.

2. A Latin novel by Lucius Apuleius, also titled *The Golden Ass,* which contains the only surviving version of the important Greek myth about Cupid and Psyche. **See** *The Golden Ass;* **also** Cupid and Psyche (Chapter 6).

Odes

1. A collection of poems in four books by the Augustan poet Horace, considered to be one of the major achievements of Roman literature. Books 1 through 3, made up of eighty-eight poems, were published in about 23 B.C.; and Book 4, comprising fifteen more poems, appeared perhaps ten years later. They are in a variety of meters and, by the author's own admission, are modeled on the works of the earlier Greek poets Sappho and Alcaeus.

The themes and subjects of the *Odes* are wide-ranging, some involving public affairs, others private aspects of Horace's life and the lives of his friends. The public ones often express his feelings of relief (presumably shared by a majority of Romans) that an age of strife and uncertainty had begun to give way to one of peace and security under the rule of Augustus (the first Roman emperor). "Jupiter's thunder confirms our belief that he is the lord of

heaven," Horace writes. "Augustus shall be held an earthly God." (*Odes* 3.5) Horace's patriotism also takes the form of praising traditional Roman values of austerity, courage in the face of hardship, and loyalty to country (values widely felt to have been lost in the turbulent years of the late Republic). "Let every Roman boy be taught to know hardship as a friend," one of the odes begins. "Yes, let him live beneath the open sky in danger. . . . For country is a sweet and seemly thing to die for." (*Odes* 3.2)

Horace's more private odes deal with love, the changing seasons, the beauties and virtues of country living, and the need to live life to its fullest since life is so short. At the same time, he advocates, one should not seek life's extremes but rather learn to live moderately; that way real happiness is easier to achieve. "He that holds fast to the golden mean," he says, "and lives contentedly between the little and the great, feels not the wants that pinch the poor, nor plagues that haunt the rich man's door." (*Odes* 2.10) Most of these pieces are charming and witty, and some have surprise endings. They also make frequent references to mythological characters and stories. Overall, the odes display the author's extraordinary talent for expressing himself concisely and always with just the right emotional tone and choice of words. **See** Horace.

2. A series of poems written by the fourth-century B.C. Greek poet Pindar to honor winning athletes at the "big four" Greek athletic competitions held at Olympia, Delphi (home of the famous oracle, or Pythia), Isthmia, and Nemea. (Accordingly, each ode is titled either "Olympian," "Pythian," "Isthmian," or "Nemean.") Forty-five of these victory odes (*epinikia*) have survived. They were originally commissioned by the athletes themselves or their families and performed by choirs in their hometowns. The poems are valuable not only for their literary merits but also as rich sources of mythological allusions, which Pindar utilized often. The following example, one of several hundred, describes Jason and his Argonauts braving the Symplegades (Clashing Rocks) and entering Colchis, where the local king, Aeetes, guards the Golden Fleece:

> They [the Argonauts] were running toward deep danger and prayed to the Lord of Ships to escape the awful onset of the Clashing Rocks. Two of these rocks there were, and [they were seemingly] alive. They rolled [toward each other] swifter than the howling winds charge past. But that [successful piece of] sailing [straight between the closing rocks, performed by] the sons of gods [the Argonauts] brought them [the rocks] to an end [i.e., marked the last time the rocks clashed together]. After that, Jason and his men came to the River Phasis and matched their might among the dark-faced Colchians, in the very presence of Aeetes. (*Fourth Olympian Ode* 207–216)

See Pindar; **also** Symplegades (Chapter 3); Delphi; Olympia (Chapter 4).

Odyssey

An epic poem attributed to the Greek poet Homer, probably completed in the late eighth century B.C. The title derives from the name of the main character, Odysseus, ruler of the island kingdom of Ithaca (located off the western coast of mainland Greece).

The story begins ten years after the conclusion of the Trojan War, in which Odysseus played a key role. All of the leaders of the Greek expedition to Troy have made it home (or were killed), except for Odysseus. He is on the remote island of Ogygia, where the nymph Calypso has kept him a virtual prisoner for some seven years. Back in Ithaca, almost everyone assumes that Odysseus is dead. His faithful wife, Penelope, and now grown son, Telemachus, are among the few who continue to hold out hope that he still lives. Penelope is beset by a pack of suitors, local nobles, each of whom wants her to marry him and make him king.

While Penelope keeps the suitors at bay and pines away for her lost husband, Zeus, ruler of the gods, finally decides to free Odysseus from Calypso's island. The man builds a raft and sails away, but the sea god Poseidon (who is angry at Odysseus for blinding his son a few years earlier) creates a storm and wrecks the small vessel. Odysseus washes ashore in the land of the Phaeacians, a happy people ruled by King Alcinous.

At a banquet given by Alcinous, Odysseus tells the story of his wanderings during the preceding ten years. After sailing from Troy and heading for home, he recalls, he and his men visited the land of the Lotus-eaters, who ate a local fruit that made them lazy and forgetful. He would have lost many of his men there had he not dragged them away. Not long afterward, the party went ashore to look for supplies on the island of the Cyclopes (one-eyed giants). Odysseus and several men were trapped in the cave of a Cyclops named Polyphemus, whom they blinded to facilitate their escape. (Unfortunately, Polyphemus turned out to be a son of Poseidon, who later exacted revenge by wrecking Odysseus's raft.)

In the adventures that followed, Odysseus tells the Phaeacians, he slowly but surely lost all of his companions. First, he and his followers had another run-in with giants, in this case cannibalistic ones who wrecked eleven out of twelve of the party's ships. The last ship made it to the island of Aeaea, home of the sorceress Circe. She changed Odysseus's men into pigs, but he was protected by a special herb provided by the god Hermes. After a year, Circe released the Greeks, who next landed on the shore of the Ocean (the wide river running around the outer edge of the earth). There, Odysseus visited a group of spirits who rose up from the Underworld. Among them were the blind prophet Tiresias and Achilles, one of the greatest heroes of the Trojan War. Finally, Odysseus and his remaining men had to sail past the monsters Scylla and Charybdis (on the shores of Sicily's Strait of Messina) and the island of the Sirens (women whose songs lured sailors to their deaths). A thunderbolt hurled by Zeus destroyed the last of Odysseus's ships, and he alone made it to Calypso's island, where he spent the next seven years.

After Odysseus finishes his tale, the kindly Phaeacians provide a boat to carry him home to Ithaca. The goddess Athena disguises the man as an old beggar so that he can survey the present situation on the island without alerting anyone to his presence. Odysseus reveals his true identity only to his son, Telemachus, and a faithful servant. They plot and carry out the death of the suitors, which takes place in a bloody battle in the palace banquet hall. Odysseus finally reveals himself to Penelope, and the lovers are reunited. **See** Homer; *Iliad;* **also** Calypso; Circe; Poseidon (Chapter 2); Charybdis; Cyclops; Polyphemus; Scylla; Siren (Chapter 3); Ithaca; Ogygia (Chapter 4); and, for a more detailed account of the story told in the *Odyssey,* **see** The Wanderings of Odysseus (Chapter 6).

Oedipus at Colonus

A tragic play by Sophocles, written in 406 B.C., shortly before the writer's death, and first produced in 401 B.C. by his grandson, also named Sophocles. Oedipus, once king of Thebes and now a blind beggar, has been banished from the city and wanders the countryside attended by his faithful daughter Antigone. They reach Colonus, a village just outside Athens's city walls. Realizing who he is, the local people ask him to go away; however, an oracle has fore-told that Oedipus will die in Colonus, so he refuses to leave. Theseus, king of Athens, hears that Oedipus has arrived and promises the blind man protection and a decent burial after he dies.

At this juncture, Oedipus's other daughter, Ismene, appears in Colonus. She tells her father and sister about a terrible quarrel that recently erupted between Oedipus's sons—Eteocles and Polynices—over the throne of Thebes. The young men rebelled against the city's regent, Creon, Oedipus's former brother-in-law; at first they agreed to share the throne, each ruling in alternate years, but Eteocles now refuses to give up the throne and Polynices plans to retaliate by attacking the city. In addition, an oracle has proclaimed that Oedipus's presence in the vicinity of Thebes will ward off anyone approaching the city with hostile intentions.

Creon arrives in Colonus and confirms this state of affairs. He has come to take Oedipus back to Thebes with him to protect the city from Polynices' assault. When Oedipus refuses to go, Creon attempts to force him by taking Antigone and Ismene as hostages. But Theseus and his soldiers intervene and hold Creon prisoner until he returns the young women, after which the Athenian king orders Creon to leave Attica.

Still another Theban now arrives at Colonus—Oedipus's son Polynices. The young man tells his father that he has married the daughter of Adrastus, king of Argos, who has raised an army to help him attack and dethrone Eteocles. Polynices asks Oedipus to join him in his struggle to gain power in Thebes. Furious at both of his sons, Oedipus curses them, predicting that they will kill each other (a prophecy that later comes true). Polynices departs.

Suddenly, the people of Colonus notice that the sky has grown dark. They hear thunder in the distance, and Oedipus suspects that his time to die has come at last. Theseus arrives in time to watch the blind man walk to a remote spot and there disappear mysteriously from the face of the earth. It becomes clear to the Athenians, as well as to Antigone and Ismene, that the gods have forgiven poor Oedipus his sins and taken him to their bosom. **See** *Antigone; Oedipus the King;* Sophocles; **also** Antigone; Creon 2; Polynices (Chapter 1); The Theban Myth Cycle (Chapter 6).

Oedipus the King

(or *Oedipus Rex* or *Oedipus Tyrranos*) A tragedy by Sophocles, written in about 429 B.C. The first (in order of the mythical events) of the author's three Theban plays (the other two being *Oedipus at Colonus* and *Antigone*), *Oedipus the King* has often been called the greatest tragedy ever written. In his *Poetics,* the fourth-century Greek philosopher-scholar Aristotle praised the work as one of the supreme achievements of the tragic stage, a judgment that has stood the test of time.

Years before the events of the play, Oedipus, a prince of the city of Corinth, heard from an oracle that he would one day kill his father and marry his mother. Hoping to avoid this awful fate, the young man fled from Corinth to Thebes. There, he outwitted the Sphinx, a monster that had been terrorizing the city, and the grateful citizens made him their ruler. He married Jocasta, wife of the former king, Laius (who had been killed on a roadside on his way to consult the Delphic Oracle), and had children by her.

As the play begins, Thebes is beset by a terrible plague. Creon, Jocasta's brother, has just returned from Delphi, where he asked the oracle why his native city has been struck by pestilence. Creon tells Oedipus and a group of Thebans that the plague was sent by the gods as a punishment for the murder of Jocasta's first husband; indeed, the murderer is still at large and must be found and punished before the plague can be averted.

Oedipus vows to find and punish this murderer. But then a series of unexpected and terrible events unfolds. The blind prophet Tiresias tells the king that he, Oedipus, is the very culprit whom everyone seeks. At first, Oedipus scoffs at such a seemingly far-fetched idea. But soon, the king becomes suspicious and disturbed when he hears his wife discussing the details of her former husband's death. The scene she describes, which took place at a crossroads, sounds strangely like an incident in which Oedipus himself had killed a man on his way to Thebes several years earlier.

Before the king can pursue his suspicions any further, however, a messenger arrives from Corinth to announce that Oedipus's father, King Polybus, has died. The Corinthian people want Oedipus to return and take the throne, but he remembers the prophecy predicting that he would marry his mother and is therefore reluctant to go to Corinth. It is at this moment that the messenger reveals a dark secret. Oedipus is *not* the son of the king and queen of Corinth. As a baby, he was a Theban prince who was left outside to die, was found by shepherds, and was secretly given to Polybus and his wife to raise as their own.

The hideous truth now becomes clear to all. The old man whom Oedipus slew at a crossroads on the way to Thebes was none other than his true father, King Laius; and Jocasta, Oedipus's wife, is also his real mother. The old prophecy Oedipus had tried to escape has come true with a vengeance. Unable to face the twisted reality of having married her son and had children by him, Jocasta hangs herself. As for Oedipus, he gouges out his own eyes with a brooch pin. As the play ends, Creon assumes the throne of Thebes. **See** *Antigone; Oedipus at Colonus;* Sophocles; **also** Creon 2; Tiresias (Chapter 1); and, for a fuller account of Oedipus's adventures and tragic fate, **see** The Theban Myth Cycle (Chapter 6).

Oresteia

A trilogy of plays written by the Athenian playwright Aeschylus in 458 B.C. The only complete surviving ancient Greek trilogy, the *Oresteia* consists of *Agamemnon, Libation Bearers,* and *Eumenides,* dealing with the murder of Agamemnon (king of Mycenae and Argos) by his wife, Clytemnestra, and her subsequent murder by their son, Orestes. For synopses of the three plays, **see** under their titles; and, for a more detailed overview of the family's troubles, **see** The Curse of the House of Atreus (Chapter 6).

Ovid

(Publius Ovidius Naso, 43 B.C.–A.D. 17) One of Rome's finest and most popular poets, known for his light-hearted poems about love and also for his huge compendium of myths. Much younger than his celebrated contemporaries Virgil and Horace, Ovid was never invited into the elite literary circle sponsored by Gaius Maecenas, friend of the first emperor, Augustus. Ovid's mentor was another wealthy arts patron named Corvinus Messala.

Although he utilized and excelled in a number of different poetic forms, including the love letter, Ovid is perhaps best known as a master of the love elegy. His love poems were generally witty and full of delicate, colorful description; but despite their beauty, many discussed private sexual matters in a manner too open and graphic for conservative Romans like Augustus, and this inevitably got the poet into trouble. The emperor was apparently disturbed by Ovid's first book of poems, the *Amores* (written ca. 20 B.C.), a bold and witty account of the author's love affair with a married woman named Corinna.

This modern rendering of the Roman poet Ovid captures his wit and sophistication. His Metamorphoses *is one of the most important sources of ancient myths.*

Ovid followed this with *The Art of Love* (ca. 1 B.C. and after), a charming, humorous, and sophisticated but often sexually graphic book of advice on the art of seduction, some of it addressed to men, the rest to women. Although the work convinced the prudish Augustus that Ovid had loose morals, the emperor tolerated the poet's audacity for a number of years.

Eventually, though, the ax fell. For reasons that remain unclear (some rumors claiming the poet was somehow involved with Augustus's daughter Julia), in A.D. 8 Ovid was exiled to Tomis, a bleak frontier town on the shores of the Black Sea. He died there nine years later. His other works included a tragic play, *Medea,* now lost; some collections of letters; and one of his masterpieces, the *Metamorphoses,* a long narrative poem combining over two hundred myths and legends. Ovid not only exerted a strong influence on later Roman writers, but he also became the most popular Latin poet of the European Renaissance and also influenced Shakespeare. **See** *Metamorphoses* 1.

The Phoenician Women

A tragedy by Euripides, first produced between 412 and 408 B.C. The play, the longest surviving ancient Greek drama, deals with the same subject matter as Aeschylus's *Seven Against Thebes*—the quarrel between Oedipus's sons, Eteocles and Polynices, and Polynices' failed assault on the city of Thebes. The title of the play comes from a group of women sent by the king of the Phoenician city of Tyre on a mission to Delphi, home of Apollo's famous oracle. The women stop in Thebes on their way to Delphi and witness the events of the play, though they do not take part in them.

These events begin shortly after Oedipus has fallen from power in Thebes. His sons had agreed to rule the city jointly, each sitting on the throne in alternate years. But Eteocles recently refused to allow Polynices his due share of power, and Polynices has come to Thebes with an army organized by Adrastus, king of Argos, to unseat Eteocles. Eteocles' and

Polynices' mother, Jocasta (wife and mother of Oedipus) tries to get her sons to patch up their feud, but they refuse.

The Thebans are desperate to find a way to repel the attackers. So they listen with interest to the blind Theban prophet Tiresias, who claims that victory will be assured if Creon (Jocasta's brother) sacrifices one of his sons. Creon is reluctant to do so, but his son Menoeceus steps forward and courageously gives up his life to save the city. The young man's sacrifice appears to work, for the Thebans drive the invaders back.

The two sides now agree that the war will be settled by single combat between Eteocles and Polynices. The brothers proceed to kill each other, and Jocasta, consumed by grief, grabs one of their swords and falls on it. Creon assumes the throne and ordains that Polynices' body will remain unburied; furthermore, Oedipus, now a blind beggar, will be exiled to rid the city of the taint of his earlier crimes (killing his father and marrying his mother). Antigone, Oedipus's daughter (and Eteocles' and Polynices' sister) accompanies her father into exile, hinting as she leaves that she will return to give Polynices a proper burial (the subject of Sophocles' play *Antigone*). **See** *Antigone;* Euripides; *Oedipus the King; Seven Against Thebes;* **also** The Theban Myth Cycle (Chapter 6).

Pindar

(ca. 518–ca. 438 B.C.) One of Greece's greatest poets, who became famous for his victory odes composed to honor the winners of the athletic games at Olympia, Delphi, Nemea, and Isthmia. Little is known about Pindar's life, except that he was born in Boeotia, studied music in Athens, and went to Delphi, where he may have been a priest of the god Apollo. **See** *Odes* 2.

Plato

An Athenian philosopher-scholar whose works remain among the most famous and influential of all times. Plato was born circa 427 B.C. into a well-to-do family that (through his mother) traced its descent from the renowned Athenian lawgiver Solon. Little for certain is known about Plato's early life except that he grew up during the disruptive Peloponnesian War (in which he may have served as a cavalryman in its final years), and that, through his relatives Critias and Charmides, he became a follower of the eccentric philosopher Socrates. When Athens was defeated in 404 B.C., Critias and Charmides figured prominently in the short-lived dictatorship that followed. And because of his association with these unpopular characters, Socrates was executed in 399 B.C.

Devastated by these events, Plato left Athens. For the next several years he traveled widely through the Greek world. In 386 B.C. he returned to Athens and established the Academy, a university-like school dedicated to philosophical inquiry and the preparation of future political leaders. There, he became mentor to the brilliant young Aristotle. Except for a journey to Sicily in the 360s B.C., Plato spent the rest of his life in Athens running the school and writing. He died there in 347 B.C. at about the age of eighty.

Plato is nearly unique among the ancient Greek writers because all of his major works have survived to the present. They cover a wide range of topics but are especially concerned with ethical, moral, political, and legal issues. His *Republic* (ca. 380 B.C.), widely viewed as his masterpiece, for example, begins by attempting to define the concept of justice and then proceeds to lay out his plan for an ideal state and its government, which would be ruled by philosopher-kings.

The majority of Plato's works take the form of a dialectic, or dialogue, in which two or more characters engage in a session of questions and answers. The central character is usually Socrates, Plato's old mentor, who directs the discussion; in the course of the discussion, several preconceived notions about the topic in question are refuted by logical means. The remaining notion is assumed to be the truth, or a rough approximation of it. This became known as the Socratic method in Socrates' honor. Besides the *Republic,* some of the most famous of Plato's dialogues are the *Crito,* set in Socrates' jail cell as he awaits execution, which addresses the issue of respect for law; the *Phaedo,* which describes Socrates' death and deals with the nature of the soul; the *Protagoras,* concerned with the nature of virtue; and the *Symposium,* which seeks to understand the nature of love.

Plato's works are filled with short references to various gods, myths, and mythological characters. But his chief contributions to mythology are his dialogues *Timaeus* and *Critias,* which contain the

In his Timaeus, *Plato, seen in this fanciful drawing, told the myth of the lost empire of Atlantis.*

most detailed ancient account of the myth of Atlantis. Plato based the details of the legend on tales brought back from Egypt by one of his ancestors, the lawgiver Solon. As envisioned by Plato, Atlantis was a full-size continent located in the Atlantic Ocean; however, modern scholars believe that the land that sank into the sea was really the Greek island of Thera (lying north of Crete), which was destroyed by a volcanic eruption in the second millennium B.C. **See** Atlantis (Chapter 4).

Plutarch

(ca. A.D. 46–ca. 120) A Greek biographer, essayist, and moralist who became one of the most widely read and best-loved writers in history. Born at Chaeronea (in Boeotia), Plutarch was active in local affairs in his native city as well as the priesthood of the shrine at Delphi. He also became a Roman citizen and resided for a time in Rome.

Plutarch is most famous for his biographies of prominent Greek and Roman figures, collectively known as the *Parallel Lives*, fifty of which survive. Although he was not a historian by trade, Plutarch's sources included hundreds of ancient historical works that are now lost; therefore, for modern historians, these colorfully written biographies constitute priceless mines of information about Greco-Roman history from about 600 to 200 B.C. The sixteenth-century translation of the *Lives* by Sir Thomas North was the main source for Shakespeare's plays *Coriolanus, Julius Caesar,* and *Antony and Cleopatra*. Plutarch's equally large output of commentary on literary, scientific, and moral issues was collected as the *Moralia* (*Moral Essays*).

Plutarch's works contain many passing references to mythological characters and events. In addition, the subjects of four of his biographies are mythological characters, and these works are among the major surviving primary sources about these charac-

ters and their deeds. The four lives are those of Theseus (the Athenian hero and king), Romulus (founder of Rome), Numa Pompilius (Rome's legendary second king), and Lycurgus (a legendary Spartan lawgiver). **See** The Exploits of Theseus; The Founding of Rome (Chapter 6).

Prometheus Bound

A grand and moving tragedy by Aeschylus, dated roughly to 460 B.C. (although some scholars suggest that it remained incomplete until after his death four years later and that another playwright finished it). The play deals with the unique fate of the Titan Prometheus, who incurred the wrath of Zeus by championing human beings, which the Titan had created. The ruler of the gods did not mind Prometheus's first gift to humanity, namely the physical form of the divine Olympians. But Zeus had expressly forbidden the second gift—the secret of fire, which he wanted always to remain a possession of the gods and no one else. However, Prometheus had a soft spot in his heart for the little beings he had created. He wanted them to be able make weapons to defend themselves from wild beasts and to learn various basic and essential crafts, all of which required the use of fire. So he defied Zeus, stole fire from heaven, and presented it to the still-primitive humans.

The play begins shortly after Zeus's discovery that Prometheus has disobeyed him. The ruler of Olympus orders his trusty servants, the giants Force and Violence, to seize Prometheus and take him to the remote Caucasus region, far northeast of Greece. There, accompanied by Hephaestos, god of the forge, they bind the Titan to a jagged rock. Then they leave him alone to suffer as long as Zeus pleases. A group of Oceanids (daughters of the Titan Oceanus, who make up the play's chorus) arrive and try to comfort Prometheus. Soon, Oceanus himself arrives and offers to try to talk Zeus into letting Prometheus go; all that the bound Titan has to do is admit that he was wrong in defying Zeus. Prometheus flatly rejects this idea since he is proud of helping the humans he has come to love.

After Prometheus had suffered for some unknown number of years, Zeus sends his messenger, Hermes, to offer the bound Titan a deal. Zeus has heard a prophecy claiming that someday a son will be born to him, a child who will end up driving him off his throne on Olympus. Because Prometheus possesses the gift of foresight, he alone knows the identity of the woman who will become the boy's mother. (The woman is the nymph Thetis; the prophecy never comes true because Zeus ends up marrying her off to a mortal, Peleus; their son, Achilles, becomes a great hero but poses no threat to Zeus.) If Prometheus will reveal the name of this woman, Hermes says, the king of the gods will free the Titan from his torments. But Prometheus refuses this offer. He knows that in the past he has served Zeus well and that taking pity on the humans and giving them fire was the right thing to do. The chained god asserts that Zeus's punishment is cruel and unjust and that he will never submit to his tyranny.

Hermes now warns Prometheus that if he does not submit to Zeus's will, he will never enjoy a single moment of sleep or relief. First, the mountaintop on which the Titan is chained will collapse into the earth, where Prometheus will remain buried for many centuries. Then he will rise, still bound to the rock, back into the light of day, where a new torture will begin. Each morning a huge, bloodthirsty eagle (in some accounts a vulture) will swoop down and gnaw away at his liver. At night the organ will grow back, but the next day the eagle will return to repeat its grisly task. And this cycle will be repeated endlessly, so that the Titan will know only agony for all eternity.

Even in the face of this terrible fate, the stalwart Prometheus refuses to give in.

And because of this stubbornness, Zeus follows through with the threats he has made. As Prometheus bravely roars his continued defiance, the play comes to a shattering end as the rock and its chained prisoner collapse and disappear into the depths.

The Greeks who watched this titanic drama unfold were not likely to have been satisfied with the valiant Prometheus losing to the tyrannical Zeus and spending eternity in torment. There had to be a satisfactory resolution to the story, one in which the Titan's courage, goodness, and steadfast patronage of mankind would be ultimately rewarded. Indeed, some evidence suggests that *Prometheus Bound* was intended as the second play in a trilogy that Aeschylus never finished. The plot of the third play, *Prometheus Unbound,* is not known for certain; but it is likely that it followed the popular myths associated with the famous Titan. Aeschylus probably had Prometheus reappear from the depths, as Hermes said he would. Next, the eagle would tear at the chained god's liver for untold years; Prometheus would realize that he could end his suffering simply by calling out to Zeus and revealing the information the ruler of Olympus seeks. Yet he would remain resolute and refuse to give in to Zeus. Eventually, though, the courageous Prometheus would gain his freedom in one of two ways. Either the kindly centaur Chiron would offer to die in exchange for Prometheus's release and Zeus would accept this offer, or the famous hero Heracles would happen by, slay the eagle, and release the Titan. Either way, the leader of the gods would ultimately end up allowing Prometheus to be free once more, which means that Zeus, and not the long-suffering and heroic Prometheus, would be the one who submits in the end. **See** Aeschylus; **also** Prometheus; Zeus (Chapter 2); The Creation of the Gods and Humans (Chapter 6).

Sappho

(late seventh century B.C.) A prominent lyric poet and one of the few female literary figures of ancient Greece. Sappho was born in Mytilene, on the island of Lesbos. Little is known about her life, except for a few clues she reveals in her verses; for instance, the fact that she had a daughter whom she loved dearly. The story that Sappho jumped to her death from a cliff because of her unrequited love for a boatman is most likely a fable. Her surviving works (two complete poems and about 150 fragments), mostly describing the other young women in the local cult of Aphrodite to which she belonged, display unusual intensity, directness, honesty, and often erotic qualities. Sappho make numerous references to mythological characters, especially the love goddess, Aphrodite (to whom her main surviving work is addressed), and the Muses (goddesses of the fine arts).

Seven Against Thebes

A tragic play by Aeschylus, written in 467 B.C. The work was the third part of a trilogy, the first parts of which—*Laius* and *Oedipus*—are lost. *Seven Against Thebes* deals with the ill-fated expedition led by Polynices (Oedipus's son) to dethrone his brother, Eteocles, the same subject Euripides addressed in his *Phoenician Women.*

When old enough to rule, Eteocles and Polynices had agreed to share the Theban throne, each reigning in alternate years. But at the end of his first term, Eteocles refused to surrender the kingship. Aided by Adrastus, king of Argos, and five other champions, Polynices has marched an army to Thebes, intending to assault the city and wrest control from Eteocles. A messenger enters the throne room, gives Eteocles a breakdown of the besieging army, and tells how each of its seven leaders is preparing to assault one of Thebes's famous seven gates.

To meet this challenge, King Eteocles appoints a Theban champion to defend each gate, making sure that he himself will defend the one his brother, Polynices, attacks. A huge battle ensues, and the attackers suffer defeat. Eteocles and Polynices meet in single combat and slay each other, fulfilling a curse their father, Oedipus, had laid on them earlier. Soldiers soon bear the bodies of the dead brothers inside the city, where a chorus of Theban women mourns their tragic fate. A herald then enters and announces the decision of the regents, who are in temporary control of the city. Eteocles will be given a proper funeral, but Polynices will be left unburied. "So shall he bear even in death the pollution of his sins against his father's gods," the herald says,

> whom he . . . insulted, launching a foreign army upon our town to overthrow it. His reward shall be dishonor, vagrant birds [i.e., vultures] his only tomb; no troops of slaves shall heap the earth above his corpse; no shrill melodious song of lamentation shall be chanted in his honor, nor any funeral rite performed by next of kin. (*Seven Against Thebes* 1017–1024)

Hearing this decree, Antigone, sister of Eteocles and Polynices, asserts that she will defy it and bury her brother. **See** Aeschylus; *The Phoenician Women;* **also** Adrastus; Antigone; Eteocles; Polynices (Chapter 1); Thebes (Chapter 4); The Theban Myth Cycle (Chapter 6).

Sophocles

(ca. 496–406 B.C.) One of the four great fifth-century B.C. Athenian dramatists and the author of *Oedipus the King,* often called the greatest tragedy ever written. Sophocles was born in the small Athenian village of Colonus, whose name he later immortalized in his play *Oedipus at Colonus.* A friend of the noted Athenian statesman Pericles and the historian Herodotus, the playwright took an active role in public life, serving in 443 B.C. as treasurer of the federation of states that made up Athens's maritime empire and possibly as a military general in 440 B.C.

However, the main focus of Sophocles' long life was the theater, for which he reportedly wrote 123 plays. Unfortunately, only seven of these have survived: *Ajax* (ca. 447 B.C.), *Antigone* (ca. 441), *Oedipus the King* (ca. 429), *The Women of Trachis* (ca. 428), *Electra* (ca. 415), *Philoctetes* (ca. 409), and *Oedipus at Colonus* (406). Some substantial fragments of his satyr play, *The Trackers,* also exist.

A master of characterization, Sophocles was the first playwright to use a third actor (and may also have employed a fourth toward the end of his career). This significantly increased the amount of character interaction in drama. Another result of this development was a reduction in the importance of the chorus, the size of which the playwright fixed at fifteen members.

Sophocles' plots generally revolve around central characters whose personal flaws (often called "tragic flaws") lead them to make mistakes that draw them and those around them into crises and suffering. During the climax of a Sophoclean tragedy, the main character recognizes his or her errors or crimes and accepts the punishment meted out by society and/or the gods. The most famous example is the plight of the title character in *Oedipus the King.* Through the events of the story, Oedipus gradually learns that, unknowingly, he has killed his father and married his mother. Overwhelmed by the horror of these deeds, he accepts responsibility for them, blinds himself, and is doomed to wander the countryside as a moral leper.

Sophocles was the most honored of all Greek playwrights, winning eighteen victories at the City Dionysia (Athens's main dramatic festival, dedicated to the god Dionysus). Indeed, in his *Poetics,* Aristotle praised Sophocles above all other dramatists. The widespread respect and admiration for him, not only as a dramatist but also as an upright, kind, and caring individual, is testified in the tribute paid him shortly after his death by his colleague Aristophanes: "Sophocles, gentleman always, is a gentleman still." (*Frogs* 81–82). **See** *Ajax; Antigone; Electra* 1; *Oedipus at Colonus; Oedipus the King;* **also** The Theban Myth Cycle (Chapter 6).

Statius, Publius Papinius

(ca. A.D. 45–ca. 96) The son of a teacher and poet, Statius was a Roman poet whose talent gained him the patronage and friendship of the emperor Domitian (reigned A.D. 81–96). Statius's best-known works were the *Thebaid* (published ca. 91), an epic poem about the quarrel between Eteocles and Polynices, the sons of the legendary Greek figure Oedipus; and the *Silvae,* a collection of thirty-two short poems (published in installments beginning in 91). The last poem of the *Silvae* is a hauntingly beautiful expression of his grief over the death of his adopted son.

The Suppliant Women

1. A tragedy by Aeschylus, of uncertain date but likely first produced in about 463 B.C. The women of the play's title are the fifty daughters of Danaus, son of the Egyptian king Belus and the twin brother of Aegyptus. Belus had given Aegyptus control of the kingdom of Arabia and Danaus the throne of Libya. Aegyptus had fifty sons and had offered to marry them to Danaus's fifty daughters, the Danaids. However, suspecting that this was a trick by Aegyptus to gain control of Libya, Danaus took his daughters and fled northward to Greece.

The play opens shortly after the travelers have landed at Argos, a city from which, they say, their ancestor Io had hailed. Aegyptus's fifty sons soon follow and demand that the brides they were promised go with them, marry them, and thereafter do their bidding. The fearful maidens plead for the protection of the Argives, led by their king, Pelasgus. After much deliberation by the Argives and numerous threats by the fifty suitors, Pelasgus announces that Argos will give sanctuary to Danaus and his daughters. Pelasgus tells the herald of the sons of Aegyptus to leave Argos or risk war. **See** Aeschylus; **also** Danaus (Chapter 1).

2. A tragic play by Euripides, written in about 422 B.C. The plot deals with the events immediately following the failed attack on Thebes by the Seven Against Thebes, led by Polynices (son of Oedipus) and Adrastus (king of Argos). The Theban people have refused to allow the burial of the leaders of the defeated army. Because such a policy goes against a long-standing, sacred custom, most other Greeks view it as unfair, even barbaric.

To protest the Theban decree, Adrastus, the only leader of the Seven who has survived, accompanies the mothers of the others to Eleusis, in western Attica (about twelve miles from Athens). There, they pray at the shrine of the goddess Demeter and appeal to Theseus, king of Athens, to intervene and ask Thebes to change its policy. (The play's title derives from the fact that the women supplicate, or humbly beg, for justice.)

Theseus agrees to help and requests that the Thebans hand over the corpses. But Theban leaders refuse and also demand that Theseus expel Adrastus so they can arrest him. Furious at this arrogant reply, Theseus resorts to force, defeats the Thebans, and recovers the bodies, which are given proper burial rites and are cremated. **See** Euripides; *The Phoenician Women; Seven Against Thebes;* **also** The Exploits

of Theseus; The Theban Myth Cycle (Chapter 6).

Theogony

A long poem (just over a thousand lines) by the eighth-century B.C. Greek poet Hesiod, important for its systematic account of the origins of the Greek gods. This account is one of the two principal early descriptions of the gods (the other being that of Homer in his epics the *Iliad* and the *Odyssey*); and later Greek writers, including the great Athenian playwrights, frequently drew on Hesiod's material.

The *Theogony* begins with the author's assertion that the Muses (goddesses of the fine arts) visited him one day on the slopes of Mt. Helicon (in Boeotia) and inspired him to write a poem about the gods. The *Theogony* starts at the dawn of creation. From Chaos, Hesiod says, emerged the deities/forces Gaia (Earth), Tartarus (the darkest region of the Underworld), and Eros (Love). Gaia gave rise to Uranus (Sky), and these two mated to produce the Titans (the first race of Greek gods), Cyclopes, and other giants.

Next, the work describes the emergence of Cronos as leader of the Titans and how he sired the first of the Olympians, including Zeus; how Zeus overthrew Cronos; how the Titan Prometheus created the human race and defied Zeus by giving the humans fire; and how Zeus punished Prometheus and also punished the humans by creating the first woman (Pandora).

Finally, the *Theogony* tells about the war between the Titans and the Olympians, which the Olympians won; how Zeus banished most of the Titans to

Tartarus; and how Zeus, now king of the gods, had children by various goddesses and married Hera. **See** Hesiod; *Works and Days;* **also** Cronos; Gaia; Prometheus; Titans; Zeus (Chapter 2); The Creation of the Gods and Humans (Chapter 6).

Valerius Flaccus, Gaius

(first century A.D.) A Roman writer whose only surviving work is a Latin epic poem—the *Argonautica*—a version of the famous story of the quest for the Golden Fleece by Jason and the Argonauts. Almost nothing is known about Valerius's life; even the time and place of his death are uncertain. In a work published sometime between A.D. 93 and 95, another Roman man of letters, Quintilian, said that the recent death of Valerius had been a great loss to Rome, so most modern scholars date the event to circa A.D. 90–93. **See** *Argonautica* 2.

Virgil

(or Vergil; Publius Vergilius Maro) Perhaps the finest and certainly the most popular and influential literary figure of Rome's Augustan age of literature and the author of one of the greatest of all mythological works—the *Aeneid.* Virgil was born in 70 B.C. on a farm in northern Italy. Like most rural Romans, he came to love the land and the virtues of agricultural life, which later became major themes in his works. Shortly after the Battle of Philippi in 42 B.C. (in which the assassins of Julius Caesar were defeated), Virgil met the literary pa-

tron Gaius Maecenas and, through him, the young Octavian (the future Augustus). The poet soon made his name with the *Eclogues,* a collection of short poems about country life, and then he worked for seven years on another set of pastoral verses, the *Georgics,* finished just in time for Octavian's triumphant return to Rome in 29 B.C. Thereafter, until his death ten years later, Virgil was the most respected and imitated writer in the known world.

Virgil had many literary talents, but his greatest was his ability to capture a vision of and make people feel genuine nostalgia for the "good old days." As historian John Firth puts it in his biography of Augustus,

> The great secret of the power which he [Virgil] wielded over his contemporaries and over the ages which were to follow lies not so much in . . . his moral earnestness and in

A modern drawing of Virgil as a young man. His Aeneid *is the chief source of the story of the founder of the Roman race.*

the spirit of humanity . . . which permeates his work. . . . Deep religion and intense burning patriotism—in these lie the secret of Virgil's influence. . . . He looked back with regret to the bygone days when men lived simpler lives, and not only feared, but walked with, the gods.

Virgil's talent for dramatizing the heroic characters and events of past ages reached its zenith in his masterpiece, the epic poem the *Aeneid.* This definitive version of the Roman legend of the Trojan prince Aeneas's founding of the Roman race became Rome's national patriotic epic. This is not surprising, for in it Virgil put into stirring words and verses the Romans' deep pride in their past and their belief that they had a superior destiny. **See** *Aeneid; Eclogues;* **also** Aeneas's Journey to Italy (Chapter 6).

Works and Days

A long poem (consisting of more than eight hundred lines) by the eighth-century B.C. Greek poet Hesiod. The main themes of the work are justice and the work ethic, both of which he seems to feel that his brother lacks. That brother, Perses, took more than his fair share of the family land when their father died.

In the opening of the *Works and Days,* Hesiod calls on Perses to end the feud that has separated the two brothers of late and launches into a series of myths to illustrate the importance of justice and hard work. In this section of the poem, making up about the first third, Hesiod tells how the Titan Prometheus hoodwinked Zeus by stealing fire and giving it to humans and how Zeus retaliated by creating Pandora, the first woman, who unleashed disease and troubles on mankind. Hesiod also explains how the gods created various races of humans in the past, all of them better than the people living in Hesiod's time, which he calls the "Age of Iron." "Now, by day," he says, "men work and grieve unceasingly; by night they waste away and die." (*Works and Days* 181–183) Only through acting with justice and working hard, Hesiod insists, can people hope to make the best of this thankless life and avoid being completely eradicated by Zeus, who is ever vigilant for sinners.

In the last two-thirds of the work, Hesiod gives his brother advice on how to be a successful farmer as well as how to be a good citizen. He explains how to construct a plow and how to sell one's goods to traders, and he offers practical advice, including an almanac listing which days are lucky and which are unlucky for planting and other activities. Like Hesiod's other major work, the *Theogony,* and Homer's epics poems, the *Works and Days* exerted a strong influence on Greeks in succeeding generations, helping them to understand what the gods were like and what these divinities expected of human beings. **See** Hesiod; *Theogony;* **also** Pandora (Chapter 1); Epimetheus; Prometheus; Zeus (Chapter 2); The Creation of the Gods and Humans (Chapter 6).

CHAPTER 6

TWELVE MAJOR GREEK AND ROMAN MYTHS

The Adventures of Heracles

Heracles (whom the Romans called Hercules) was without doubt the most famous and popular ancient Greco-Roman hero. Not only were his physical strength and prowess unmatched, but he was also a humble man who owned up to his mistakes and willingly endured all manner of punishments, usually self-inflicted, as penance. Still, he was not a completely perfect hero. This was because he possessed two character flaws, the first being a lack of keen intelligence like that of his friend the Athenian hero Theseus. As the famous modern scholar Edith Hamilton explains in her classic book on mythology, Heracles

> could never have thought out any new or great idea as the Athenian hero was held to have done. Heracles' thinking was limited to devising a way to kill a monster which was threatening to kill him. Nevertheless, he had true greatness. Not because he had complete courage based on overwhelming strength, which is a matter of course, but because, by his sorrow for wrongdoing and his willingness to do anything to expiate [atone for] it, he showed greatness of soul. If only he had had some greatness of mind as well . . . he would have been the perfect hero.

Heracles' other flaw was his temper. On occasion he flew into uncontrollable rages, during which he struck out at and hurt whoever was near him, even family, friends, and innocent bystanders.

Heracles' Birth and Youth

Heracles' few character flaws were not at all apparent in his infancy and childhood. His mother was Alcmena, wife of Amphitryon, king of Tiryns (in the northeastern Peloponnesus). After Amphitryon accidentally killed his father-in-law, he was accused of murder and fled with his wife to Thebes, where the local king, Creon, purified him. Thebes, therefore, became Heracles' birthplace. Zeus, ruler of the Greek gods, needed a strong son to help him in the impending battle with the giants. Therefore, the god came to Alcmena in Amphitryon's form and made love to her. Later that night, Amphitryon himself made love to Alcmena, too, so she became pregnant with twins boys—Zeus's son, Heracles, and Amphitryon's son, Iphicles.

As almost always happened when Zeus slept with goddesses or mortal women behind his wife's back, that wife—Hera—became jealous and angry. Often, she tried to harm her husband's mistresses and their children, and the case of Heracles was no exception. Hera learned of Alcmena's pregnancy and sent Eileithyia, goddess of childbirth, to thwart the birth. Eileithyia sat outside Alcmena's bedchamber for several days with her arms, legs, fingers, and toes crossed, hoping that this charm would prevent the babies from being born. But one of Alcmena's servants suddenly screamed, startling Eileithyia and causing her to uncross her appendages. In this way, the charm was broken and Alcmena gave birth to Heracles and his brother.

Having failed to stop Heracles' birth, Hera determined to kill him while he was still an infant. She unleashed a pair of serpents, which crawled into Heracles' and Iphicles' nursery in the middle of the night. Iphicles shouted out when he saw the creatures, awakening his brother. Wasting no time, the baby Heracles grabbed hold of the serpents, one in each hand, and strangled them to death. Amphitryon ran into the nursery in time to see this incredible feat and immediately realized that Heracles was no ordinary mortal. The blind Theban prophet Tiresias soon confirmed to Amphitryon that the child was indeed the son of a god—none other than Zeus himself.

Proud of his unusual foster son, Amphitryon made sure that the boy received the best education possible. He taught Heracles how to drive a chariot, and renowned experts from all over Greece instructed the boy how to shoot a bow, wrestle, fight with a sword, and throw a spear. The bow became Heracles' favorite weapon, one he would later use to vanquish many an enemy. In addition to his prowess in these fighting disciplines, the young man repeatedly showed that he possessed enormous, superhuman strength. The first dramatic test of his strength came when he was about seventeen. Hearing that a huge lion was terrorizing and killing the sheep belonging to his father, Amphitryon, Heracles left Thebes and journeyed to nearby Mt. Cithaeron, where the lion had its lair. After slaying the beast, the young man skinned it and thereafter wore its pelt, as one of his trademarks, over his tunic.

When Heracles returned to Thebes from Mt. Cithaeron, he found that Erginus, king of the nearby Boeotian city of Orchomenus, had defeated the Thebans and now demanded that Thebes pay him large sums of money. Enraged, the young strongman armed his fellow Thebans (including his father, Amphitryon, and brother, Iphicles) with swords and spears stored in the city's temples and led them against Erginus's troops. The Thebans were victorious, after which Heracles torched Erginus's palace and flooded Orchomenus's cornfields. Thereafter, Thebes overshadowed Orchomenus and remained always the leading city of Boeotia.

The Madness of Heracles

These deeds made Heracles a hero of tremendous stature in the eyes of his countrymen. They lavished honors on him, and Creon rewarded him by giving him the hand of his daughter, Megara, in marriage. (Megara's younger sister married Iphicles at the same time.) Heracles came to love Megara deeply, and she bore him eight children, all of whom he cared for just as much.

Unfortunately, the goddess Hera was watching these events. She still bore Heracles a grudge and deeply resented his recent good fortune and happiness. Observing his deep feelings for his family, the jealous goddess caused him to fall into a fit of madness; in this state of temporary insanity, Heracles killed his wife and six of his children. He would have slain his other two children and Iphicles' offspring as well had not the goddess Athena intervened by knocking him out with a rock.

When Heracles finally came to his senses and saw his mangled family members lying at his feet, he was beside himself with guilt and anguish. In his tortured mind, killing himself seemed the only just punishment for so terrible a crime. But just as he was about to do away with himself, his friend Theseus arrived and took his bloody hands in his own. The Athenian king implored the strongman not to take his own life. Heracles responded that he had committed a horrible crime and should suffer death himself so that the deaths of his loved ones might be properly avenged. But Theseus argued that what Heracles had done was not murder since he had been bewitched by Hera and therefore did not realize what he was doing. He urged the strongman to go with him to Athens, where a champion of his caliber was badly needed.

Heracles reluctantly agreed to go to Athens with Theseus. But though the people of that great city welcomed the strongman and told him that the deaths of his wife and sons were not his fault, he could not bring himself to agree with them. In his own mind, he remained a criminal who must be punished. Seeking advice on what he might do to atone for the killings, he left Athens and journeyed westward to Delphi, home of Apollo's oracle. The oracle told Heracles to go to Argolis (the region of the Peloponnesus containing Argos, Mycenae, and Tiryns) and seek out its king, Eurystheus. He would devise a series of extremely difficult tasks, and only after Heracles had completed them would he be cleansed of the guilt of his terrible crime.

The Twelve Labors Begin

Following the oracle's advice, Heracles made his way to the fortress-town of Mycenae, whose mammoth stone walls perched atop a rocky crag overlooking a fertile valley in southeastern Greece. Eurystheus welcomed the strongman and told him that he must perform a number of labors that an ordinary person would find daunting or even impossible. The first was to kill the Nemean Lion, a huge creature that could not be wounded by weapons. Heracles walked to Nemea (which lay a few miles northwest of Mycenae) and there found the huge and fearsome creature guarding its lair in a cave on the side of a mountain. The strongman first tried

shooting it with his bow, but sure enough, the arrows from the weapon had no effect. Since weapons would not work, Heracles decided to fight without them. He charged forward, grasped the lion around its neck, and strangled it.

When Heracles returned to Mycenae carrying the carcass of the Nemean Lion on his back, the people were astounded. Eurystheus praised him for a job well done, but he was careful to point out that Heracles' labors had only just begun. Next, the king declared, Heracles must slay the Hydra, a monster that lived in a swamp in Lerna (several miles southwest of Mycenae) and periodically went out into the countryside killing cattle and laying waste to the land. According to the ancient myth teller Apollodorus of Athens,

> The Hydra had an enormous body and nine heads, one of which was immortal. Heracles went to Lerna . . . and found the Hydra on the brow of a hill . . . where it had its den. Shooting at it with flaming arrows, Heracles drove the creature out, and then, when it came close, he grabbed it and held it tight. But the Hydra wrapped itself around his foot, and he was not able to get free by striking off its heads with his club, for as soon as one head was cut off, two grew in its place. In addition, a huge crab came to the aid of the Hydra and kept biting Heracles' foot. He therefore killed the crab and . . . set fire to the woods nearby and, by burning the stumps of the Hydra's heads with firebrands, kept them from growing out again. Then Heracles cut off the immortal head, and when he had buried it in the ground, he put a heavy rock over it. (*Library* 2.4)

After overcoming the Hydra, the hero split open its body and dipped his arrows in its deadly poison. In the years that followed, this poison made Heracles' bow and arrows one of the most formidable weapons in the known world.

Heracles grapples with the Hydra. Each time one of the creature's heads was cut off, two more grew in its place.

Heracles returned in triumph to Mycenae once more, and he asked Eurystheus if there was a third labor to perform. Indeed there was: to bring back alive the Cerynitian Hind, a fabulous deer with horns of gold, a creature sacred to the goddess of the hunt, Artemis. Although the strongman managed to complete this difficult task, it took him an entire year. He finally tracked down the hind in Arcadia (in central Greece) and captured it with a net while it slept. On the way back to Mycenae, the strongman encountered Artemis, accompanied by her brother, Apollo. The gods demanded that Heracles release the hind, but he argued that he was only acting on the order of King Eurystheus, as part of his penance for slaying his wife and children. Hearing this, Artemis allowed him to continue on; and once the hero reached Mycenae and showed the hind to the king, he let the creature go.

Adventures with Centaurs and Argonauts

Eurystheus then proceeded to heap still more labors on Heracles, who patiently and humbly accepted them all without complaint. For his fourth labor, the strongman set out to track down and capture a large and vicious boar that was destroying the villages and the farmlands near Mt. Erymanthos, in a desolate region many miles to the west of Mycenae. On his way to that region, he stopped to talk to a centaur (a creature half man and half horse) named Pholus, who invited him to dinner. Pholus turned out to be a poor host, however. He refused to give Heracles any wine. And when the man complained, a fight broke out. In self-defense, Heracles was forced to kill a large number of the centaurs, including Pholus, with his mighty bow and poisoned arrows. (One of the surviving horse-men, Nessus, would eventually achieve a sort of revenge on Heracles for slaying his fellow centaurs.) After this run-in with the centaurs, Heracles used his net to capture the Erymanthian Boar and carried the struggling beast back to King Eurystheus. (Legend held that the king was so afraid of the boar that he hid inside a large bronze jar until his attendants took the creature away.)

It was shortly after Heracles had completed his fourth labor that news came that the hero Jason was scouring Greece looking for champions to accompany him on a quest to find the fabulous Golden Fleece. Eurystheus allowed the strongman to take a break from his arduous labors, and Heracles joined the crew of Jason's ship, the *Argo*. When the vessel sailed from Pagasae (on the coast of Thessaly, near Iolcos), Heracles took along a young friend, Hylas, as his squire. The two became inseparable and proved themselves on more than one occasion during the Argonauts' early adventures. Heracles' greatest single feat on the voyage was killing a tribe of giants who were terrorizing the Doliones, a people who lived in Mysia (in northern Asia Minor).

Unfortunately, not long after this exploit, Heracles accidentally broke his oar. And when he and Hylas went ashore to cut down a tree to make a new one, Hylas got lost and some water nymphs suddenly captured him and pulled him down into their spring. Frantic, Heracles searched long and hard for his friend and refused to leave until he succeeded. The Argonauts finally had no choice but to leave him and continue with their voyage. (Before turning back for Greece, the strongman persuaded the local people to conduct a fresh search for the youth each year.)

Deadly Birds, a Savage Bull, and Man-Eating Horses

Reaching Mycenae a few weeks later, Heracles told Eurystheus that he was ready to perform his fifth labor. The king ordered him to clean out the stables of Augeas, king of Elis (a city lying west of Mt. Erymanthos), which were unbelievably filthy after thousands of cattle had lived in them for years. To accomplish this task, Apollodorus says, Heracles "tore away part of the foundations of the stable and diverted the Alpheus and Peneus rivers into the stables, letting them run out through an opening he had made on the other side." (*Library* 2.4)

In his sixth labor, Heracles drove away a flock of huge birds that were plaguing

the people of Stymphalus (northwest of Nemea). These dangerous creatures had been killing both humans and animals by shooting them with the tips of their feathers, which had metal tips and flew through the air like arrows. To destroy these pests, Heracles shook a bronze rattle (made by Hephaestos, god of the forge), which frightened them out of their treetop nests, and he then shot them with his poisoned arrows.

To complete his seventh task for Eurystheus, Heracles journeyed to Crete and captured a beautiful but savage bull that the sea god Poseidon had given to that island's king, Minos. (Minos did not interfere with the strongman since this was the bull with which his wife had mated to produce the fearsome Minotaur; the Cretan king was glad to be rid of it.) Heracles carried the bull all the way back to Mycenae and, after showing it to Eurystheus, released it. (The bull then found its way to Marathon, northeast of Athens, where Heracles' friend Theseus ended up slaying it.)

The eighth labor Eurystheus ordered the strongman to perform was to go to Thrace (in extreme northern Greece) and bring back a herd of man-eating horses belonging to Diomedes, the king of a powerful Thracian tribe. On the way to Thrace, Heracles passed through Pherae, in Thessaly, where he visited the palace of the local king, Admetus. The hero was surprised and perplexed when he found the outside of the palace nearly deserted and heard sounds of wailing from inside. Then he learned that Admetus's courageous and loyal wife, Alcestis, had just given her life so that her husband might live. (The god Apollo had granted Admetus the privilege of escaping death as long as he could find another mortal who would willingly take his place when it was time for him to die.) Filled with admiration for Alcestis, as well as pity for Admetus, the big-hearted Heracles determined not to allow Thanatos, god of death, to take the woman to the Underworld. In a titanic struggle, the strongman wrestled Thanatos and drove him away, then reunited Admetus and Alcestis.

Leaving Pherae, Heracles made his way to Thrace and captured Diomedes' man-eating horses. The strongman did not wish to hurt Diomedes or his people, but this became necessary when the king ordered his subjects to attack Heracles and recover his horses. After defeating or driving away these attackers, Heracles found Diomedes, bound him, and fed him to his own horses, after which the animals became tame.

Hippolyte's Girdle and Geryon's Cattle

Even after Heracles had delivered the once bloodthirsty horses to Eurystheus in Mycenae, his penance was not over. For his ninth labor, Heracles delivered to Eurystheus the girdle of Hippolyte, queen of the Amazons, a tribe of warrior women who inhabited the wild steppes of the region north of Thrace. When the strongman approached the queen and asked her for the girdle, she surprised him by handing it over without a fuss. But Heracles' assumption that this labor would require no fighting or great physical effort turned out to be wrong. The goddess Hera, still trying to impede the hero whenever she could, disguised herself as an Amazon; she stirred up the warlike women, telling them that the man had come to kidnap their queen, and they assaulted him. Having no choice but to fight back, Heracles ended up slaying Hippolyte, an act he regretted.

During his return voyage from the land of the Amazons, Heracles stopped to rest on the coast of Asia Minor, near Troy. There, he received greetings from Laomedon, the city's king. Laomedon begged the renowned hero to save his daughter, Hesione, who was about to be eaten by a huge sea monster (sent by Poseidon to punish Laomedon for refusing to pay the god for helping to erect Troy's defensive walls). Heracles agreed to destroy the monster in exchange for some prize horses that Zeus had given Laomedon. But after the hero had managed to slay the creature, Laomedon reneged and did not deliver the horses. For this offense, Heracles promised to come back someday and punish the Trojan king.

Returning to Mycenae with Hippolyte's girdle, Heracles had to agree to still another labor, his tenth. Eurystheus ordered him to travel all the way to the western end of the Mediterranean Sea and from there out into the great unknown sea that lay beyond until he reached the fabulous island of Erythea. There, the strongman had to capture the cattle of a monster named Geryon, who had three bodies and three heads. Geryon's cattle were guarded by a huge herdsman, Eurytion, and a two-headed dog, Orthus. According to Apollodorus,

> Because he was hot from the sun on his journey, he [Heracles] shot an arrow at the sun god Helios, who in wonder at his daring, gave him a golden goblet in which he crossed the sea. And when he came to Erythea . . . the dog [Orthus] found him and attacked him, but he struck the creature down with his club, and he also killed the herdsman Eurytion when he came to the rescue of the dog. When Geryon heard what had happened, he caught up to Heracles . . . and Geryon was killed by an arrow as he tried to fight him. Then Heracles loaded the cattle into the goblet, and when he had crossed over to Europe, he gave the goblet back to Helios. (*Library* 2.5)

Having reached the mouth of the Mediterranean once more, Heracles commemorated his success by setting up two gigantic rocks, which became known as the Pillars of Heracles (or Pillars of Hercules, today called Gibraltar).

Getting the cattle back to Greece proved a more formidable task than Heracles had expected, though. As he drove the cattle southward through Italy, he visited the future site of Rome; there, he encountered Cacus, a fire-breathing creature that lived on human flesh and piled up the skulls and bones of its victims inside its cave. Heracles stopped for a nap on the bank of the Tiber River, after which Cacus saw the cattle and stole four bulls and four heifers. When the strongman woke up, he searched for the missing cattle and found them in Cacus's cave. In the battle that ensued between man and monster, Heracles ripped away the top of the hill to force his opponent into the light, then strangled the creature and recovered the cattle.

Heracles had to preserve and defend Geryon's cattle in three other incidents on the way back to Mycenae. In the first, one of the bulls escaped and swam from southern Italy to Sicily, where a local king, Eryx, captured it and refused to give it up. Heracles wrestled Eryx, winning three falls, and then killed him before retrieving the escaped bull. Later, when crossing the Isthmus of Corinth, the strongman was attacked by a giant named Alcyoneus, who wanted to steal the cattle. Heracles killed Alcyoneus with a rock. Finally, Hera struck again, sending a gadfly, which stung the cattle and caused them to scatter. Only with great difficulty was Heracles able to round up all the cattle and deliver them to Eurystheus.

The Golden Apples and the Descent into the Underworld

To complete his eleventh labor, Heracles had to bring back a treasure, namely the golden apples of the Hesperides (in some accounts, the Hesperides were the daughters of the Titan Atlas, who held up the sky in a remote land near the Hesperides' garden). To find the Hesperides' legendary garden, Heracles consulted Nereus, a reclusive sea god who was known to change his shape repeatedly to avoid having to deal with people. Holding onto the

slippery deity throughout all its transformations, the strongman was finally able to force Nereus to reveal the location of the Hesperides' garden.

The journey to the garden was long, however, and Heracles experienced several adventures on the way. Perhaps the most famous involved his freeing of the Titan Prometheus after slaying the giant eagle that Zeus had ordained should tear out Prometheus's liver each day. The strongman also encountered a giant named Antaeus, who challenged all passersby to wrestle him and then killed them; Heracles accepted the giant's challenge and proceeded to squeeze the life out of him.

Finally reaching the land of the Hesperides, Heracles saw the mighty Atlas holding up the far edge of the sky and told the Titan why he had come. Atlas offered to go collect the golden apples if Heracles would do him the favor of holding up the sky while he was away. But when the god returned with the apples, he would not uphold his part of the bargain and told Heracles that he would have to go on holding up the sky forever. However, though certainly no mental giant, Heracles was smarter than Atlas and was able to trick him. He claimed that he needed to adjust the weight better on his shoulders and asked for some help; the dim-witted Atlas obliged and resumed holding up the sky, after which Heracles took the apples and left.

On returning to Mycenae, Heracles offered the golden apples to Eurystheus. The king refused to touch them, however, fearing the wrath of the gods; this turned out to be a wise move, for the goddess Athena suddenly appeared and took possession of the treasure, which she duly returned to the Hesperides' garden.

The twelfth and last of Heracles' labors witnessed his descent into the dark and forbidding Underworld to capture Cerberus, the monstrous and vicious three-headed dog that guarded the realm of the dead. The god Hermes and goddess Athena guided the man down into the Underworld and to the edge of the River Styx. There, the ghastly boatman Charon, who had heard of the strongman's exploits and feared him, wasted no time in rowing him across the river. (Later, Hades, lord of the Underworld, chained Charon for a year to punish him for allowing Heracles to enter the realm of the dead.) On the far bank of the Styx, Heracles found Hades waiting to bar his way; and the two got into a fight. After the man wounded him, the god agreed to let him take Cerberus, provided that he could capture the creature without the use of weapons; Hades also agreed to allow Heracles to rescue the Athenian champion Theseus, whom the god had imprisoned in one of his Chairs of Forgetfulness (after Theseus and his friend Pirithous

had attempted to abduct Hades' wife, Persephone). Then, the ruler of the Underworld hurried off to Mt. Olympus to receive medical treatment.

After having defeated Hades, Heracles had little trouble capturing Cerberus. Carrying the hideous creature up to the earth's surface, the strongman brought it to Eurystheus (who was so terrified that he once again hid inside his bronze jar). The king had no intention of keeping the dangerous creature, of course, so Heracles dutifully lugged it back to its place in the Underworld.

Heracles' Last Exploits and Deification

Heracles had finally completed all twelve of these seemingly impossible labors—a task that had consumed many years and

On a Greek vase, Heracles, brandishing his signature club, presents Cerberus to King Eurystheus, who retreats into his bronze jar.

had taken him to the ends of the earth. During all that time he had never wavered because he still felt strongly that he must atone for killing his wife and sons. Now that he had atoned, however, his adventures were far from over; in the years that followed, he performed numerous other formidable and wondrous deeds.

Among these adventures were several in which Heracles gained vengeance on various individuals who had cheated or otherwise wronged him in the past. He returned to Troy, for example, and slew King Laomedon (who had refused to give him his horses in exchange for saving his daughter from the sea monster). The strongman also returned to Elis and punished its king, Augeas, whose stables he had earlier cleaned. Augeas had agreed to pay the hero a fee of one-tenth of his cattle for the job, but he had gone back on the deal; now that king paid for his bad faith with his life.

Heracles also helped the Olympian gods defeat the giants who had sprung from the blood droplets that fell after the Titan Cronos castrated his father, Uranus. Gaia (the earth) had gathered them for an attack on Zeus and his fellow gods; but athough the Olympians were incredibly strong and resourceful, the giants were immune from death at the hands of any god. To win the battle, therefore, Zeus needed the aid of a mortal hero. And having foreseen this need long before, he had sired the tremendously strong and valiant Heracles, who now made possible his father's great victory over the giants.

In a way, this heroic stand that Heracles took beside Zeus and the Olympians foreshadowed his eventual deification, for he was not fated to remain merely an earthly hero. While undertaking his last labor—the trip to the Underworld to fetch Cerberus—Heracles had met the shade (soul) of Meleager, a prince and hero of Calydon (in western Greece). And when Meleager had urged him to go to his hometown and marry his sister, the beautiful Deianira, Heracles had promised him he would do so. Later, the strongman remembered this promise, journeyed to Calydon, and married Deianira, who gave him several children, including a son, Hyllus.

Heracles and Deianira remained happy for a number of years. But then Heracles won a young girl named Iole in an archery contest. (Iole's father refused to hand her over, and the strongman slew him and took her prisoner.) Worried that Heracles had come to love this girl more than his own wife, Deianira found a vessel containing the blood of Nessus, one of the centaurs Heracles had slain in Arcadia many years before. She smeared the blood on a tunic and gave the garment to her husband to wear; and when Heracles donned the tunic, it badly burned his flesh (thereby fulfilling Nessus's vengeance on the strongman for killing his fellow centaurs).

Mortally wounded, the great hero sent a messenger to the Delphic Oracle to ask the gods for guidance. Their answer was that he should erect a funeral pyre on Mt. Oeta, in Thessaly, lie on the pyre, and wait for Zeus's intervention. At Heracles' bidding, his son Hyllus built the pyre. But when the dying hero lay down on it, none of his relatives or friends had the heart to light it. As fortune would have it, at that moment Poeas, father of Philoctetes (who would later become a hero of the Trojan War), happened by; in exchange for Heracles' famous bow and poisoned arrows, Poeas set the pyre ablaze. A few moments later the sad mourners were startled by a huge bolt of lightning that exploded above the pyre, after which they witnessed a column of smoke rise swiftly into the sky. When they looked back at the pyre, the body of their friend was nowhere to be seen, and they suddenly realized, with great joy, what had happened. The gods had taken the mighty and generous Heracles into their realm, granting him the gift of eternal life.

Aeneas's Journey to Italy

Aeneas's fateful story, as told in Virgil's *Aeneid,* begins seven years after the fall of Troy. The Trojan prince's small fleet of ships was plying the calm waters near the large Mediterranean island of Sicily, when the goddess Juno (wife of Jupiter, leader of the gods) intervened. She had favored and aided the Greeks during the Trojan War, so she naturally did not want to see Aeneas or any other Trojans succeed in their ventures. Moreover, with her divine powers she could foresee the awful possibility that Aeneas's descendants might destroy her favorite city, the lovely and prosperous North African metropolis of Carthage. (This turn of events actually occurred many centuries later, when the Romans defeated the Carthaginians in the three devastating Punic Wars.) So Juno mustered up a violent storm, hoping to scatter and destroy Aeneas's vessels. According to Virgil,

> The winds . . . swirled out and swept the land in a hurricane, whirled on the sea and whisked it deep to its bed, from every quarter hurling the breakers shoreward. . . . From Trojan sight, darkness descended on the deep, thunder shackled the poles, the air crackled with fire, everywhere death was at the sailor's elbow. Terror played fast and loose with Aeneas's limbs and he moaned and lifted his arms to the stars in prayer. . . . The waves towered to the stars; the oars were smashed, the bow yawed . . . and a huge mountain of toppling water battered the vessels' beams. (*Aeneid* 1.82–106)

When the tempest finally subsided, Aeneas and his surviving followers made their way to the nearest shore, which, as fate would have it, turned out to be the coast near Carthage. The men entered the city, and soon Aeneas met its queen, Dido, who fell madly in love with him. (This happened partly because the love goddess,

Venus, willed it. Venus was Aeneas's mother, who had mated with a mortal man—Anchises, of the royal house of Troy—to produce him; and she wanted Aeneas to stay in Carthage and live a safe and happy life there.) As Dido got to know the Trojan prince, Virgil writes,

> Again and again there rushed into her mind thoughts of the great valor of the man and high glories of his [family] line. His features and the words he had spoken had pierced her heart and love gave her body no peace or rest. . . . She spoke these words from the depths of her affliction to her loved and loving sister: "O Anna, what fearful dreams I have as I lie there between sleeping and waking! What a man is this who has just come as a stranger into our house! What a look on his face! What courage in his heart! What a warrior! I do believe, and I am sure it is true, that he is descended from the gods." (*Aeneid* 4.3–14)

Aeneas Describes Troy's Fall

At a great banquet in the Carthaginian court, Dido begged Aeneas to describe his recent adventures to her and her noble courtiers. She implored the brave soldier to tell them about the end of that mighty city, Troy, and how he had escaped its flames carrying his aged father, Anchises, on his back. Silence then fell on the crowded hall as everyone focused their attention on the noble Aeneas. "O Queen," he said,

> the sorrow you bid me bring to life again is past all words. . . . No man could speak of such things and not weep. . . . But if you have such a great desire to know what we suffered, to hear in brief about the last agony of Troy, although . . . I shudder to remember, I shall begin. (*Aeneid* 2.2–14)

Aeneas proceeded to tell his listeners how his brother, Hector, the greatest Trojan champion, had been slain by the mighty Greek warrior Achilles. Then, after having besieged the city for ten years, the Greeks had suddenly appeared to give up the siege. They had sailed away, leaving one of their number, Sinon, behind, along with a huge wooden horse that towered over the plain of Troy. Sinon claimed he was a deserter and that the horse was an offering to the goddess Minerva (the Greek Athena). If the Trojans brought the horse into their city, he said, it would bring them good fortune. But one Trojan priest, Laocoön, warned his countrymen that the Trojan Horse was only a ruse. He said that Sinon was lying and urged the Trojans not to touch the horse. Barely had these words left his lips when two monstrous serpents rose up from the nearby sea and killed Laocoön and his two young sons.

The Trojans assumed that Minerva had sent the serpents to punish Laocoön for doubting the sincerity of her offering. So they believed Sinon's story and proceeded to drag the horse into the city. This only sealed their doom, however, for Laocoön had been right. Later that night a band of Greek warriors, who had been hiding inside the horse, crept out and opened the gates for the rest of their army, which went on a killing spree and torched the city. Meanwhile, Aeneas explained, he and some close kin and followers managed to escape. Having lost their home, they now had no other choice but to search for another, so they built some ships and set out into the blue-green waters of the Aegean Sea.

A Journey Guided by Prophecies

The Trojan refugees, Aeneas continued, first stopped in Thrace (the land lying along the northern rim of the Aegean Sea); however, when the Trojans built an altar and pulled up some plants to cover it, they were disturbed to see the roots of the plants dripping blood. Then they heard a voice that seemed to come from thin air. It warned them that Thrace was not a friendly place and that they would surely come to grief if they stayed there. (The voice turned out to be that of the son of Troy's Queen Hecuba—Polydorus, who had recently been murdered by a king of Thrace.)

Heeding Polydorus's warning, Aeneas and his followers next sailed to the tiny sacred island of Delos (birthplace of the deities Apollo and Diana), which lies at the center of the Aegean. There, an oracle gave them a message from Apollo, god of prophecy. The Trojans should seek out their "ancient mother," the message said, the land from which their distant ancestors had originally come. But Aeneas and his companions had no idea where this ancient motherland might be, and the oracle had given no substantial clue. Thinking that it might be the island of Crete (which lies southeast of the Greek mainland), Aeneas led his followers there. But after they had landed, they received another message from Apollo, this one informing them (according to Virgil),

> Since Troy was consumed by fire, the gods have followed you and your arms. We have been with you through every . . . crest of ocean your fleet has weathered, and we shall raise your prosperity to the stars and give to your city its mighty sway. . . . You must move your habitation—it was not these shores that I commended to you. . . . There is a place the Greeks have called Hesperia—the western land—an ancient country powerful in war and rich of soil. . . . The inhabitants call themselves "Italians" after Italus—one of their leaders. There lies your true home. (*Aeneid* 3.157–167)

In this way, Aeneas learned that his fate was to sail to Italy and there to establish a new home for his people.

Unfortunately, the voyage to faraway Italy had been neither quick nor easy, Aeneas told Dido and the others. With a heavy sigh, he explained how it turned out to be a long, complicated, and dangerous venture. Sailing westward into the larger reaches of the Mediterranean, the Trojans stopped on one of a group of islands known as the Strophades. No sooner had they slaughtered some cattle, cooked the meat, and settled down for a meal, when a flock of Harpies appeared seemingly out of nowhere. These hideous, smelly, birdlike creatures, which had large, sharp claws and women's faces, descended on the gathering and fouled the food by covering it with their sickening stench. Aeneas and his followers managed to drive the creatures away, but the retreating Harpies uttered a combination of prophecy and curse. Aeneas would make it to Italy, they said, but he would not be allowed to establish a walled city of his own until hunger had driven him to devour his tables. (When Aeneas and his followers later sailed up the Tiber River in Italy, they stopped to eat and were so hungry that after finishing their meal they ate the thin bread cakes they were using as platters; Aeneas interpreted these as their "tables" and concluded that the Harpies' prophecy had been fulfilled.)

After the Harpies had departed, Aeneas continued westward, constantly harassed by the goddess Juno, who still harbored resentment toward him and the other Trojans. The travelers soon came to the shores of Epirus (in northwestern Greece). There, to their great surprise, they found that the ruler was Helenus, a Trojan and one of Aeneas's kinsmen. Helenus was also gifted with the ability to see into the future. Taking Aeneas aside, he told him that the gods had fated that he would succeed in his great quest, but only if he did certain specific things to help overcome the obstacles along the way. First, said Helenus, Aeneas should avoid a channel bordered by some dangerous falling rocks. (This was one of the same danger spots that the Greek king Odysseus had encountered during his own perilous journey

following Troy's downfall.) Second, after reaching Italy, Aeneas must seek out and get the advice of a renowned local priestess and prophetess, the Sibyl. And third, a great city will eventually rise on a riverbank where Aeneas sees a white sow and her thirty babies resting.

Dido's Rage

Thanking Helenus, Aeneas gathered his followers and once more sailed toward the setting sun. Although the travelers managed to avoid the dangerous rocks Helenus had warned them about, they made the mistake of stopping on an uncharted island to gather provisions. There, they came on a bedraggled old Greek. Claiming to be one of Odysseus's men who had been left behind accidentally, he informed them that this was the land of the Cyclopes, a race of frightening one-eyed giants. Moreover, the Greek said, Polyphemus, the Cyclops whom Odysseus and his men had blinded, lived nearby. "He is hideous to look on," said the Greek (according to Virgil),

> nor can his mind be moved by human speech. He feeds on the entrails [insides] and the dark blood of his unhappy victims. With my own eyes I have seen him snatch up two of our number in his colossal hand and brain them on a rock. . . . I have seen all the floor awash with spurting blood. I have seen him crunch their limbs up dripping with dark blood and their joints warm and twitching still as his jaws closed over them. (*Aeneid* 3.622–628)

Only seconds later, the subject of this grisly tale, the giant Polyphemus, appeared and threatened Aeneas and his band. Luckily, the Trojans managed to elude the creature's clutches and made it to the shore of Sicily (which lies just south of the Italian peninsula). However, their happiness at having escaped a gruesome death was now overshadowed by an unexpected bout of grief. Old Anchises, Aeneas's father, by now very frail and exhausted by the arduous trek, died, leaving his son and the others weighed down by a heavy sadness.

It was directly after leaving Sicily, Aeneas said, finishing the story of his adventures, that the terrible storm struck and drove the Trojans to the beaches of Carthage and their meeting with their goodly host, Dido. The queen was delighted with the tale and was now even more in love with Aeneas than she had been before. She begged him to stay with her and make Carthage, rather than Italy, his new home. The Trojan prince came to care deeply for Dido, and for a while it looked as though he might forget about his prophesied Italian destiny and become the king of the North African kingdom she ruled.

However, mighty Jupiter did not desire for Aeneas to settle down in Carthage. The leader of the gods sent his messenger, the swift-footed Mercury, to remind Aeneas that he had a duty to future generations of Italians. "You forget, it seems, your true kingdom, your destiny!" Mercury told Aeneas.

Aeneas (left) relaxes with his lover, Dido, queen of Carthage. After he left her to complete his mission to Italy, she committed suicide.

> Now mighty Jupiter, the absolute monarch of the gods, has sent me, he who holds heaven and earth in the palm of his hand. . . . What are you doing? Why do you linger here in north Africa? If no ambition spurs you, nor desire to see yourself renowned for your own deeds, what about Ascanius [Aeneas's son]? The realm of Italy and the Roman inheritance are his due. (*Aeneid* 4.268–277)

Hearing this appeal, Aeneas came to his senses and made preparations to leave Carthage. Not surprisingly, Dido was both grief-stricken and angry that he would

suddenly leave her this way; despite her love for him, she hurled harsh words at him. "You traitor!" she screamed.

> Did you hope to mask such treachery and silently slink from my land? Is there nothing to keep you? Nothing that my life or our love has given you, knowing that if you go, I cannot but die? . . . Why, if Troy still stood, would you seek Troy across these ravening waters? Is it unknown lands and unknown homes you seek, or is it from me you flee? You see me weep. I have nothing else but tears and your right hand to plead with. . . . If you ever found in me any sort of sweetness, pity me now! . . . If prayer has any potency [strength] change your mind! . . . [When he refused to change his mind, she screeched:] "Oh God, I am driven raving

mad with fury! . . . Go! Seek Italy on a tempest, seek your realms over the storm-crests, and I pray if the gods are as true to themselves as their powers that you will be smashed on the rocks, calling on Dido's name! (*Aeneid* 4.306–386)

She then pronounced a terrible curse: May future Carthaginians and Aeneas's descendants always hate one another, she said. Let there be no treaties between the two peoples, and let generation after generation be consumed by weapons and war! (This curse was fulfilled when the Carthaginians and Romans later came to death grips in the bloody Punic Wars.) Soon afterward, as Aeneas's ships sailed from Carthage's harbor, the livid, grieving queen grasped a sword and plunged it into her breast, ending her life.

Italian Landfall

After departing Africa, Aeneas and his company sailed back to Sicily, arriving about a year after old Anchises had died there. The local ruler welcomed the travelers and helped them to stage athletic games to honor Anchises; and during the celebration, the Trojan women mourned the loss of their homes and loved ones years before at unlucky Troy.

Meanwhile, the goddess Juno was secretly watching. She still wanted to thwart Aeneas's plans to reach Italy, so she hatched a sinister plan designed to force him and his followers to remain in Sicily. She sent down the rainbow goddess, Iris, disguised as one of the grieving Trojan women. Iris gathered the women around her and told them that their unhappiness over losing their homes was perfectly understandable. Aeneas had only prolonged their agony and that of their poor children, she said, by refusing to stay in one place. For years he had forced them to wander from one end of the great sea to another, passing up many opportunities to establish new homes in friendly, pleasant climates. Aeneas's followers should put a stop to this nonsense, she said. The ruler of this fair land of Sicily had welcomed them, and they should accept his hospitality and make their new home there, where they knew it was safe, rather than continue on to unknown and potentially dangerous lands. Having said all this, the disguised goddess incited the women to light torches and burn the ships. Then, she exclaimed, Aeneas would have no choice but to give the order to stay!

As the women, roused to anger by the words of the disguised goddess, began to burn the ships, Aeneas was horrified. He cried out to mighty Jupiter, saying that if the ships were destroyed his people would lose the will to go on. And in that case, the great mission that the chief god had foreseen for Aeneas and them would never come to pass. Hearing this plea, Jupiter sped through the sky towing some huge, dark storm clouds, which soon released torrents of rain that doused the fires. Most of the ships were saved. However, four were beyond repair; and because of a lack of room in the surviving vessels, Aeneas decided to leave the crews of the lost ships, along with their families, to make new homes in Sicily.

The two groups of Trojans said their tearful good-byes. Then, guided and protected by Venus, who kept a wary eye out for Juno, Aeneas crossed from Sicily to Italy, making landfall near Cumae, on the peninsula's southwestern coast. This location was no random choice. Indeed, Cumae was the home of the Sibyl, the wise woman and seer whom Aeneas's kinsman, Helenus, had instructed him to find and consult.

The Sibyl and the Golden Bough

Aeneas made his way to Cumae's impressive Temple of Apollo and arranged an audience with the Sibyl, who, he learned, lived in a deep, forbidding cavern near the temple. After entering the cavern, the Trojan leader found the woman sitting on a rock and dressed in a black robe that covered most of her body. She greeted him as if she knew him (since, being a prophetess, she was well aware of who he was and why he had come) and bade him sit down. She had communicated with the gods about him, she said, and in their view he had done well in making it this far. Moreover, if Aeneas remained steadfast in his courage and resolve, he would make it farther. The fair and fruitful plain of Latium, which lay many miles north of Cumae, awaited him, the Sibyl said. It was there that he should attempt to establish a kingdom.

However, the Sibyl continued, Aeneas should be warned that the goddess Juno still opposed him, so his path was still strewn with potential dangers. Among those dangers that the prophetess could foretell, he was destined to fight a bloody war over the right to marry an Italian bride, and he would have to engage in a fight to the death with a warrior nearly as formidable as Achilles, the Greek hero who slew Aeneas's valiant brother, Hector, before the towering walls of Troy.

Aeneas's eyes went wide and then he sighed, for this new and momentous information was a great deal to absorb and sort out. He thanked the priestess for her insights and prevailed on her for one other favor. He asked her to find him a way into the Underworld so that he might once more see his beloved father, who had died during the long journey across the sea from Troy. The Sibyl agreed to do so. But first, she said, Aeneas must go out and find the Golden Bough—the branch of a magical tree—or else Proserpina (the Greek Persephone), queen of the Underworld, would not allow him, a living mortal, to enter her kingdom. As for the tree, the Sibyl said,

A whole grove conceals it and the shades of a dark, encircling valley close it in. But

no man may enter the hidden places of the earth before plucking the golden foliage and fruit from this tree. . . . So then lift up your eyes and look for it, and when in due time you find it, take it in your hand and pluck it. If you are a man called by the Fates, it will come easily of its own accord. (*Aeneid* 6.139–148)

Aeneas immediately set out to find the Golden Bough. And thanks to two white doves, sent by his mother, Venus, to guide him, he found the tree and plucked the branch.

The Descent to the Underworld
When Aeneas, carrying the Golden Bough, returned to the Sibyl, she led him to a forbidding-looking cave on the shore of the mist-shrouded Lake Avernus, which lay not far from Cumae. This was one of the few entrances to the Underworld that existed on the earth's surface. After winding their way through dark passageways for what seemed like a long time, Aeneas and the Sibyl reached the River Styx, the boundary of the realm of the dead. They approached Charon, the gloomy boatman whose job it was to ferry souls across the river; but he shrank back and refused to allow them into his boat. They were not dead, he exclaimed, but still living, and they therefore had no business in this place. Anyway, Charon said, the last living mortal to make it across the Styx, the hero Hercules (the Greek Heracles), had proved nothing but trouble; he had even stolen Cerberus, the three-headed dog that stood guard to make sure no souls escaped from the Underworld. When Aeneas showed Charon the Golden Bough, however, he abruptly changed his tune. Recognizing that the branch bore Proserpina's stamp of approval, the boatman carried the man and the priestess across the river, after which the Sibyl threw a drugged honey cake to Cerberus to keep the ghastly watchdog quiet.

Continuing on into the gloomy darkness, Aeneas began to see the souls of people both long and recently dead. There were ghosts of old people, who had been fortunate enough to have lived long lives, and also those of infants, still crying for their mothers left behind on the earth. But saddest of all for Aeneas was his unexpected encounter with a pale, thin form that he recognized as the spirit of Queen Dido, who had loved him so. "The tears rose to his eyes," Virgil writes,

> and in soft loving tones he said to her: "Oh Dido, unhappy one, was the story true that was brought to me? They told me you had used a sword to end your life. . . . I swear by the stars, by the gods above . . . it was not of my own desire that I left your land. Oh Queen, it was the inescapable bidding of heaven. . . . Do not withdraw yourself from my sight, I beg you! . . . These are the last words I shall ever speak to you; fate allows me no more.". . . But she, with her head averted, and eyes fixed on the ground . . . flung herself away and fled into the shadows. (*Aeneid* 6.455–474)

Shocked and grieved at Dido's unjust fate, Aeneas, still accompanied by the silent Sibyl, continued on until he found his father. Following their joyful reunion, the old man offered to reveal the future of the grand and blessed race Aeneas would sire. "Come, my son," said Anchises, "I shall show you the whole span of our destiny." First, he said, Aeneas would build a city on the plain of Latium, south of the Tiber River. Later, his offspring would establish the city of Alba Longa in the same region, and the line of Alba's noble rulers would lead to a young man named Romulus, who himself would establish a city—none other than Rome. "Under his tutelage," Anchises predicted, "our glorious Rome shall rule the whole wide world, and her spirit shall match the spirit of the gods." (*Aeneid* 6.756–784) Anchises

showed his son a vision of the long line of noble Romans, finally culminating in the greatest of them all—Augustus Caesar—who was destined to bring about a new golden age for Rome and humanity. (Indeed, it was Augustus who established the Roman Empire.)

The War with the Latins

After Aeneas and the Sibyl returned from their journey through the lower regions, the hero traveled northward to Latium to fulfill the destiny that had been revealed to him. He met the local ruler of Latium, Latinus, who soon offered him an alliance and the hand of his daughter, Lavinia, in marriage. But Turnus, prince of a neighboring Latin people, the Rutulians, had already asked for Lavinia's hand. This fact immediately caught the attention of the goddess Juno, who recognized the opportunity to cause more trouble for Aeneas. She filled Turnus's heart with jealousy, causing him to declare war on the Trojans and organize the local Latin tribes as his allies. In this way, the Sibyl's prophecy that Aeneas would have to fight over the right to marry an Italian bride was fulfilled.

One day, as Aeneas anxiously awaited the attack of the Latins, who were massing for war against him, he had a dream in which a river god came to him with vital information. If Aeneas would sail up the Tiber River, the god said, he would find a needed ally—Evander, a Greek who had established a settlement in the area. Aeneas followed the god's advice and journeyed up the Tiber, where he suddenly saw a white sow and her thirty piglets on the riverbank, just as the prophet Helenus had foretold he would. And nearby, the Trojan met Evander and the people of his village nestled on the Palatine Hill (the future site of Rome). Evander entertained Aeneas with much goodwill and hospitality, then offered to help him. "Great leader of the Trojans," the Greek said, while you are alive, I shall never accept that Troy and its kingdom are defeated. Beside your mighty name, the power we have to help you in this war is as nothing. . . . But I have a plan to join vast peoples and the armies of wealthy kingdoms to your cause. A chance that no man could have foreseen is showing us the path to safety. Fate was calling you when you came to this place. (*Aeneid* 8.470–478)

True to his word, Evander enlisted the aid of a neighboring Etruscan king, Tarchon. Meanwhile, Venus, who was worried about her son's safety, prevailed on her husband, Vulcan, god of the forge, and his assistants, the Cyclopes, to create a magnificent array of armor and weapons for Aeneas. She also presented her son a shield engraved with some of the major future events of Roman history (ending with the Battle of Actium, Augustus's great victory over his last rivals).

Venus had good reason to be worried. While Aeneas was away visiting Evander, Turnus took the initiative and attacked the Trojan camp. The Latins also attempted to burn Aeneas's ships. But these hostile assaults ended in failure, and before Turnus could mount another attack Aeneas and his allies appeared. Turnus's army eventually suffered defeat, and Turnus himself fled. Hoping to end the war without further unneeded bloodshed, Aeneas then challenged Turnus to single combat, much as Achilles and Hector had faced each other outside the towering walls of Troy. (In this way, another part of the Sibyl's prophecy—that Aeneas would have to fight a champion almost as mighty as Achilles—came to pass.)

Final Victory and a Destiny Fulfilled

When the day of the proposed battle came, Aeneas mounted his chariot and drove out onto the battlefield to meet his foe, Turnus. "Now at last," as Virgil tells it,

the Rutulians and the Trojans and all the men of Italy . . . turned their eyes eagerly to see and took the armor off their shoulders. King Latinus himself was amazed at the sight of these two huge heroes born at opposite sides of the earth coming together to decide the issue [i.e., the war] by the sword. There, on a piece of open ground on the plain, they threw their spears at long range as they charged, and when they clashed the bronze of their shields rang out and the earth groaned. Blow upon blow they dealt with their swords as chance and courage met and mingled in confusion. . . . Turnus leapt forward, thinking he was safe, and lifting his sword and rising to his full height, he struck with all his strength behind it. . . . But in the height of his passion the treacherous sword broke in mid-blow and left him defenseless. (*Aeneid* 12.705–735)

At a fatal disadvantage, Turnus fled; but Aeneas pursued him, eventually caught up, and wounded him in the thigh. The leader of the Rutulians pleaded for Aeneas to spare him, and the Trojan champion had a mind to do so. But then Aeneas noticed that his opponent was wearing the sword belt belonging to Pallas, son of Evander. Turnus had earlier slain Pallas, and Evander had pleaded with Aeneas to avenge his son. Aeneas now remembered that heartfelt request and plunged his sword into Turnus's chest, killing him and thus ending the terrible conflict between the Trojans and the Latins.

Afterward, Aeneas established a city in Latium, naming it Lavinium after Lavinia, whom he married. And from the union of the Trojan and the Latin races, fulfilling the destiny ordained by Jupiter, sprang the lineage of the noble Romans, who would one day rule the known world. For the Romans, Jupiter had earlier told Venus, "I see no measure nor date, and I grant them dominion without end. Even Juno . . . will mend her ways and vie with me in cherishing the Romans, the master race, the wearers of the toga. So it is willed!" (*Aeneid* 1.277–284)

The Creation of the Gods and Humans

In the beginning, uncounted ages ago, there was only a great hollow void in which the seeds and basic elements of all things swirled randomly together in a shapeless mass. This void was called Chaos. After a very long time—just how long no god or human can say—Chaos gave birth to two children, Nyx (Night) and Erebus (Darkness), the latter being the still depths where death resides. Both Nyx and Erebus were black, silent, and endless.

More long ages passed; and then suddenly, and in some mysterious way that no one can explain, from the terrifying blackness of Nyx and Erebus sprang Eros, or Love. Some say that Eros may have hatched from an egg. According to Aristophanes in his play *Birds,* for example,

> Night of the black wings brought forth in her nest within Erebus's breast an Egg, sired by the whirlwind, from whence was born, as the months rolled on, great Eros, the ever desired, with wings on his shoulders of shining gold, as swift in the storm in his flying. . . . No gods were above us until turbulent Love had affected a cosmic communion. (*Birds* 695–701)

Indeed, Eros made all communion—or the coming together of things—possible. He brought light to pierce the darkness, and through his influence, order began to appear in the void. The heavier elements slowly settled out and became the earth, and the lighter parts drifted upward and became the sky. Far under the earth, remained a dark region, called Tartarus. But above the earth, in the heavens, the sun, moon, and stars appeared; and on the earth itself the land and sea became separate, rivers flowed to the sea, and trees and plants grew and multiplied across the face of the land. And the earth was endowed with the personality of Gaia, Mother Earth, and the heavens personified the spirit of Uranus, Father Heaven.

The Children of Gaia and Uranus

Gaia and Uranus had many children, the first beings recognizable as living creatures. But these were quite unlike any creatures now known. They were huge and misshapen and possessed the tremendous strength of earthquakes, hurricanes, and volcanoes. In a way, each was a combination of a living being and an irresistible force, able to perform tasks no ordinary living being ever could. The first three of the brood were horrifying monsters, each possessing fifty heads and a hundred hands (so that they became known as the "Hundred-handers"). Their names were Cottus, Gyes, and Briareos. Next came three huge and powerful creatures, each bearing a single eye in the middle of its forehead, who became known as the Cyclopes, which means "Wheel-eyed."

Finally, Gaia and Uranus produced the twelve Titans, who looked similar to humans but who were much larger and stronger. Among these were Oceanus and Tethys, who took charge of the sea; Hyperion and Thea, deities of the sun and moon, respectively; Rhea, who would later come to be called "the Great Mother"; and Cronos (whom the Romans called Saturn), the youngest and most powerful of all.

Like nearly all mothers, Gaia loved all of her children, no matter how ugly; but Uranus hated his children, especially the six extremely ugly monsters. So he swept them up and hid them in secret dark places in Tartarus, deep beneath the earth's surface. This distressed Gaia greatly, and she conspired with Cronos and the other Titans to stage a rebellion against Uranus. In the ensuing fight, Cronos castrated his father and drops of Uranus's blood showered down. Those drops that landed in the sea gave rise to Aphrodite (the Roman Venus), goddess of love, and the drops that touched the earth spawned two races of fearsome creatures: the giants, primitive beings who wore animal skins, and the serpent-haired Furies, who would later become the merciless tormentors of humans who shed blood. The bleeding Uranus finally lost the battle, and Cronos imprisoned him in the shadowy regions of Tartarus, the lowest region of the Underworld.

The Battle for the Universe

Now that Uranus was out of the way, mighty Cronos assumed the kingship of heaven and married his fellow Titan Rhea. They began to have children of their own, but Cronos feared that his offspring might rebel against him just as he had rebelled against Uranus. Thus, as soon as each child was born, Cronos swallowed it whole, storing it deep within his gigantic body. This occurred five times in a row and finally poor Rhea, despairing over the loss of so many children, determined to put an end to this grisly practice. When she gave birth to her sixth child, Zeus (the Roman Jupiter), she hid the baby in a cave on the island of Crete. She knew that Cronos would expect her to hand over a child for him to devour, of course, but she also knew that he was somewhat dull-witted and would therefore be easy to hoodwink. According to the Greek poet Hesiod,

> To the great lord, the son of Heaven, the past
> king of the gods [Cronos], she handed,
> solemnly, all wrapped in swaddling-clothes,
> a giant stone. He seized it in his hands
> and thrust it down into his belly, the fool!
> He did not know that his son, no stone,
> was left behind, unhurt and undefeated,
> who would soon conquer him with violence and force, and drive him out from
> all his honors, and would rule the gods.
> (*Theogony* 485–492)

Indeed, in accomplishing her ruse Rhea had unwittingly set in motion a momentous series of events. Zeus's preservation and safekeeping in Crete set the stage for the downfall of the Titans and the rise of the Olympian gods. As Zeus grew into manhood, he learned about the horrible fate of his brothers and sisters who had come before him, and he made up his mind to remedy the situation. Conspiring with his grandmother, Gaia, the young god secretly fed Cronos a dose of very strong medicine that made the king of the Titans feel nauseated. Cronos then began vomiting up all those he had swallowed. First came the stone that had been substituted for Zeus, an object that humans later found and placed in the sacred sanctuary of Delphi in central Greece. Then out popped Cronos's and Rhea's first five children, all now grown into adults like Zeus. These were Hestia (the Roman Vesta), Demeter (the Roman Ceres), Hera (the Roman Juno), Hades (the Roman Dis), and Poseidon (the Roman Neptune).

Zeus and his five siblings eventually joined forces and waged war on Cronos and most of the other Titans; but after ten years of this battle for the universe, neither side had managed to get the upper hand. It was then that one of the Titans, Prometheus, whose name means "Forethought," advised Cronos to release his monstrous brethren from Tartarus. With the hundred-handed creatures and the Cyclopes fighting on their side, said Prometheus, they might gain the advantage over the enemy. But Cronos showed his stupidity once more by refusing to take this advice.

So the frustrated Prometheus, along with his brother, Epimetheus (meaning "Afterthought"), abandoned Cronos and went over to Zeus's side. Prometheus gave Zeus the same advice about releasing the monsters, and Zeus, who was a good deal smarter than Cronos, did so. After ages of imprisonment, the Cyclopes, whose names were Thunderer, Shiner, and Lightning-

A very early sculpture of Zeus. His right hand originally held a thunderbolt, with which he vanquished the Titans.

gods and those whom Cronos sired and those whom Zeus had brought to light from . . . beneath the earth, strange, mighty ones, whose power was immense, each with a hundred arms darting about. . . . They stood against the Titans in the grim battle, with giant rocks in their strong hands, while on the other side the Titans eagerly strengthened their ranks, and both at once displayed the mightiest efforts their hands could make. The boundless sea roared terribly around, the great earth rumbled, and broad heaven groaned, shaken; and tall Olympus was disturbed down to its roots, when the immortals charged. The heavy quaking from their footsteps reached down to dark Tartarus, and piercing sounds of awful battle, and their mighty shafts. They hurled their wounding missiles, and the voices of both sides, shouting, reached the starry sky. . . . The fertile earth, being burnt, roared out, the voiceless forest cried and crackled with fire; the whole earth broiled . . . [and] flame, unspeakable, rose to the upper air. . . . To the ear it sounded, to the eye it looked as though broad heaven were coming down upon the earth. (*Theogony* 666–703)

Maker, were so grateful to be free that they each gave Zeus a present—the thunder, the thunderbolt, and the lightning, respectively. They also gave Hades a special cap that rendered him invisible while wearing it; and to Poseidon they presented a trident, or three-pronged spear, which became his symbol from then on.

The war then resumed with a frightful vengeance. Hesiod describes it in the following way:

On that day they joined in hateful battle, all of them, both male and female, the Titan

At last, after the forests had burned and the seas and rivers boiled, Zeus and his forces were triumphant. They cast Cronos and most of the other Titans down into dark Tartarus, bounded by Styx, the black river of death, and guarded by the Cyclopes, the Hundred-handers, and also by a fearsome three-headed watchdog named Cerberus. Because they had helped Zeus, Prometheus and Epimetheus, as well as Oceanus, Tethys, and a few other Titans, were allowed to remain free.

Dwellers on Olympus

Zeus and his companions now divided up the earth among themselves. They became known as the Olympians because they often dwelled in a magnificent palace high atop Mt. Olympus (in northern Thessaly). Zeus, who had led the rebellion, assumed control of the Olympians and took his sister, Hera, as his wife. Zeus not only ruled the gods and the earth but also became chief administrator of justice and protector of oaths sworn in his name. Though known for his justice and tremendous power (in Homer's *Iliad* he boasts that in a tug-of-war he could easily best of all the other Olympians put together), Zeus had his faults and vices, perhaps the worst being his tendency to lust after human women. On many later occasions he would descend to earth in disguise and have love affairs; Hera would usually find out and achieve her revenge by punishing the mortal women involved. Out of her constant concern for the sanctity of marriage, she appropriately became the guardian of that institution and also of childbirth.

Meanwhile, Zeus's brothers acquired their own, although lesser, realms. Poseidon took control of the sea. He was also the bringer of earthquakes, hence his frequent title "Earthshaker"; and because he ended up giving humanity its first horse, he also became the god of horses. Hades became ruler of the Underworld, from which he only rarely departed to visit Olympus or the earth's surface. Although he ruled harshly and with little pity, he was not an evil god and was known for his sense of justice.

Zeus's sisters had their own important roles. Hestia, who remained always a virgin, became protector of the hearth and home, and every Greek town honored her with a public hearth in which the fire was never extinguished. Her sister Demeter oversaw agriculture and later, when humans began to worship her, the chief festival in her honor was at harvest time. After her daughter, Persephone (the Roman Proserpina), was abducted into the

Underworld by Hades, Demeter left Olympus and dwelled thereafter on the earth, often inside the sacred temple the Greeks erected to her in Eleusis (twelve miles west of Athens).

Though Demeter seemed to have abandoned Olympus, a number of other important gods soon came to reside there. Aphrodite, goddess of love, who had earlier risen from the sea foam that had grown from Cronos's blood droplets, was one of them. Depending on the situation, she showed one of the two sides of her personality: the first side soft, lovely, and pleasant, befitting her stunning physical beauty; and the second side spiteful, calculating, and malicious, as when she manipulated males, both mortal and immortal.

Most of the other powerful Olympians were Zeus's children. These included Ares (the Roman Mars), god of war, whose bird, the vulture, befitted his hateful, ruthless personality; stately Athena (the Roman Minerva), goddess of wisdom and war and protector of civilized life, who sprang fully clothed in armor from Zeus's head, and who later became the patron deity of Greece's greatest city—Athens; the incredibly handsome Apollo (the Romans called him this too), lord of prophecy, truth, the healing arts, and also of music and poetry, his greatest shrine at Delphi, site of the famous oracle; swift and cunning Hermes (the Roman Mercury), the messenger god and patron of travelers, who also guided the souls of the dead to the Underworld; Apollo's twin sister, Artemis (the Roman Diana), virgin goddess of the moon and the hunt, who also protected young girls and pregnant women; and Hera's son, the kind and peace-loving Hephaestos (the Roman Vulcan), god of fire and forges and also patron of craftsmen.

The Five Races of Men
In this bygone era when the gods established themselves in their various roles,

there were still no humans on the earth. The Greeks told two different stories explaining the creation of people. In one, the gods made a series of five human races—those of gold, silver, bronze, heroes, and iron—each succeeding race less admirable than those preceding it (except for the heroes). According to Hesiod,

> [The gods] first fashioned a golden race of mortal men. . . . Like the gods, they lived with happy hearts untouched by work or sorrow. Vile old age never appeared. . . . All good things were theirs; ungrudgingly, the fertile land gave up her fruits unasked. . . . And then this race was hidden in the ground, but still they live as spirits of the earth, holy and good, guardians who keep harm away. . . . The gods . . . next fashioned a lesser, silver race of men, unlike the gold in stature or in mind. . . . They lived brief, anguished lives because of their foolishness, for they could not control themselves, but recklessly injured one another and forsook the gods. . . . The earth then hid this second race, and they are called the spirits of the Underworld. . . . And Zeus the father made a race of bronze . . . worse than the silver race, but strange and full of power. They loved the groans and violence of war; they ate no bread; their hearts were flinty-hard; they were terrible men. . . . Their weapons were of bronze, their houses bronze, their tools were bronze. . . . They died by their own hands, and nameless, went to Hades' chilly house. . . . But when this race was covered by the earth, Zeus made another, fourth race, upon the fruitful land, more just and good, a god-like race of heroes, who are called the demigods—the race before our own. . . . Some, who crossed the open sea in ships, for fair-haired Helen's sake, were killed at Troy. These men were covered up in death, but Zeus gave the others life and homes apart from mortals, at earth's edge. And there they live a carefree life, beside the whirling Ocean, on the Islands of the Blessed. . . . Far-seeing Zeus then made another race, the

> fifth, who live now on the fertile earth. . . . This is the race of iron. Men [of this race] work and grieve unceasingly. (*Works and Days* 109–181)

The classical Greeks, who believed that they lived in the unwholesome Iron Age, looked back with awe and longing to the Age of Heroes, which had produced a long series of stalwart characters, including Achilles, Ajax, Hector, Odysseus, and others who had fought in the famous Trojan War.

The Creatures of Prometheus

The more popular story for the creation of humans involved the Titans Prometheus and Epimetheus, who had been allowed their freedom after the great war. Prometheus was very wise—supposedly the wisest of all gods—and for that reason he served for many years as Zeus's adviser. Duly impressed with Prometheus's abilities, Zeus delegated to him and his brother the task of making races of mortal animals and humans. Unfortunately, the scatter-brained Epimetheus, living up to the name Afterthought, acted without thinking and gave most of the choicest physical traits, including swiftness, strength, fur, wings, protective shells, and so on, to the animals; thus, when it came time to make humans, little was left that would help them to survive in a hostile world.

Prometheus tried hard to find a way to rectify his brother's mistake. First, he fashioned some humans from mud, which still contained sparks of life left over from Chaos (which had not yet completely sorted itself out). As an initial special gift to set them apart from the animals, Prometheus endowed the mud creatures with the physical form of the divine gods. But this was clearly not enough. He observed that these unfortunate mortals had to struggle hard, not only against wild beasts but also against harsh extremes of weather. Life would be so much better for

The shrewd Titan Prometheus fashions human beings on his potter's wheel while the goddess Athena looks on.

them, he reasoned, if only they possessed fire and understood how to use it. So Prometheus approached Zeus with the idea of giving humans the gift of fire. But the king of the gods declared bluntly that these creatures were not worthy of the divine spark of fire and decreed that they could not have it.

Though Zeus had forbidden it, Prometheus decided to give his precious creations fire anyway. The former Titan snatched a bit of fire from the sun and hid it in a hollow reed, which he carried with him to the earth. There, he taught the humans the uses of fire, including how to cook their food, how to make weapons for defense, and how to fashion tools to make houses, ships, utensils, and all manner of other things. Prometheus also taught people the use of the calendar, how to write, and some of the healing arts.

The Wrath of Zeus

When Zeus saw that Prometheus had disobeyed him and that humans were beginning to build an impressive civilization, he was very angry. The chief Olympian made up his mind to punish both the humans and the Titan, in that order. Zeus noticed that all of the "creatures of Prometheus" were of a single sex—all of them men; and he devised a plan to introduce among them a second sex, one that would seem very charming but whose devious and manipulative nature would cause them trouble and grief. The ruler of Olympus sent for Hephaestos, the skilled craftsman, and ordered him to make a woman. Taking a piece of clay, Hephaestos molded it into the shape of one of the immortal goddesses, creating a lovely creature. All of the gods and goddesses gave the woman gifts: Athena outfitted her with beautiful clothes and taught her spinning and weaving, Aphrodite instructed her in how to act gracefully and appear alluring to men, and Hermes taught her how to speak well and act deviously when it suited her. Appropriately, they gave her the name Pandora, meaning "All-Gifts."

Then Zeus ordered Hermes to take Pandora down to the earth and to present her to the dim-witted Epimetheus. Prometheus had earlier warned his brother not to accept any gifts from Zeus, but Epimetheus, as usual, acted without thinking. He welcomed Pandora into his home as his wife, along with a large sealed jar she had been told was her dowry, although she was unsure of the container's contents. Eventually her curiosity got the better of her, and with Epimetheus's help, she broke the seal and opened the jar. Immediately, out rushed a swirling torrent of evils—disease, hatred, worry, greed, and all of the other troubles that plague humanity to this day, for once they had been loosed from the jar they could never be forced back in. Thus did Zeus accomplish the first part of his punishment.

Zeus aimed the second part of his wrath directly at Prometheus, who had had the gall to bring down fire from heaven. At Zeus's order, two giants seized the Titan, and Hephaestos, much against his kindly nature, bound him to a huge rock on the summit of a faraway mountain. There, each day a gigantic eagle (in some versions a vulture) gnawed at Prometheus's liver. At night, when the bird was gone, the liver grew back and the next day the chained god had to endure the same agonies again.

A Great Flood

One version of these tales holds that Pandora's unleashing of troubles on humankind and Prometheus's grisly tortures were not enough to quench Zeus's anger. Only by destroying humanity once and for all would the chief god be satisfied; therefore, he caused an immense flood that threatened to overwhelm the entire earth. Luckily, Prometheus, though he was chained, still possessed the gift of foresight, and he managed to warn his son Deucalion about the impending disaster. Deucalion and his wife, Pyrrha, climbed atop Mt. Parnassus (near Delphi in central Greece), hoping to escape the rising waters. After all of the other humans had perished, Zeus's anger was at last extinguished, and he took pity on the couple and allowed their survival.

Soon afterward, on the advice of a mysterious voice, Deucalion and Pyrrha gathered together many small stones, veiled their heads, and walked along, casting the stones behind them as they went. The stones Deucalion cast grew into men, and the stones Pyrrha tossed grew into women; in this way, they repopulated the earth.

With the transformation of Chaos into order, and the birth of Gaia and Uranus, who gave rise to the Titans, who themselves produced the Olympians; the great war in which the Olympians emerged victorious; the rise of the creatures of Prometheus and the gift of fire he gave them; and finally the great flood and the birth of a new race of humans, at long last the creation of the earth and heavens and the gods and mortals was complete.

Cupid and Psyche

According to the Roman novelist Lucius Apuleius, true love overcame Venus's anger in the following manner. A certain city was ruled by a king and queen who had three lovely daughters, the youngest of whom, Psyche, was so strikingly beautiful that people journeyed from far and wide just to gaze at her. In fact, the local residents were so taken with the maiden that they began the custom of giving her wreaths and flowers when she walked through the streets. Soon, they neglected their usual worship of the goddess Venus and started offering their prayers to Psyche in her place.

It did not take long for Venus to see what was happening. "Since divine honors were being diverted in this excessive way to the worship of a mortal girl," writes Apuleius,

> the anger of the true Venus was fiercely kindled. She could not control her irritation. She tossed her head, let out a deep growl, and spoke to herself: "Here am I, the ancient mother of the universe . . . the Venus that tends the entire world, compelled to share the glory of my majesty with a mortal maiden, so that my name which has its niche in heaven is degraded by the foulness of the earth below! Am I then to share with another the supplications to my divine power, am I to endure vague, indirect adoration, allowing a mortal girl to strut around posing as my double? . . . This girl, whoever she is, is not going to enjoy appropriating the honors that are mine; I shall soon ensure that she rues the beauty which is not hers by rights!" (The Golden Ass 4.29–30)

The irate goddess summoned her handsome son, Cupid, and bade him help her exact her revenge on Psyche. Venus ordered Cupid to make the girl fall madly in love with the vilest, most despicable, most disreputable man on Earth; that way her great beauty would be wasted and her life miserable.

Love at First Sight

At first, Cupid had every intention of helping his mother. But when he first caught sight of Psyche, his heart melted with love for her, almost as if he had been shot by one of his own love arrows. Thus, the fate he arranged for the maiden was not exactly the kind Venus had intended. Time passed and Psyche's sisters each married wealthy kings; but strangely, no man asked to marry Psyche. "She remained at home unattached," Apuleius writes, "lamenting her isolated loneliness. Sick in body and wounded at heart, she loathed her beauty which the whole world admired." (*The Golden Ass* 4.32) Psyche's parents became so confused and disturbed by this turn of events that they consulted an oracle of Apollo, not realizing that the god was cooperating in Cupid's scheme to keep Psyche from acquiring a human husband. Through the oracle, Apollo declared that the maiden would have to be dressed in black and left alone on a mountain, where a frightening winged serpent would descend and take her for its mate. Fearing to defy the god's will, Psyche's parents obeyed.

But once the girl was alone on the mountain, instead of a deadly serpent she found a pleasant valley, a placid stream, and a small but beautifully crafted palace. Upon entering, she found the building's interior lush with gold and silver trim, comfortable furnishings, and storerooms filled with gleaming jewels and other treasures. Then she heard a voice that seemed to float to her out of thin air. "Why, my lady," it asked,

> do you gaze open-mouthed at this parade of wealth? All these things are yours. So retire to your room, relieve your weariness on your bed, and take a bath at your leisure. The voices you hear are those of your hand-

> maidens, and we will diligently attend to your needs. Once you have completed freshening up, a royal feast will at once be laid before you. (*The Golden Ass* 5.2)

Psyche had no clue as to where the voice was coming from. But she was relieved that she had not been sacrificed to the serpent, and therefore she did what she was told and enjoyed a magnificent feast. That night, as she lay awake in bed, she felt someone climb into the bed with her. She could not tell who it was because the visitor was invisible in the dark, but she immediately recognized the soothing voice she had heard earlier. The two made love, and in the weeks that followed, they entered into a tender and loving relationship, crowned by the invisible lover taking Psyche as his wife. All would be well, he said, as long as she made no attempt to try to see what he really looked like. And to maintain his anonymity, after each night he spent with her he departed swiftly just before the breaking of dawn.

Jealousy, Fear, and Betrayal

The lovers' happy relationship was interrupted, however, when Psyche's two sisters came to the mountain looking for her. Her husband warned her not to make contact with them, for they would only bring trouble; but she saw them crying, apparently over having lost her, and soon greeted them. When they seemed glad to see her alive, Psyche showed them the magnificent palace in which she had been living and eventually told them about her invisible husband.

Unbeknownst to Psyche, her sisters were consumed with jealousy about her palace, treasures, and marital bliss, all of which were far greater than their own. One of them complained,

> Fortune, how blind and harsh and unjust you are! Was it your pleasure that we, daughters of the same parents, should en-

dure so different a fate? Here we are, her elder sisters, and nothing better than maidservants to foreign husbands . . . while Psyche, the youngest . . . has obtained all this wealth, and a god for a husband! She has not even a notion of how to enjoy such abundant blessings. (*The Golden Ass* 5.9)

The sisters were indeed so filled with envy that they hatched a nefarious plan to bring Psyche ruin and unhappiness. They convinced her that there was something sinister about her husband's never showing himself and that he must in reality be the very hideous serpent of which Apollo's oracle had spoken. Psyche must destroy this deceptive creature, they advised. She must wait until it fell asleep, illuminate it with a lamp, and then stab it to death with a sharp razor.

Unfortunately, Psyche became so afraid that her sisters might be right that she decided to follow their advice. That night, her husband reclined on a comfortable couch and fell into a deep sleep. Gathering her courage (according to Apuleius),

she uncovered the lamp, seized the razor, and showed a boldness that belied her sex. But as soon as the lamp was brought near, and the secrets of the couch were revealed, she beheld of all beasts the gentlest and sweetest, Cupid himself, a handsome god lying in a handsome posture. Even the lamplight was cheered and brightened on sighting him. . . . As for Psyche, she was awe-struck at this wonderful vision, and she lost all of her self-control. She swooned and paled . . . [and] her knees buckled. . . . She gazed down on him in distraction, and as she passionately smothered him with wanton kisses from parted lips, she feared that he might stir in his sleep. But while her wounded heart pounded on being roused by such striking beauty, the lamp disgorged a drop of burning oil from the tip of its flame

upon the god's right shoulder. . . . The god started up on being burnt; he saw that he was exposed [to her sight], and that his trust was defiled [betrayed]. Without a word, he at once flew away from the kisses and embrace of his most unhappy wife. (*The Golden Ass* 5.22–23)

Venus's Revenge

Realizing she had betrayed Cupid's trust, the distraught Psyche determined to find him and somehow make it up to him, even if she had to search for him for the rest of her days. Meanwhile, having learned that her son had lavished wealth and love on this insolent mortal, Venus was angrier than ever. The goddess rushed to the handsome young god and screamed at him, saying,

This is a fine state of affairs, just what one would expect from a child of mine, from a decent man like you! First of all you trampled underfoot the instructions of your mother . . . and then mark you, a mere boy of tender years, you hugged her close in your wanton, stunted embraces! . . . You take too much for granted, you good-for-nothing, loathsome seducer! (*The Golden Ass* 5.29)

Knowing the angry Venus was searching for her, Psyche appealed to the goddesses Ceres and Juno to intercede on her behalf. But they did not want to get on their fellow goddess's bad side, so they refused to help. Eventually, Psyche thought it best to confront Venus and beg her forgiveness. Still fuming with rage, the goddess yelled at her, slapped her, tore her dress, and proceeded to assign her a series of difficult tasks. The goddess claimed that if Psyche completed these tasks successfully she would forgive her, but Venus knew full well that the tasks were seemingly impossible for a mortal, so that the maiden was surely doomed to fail.

To the goddess's surprise, however, Psyche managed to complete the first three tasks, in each case aided by some sort of kindly woodland creature. A group of ants helped the girl sort through a huge pile of mixed seeds, separating the different types into neat piles; a river reed showed Psyche how to obtain the wool from a flock of golden sheep; and an eagle filled a jug with water that Venus had ordered the girl to fetch from a stream flowing from the pinnacle of an impossibly steep mountain. In each case, Venus realized that Psyche had not completed the task alone, but the goddess assumed, quite mistakenly, that her son, Cupid, was somehow involved.

It was then that Psyche made her most unfortunate mistake. Venus gave her still another task: to carry a box into the Underworld; ask Dis's mate, Proserpina, to fill it with some of her beauty; and bring the box back to Venus. Everything went smoothly until after Psyche, bearing the box, returned to the earth's surface. She could not resist the temptation look inside; and when she did, Venus punished her by making her fall into a deep sleep. At last, the goddess felt as though she had exacted her full revenge on the girl.

The Lovers Are Reunited

Luckily, Psyche's story did not end unhappily. Not long after she had fallen into her drowsy slumber, Cupid finally intervened. Despite the earlier breach of trust, he still deeply loved Psyche and had been pining away for her for weeks. Finding her, he released her from the spell and then approached Jupiter, who agreed to help him. According to Apuleius, Jupiter gathered together all of the gods, including Venus, and proclaimed,

> "You certainly all know this young man, whose impetuous youth, I believe, should be curbed by some kind of bridle. He has chosen a girl and made her his wife. Let him keep her and possess her, and as he embraces Psyche may he always enjoy his love." Then, turning his eyes toward

Venus, Jupiter said, "And you, my daughter, must not be saddened at all nor have any fear because of this marriage with a mortal, for I shall declare the union lawful, and in keeping with the civil law." (*The Golden Ass* 6.23)

Having said this, Jupiter ordered that Psyche be brought before the gods and given a cup of ambrosia, the magical food of the gods that would make her immortal and one of their number. And by this means, Venus's anger turned to delight, and the deep bond between Cupid, god of love, and Psyche, whose name means the soul, became unbreakable and eternal.

The Curse of the House of Atreus

The most famous curse in the annals of Greco-Roman mythology began long ago, in the days when King Tantalus ruled the region around Mt. Sipylus in Lydia (in western Asia Minor). Tantalus was a mortal son of Zeus, and as a young man he was so liked and respected by all of the gods that they allowed him regularly to dine with them in their banquet hall on Mt. Olympus. They even extended to him favors no other human enjoyed, such as letting him taste their mystical ambrosia (which made him immortal, like them) and dropping in to dine with him in his palace on Earth.

But for reasons that to this day no one can fathom, Tantalus horribly betrayed the kindness and trust the gods had extended to him. Perhaps he secretly hated them, or maybe he thought himself their better and wanted to show how easily he could deceive them. Whatever his twisted motives, one day when the divinities had arrived at his palace for supper, he had his son, the admirable young Pelops, slain, boiled in a large pot, cut into pieces, and served to his guests. They would, he reasoned gleefully, indulge in one of the lowest and uncivilized of all practices—cannibalism—without even knowing it.

But Tantalus's assumption that he could so easily fool the gods was a serious miscalculation. When they saw and smelled the dish he had served them, they realized full well what it was and recoiled with a mixture of horror and seething anger. They could have killed Tantalus instantly, of course, but they felt that a quick death was too lenient for so reprehensible a crime. So they hurled him into the depths of the Underworld. There, many eons later, the Greek Odysseus, while engaged in his famous ten years of wandering after the Trojan War, observed Tantalus's continuing and eternal punishment:

> The old man was standing in a pool of water which nearly reached his chin, and his thirst drove him to unceasing efforts; but he could never get a drop to drink. For whenever he stooped in his eagerness to lap the water, it disappeared. The pool was swallowed up, and all he saw at his feet was the dark earth, which some mysterious power had parched. Trees spread their foliage high over the pool and dangled fruits above his head—pear trees and pomegranates, apple-trees with their glossy burden, sweet figs and luxuriant olives. But whenever the old man tried to grasp them in his hands, the wind would toss them up toward the shadowy clouds. (Homer, *Odyssey* 11.554–564)

(The Greek poet Pindar offered an alternate version of Tantalus's eternal punishment, in which the man had to hold a large rock over his head and struggle to keep it from crushing him.)

Casting the Curse

As for poor Pelops, the gods took pity on him and restored him to life. Unfortunately, one of them, perhaps Demeter, had in haste taken a tiny taste of the dreadful meal Tantalus had served, and the result was that when the young man was reassembled, one shoulder was missing; so the gods fashioned him a replacement shoulder made of the finest ivory.

By some accounts, Pelops went on to have a happy and productive life. He eventually left Lydia and journeyed to Greece, where he became the able king of Elis, in the southwestern area of the country. And after his death, the large peninsula making up the southern third of Greece, in which Elis lies, became known as the Peloponnesus, or "Isle of Pelops," in his honor. In these accounts, Pelops was one of only a handful of his family members and descendants to have a happy life; for the gods never got over the crime Tantalus had attempted to perpetrate. And they cast a terrible curse on the family, an assurance that arrogance, abuse, and death would haunt its members for eternity.

Another, more common version of the origin of the curse held that Pelops himself brought it down on the family. In this

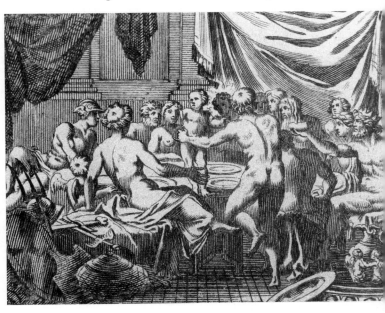

The gods attempt to put poor Pelops back together after foiling Tantalus's nefarious plot. But alas, one shoulder is missing.

story, once the gods had restored him to life, Pelops became a conceited, troublesome individual, and Ilus, king of Troy, drove him out of Asia Minor. Pelops then settled in Pisa (near Elis, in the western Peloponnesus). There, he sought to marry Hippodameia, daughter of the local king, Oenomaus; the king agreed on the condition that Pelops could beat him in a chariot race. After bribing the king's charioteer, Myrtilus, to rig one of Oenomaus's chariot wheels to break in the middle of the race, Pelops won the race and the king was killed. Perhaps to keep Myrtilus from implicating Pelops in the murder, Pelops killed Myrtilus, too; and with his last breath, Myrtilus cursed Pelops and all of his descendants. The gods heard this curse and confirmed that it would take hold.

Niobe's Tears

After Pelops (or Tantalus) brought down the curse, his sister, Niobe, was the first member of the family to suffer its dire consequences. At first, Niobe seemed to enjoy a pleasant and productive life, helping her husband, Amphion, to rule ancient Thebes in peace and prosperity. She bore seven handsome, strong sons and seven beautiful, graceful daughters. But Niobe had inherited Tantalus's and Pelops's overbearing pride, and in time this dangerous emotion began to guide and distort her actions. One day she approached a temple where some Theban women were praying and sacrificing to Leto, the Titan, mother of the gods Apollo and Artemis. Why did they bother worshiping Leto, she asked them, when she, Niobe, was more worthy of such worship? Niobe claimed to be just as beautiful as any goddess; and besides, she had fourteen wonderful children while poor Leto had only two. The women should forget about Leto, Niobe insisted, and lavish their attentions on the Theban queen instead.

It was not long before Leto found out about this grave insult to herself and her

divine children. The goddess immediately went to Apollo and Artemis and asked them to help her exact a suitable punishment. And they just as quickly agreed. They sped down from towering Olympus to Thebes and, in a savage bloodbath, used their mighty bows and arrows to slay all of Niobe's noble sons before her very eyes. The gods might have been satisfied with this load of vengeance had not Niobe continued to defy them. As the Roman poet Ovid tells it,

> Niobe bent over the bodies of her sons, now cold in death, showering them in kisses. Then, raising her arms toward the heavens, she cried, "Feed, cruel Leto, on my grief. Feast your heart on my sorrow! Exult and triumph over your victory! But why do I say victory? Even in my misery I have more left to me than you have in your glory. Even after so many deaths I am the victor!" As she spoke the twang of the bowstring rang out, bringing terror. The sisters [Niobe's seven daughters], with their hair flowing and dressed in black, were standing where their brothers lay in death. One, as she pulled the arrow from his flesh, fell dying as she tried to kiss her brother's lips. A second, endeavoring to console her mother in her misery suddenly fell silent and doubled up with a hidden wound. One sank down as she tried in vain to escape; another fell dead upon her sister. One tried to hide; another stood there trembling. When six had been taken by death, suffering various sorts of wounds, only one remained alive. Then the mother, shielding this last child with her body . . . cried out, "Leave this one for me, leave me the youngest one! I pray you, leave the smallest, leave one!" But even as she prayed, the one she prayed to save fell dead. (*Metamorphoses* 4.284–304)

Struck dumb with overpowering grief at the merciless slaughter of all her children, Niobe burst into tears. And even as she did so she steadily solidified into stone, her final punishment from the divinities she had offended. Thereafter, both night and day, tears continued to spring from the stone and kept its surface moist, a warning to all who might contemplate insolence against the gods.

The Curse Passes to a New Generation

The family curse next fell on Pelops's two sons, Thyestes and Atreus, who, through their own terrible deeds, passed it along to the succeeding generation. Thyestes fell in love with his brother's wife, Aerope, and had sexual relations with her behind Atreus's back. On learning of the affair, the enraged Atreus, taking inspiration from his grandfather Tantalus, killed Thyestes' two small children, cut them up, boiled them, and served them to their unsuspecting father.

Because Atreus was king and had all of the power, the distraught Thyestes could not retaliate, at least not at first; over time, however, he had his revenge. Thyestes went to the Delphic Oracle and asked the god Apollo how he could gain vengeance on Atreus; and the god, keeping in mind his obligation to see that the curse continued in force, informed Thyestes that he should rape his own daughter, Pelopia, and have a child by her. Reluctantly, the man did so, making sure to disguise himself so that the girl would not know his true identity; however, she had the presence of mind to steal and hide his sword before he departed in haste.

Meanwhile, a famine struck the land of Argolis, where Atreus reigned. He consulted an oracle, which said that the famine might be averted if he brought his brother, Thyestes, back home. So Atreus went looking for his brother. Instead of Thyestes, however, he found young Pelopia, who was pregnant with Thyestes' child, and, not realizing who she was, fell in love with and married her. When the baby was born, Atreus raised it as his own, naming it Aegisthus.

Years went by and Aegisthus grew into a young man, as did Atreus's true sons, Agamemnon and Menelaus. One day Agamemnon and Menelaus accidentally discovered the whereabouts of their uncle, Thyestes, captured him, and brought him to Atreus, who locked him up in a cell. Then the king ordered Aegisthus to go into the cell and kill Thyestes, by chance giving the youth the very sword that Pelopia had taken from Thyestes years before. Thyestes immediately recognized the weapon and told Aegisthus and Pelopia the truth about the vile incest he had perpetrated on them. In her shame and grief, Pelopia grabbed the sword and fell on it. But Aegisthus refused to kill Thyestes, his true father; instead, the disturbed and grief-stricken young man left the cell and slew Atreus, whom he saw as the real villain behind the crime.

The Blood of Agamemnon and Clytemnestra

Even after ruining the lives of Thyestes, Atreus, and Pelopia, the curse (which came to be called the curse on the house of Atreus, though Atreus himself did not cause it) continued, unabated, to afflict further generations of the family. Atreus's son Menelaus, ruler of Sparta and husband of Helen (whose flight with Paris instigated the Trojan War), lived a reasonably uneventful and happy life once back in Greece after the fall of Troy. Thus, the family curse appeared to skip over Menelaus.

However, the plague on the family and its fortunes fell with full force on Atreus's other son—Agamemnon, king of Mycenae (in Argolis). After leading the Greeks to victory at Troy and then surviving the storm sent by Poseidon to punish Greek sacrilege during the city's fall, Agamemnon returned to Mycenae in triumph. Huge crowds greeted the conquering hero as he disembarked his ship on the coast and accompanied him as he made his way across the fertile plain to his magnificent fortress-palace.

To the king, all seemed festive and hopeful. But in the crowd were elder Mycenaeans who remembered with foreboding what had occurred before Agamemnon had departed for Troy. They recalled his pitiless slaughter of his daughter Iphigenia (whom he had sacrificed to obtain fair sailing winds for the voyage to Troy) and worried that this deed might be part of the continuing cycle of evil that was rumored to hang over the royal house of Atreus. Ten years had gone by since Iphigenia's sacrifice, but the memory of her death lingered to the present. In their wisdom, the elders realized that one sin often leads to another. Still, though the crime of sacrificing the girl had not been forgotten, the elders held out some small ray of hope that Agamemnon would not have to pay a terrible price for his crime.

But the happy ending the elders hoped for never materialized, for Agamemnon was already doomed. Waiting for him inside the palace was his wife, Clytemnestra, who had all of these long years harbored deep-seated hatred and resentment toward him for the death of their innocent daughter. In the king's absence, she had taken a lover—Aegisthus, the son born out of Thyestes' incest with Pelopia; and now, with Aegisthus to help her, she put her plan for revenge into action. The elders who had gathered outside the palace heard Agamemnon's death cries, and only minutes later the queen appeared, her gown spattered with fresh blood, the dripping knife still in her hand. In his play *Agamemnon,* the Athenian playwright Aeschylus has her say,

> I struck him twice. In two great cries of agony he buckled at the knees and fell. When he was down I struck him a third blow. . . . Thus he went down, and the life

struggled out of him; and as he died he spattered me with the dark red and violent driven rain of bitter savored blood. . . . For me, I glory. Were it religion to pour wine above the slain, this man deserved, more than deserved, such sacrament. He filled our [family's] cup with things unspeakable and now, himself come home, has drunk it to the dregs. (*Agamemnon* 1384–1398)

Orestes' Revenge

Clytemnestra and Aegisthus felt no guilt for what they had done, just as Agamemnon, Atreus, Niobe, and Tantalus had felt no guilt for their crimes; and because only guilt and suffering could cleanse the stains of such terrible acts, they, in their self-righteousness, inadvertently allowed the curse to continue to still another generation. Clytemnestra and Aegisthus ruled for many years, thinking that all was finally well in their land. But two of Agamemnon's children—his son Orestes and his daughter Electra—were still living. The young man grew up in a foreign land, safe from his mother and stepfather, who feared him and would surely have killed him if they had the chance. Electra grew up in the palace, miserable at having to live with her father's murderers, and she dreamed of the day when her brother might return home and exact vengeance.

That day finally came. Orestes, now fully grown and aching to avenge his father's murder, slipped into the palace and revealed himself to Electra. Together, they plotted to kill Clytemnestra and Aegisthus, and Orestes actually executed these bloody deeds. But as he stood on the palace steps, the gore-spattered bodies sprawled behind him, he beheld something terrifying that no others present could see: the snake-haired Furies, the tormentors of murderers, who had come to haunt and pursue him. He realized that, having perpetrated the awful family curse, he could

Orestes and his friend Pylades slay Aegisthus, Clytemnestra's lover, in this painting on a Greek vase.

not stay to sit on the throne that was rightfully his. According to Aeschylus, Orestes cried out,

> I go, an outcast wanderer from this land, and leave behind, in life, in death, the name of what I did. . . . [The Furies] come like gorgons [hideous women with snakes for hair], they wear robes of black, and they are wreathed in a tangle of snakes. I can no longer stay. . . . These are no fancies of affliction [i.e., illusions]. They are clear and real, and here right now! They are the bloodhounds of my mother's hate! . . . Ah, Lord Apollo, how they grow and multiply, repulsive for the blood drops of their dripping eyes. . . . You cannot see them, but I see them! I am driven from this place. I can stay here no longer! (*Libation Bearers* 1042–1062)

Orestes wandered through many lands, always pursued by the fearsome Furies. Finally, having long felt great guilt for his acts, he journeyed to the temple of Athena in Athens and there asked the goddess for guidance and the purification of his sins. The wise Athena saw how Orestes was the first of the long line of killers in his family to suffer from his guilt, seek absolution from the gods, and throw himself on their mercy. Thus, she accepted his plea. Moreover, at the conclusion of his trial, held near the city's Acropolis, she voted to acquit him. In this healing atmosphere of mercy and forgiveness, a wondrous thing happened: Athena transformed the hideous and vengeful Furies into the kindly and graceful Eumenides, protectors of all who beseech the gods. And from that day forward, none of Orestes' descendants were doomed to perpetuate the sins of the past; the destructive curse that had hung so long over the house of Atreus was at last extinguished.

The Exploits of Theseus

Long before the advent of the great war at Troy, there arose in Greece one of its finest and most valiant early champions— Athens's national hero, the brave and quick-witted Theseus. To understand how he first became a hero, we must begin in the days shortly before his birth. Aegeus, king of Athens, was traveling through southern Greece, heading for home after a long journey, and he stopped for the night at the house of a friend, Pittheus. That night Aegeus slept with Pittheus's daughter, Aethra, who then became pregnant. Before leaving for Athens, Aegeus placed one of his swords under a large stone and instructed Aethra that, if the child was a boy, she should tell him about the sword. When he grew old and strong enough to lift the stone and retrieve the sword, the king said, she should send the boy to Athens to seek out his father and his rightful destiny.

Aegeus returned to Athens and many years passed. The child, indeed a boy whom Aethra named Theseus, grew into a handsome, exceedingly intelligent, and admirable young man. When he felt he was ready, he easily lifted the stone and took possession of the sword, then eagerly set out for Athens. On the way, he decided that it would be best if he could prove himself a great champion before arriving, so that the father he had never met would be both impressed and proud of him. The young man had heard that several murderous bandits roamed the countryside on the road to Athens, terrorizing and killing travelers, farmers, and other innocent people. Setting himself the challenge of ridding the land of these brigands, one by one he met and defeated them. According to the ancient writer Apollodorus of Athens, Theseus first overcame Periphetes,

who, because of the club that he carried, was called *Corynetes,* the "club-bearer." Since his legs were weak, Periphetes carried a club of iron and used it to kill passers-by. After he took the club away from him, Theseus continued to carry it himself. Second, Theseus killed Sinis . . . who was called the pine-bender, for he haunted the Isthmus of Corinth and forced travelers to hold onto pine trees he had bent down. They, however, were not strong enough to do this and so they were pulled up to their deaths by the trees. Theseus killed Sinis in this same way. (*Library* 3.15.14–16)

Theseus also defeated and slew several other unsavory characters. One was Sciron, who kicked passersby over the edge of a cliff; the young hero tossed him off the same cliff. Another offender, Cercyon, was a skilled wrestler who forced travelers to fight him and almost always ended up killing them. Theseus accepted this challenge and smashed his opponent against some rocks. Still another villain Theseus eliminated was Damastes, also known as Procrustes, "the Stretcher." "Beside the road Damastes had his dwelling place," Apollodorus writes,

where he made up two beds, one small and the other large, and extended hospitality to the passers-by. But he laid the short men on the large bed and beat them with a hammer to the size of the bed; and the tall men he put on the small bed and sawed off whatever parts of the body hung over it. (*Epitome* 1.3)

Theseus dispatched Damastes by his own methods, laying him in a bed that was too short and cutting off his head, which hung over the end.

Facing Rebels and a Giant Bull

Because of these impressive deeds, Theseus's reputation preceded him, and when he reached Athens the people of that city welcomed him with open arms. Of course, neither they nor their king, Aegeus, were yet aware of the young man's true identity. This was revealed at a banquet thrown by the king in honor of Theseus's heroic slaying of the bandits. At the time, King Aegeus was living with Medea, the sorceress whom the hero Jason had brought back from Colchis along with the fabulous Golden Fleece. (Jason and Medea had ended up in Corinth, where he had jilted her for another woman and she had killed her own children to get revenge; afterward, Aegeus had given Medea sanctuary in Athens.) Because of her abilities in the black arts, the evil Medea recognized Theseus's true identity. She persuaded Aegeus that this young stranger was actually one of a group of men who were then secretly plotting to usurp the Athenian throne and that Theseus should be poisoned before he could do any harm. Aegeus agreed to this plan. But just as Theseus was about to drink some poisoned wine, the young man drew his sword to cut his meat; Aegeus instantly recognized the weapon as the one he had placed under the stone years before. The king quickly spilled out the wine and joyfully announced that Theseus was his son and heir, and Medea skulked away and fled the city, never to be seen again.

Now that Theseus and his father were reunited and the young man was securely in line for the throne, the plotters became open rebels and tried to overthrow the government. Half of their force marched on Athens while the other half hid outside the city, hoping to ambush Theseus as he rode by on his horse. Thanks to an alert herald, who saw the rebels preparing the ambush, Theseus attacked them from behind and wiped them out; when the other rebels heard what had happened, they fled for their lives.

No sooner had Theseus eliminated this threat to Athens, when he had to face another. Aegeus informed his son that for over two years a huge wild bull had been ravaging the countryside near Marathon (a village and plain lying about twenty-five miles northeast of Athens). This was the same beast that had mated with Pasiphae, wife of King Minos of Crete, a union that had produced the fearsome Minotaur, a creature half man and half bull. The famous hero Heracles had captured the bull as one of his twelve labors, Aegeus told Theseus; however, once that labor was completed, the strongman had released the beast on the Greek mainland, and it had eventually made its way to Marathon. Then, Androgeos, King Minos's son, had paid a visit to Athens. Aegeus had sent Androgeos to kill the bull and the youth had died in the attempt. Having heard all of this, Theseus wasted no time in going to Marathon and capturing the great bull. Leading the shackled creature back to Athens, the young hero sacrificed it to the god Apollo.

Theseus in the Labyrinth

But Theseus soon learned, to his dismay, that killing the bull of Marathon had eliminated only part of the threat to Athens by Cretan bulls. Aegeus explained that King Minos had blamed the Athenian king and his city for the loss of his son, Androgeos; and to get revenge, Minos had invaded Athens. He had threatened to destroy the city if Aegeus did not agree to send seven young men and seven young women to Crete every year (some ancient sources said it was every nine years) as tribute (payment acknowledging submission). Once they arrived in Crete, these hostages were locked in the labyrinth, a mazelike dungeon inhabited by the hideous, bloodthirsty Minotaur. One by one, the Minotaur would hunt down and devour the captives. Already, Aegeus sadly told Theseus, this grisly scenario had played out twice.

Theseus decided that he must free his city from this appalling obligation. When the time came for the third group of hostages to make their way to certain death in Crete, Theseus volunteered to become one of their number, promising to do everything in his power to slay the Minotaur. Old Aegeus was grateful, but he worried about what might happen to his son. "On the two earlier occasions," Theseus's noted ancient biographer Plutarch writes,

> there had seemed to be no hope of deliverance [for the hostages], and so the Athenians had sent out their ship with a black sail, believing that it was carrying their youth to certain doom. But this time Theseus urged his father to take heart and boasted that he would overcome the Minotaur, and so Aegeus gave the [ship's] pilot a second sail, a white one, and ordered him on the return voyage to hoist the white canvas if Theseus were safe, but otherwise to sail with the

black [canvas] as a sign of mourning. (*Life of Theseus* 17)

Bidding farewell to his father, Theseus sailed with the other hostages for Crete. There, before putting them into the labyrinth, the authorities paraded the doomed young men and women before the local populace. Among those watching was King Minos's daughter, the princess Ariadne, who fell in love with Theseus at first sight and became determined to save him somehow from the fate ordained by her father. That night she went to the young man and told him of her love. She also brought along a means by which he could find his way out of the labyrinth—a ball of twine, supplied by Daedalus, the brilliant inventor who was at the time working for King Minos. Ariadne told

A painting on a Greek black-figure vase dating to the sixth century B.C. depicts Theseus killing the fearsome Minotaur.

Theseus that he should tie the end of the twine to the door and unravel it as he walked along; later, he would be able to retrace his steps by following the trail of twine.

Unraveling the ball of twine as Ariadne had instructed, the next morning Theseus descended into the labyrinth and sought out the Minotaur. Finding the repulsive creature, he engaged it in hand-to-hand combat and succeeded in beating it to death with his fists (since he lacked a sword or other weapon). Wasting no time, Theseus led the Athenian hostages out of the maze by following the twine. Reaching the light of day, they joined the awaiting Ariadne, boarded the Athenian ship, and escaped.

On the way to Athens the party stopped to rest on the island of Naxos. There, they unfortunately lost Ariadne, who had by this time become Theseus's wife. The way this happened varies from one ancient source to another, one saying that Theseus abandoned her, another that he got lost in a storm and returned to find her dead, and still another that the fertility god, Dionysus, fell in love with her and carried her away.

All of the versions agree, however, on what happened when the ship made it back to Athens. "In his distress over losing Ariadne," Apollodorus claims,

> Theseus forgot as he was sailing back to port to hoist the white sail on his ship. Aegeus, therefore, when he caught sight of the ship from the top of the Acropolis [Athens's central, rocky hill] and saw the black sail, thought Theseus had been killed, and so he jumped to his death. (*Epitome* 1.10)

To commemorate the tragic demise of poor old Aegeus, the body of water Theseus had crossed to reach Crete became known as the Aegean Sea, the name it has borne ever since.

Uniting and Defending Athens

With the passing of Aegeus, Theseus inherited the Athenian throne. Though the young man felt that Athens was a fine town, he recognized that it held the potential to become a truly great city, perhaps the greatest in Greece. Thus, he proceeded to institute a series of reforms to make that dream a reality. The most important of these reforms was the unification of the towns of Attica (the large peninsula in which Athens is located) into a central Athenian state. According to Plutarch,

> He now traveled around Attica and strove to convince them town by town and clan by clan. The common people and the poor responded at once to his appeal, while to the more influential classes he proposed a constitution without a king. There was to be democracy, in which he would be no more than the commander of the army and the guardian of the laws. . . . He then proceeded to abolish the town halls, council chambers, and public officials in the various districts. To replace them, he built a single town hall . . . for the whole community on the site of the present Acropolis. (*Life of Theseus* 24)

Theseus also instituted the Panathenaea, a grand religious festival celebrated thereafter every four years by the people of Attica.

Theseus's unification of Attica turned out to be advantageous, partly because it significantly increased the number of able-bodied men in the Athenian army. And Athens needed all the soldiers it could muster to fight the Amazons, a race of warrior women who lived in the wild lands lying west of the Black Sea. Theseus led an expedition northward into Amazonian territory and captured Antiope, sister of Hippolyte, the Amazon queen. An army of Amazons, commanded by Hippolyte herself, then pursued the Athenians back to Attica and attacked Athens. The warrior women besieged the Acropolis, but Theseus and his troops suddenly burst forth and defeated the invaders. (Later Greeks referred to this battle as the Amazonomachy.)

Theseus's Later Adventures

Having saved Athens once more, Theseus now began expanding Athenian power and influence by intervening in the affairs of neighboring states. After the Seven Against Thebes failed in their attack on that city, for example, Theseus demanded that Creon, the new king of Thebes, allow the attackers to bury the bodies of their leaders (which Creon had forbidden, an act most Greeks viewed as barbaric). Theseus also gave the former Theban king Oedipus and his daughter Antigone sanctuary in Athens and drove away the men Creon sent to take custody of the two refugees.

Theseus was not so successful, however, in an incident that occurred closer to home. While Antiope the Amazon had been in Athenian custody, she (or, in some accounts, her sister Hippolyte) and Theseus had had a relationship and produced a son—Hippolytus. When Hippolytus had grown into a young man, Theseus's second wife, Phaedra, fell in love Hippolytus with and made sexual advances toward him. Though the youth steadfastly refused these advances, Theseus mistakenly came to believe that it had been his son who had made the advances, and he exiled the young man, who died shortly afterward. Phaedra then hanged herself, leaving Theseus grieving and lonely.

Trying to raise Theseus's spirits, his friend Pirithous, king of the Lapiths (a Greek tribe inhabiting central Greece), who had also recently been widowed, proposed that the two leaders take part in an adventure. Pirithous wanted to marry Persephone, daughter of the goddess Demeter and queen of the Underworld. To make this goal a reality, said Pirithous, the two men must descend into the realm of the dead and abduct Persephone. Perhaps because he was still grieving and not thinking clearly, Theseus agreed to help in this audacious venture. The two men made their way down into the Underworld and soon encountered Hades, the lord of that nether realm. He pretended to extend them hospitality and bade them sit down for a meal with him. But when they sat, they found themselves locked fast, for Hades had placed them in his Chairs of Forgetfulness, which made them forget who they were and why they had come. Luckily for Theseus, Heracles happened by (on his way to fetch the three-headed dog Cerberus to fulfill one of his labors) and freed the Athenian leader. Sadly, Pirithous was not as fortunate and remained in Hades' clutches thereafter.

Returning to the earth's surface, Theseus found that Athens had been invaded by the Spartans and that the city was now under the rule of an Athenian usurper backed by Sparta. For the moment, Theseus was powerless to change the situation. Therefore, he decided it would be best to find a secure place and there begin devising a plan to save Athens once more. However, the king of the place he chose, the Aegean island of Skyros, was afraid that having such a controversial figure in his land might be dangerous. So the king pushed Theseus off a cliff, killing him. (Many years later, in historic times, an Athenian general named Cimon traveled to Skyros and dug up the bones of large man, claiming they were the remains of Athens's greatest hero—the resourceful Theseus.)

The Founding of Rome

Romulus, the legendary founder and first king of Rome, and his twin brother, Remus, were the grandchildren of Numitor, king of Alba Longa (on the plain of Latium, south of the later site of Rome). When they were still infants, their great-uncle, Amulius, usurped the throne from Numitor and ordered the babies to be drowned in the Tiber River. But they fortunately washed ashore, where a she-wolf fed them and some poor shepherds eventually took them in. When the brothers grew to manhood and learned their true identities, they returned to Alba, overthrew Amulius, and restored Numitor to his throne. Then they set out to establish a new city of their own on the northern edge of the Latium plain.

As it turned out, however, Romulus ended up founding the city by himself, for he and Remus got into a petty squabble, fought, and Romulus slew his brother. According to the Roman historian Livy's account,

> Unhappily, the brothers' plans for the future were marred by the same source which had divided their grandfather and Amulius— jealousy and ambition. A disgraceful quarrel arose from a matter in itself trivial. As the brothers were twins and all questions of seniority were therefore precluded, they determined to ask the gods of the countryside to declare . . . which of them should govern the new town once it was founded, and give his name to it. . . . Remus, the story goes, was the first to receive a sign—six vultures [in some accounts eagles]; and no sooner was this made known to the people than double the number of birds appeared to Romulus. The followers of each promptly saluted their masters as king. . . . Angry words ensued, followed all too soon by blows, and in the course of the fray Remus was killed. (*History of Rome from Its Foundation* 1.6)

Livy tells of another, more common story, in which Romulus began building some city walls and Remus jumped over them. In a fit of rage, Romulus slew his brother; he soon regretted killing Remus and gave his brother a proper burial.

Laying Out the City
Romulus then continued to erect the city, which thereafter became known as Rome, after him. Realizing that he needed help,

the founder sent for masons, workers, and advisers from Etruria (homeland of the Etruscans). They instructed him in the proper steps one had to follow to construct a city and the accepted religious ceremonies that should be conducted to inaugurate it. "First," Romulus's ancient biographer Plutarch writes,

> they dug a round trench . . . and into it solemnly threw the first-fruits of all things either good by custom or necessary by nature; lastly, every man taking a small piece of earth of the country from whence he came, they all threw [the pieces] in randomly together. Making this trench . . . their center, they laid out the boundary of the city in a circle round it. Then the founder fitted to a plow a metal plowshare [blade], and, yoking together a bull and a cow, drove himself a deep line or furrow round the boundary. (*Life of Romulus* 296–308)

Using this line in the dirt as a guide, on April 21, 753 B.C. (which became the birthday of the Roman nation), Romulus and the others laid out the city's outer defensive wall around the Palatine, one of the seven low hills on which, over time, Rome would rise.

Once he had established Rome, Romulus proceeded immediately to deal with some important religious, legal, and social matters. According to Livy,

> Having performed with proper ceremony his religious duties, he summoned his subjects and gave them laws, without which the creation of a unified people and government would not have been possible. . . . Meanwhile Rome was growing. . . . To help fill his big new town, [Romulus] threw open . . . a place of asylum for fugitives. Here fled for refuge all the outcasts from the neighboring peoples; some free, some slaves, and all of them wanting nothing more than a fresh start. That mob was the first real addition to

the city's strength, the first step toward her future greatness. (*History of Rome from Its Foundation* 1.8–9)

The Rape of the Sabine Women

Unfortunately, most of those who initially settled in the city were men, and they had difficulty obtaining brides. To solve this problem, Romulus came up with an audacious plan. He invited the residents of a number of neighboring towns, all inhabited by a Latin people called the Sabines, to a great religious festival where athletic games and theatrical performances would be staged. His real intention, however, was not to foster friendship but rather to steal the Sabine women. "On the appointed day," Livy writes,

> crowds flocked to Rome, partly, no doubt, out of sheer curiosity to see the new town. . . . All the Sabines were there . . . with their wives and children. . . . Then the great moment came; the show began, and nobody had eyes or thought for anything else. This was the Romans' opportunity. At a given signal, all the able-bodied men burst through the crowd and seized the young women. Most of the girls were the prize of whoever got hold of them first. . . . By this act of violence, the fun of the festival broke up in panic. The girls' unfortunate parents made good their escape, not without bitter comments on the treachery of their hosts. . . . The young women were no less indignant and full of foreboding about the future. (*History of Rome from Its Foundation* 1.9)

But Romulus assured the captured brides that they would be well treated and tried to talk them into accepting their new situation.

Soon, however, the male Sabines reorganized and attacked Rome in an effort to win back their women. Romulus and his troops managed to defeat the first several groups that marched on the city. But the Sabines of the city of Cures, led by their

king, Titus Tatius, managed to surround the city. A great battle occurred on the flat ground between the Palatine and Capitoline Hills, and many on both sides were killed before the former Sabine women rushed out and demanded a truce. They could not simply stand by, they declared, and watch their fathers, brothers, and husbands slaughter one another. The result was a treaty in which the two sides agreed to merge as one people, with Romulus and Titus Tatius as joint rulers. Rome had made it first conquest and absorption of neighboring people, opening the way for the newly founded city's spectacular rise to greatness.

Perseus and Medusa

If ever a monstrous creature needed killing, it was Medusa, who gained her terrifying and murderous physical appearance in the following way. Gaia (the earth), mother of the Titans, mated with her own son Nereus, producing the sea gods Phorcys and Ceto; and the latter two in their turn mated and had six female offspring. The first three, the Graiae, were, from the moment of their birth, old hags who shared a single eye and a single tooth among them. The other three sisters were the Gorgons—Stheno, Euryale, and Medusa. When she was a young woman, Medusa was quite lovely. But then she had an affair with Poseidon, god of the seas, and the two made the mistake of making love inside a temple dedicated to the goddess Athena. The angry Athena turned Medusa into a creature with snakes for hair and an appearance so grotesque that any animal or human who looked directly at her turned to stone.

Thereafter, Medusa lived with her sisters, who were almost as hideous as she was, on an island on the far edge of the known world. (Some ancient accounts claimed that all three Gorgons turned those who gazed at them to stone; other sources say that only Medusa possessed this power.) Many a traveler who was lost or blown off course and accidentally encountered the dreaded sisters ended up as a pillar of solid stone. For a long time, no one dared even to think about traveling to the faraway land where the Gorgons lived and attempting to kill them. To fight these creatures, went the conventional wisdom, one had to look at them; and looking at them seemed the same thing as signing one's own death warrant. In short, eliminating just one, let alone all, of the Gorgons seemed an impossible task for any human being.

Perseus's Early Years

In time, however, there arose a champion who possessed the special combination of physical prowess and shrewd wit that was needed to defeat the worst of the three hideous sisters—Medusa. This hero was Perseus, whose circumstances even before he was born suggested that he was destined for greatness. An oracle had informed Acrisius, king of Argos (in the eastern Peloponnesus), that one of his grandchildren would one day kill him. To avoid such a fate, Acrisius locked his daughter, Danae, in a cell made of bronze until she was too old to have children.

Nevertheless, Danae soon became miraculously pregnant, which shocked her father. He had no way of knowing that Zeus, leader of the gods, had taken the form of a beautiful shower of gold dust, which seeped into Danae's cell one night through an air vent in the roof. Nine months later, the young woman gave birth to a son, whom she named Perseus. Enraged at this turn of events, King Acrisius ordered both mother and child to be thrown into the sea in a wooden chest. Luckily, Danae and Perseus survived the ordeal and washed up on the island of Seriphos (about a hundred miles south of Athens), where a friendly fisherman named Dictys gave them shelter. After Perseus had grown into a handsome, powerful young man, Danae told him the identity of his father.

Now, it so happened that Dictys's brother was Polydectes, the king of Seriphos. An unsavory, overbearing character, Polydectes took a fancy to Perseus's mother and insisted that she marry him. She refused. But the king kept badgering her until Perseus finally stepped in and warned Polydectes to break off his pursuit. Angry at being rebuffed, the king vowed to get revenge on Danae and Perseus when the chance presented itself.

The chance for revenge came much sooner than Polydectes had expected. He proposed marriage to another woman, named Hippodameia, and he demanded that every man on the island provide a horse that the king would present as a gift to his prospective bride. Because Perseus owned no horses, he went to Polydectes and offered to give him an alternative gift; in the course of their conversation, they discussed the idea of Perseus bringing back a truly novel gift—the head of the Gorgon Medusa.

The Divine Visitors

Only after committing himself to the goal of killing the Gorgon did Perseus truly realize the tremendous difficulty of the task. First, he did not know where to find the monster. Second, even if he could find her, he lacked a sword strong enough to penetrate her tough hide. And third, there was the problem of devising a way to fight her without having to look directly at her. Hoping to discover the whereabouts of the Gorgons, Perseus sailed to the Greek mainland and journeyed to Delphi, home of the renowned oracle of Apollo. The priestess was not very helpful, however. All she said was that he should seek out a land where people ate acorns instead of wheat (which suggested an area of forests rather than plains). So the young man traveled farther north, to another famous oracle—that of Zeus at Dodona. The priest of Zeus did not know where the Gorgons lived either, but he did provide Perseus with a crucial piece of information. From now on, he told the young man, he would be under the special protection of some powerful gods.

Fortunately for Perseus, this protection became apparent almost immediately. He was riding his horse along a country road less than an hour after departing Dodona when he encountered an unusually handsome young man carrying a golden staff with little wings on it. The young man greeted Perseus warmly as if he knew him. And stopping his horse, Perseus asked if the two had met at some time in the past. The young man answered that a small demonstration seemed to be in order and suddenly rose into the air and flitted like a bird around Perseus's head.

It was then that Perseus recognized the young man as Hermes, the swift-footed messenger god and protector of travelers. Landing back on his feet, Hermes told the man that the task he had undertaken was both difficult and perilous, but not impossible. The god would show him where the Gorgons dwelled. However, to fight and defeat Medusa he would need some very special equipment, which only a group of young maidens—the Nymphs of the North—possessed. The problem was that the only ones who knew where the Nymphs lived were the grizzled old Graiae, who shared an eye among themselves. Because they were the Gorgons' sisters, it was unlikely that they would agree to help Perseus, so he would have to devise a way to force the information from them. In the meantime, Hermes produced a magnificent sword seemingly out of thin air and handed it to Perseus. With it, the god said, the man would be able to cut through Medusa's thick hide.

Perseus still had one very important question: How would he be able to avoid the Gorgon's gaze and keep himself from becoming a pillar of stone, as so many

men and women had been before him? The answer to this question did not come from Hermes, however; for at that moment the startled Perseus looked up and beheld a radiant golden ball descending from the sky. Suddenly, the ball seemed to burst, revealing the goddess Athena, dressed in her splendid suit of armor. She greeted Perseus and then removed a shield of polished bronze from her chest. He should use this shield, she said, when he approached the Gorgon, for the simple reason that, though her image was lethal when viewed directly, her reflection in the shield would be harmless. She explained that Hermes would take Perseus to the withered ones— the Graiae. They would tell him how he could find the Nymphs and acquire the rest of his equipment. After wishing the young hero good luck, the goddess became a radiant ball once more and ascended into the sky.

Outwitting the Graiae
Guided by Hermes, Perseus journeyed to the gray, dismal land where the Graiae lived. Eventually the god pointed to three figures huddled near the entrance to a large cave. At first glance, Perseus thought that the creatures resembled large birds, but on closer inspection he could see that they had human heads and hands, which were covered with wrinkles and age spots. The man and his divine companion hid behind a rock and watched the weird sisters closely. Each time one of them wanted to look at something, she took the eye out of her sister's forehead and placed it in an empty socket in her own forehead. In this manner, they swapped the eye back and forth every minute or so. A plan began to take shape in Perseus's mind, and soon he knew what he had to do.

The young man suddenly stepped forward and revealed himself to the Graiae, who regarded him warily. One of them demanded to know what the stranger wanted. Perseus answered that he sought the location of the Nymphs of the North. Recoiling in horror, the sisters wailed in unison, refused to give him this information, and ordered him to go away. Perseus had fully expected this reaction, of course, and now he put his plan into action. He moved abruptly to one side, then to the other, forcing the sisters to pass the eye hastily back and forth to keep track of him, and as they did so, he suddenly snatched the organ from one of their hands. If they wanted the eye back, he said, they must tell him how to find the Nymphs.

Needless to say, the Graiae, who had been stricken blind by the loss of their only eye, relented and gave Perseus the information he sought. Accompanied by the faithful Hermes, he followed their directions northward to the land of a happy people called the Hyperboreans. There, the travelers found the Nymphs of the North, who gave Perseus three gifts. The first was a pair of winged sandals similar to those Hermes wore. The second was a special sack that conformed in size to whatever one put into it. And the third gift was a cap that made its wearer invisible. At last, Perseus was ready to confront the monstrous Medusa.

Medusa's Death

In the words of the ancient Roman myth teller Ovid, Perseus, guided by Hermes, now flew

> through unknown ways, thick-bearded forests, and tearing rocks and stones, until he found the Gorgons' home. And as he looked about from left to right, no matter where he turned, he saw both man and beast turned into stone, all creatures who had seen Medusa's face. (*Metamorphoses* 777–781)

Finally, by their reflection in his shield, Perseus beheld the three Gorgons, who lay sleeping on a large rock. The man was startled when, without warning, Medusa awakened. Thanks to the keen senses of the writhing green serpents on her head, she could tell that danger was near; but because of her stalker's cap of invisibility, she could not see him. Being careful to look at her only by reflection, Perseus swooped down at her, his mighty sword raised to strike. Guided by Athena, who appeared on the scene at the crucial moment, the weapon sliced through Medusa's neck, severing her monstrous head from her equally repellent body. Skillfully, Perseus caught the head in his magic sack. At that moment, the other two Gorgons woke up, and, seeing that their sister had been slain, they searched frantically for the killer. But Perseus was still invisible, so they could not find him.

As Perseus sped away, carrying Medusa's blood-spattered head, he glanced back and saw a wondrous sight. At the time of her death, the Gorgon had been pregnant with two of Poseidon's offspring, and these creatures now sprang from Medusa's decapitated body. One was Pegasus, a magnificent winged horse (who would later aid another hero, Bellerophon, in slaying a monster called the Chimaera); the other was Chrysaor, a sadly misshapen creature.

An Encounter with a Titan

On his way back to Greece, Perseus encountered heavy winds that blew him toward northern Africa. Finally, because it was getting dark, he decided to stop to rest and found himself in the region where the great Titan Atlas held up the edge of the sky and guarded the golden apples of the Hesperides (minor goddesses). Approaching Atlas, Ovid writes,

> Perseus asked for permission to sleep and refresh himself. . . . "My friend," he said to Atlas, "if you are impressed by those of noble birth, you should know that Zeus himself is my father. Or if you admire heroic deeds, you will surely admire mine. I ask you to give me hospitality and

a chance to rest." Atlas, however, remembered an ancient prophecy that the goddess Themis had uttered long before:
"The time will come, Atlas, when you
will be robbed of your gold by the son of
Zeus, who will gain glory by stealing it."
(*Metamorphoses* 4.636–645)

Atlas did not realize that the son of Zeus
who was fated to steal the golden apples
was the strongman Heracles. Mistakenly
assuming that Perseus was the potential
thief, Atlas told the young man to leave at
once; when Perseus tried to calm him
down, the Titan swung one of his huge
legs at him, a blow that would have
crushed the man had his winged sandals
not allowed him to dodge it in the nick of
time. Deciding that he must fight back,
Perseus reached into his sack, pulled out
Medusa's head, and displayed it to the
startled Atlas, who speedily turned to
stone. Thereafter, his craggy body remained as the Atlas Mountains, which
continued to hold up the far edge of the
sky.

The Princess Andromeda
The next morning Perseus took flight once
more and headed west along the African
coast. He passed over Egypt, then turned
northward and soon saw the coast of Palestine below. Suddenly the young man halted
in midair, greatly disturbed by the sight of
a beautiful young woman chained to the
side of large rock on the seashore. Swooping down, Perseus approached the maiden
and asked the reason for her predicament.
She told him that she was Andromeda,
daughter of Cepheus, king of Joppa (in
Palestine), and his wife, Cassiopeia. The
queen had recently angered Poseidon, and
to punish her the god had sent a horrible
sea monster to ravage the countryside
around Joppa. Desperate, Cepheus had
consulted an oracle, who told him that sacrificing Andromeda to the creature was the
only way to make it leave.

As Perseus listened to this pitiable story,
he heard a loud snorting sound behind him
and turned to see the monster approaching
from the churning surf. Determined to
save the princess, the man sprang into the
air and flew straight at the creature. According to Ovid's account,

Swooping swiftly through the sky, Perseus
attacked the monster's back and, to the
sound of its bellowing, buried his sword up
to its crooked hilt in the beast's right shoulder. Tormented by this deep wound, the
creature now reared itself upright, high in
the air, now plunged beneath the waters,
now turned itself about like some fierce
wild boar encircled by a pack of baying
hounds. The hero, on his swift wings,
avoided the greedily snapping jaws, and
dealt blows with his curved sword. . . .
From its mouth, the monster spat out waves
dyed red with blood. . . . [Then mighty
Perseus] drove his sword through the
beast's flanks, striking it again and again.
The shores of the sea, and homes of the
gods in heaven echoed with shouting and
applause at the exciting spectacle. (*Metamorphoses* 4.718–735)

Thrilled that Perseus had rescued his
daughter, King Cepheus gave Andromeda
in marriage to the young hero. And she
bore Perseus a son, Perses. After spending
a year in Joppa, however, Perseus felt
compelled to return to Seriphos to see how
his mother was faring. Leaving Perses
with his grandparents, Perseus and Andromeda journeyed northwestward toward
Greece.

Pillars of Stone
On reaching Seriphos, Perseus learned that
King Polydectes was persecuting his
mother. Having decided not to marry the
princess Hippodameia, Polydectes had re-
sorted to threats to force Danae to marry
him. Furious, Perseus flew to the palace.
There, he removed the cap of invisibility

The Quest for the Golden Fleece

The great quest for the Golden Fleece arose not long after an oracle had delivered a prophecy to Pelias, king of Iolcos (in southeastern Thessaly). The oracle warned Pelias to beware of any stranger who arrived in Iolcos wearing only one sandal, for this man would cause Pelias to lose both his throne and his life. Because the king had usurped the throne from his half brother, clearly an illegal act, he felt that the prophecy was ominous and worrisome; it might mean that the gods were angry with him for his crime.

Pelias had good reason to be worried. It came to pass that just such a one-sandaled man appeared at the palace, having lost a sandal while crossing a flooded stream. The stranger informed Pelias that he was his cousin Jason, the son of the rightful king. Jason had come to claim his birthright and to bring back enlightened rule to Iolcos, which Pelias had administered harshly. Because the two men were kin, Jason did not seek to fight or harm Pelias. Instead, the younger man simply called on the king to do the right thing and step down from the throne. He could keep all of the wealth that he had recently accumulated, along with his flocks of sheep and other livestock. However, he must transfer the royal crown of Iolcos to Jason, after which the latter would gladly make Pelias the chief royal adviser.

Pelias had to think fast on his feet. He did not want to give up the throne, but he knew he had to find some way to appease this young royal claimant or else risk violence or even civil war. After all, the prophecy had stated that Pelias would lose his life to a one-sandaled man. And it seemed logical that the way to keep the

This painting, found at the House of the Dioscuri, in the buried city of Pompeii, shows Perseus rescuing the princess Andromeda.

and confronted the king and his supporters, who drew their swords and prepared to attack him. Reaching into the sack at his side, Perseus pulled out the repulsive snake-haired head and held it up. Instantly, the king and his courtiers froze in their tracks, the light of life faded from their eyes, and their bodies quickly calcified into motionless stone pillars. The eerie truth was that, even in death, the monster Medusa retained her terrible power.

prediction from coming true was to avoid getting into a fight with Jason. Therefore, the king deviously pretended to agree with Jason's claim to the throne while secretly plotting to rid himself of the young man. Jason was right in his claim to the throne, Pelias said, lying through his teeth, and Jason would indeed become king of Iolcos. First, however, he had to accomplish a special task that would prove to the people that he was worthy of ruling them.

Jason grasped the hilt of his sword and promised gladly to perform any task that Pelias named. Smiling, Pelias told him that he was continually vexed by a spirit who bade him bring the fabulous fleece of the legendary Golden Ram back to Iolcos, its rightful home. At that time, the fleece hung in a tree in the faraway land of Colchis (on the far shore of the Black Sea), and since Pelias was too old and weak to make the journey, Jason must do so. When the young man returned with the fleece, Pelias swore by Zeus, he would willingly abdicate and make Jason king. This was another lie, of course. Pelias knew full well that the voyage to Colchis was long and extremely treacherous and that in all likelihood Jason would never return.

Preparations for the Voyage

As for Jason, he never even considered the idea that he might never come back. Indeed, he felt supremely confident that he could bring back the fleece, which would, through its magical properties, bring good fortune to the city and its people. However, to succeed in this endeavor, Jason realized, he would need a special ship. Under the direction of the goddess Athena, the master shipbuilder Argus came to Iolcos and there constructed the mighty *Argo*. According to the Roman poet Gaius Valerius Flaccus's account,

A large gathering of men worked busily. At the same time . . . a grove of trees had been

felled on all sides and the shores were resounding with the steady blows of the double-edged ax. Already Argus was cutting pines with the thin blade of a saw, and the sides of the ship were being fitted together. . . . Planks [were] being softened over a slow fire until they bent to the proper shape. The oars had been fashioned and Pallas Athena was seeking out a yardarm for the sail-carrying mast. When the ship stood finished, strong enough to plow through the pathless sea . . . Argus added varied ornamental paintings. (*Argonautica* 1.62–73)

Such a superior ship needed a superior crew, and Jason soon gathered together many of the strongest, ablest, and noblest men of Greece. Among their number was the mighty hero Heracles (whom the Romans called Hercules), the strongest man in the world and a renowned warrior and monster killer. He was accompanied by his faithful armor-bearer Hylas. "In the first bloom of youth," says the Greek poet Apollonius in his account of the voyage, Hylas "went with Heracles to carry his arrows and serve as keeper of the bow." (*Argonautica* 1.131–132) Other prominent Argonauts included the master musician and singer Orpheus, the warrior Peleus (father of Achilles, who would become the most famous hero of the Trojan War), and Zeus's twin sons Castor and Polydeuces.

Finally, there was the matter of who should be the commander of the expedition. Jason felt that this honor should go to the strongest and most valuable man in the crew and called on the men to choose that champion. According to Apollonius,

The young men's eyes sought out the dauntless Heracles where he sat in the center, and with one voice they called on him to take command. But he, without moving from his seat, raised his right hand and said: "You must not offer me this honor. I will not accept it for myself, nor will I allow another man to stand up. The one who assembled this force must be its leader too." The generosity that Heracles had shown won their applause and they accepted his decision. (*Argonautica* 1.341–346)

Smelly Women and Six-Armed Giants

Having chosen their leader and stored sufficient provisions for the voyage, Jason and his Argonauts finally embarked from Pagasae (on the sea coast a few miles south of Iolcos) and sailed out into the blue-green waters of the Aegean Sea. Their first stop was the island of Lemnos, where they discovered the local inhabitants in a peculiar state of affairs. The love goddess, Aphrodite, had recently caused the women of the island to give off a sickening smell, and their husbands had all abandoned them. The angry women had then retaliated by killing their husbands, along with all other men on the island. However, the women now regretted the loss of the men and asked the Argonauts for help. The god Hephaestos convinced Aphrodite to eliminate the stench from the women; and the Argonauts proceeded to spend a whole year on Lemnos helping these women to repopulate their land.

Finally, Jason informed the Lemnian queen that he and his men had to continue on their voyage to faraway Colchis. After a tearful parting with their temporary brides, the Argonauts left Lemnos and sailed through the Hellespont (now the Dardanelles Strait) and into the Propontis (now the Sea of Marmara). There, they stopped at Bear Island, where Cyzicus, king of a local people called the Doliones, greeted them warmly. While the crew was feasting in the king's palace, however, a group of giants, each with six arms, attacked the *Argo*. Luckily, the crewman who had volunteered to stand guard at the ship was none other than the mighty Heracles. He easily defeated and slew the giants and piled up their bodies neatly on the beach, where the local people marveled at the incredible sight.

Moving farther north, the Argonauts reached the coast of Bithynia. There, Heracles' oar broke and he and his faithful companion Hylas went ashore to find a suitable tree from which to cut a new one. Unfortunately, Hylas lost his way and some water nymphs took a fancy to him and pulled him down into their spring. Distraught, Heracles searched long and hard for his friend and refused to leave until he had found him. The Argonauts finally had no choice but to leave him and continue with their voyage. (Later, before he returned to Greece, the strongman asked the local people to conduct a new search for the youth each year; they complied and continued to do so for centuries afterward; but alas, they never found poor Hylas.)

Old Phineus and the Vile Harpies

Heracles therefore missed the Argonauts' subsequent adventures. In one of the most exotic of these episodes, the Argonauts tangled with the terrifying Harpies, flying creatures endowed with pointed beaks and claws and a sickening stench. One evening the Argonauts came ashore on the European coast of the Bosphorus Strait (connecting the Propontis to the Black Sea). There, they found an old man named Phineus, who was so starved and emaciated that all that was left of him was quite literally skin and bones. Jason asked what had happened to the poor fellow. Phineus answered that the god Apollo had once granted him the gift of prophecy, but Zeus, ruler of the gods, did not like the idea of humans knowing what he was going to do next, so he had inflicted a punishment on Phineus. Every time the man began to eat a meal, the Harpies, whom some people called "Zeus's Hounds," would swoop down and either steal his food or cover it with their vile stench, making it too disgusting for him to eat.

Jason and his men decided to help poor old Phineus. Two of the Argonauts, Zetes and Calais, were the sons of Boreas, the north wind. Therefore, they possessed the ability to fly through the air, which gave them the best chance in a fight against flying creatures like the Harpies. Jason and the others gathered a huge amount of food and prepared a magnificent banquet for Phineus. Meanwhile, Zetes and Calais stood on either side of the old man, their swords drawn and ready in case the Harpies appeared. Sure enough, as Apollonius tells it

> Phineus had scarcely lifted the first morsel [of food], when, with as little warning as a whirlwind or a lightning flash, the Harpies dropped from the clouds proclaiming their desire for food with raucous cries. [Before the warriors could react], the Harpies had devoured the whole meal and were on the wing once more, far out to sea. All they left behind was an intolerable stench. . . . Raising their swords, the two sons of the North Wind flew off in pursuit. (*Argonautica* 2.271–278)

Zetes and Calais eventually caught up to the disgusting creatures. And the men would surely have cut them to pieces if the goddess of the rainbow, Iris, had not intervened. Iris was sister to the Harpies and sought to protect them. Zetes and Calais must not kill the Hounds of Zeus, she said. If they would spare the creatures, she would promise to keep them away from old Phineus. The two warriors spared the Harpies, and Iris did indeed keep her word; so thereafter Phineus was able to eat his fill without harassment. Jason and his men continued on their voyage to faraway Colchis, taking with them some valuable advice from Phineus about the potential dangers that lay ahead.

Colchis, Aeetes, and Medea

Indeed, old Phineus's advice came in handy almost immediately. After leaving

him, the Argonauts approached one of the most dangerous places in all of the known seas—the Symplegades, or "Clashing Rocks," situated at the northern end of the Bosphorus Strait. Numerous vessels had been crushed by these giant boulders, which periodically smashed violently together. Following Phineus's instructions, Jason ordered that a dove be released ahead of the ship. The bird flew between the rocks, inducing them to smash together, then the *Argo* shot forward at full speed, hoping to make it through while the rocks were moving apart. For a while, it looked as though the ship might not make it; but at the last moment, the bright-eyed Athena appeared and gave the vessel the boost it needed to pass through unharmed.

After several more months of perilous travel, Jason and his crew finally reached their destination—the remote land of Colchis. There, Jason met with the local king, Aeetes, and asked him to give them the Golden Fleece, in exchange for which they would do him some important service, such as fighting his enemies. But Aeetes did not like foreigners. And in any case, he was not about to give up the fleece, so he concocted a plan that would surely result in Jason's death. No one could take the fleece, Aeetes claimed, unless he first proved his courage through a formidable challenge. He would have to yoke two fearsome fire-breathing bulls and use them to plow dragons' teeth into the earth. These seeds would quickly grow into a multitude of armed warriors, whom he would have to defeat.

At first, it seemed to Jason that no mortal man could pass such a test. But he soon received some unexpected and formidable aid. The goddess Hera, Zeus's wife, wanted Jason's quest to succeed. She convinced Aphrodite to send her own son, Eros, to Colchis; and Eros caused King Aeetes's daughter, Medea, to fall in love with Jason almost instantly. Indeed, Medea's love became so strong that she was willing to betray her own father for this Greek stranger. Medea, who possessed knowledge of sorcery, met Jason in secret and gave him a vial containing a magic drug. In Apollonius's version of the story, she gave Jason these instructions:

> In the morning, melt this charm, strip naked, and using it like an oil, rub it all over your body. It will endow you with tremendous strength and boundless confidence. You will feel yourself a match, not for mere men, but for the gods themselves. Sprinkle your spear and shield and sword with it as well; and neither the spear-points of the earthborn men, nor the consuming flames that the savage bulls spew out will find you vulnerable. (*Argonautica* 3.1042–1048)

Sure enough, covered in this special ointment, Jason was able to yoke the bulls, defeat the seed-warriors, and thereby pass the test. Aeetes still did not want to give up the fleece. But with more help from Medea, Jason managed to get past the huge serpent that guarded the fleece and to spirit the golden prize out of Colchis. The angry Aeetes gave chase in some ships. But before escaping with Jason, Medea had abducted the king's small son, Apsyr-tus; and now she cut the boy's body up into many pieces and every hour or so tossed one of them over the side. Aeetes kept stopping to retrieve the pieces, intending to give his son a proper burial, and these delays allowed the Argonauts to outdistance their pursuers and reach the open sea.

A Legacy of Death and Misery

Once the Argonauts returned to Greece, they disbanded and some went on to further adventures of their own. Some had sons, who, when they grew into young men, joined the great Greek expedition against Troy. Meanwhile, to give thanks to the gods for his safe return, Jason dedicated the *Argo* to the sea god Poseidon. Jason also dutifully presented the captured fleece to King Pelias, expecting that the old man would keep his end of the bargain and abdicate his throne in favor of Jason. But Pelias refused to fulfill his earlier promise to abdicate. Instead, he continued to cheat Jason out of his rights as the true heir to Iolcos's throne. While the dispute dragged on and on, Jason and Medea had two children together in Iolcos.

Finally, quite fed up with Pelias's deceit, Medea decided to help Jason attain

In this ancient sculpted panel, Jason (second from right) and Medea (far right) approach the Golden Fleece (in tree).

Having brought back the Golden Fleece, Jason (left) stands before King Pelias. Not long afterward, Medea caused Pelias's death.

both the throne and revenge on Pelias. She convinced the king's three daughters to kill their father and cut him into pieces, saying that she would supply some magic herbs and spells that would cause the pieces to reunite. Pelias would then be reborn as a young man. This fantastic story was a lie, of course, and resulted in Pelias's grisly and very permanent death.

Medea's devious plan succeeded in accomplishing only one of its intended aims, however. Jason had indeed achieved revenge on Pelias, but the young hero did not attain the throne of Iolcos, as he had desired. Pelias's son, Acastus, branded both Jason and Medea murderers and drove them and their young children from the city. The exiled family journeyed southward to the prosperous city of Corinth. Here, to Medea's surprise and dismay, Jason turned on her. He rejected her as his wife and married the daughter of Creon, king of Corinth, perhaps, as he claimed, to put himself in a better economic and political position and to thereby have a chance to inherit the city's throne someday. To punish Jason for this betrayal, Medea slew their children. Thus, the quest for the Golden Fleece left a disturbing legacy, as all of the principal characters involved—Pelias, Jason, Aeetes, and Medea—ended up either dead or miserable.

The Theban Myth Cycle

The long, eventful, and bloody saga of Thebes, one of the great cities of ancient Greece, began long ago in the legendary, colorful, and heroic age when the gods frequently descended to the earth and interacted with humans. One day, Zeus, leader of the gods, caught site of a beautiful young woman walking on the eastern shore of the wide Mediterranean Sea. She was Europa, daughter of the king of the Phoenician city of Tyre. The god was so taken with her that he disguised himself as a bull and enticed her to climb onto his back. As soon as she did so, he carried her, swimming with powerful strokes, across the sea to the large Greek island of Crete.

Back in Tyre, Europa's father, King Agenor, was distraught over her disappearance. He ordered his son, Cadmus, to go looking for her. Realizing that the world was so vast that it might take forever to find his sister, Cadmus decided to ask the oracle at Delphi, in central Greece, for help in locating her. When Cadmus asked where to look for Europa, the oracle told him that he need no longer search for her. Instead, he should pursue his own destiny, which promised to be unique and lead to momentous events. Cadmus would encounter a young cow, the oracle said. He should follow the cow until it lay down to rest, and on that spot the young man should establish a new city, which would become renowned for its heroes and kings.

Sure enough, Cadmus, who was accompanied by a few loyal companions, soon came upon the cow, and they obediently followed it as it meandered from place to place. In time, it led them across some rugged mountains, into the land of Boeotia, and finally to a windswept hillock overlooking a fertile plain. There, the beast laid down to rest and there, too, following the oracle's instructions, Cadmus founded a city. He called it Cadmea, after himself. The city later became known as Thebes, but its highest point and fortress retained the founder's name.

Part of the founding ceremony involved sacrificing the cow that had led Cadmus into Boeotia. To perform the sacrifice, he needed water, so he sent his companions to a nearby stream. Unfortunately for these young men, the stream was guarded by a fierce serpent who, it was rumored, was the son of the war god, Ares. The serpent promptly killed and ate the men, and when Cadmus saw what had happened, he angrily fought and slew the creature. According to one version of the story, Ares was so upset over the death of his serpentine son that he placed a curse on the succeeding generations of Cadmus's family. Another version maintains that Cadmus paid his debt to Ares by becoming the god's slave for a year.

In any case, soon after Cadmus had killed the serpent, Athena, goddess of wisdom, appeared before him. The man must gather up the serpent's teeth and plant them in the earth, she advised. He did so and not long afterward, to his surprise and fear, a small army of warriors sprang up from the furrows he had dug. The earth-born men paid no attention to Cadmus, however. Instead, they furiously fought one another until only five of them were left; and these survivors, whom Cadmus persuaded to become his helpers, became the founding fathers of Thebes's noble families.

Cadmus's Unfortunate Descendents
With the help of his new followers, Cadmus made Thebes a large and prosperous city, one that in time compared in power and prestige with Athens, Corinth, and other great Greek cities. Some say that Cadmus also introduced the alphabet—a Phoenician invention—to Greece. He married Harmonia, daughter of the god Ares and the goddess of love, Aphrodite. And thereafter, the royal couple enjoyed several years of happiness.

However, most of their children and grandchildren were not fated to be so happy and ended up having to endure one form of serious misfortune or another. One of their daughters, Semele, for instance, was accidentally incinerated by Zeus. At the time, she was pregnant with Zeus's son (who became the fertility god, Dionysus). Thanks to the intrigues of Hera, Zeus's jealous wife, Zeus paid a visit to Semele in the form of his symbol, the thunderbolt, killing her (although simultaneously making her child immortal).

Another daughter, Agave, had a son named Pentheus, who became king of Thebes (succeeding his grandfather, Cadmus). The young Dionysus became angry when Pentheus banned the god's followers from worshiping him in Thebes. So Dionysus made the city's women, Agave

Drawn in the nineteenth century, this sketch captures what was by then left of the site and ruins of Thebes, once one of the greatest cities of the Greek world.

among them, wander through the country-side in a frenzied trance. Perceiving Pentheus as a lion or some other beast, they hunted him down and finally cornered him in a tree. As told by the Athenian playwright Euripides,

> Thousands of hands tore the fir tree from the earth, and down, down from his high perch fell Pentheus, tumbling to the ground, sobbing and screaming as he fell, for he knew his end was near. His own mother, like a priestess with her victim, fell upon him first. . . . "No, no, Mother!" [he screamed.] "I am Pentheus, your own son, the child you bore. . . . Pity me, spare me, Mother! I have done a wrong, but do not kill your own son for my offense." But she was foaming at the mouth, and her crazed eyes rolled with frenzy. . . . Ignoring his cries of pity, she seized his left arm at the wrist; then, planting her foot on his chest, she pulled, wrenching away the arm at the shoulder, not by her own strength, for the god had put inhuman power in her hands. . . . The whole horde

of women swarmed upon him. Shouts rang out, he screaming with what little breath was left, they shrieking in triumph. One tore off an arm, another a foot still warm in its shoe. His ribs were clawed clean of flesh and every hand was smeared with blood as they played ball with scraps of Pentheus' body. (*The Bacchae* 1088–1107)

After this hideous incident, still another of Cadmus's daughters, Autonoe, had to endure her own son's death, which, unlike that of Pentheus, was quite undeserved. The demise of Autonoe's son, the unfortunate Actaeon, happened in the following manner. The youth was out hunting and grew thirsty. Finding a grotto where a little stream widened into a pool, he started to cool himself in the crystal water. Then he noticed a beautiful woman bathing stark naked on the far side of the pool, not realizing that she was no ordinary woman but the goddess Artemis. The embarrassed divinity cared little that the young man had merely stumbled on her and had not meant to spy. In a fury, she instantly turned him into a stag and he fled, only to have his own dogs see him, give chase, and tear him to pieces.

Attempting to Subvert Divine Prophecy

After Pentheus's and Actaeon's deaths, the Theban throne passed to Labdacus, who some ancient sources say was another of Cadmus's grandsons. Labdacus also died while pursuing unwise policies regarding Dionysian worship. His son, Laius, was only a small child at the time; so a nobleman named Lycus, who was a grandson of one of Cadmus's five earth-born men, assumed the role of regent, running the state for the young king. But soon Lycus got greedy and claimed the throne for himself. He ruled for twenty years but received his just rewards when his own nephews, the twin brothers Amphion and Zethus, murdered him. The twins took over the city, banishing the rightful king, Laius, who was by now about twenty-one.

Many years passed and finally Amphion and Zethus died. This allowed Laius to return from exile and reclaim his throne. Once back in power, he married his distant cousin Jocasta, and not long afterward the Delphic Oracle once more began playing a crucial role in the family's fortunes. Laius consulted the oracle about his own fate and received an answer that sorely dismayed him. He and his new wife would have a son, the prophecy stated, but that son would one day end up slaying Laius.

Because it was commonly held that Apollo's oracle never lied and that trying to change or get around one of its prophecies was both futile and an expression of distrust for the god, Laius was understandably fearful. But he was also arrogant. Despite warnings against trying to subvert the oracle, he grew determined to change the fate that had been decreed for him. When Jocasta bore him a son, he had the infant's feet bound together and ordered a servant to leave the child on the side of a mountain, where it would surely die. Confident that he had cheated fate, Laius breathed a sigh of relief and concentrated on ruling Thebes.

Many uneventful years passed. Then, the people of Thebes suddenly found themselves beset by a serious crisis brought on by their own actions. They had long diligently worshiped Dionysus, whom Cadmus's daughter Semele had carried after Zeus had impregnated her; but lately they had grown increasingly neglectful and often failed to observe the god's rites. To punish them, Dionysus sent a frightening monster to stalk the countryside around the city, a creature called the Sphinx, which had the body of a winged lion and the face of a human woman. The Sphinx would leap out at travelers and pose them a riddle; if a person could solve the riddle, the beast promised, it would let him or her go; if not, the Sphinx devoured the person alive. Because no one could solve the riddle, one Theban after another met doom in the creature's clutches and terror gripped the city. Making matters worse, news came that King Laius, now an old man, had been killed by robbers while traveling with some attendants along a road near Delphi. The widowed Jocasta and all of her subjects prayed to be delivered from their misery.

Oedipus Saves Thebes

The Thebans' prayers seemed answered when a stalwart and intelligent young man named Oedipus, a traveler from the city of Corinth, appeared on the scene. He courageously confronted the monster, which naturally demanded that he solve the riddle. According to the first-century B.C. Greek historian Diodorus Siculus,

This is what was set forth by the Sphinx: "What is it that is of itself two-footed, three-footed, and four-footed?" Although the others could not see through it, Oedipus replied that the answer was "man," for as an infant man begins to move as a four-footed being [crawling on all fours], when he is grown he is two-footed, and as an old man he is three-footed, leaning upon a staff because of his weakness. (*Library of History* 4.64.4)

On hearing Oedipus correctly solve the riddle, the Sphinx grew wide-eyed and screamed loudly. Oedipus gripped his spear and crouched, preparing to leap at the creature and strike. But then a strange thing happened. The Sphinx began shaking all over and ran in circles, crying out in despair that it had been outwitted and vanquished by a mere human. How could it live with the shame, it asked. Evidently, the monster could not live with the shame because as the man looked on in astonishment, it grabbed a sword left by one of its previous victims and plunged it into its own heart. With a great thud, the Sphinx's lifeless body struck the ground. (In another version, the Sphinx jumped off a cliff to its death.)

Thanks to Oedipus, Thebes was saved, and the grateful citizens welcomed him as their new king. He married Jocasta, who bore him two sons, Polynices and Eteocles, and two daughters, Antigone and Ismene. And there followed many years of happiness and prosperity.

A Blind Man Sees the Truth

Eventually, however, the Thebans once more found themselves in a state of crisis. A terrible plague fell on the land, a blight that killed plants, livestock, and people alike. Determined to help his people, Oedipus sent his brother-in-law, Creon, to Delphi to consult the oracle; surely, they reasoned, the far-seeing god Apollo would offer some saving piece of advice for the ailing city. And sure enough, Creon returned from Delphi with good news. The oracle had proclaimed that the plague would be lifted if and when Laius's mur-

derer was apprehended and punished. Oedipus took up this cause enthusiastically. The Athenian playwright Sophocles had him say, "I will lend my support to avenging this crime against this land and the god as well. . . . I shall leave no stone unturned, for we shall succeed with the help of the god or be destroyed if we fail." (*Oedipus the King* 135–145)

But in his search for Laius's killer, Oedipus soon discovered some odd and disturbing information. First, he spoke with the blind prophet Tiresias. This highly revered old man had already lived for several generations, during which time he had given advice to many rulers. He had not been born blind. Supposedly, as a young man he was magically transformed into a woman and then back again into a man, so that he had the unique perspective of having felt both male and female emotions. Later, when Zeus and Hera asked Tiresias to mediate in a dispute they were having, Tiresias took Zeus's side. In retaliation, the angry Hera blinded Tiresias; but Zeus compensated for this loss by granting the man great longevity and the gift of prophecy.

Thus, when Tiresias gave advice or predictions to people, they usually took what he said to heart. Tiresias told Oedipus that he, Oedipus, was the very culprit for whom the Thebans searched. "*You* are the murderer," declared Tiresias.

You are the unholy defilement of this land. . . . You are a pitiful figure. . . . You, who have eyes, cannot see the evil in which you stand. . . . Do you even know who your parents are? Without knowing it, you are the enemy of your own flesh and blood, the dead below and the living here above. The double edged curse of your mother and father . . . shall one day drive you from this land. You see straight now but then you will see darkness. You will scream aloud on that day. . . . There is no man alive whose ruin will be more pitiful than yours. (*Oedipus the King* 361, 373, 414–428)

The Horrors of the Past
Are Revealed

Oedipus knew about the old seer's reputation for correct predictions. At first, though, the Theban king angrily dismissed Tiresias's words, thinking it ridiculous that he, Oedipus, could be the killer. Jocasta also rejected this idea. She assured Oedipus that Laius had been murdered by robbers where three roads came together near Delphi; therefore, Oedipus was obviously not the guilty party. But on hearing his wife describe the specific location of the crime, Oedipus suddenly felt a small chill run up and down his spine. He asked Jocasta when exactly had this happened. She casually answered that Laius had been murdered just before Oedipus had arrived in Thebes and defeated the Sphinx.

Increasingly worried and uneasy, Oedipus proceeded to tell Jocasta about how he had come to Thebes in the first place. He had been the loving son of Corinth's king and queen, Polybus and Merope. Upon learning from the Delphic Oracle that he was fated to kill his father and marry his mother, the horrified Oedipus had attempted to escape the prophecy by fleeing Corinth. If he never saw Polybus and Merope again, he reasoned, he could never end up killing one and marrying the other. Oedipus had struck out for Thebes, and in time, as he now told Jocasta,

> I came near to a triple crossroads and there I was met by a herald and a man riding on a horse-drawn wagon, just as you described it. The driver, and the old man himself, tried to push me off the road. In anger, I struck the driver, who was shoving me. When the old man saw me coming, he grasped his water jug, aimed at my head, and hit me. But I paid him back in full. I struck him with my walking stick, knocking him backwards out of the wagon. Then I killed the whole lot of them. (*Oedipus the King* 798–813)

As Oedipus and Jocasta continued to talk, a messenger arrived from Corinth, bringing them the fateful news that old King Polybus had recently died. At first, it seemed as though this news proved that the oracle's pronouncements could indeed be false or avoided. After all, Polybus was dead and it was clear to all that Oedipus had had no hand in the deed, as the oracle had predicted he would. But then the Corinthian messenger stepped forward and told a story that made Oedipus shudder and Jocasta turn pale. Oedipus was not Polybus's son, said the messenger; Polybus and Merope had brought him up as their own after he, the messenger, had presented him to them. And where had he gotten the child? A servant of Thebes's King Laius had secretly given him the baby. Only minutes later, that very same servant, now an old man, confirmed the messenger's story. When Laius had ordered him to leave the baby outside to die, the servant had taken pity on it and had given it to the Corinthian for safekeeping.

The horrifying truth was now clear to all. Oedipus was indeed, as Tiresias had earlier claimed, the guilty man who had brought the curse of the gods down on Thebes. Both Laius and Oedipus had tried to escape their fates, and in so doing, they had sealed them. The prophecy that Laius would die by his own son's hand had been fulfilled, and the oracular prediction that Oedipus would murder his father and marry his mother had also come to pass.

Soon Tiresias's own predictions, namely that Oedipus would scream aloud and see darkness, came true as well. Unable to cope with the horror of his acts, the Theban king wailed like a mortally wounded animal, and in a fit of despair, gouged out his own eyes. As for Jocasta, the realization that she had married her own son and had had children by him was too much for her and she killed herself.

In this way, all involved learned the lesson that what the gods and fate decree no human can or should challenge. And Oedipus's fall from the heights of prosperity and happiness to the depths of wretchedness and despair illustrated another lesson: Suffering is an inevitable part of life, and it takes the ultimate measure of every person, rich or poor, mighty or humble. As Sophocles had the chorus of his great play say,

> O citizens of our native Thebes, behold;
> Here is Oedipus, who solved the renowned riddle and became ruler of our city and was regarded with envy by every citizen because of his good fortune. Think of the flood of terrible disaster that has swept over him. Thus, since we are all mortal, consider even a man's final day on earth and do not pronounce him happy until he has crossed the finish line of life without the pain of suffering. (*Oedipus the King* 1524–1530)

Oedipus's Fate and the Seven Against Thebes

After Oedipus's terrible realization and Jocasta's suicide, Oedipus resigned the Theban throne and soon afterward suffered banishment. In most people's eyes he was cursed, a polluted figure condemned to wander aimlessly from one city to another and be rejected by each. Only his daughters, Antigone and Ismene, remained faithful and cared for him. To help guide the blind man, Antigone traveled with him, and Ismene remained in Thebes and kept him informed from time to time of events in his former home. Meanwhile, Jocasta's brother, Creon (who was, under the circumstances, both brother-in-law and uncle to Oedipus), became regent in Thebes, managing the city for Polynices and Eteocles, who were still too young to rule.

After wandering for several years, Oedipus and Antigone arrived at

Colonus, a village on the outskirts of Athens. The Athenian king, Theseus, kindly allowed the fallen ruler to stay. This benefited both Oedipus, who now enjoyed a friendly, comfortable refuge, and also Athens, since the newest of Apollo's prophecies stated that the gods would grant blessings and prosperity to the land bearing Oedipus's last resting place. Ismene traveled to Colonus to inform her father of this prophecy. There, she and Antigone remained with him until he died, or, more accurately, until he mysteriously disappeared. The gods, it appears, had accepted him into their bosom and had made

Antigone and Ismene, daughters of the fallen King Oedipus. Antigone followed her father into exile.

him immortal, for in their eyes he had suffered enough; moreover, in bringing good fortune to Athens, he had redeemed himself and had become a hero once more.

Oedipus's troubles were finally over. But the same cannot be said for his unfortunate offspring. Antigone and Ismene returned to Thebes to find the city embroiled in still another crisis, this one instigated by Oedipus's sons. Polynices and Eteocles had recently come of age and had argued angrily about which of them should rule Thebes. They finally struck a deal, agreeing that Eteocles would rule for a year while his brother went into exile, after which Polynices would rule for a year while Eteocles went away, and so forth.

Once Eteocles had assumed power, however, it quickly became clear that he had no intention of keeping his end of the bargain. Deciding that he must resort to force to drive his brother from the throne, Polynices enlisted the aid of six noble warriors, led by Adrastus, king of Argos (in the eastern Peloponnesus). Each of the Argive army's seven commanders (counting Polynices) attacked one of Thebes's seven well-fortified gates; but after long rounds of bloody battle, they failed to penetrate the city's walls. Finally, both sides agreed that the war should be decided by single combat, namely a fight to the death between the rival leaders—Polynices and Eteocles. No one could have predicted the tragic outcome, about which a messenger tells the chorus of Theban women in Aeschylus's *Seven Against Thebes,*

MESSENGER: The town is safe. But the two sons of Oedipus—
CHORUS: What of them? I am bewildered—I am afraid to hear. . . .
MESSENGER: Both are dead. They killed each other.
CHORUS: Each too much like his brother in the lust to kill.
MESSENGER: Each like the other in the fate that led them both, the fate which

now annihilates their ill-starred race. . . . So, Thebes is saved. But her two brother kings are fallen; the earth has drunk their blood, shed by each other's hands. (*Seven Against Thebes* 804–823)

The Tragedy of Antigone and Haemon

With Eteocles dead, his uncle, Creon, assumed the Theban throne once more. He gave orders that, in retaliation for the brutal attack on the city, the Argive dead, including Polynices, should be forbidden proper burial. Polynices' sister Antigone would not accept this decree, seeing it as barbaric and unfair. She decided to defy Creon and attempt to bury her brother's body. A guard later told Creon that someone had disobeyed his royal decree by covering Polynices with a thin layer of earth, a symbolic burial. Furious, Creon had his guards remove the earth from the body. Dutifully, Antigone came back, intending to replace the dirt, only this time the guard caught her in the act.

When Antigone faced Creon, he condemned her to death for defying his orders. But Haemon, Creon's son, who loved and planned to marry Antigone, stepped forward to protest, and the father and son argued violently. Creon refused to be swayed by Haemon's pleas and ordered that Antigone be shut up in a cave until she died. The king *was* swayed, however, by Tiresias, the blind Theban seer who had earlier been the first to see the truth about Oedipus's guilt. Tiresias told Creon that the gods would frown on him, and Thebes, too, if he continued to leave the Argive bodies unburied, for this went against tradition and the divine will. Realizing that Tiresias never lied, Creon decided to give Polynices a proper burial and also to call off Antigone's punishment. Tragically, however, Creon's change of heart came too late. Reaching the cave, he found that Antigone had hanged herself. Moreover, the grief-stricken Haemon, who was standing over her body, spat in his father's face and then committed suicide, his body falling on top of Antigone's.

Like so many other descendants of Cadmus, the members of Oedipus's and Creon's families met with death or despair out of arrogance, lust for power, or defiance of the age-old laws and customs sanctioned by the gods. Later generations of Thebans could look back on their larger-than-life founding fathers and mothers and learn valuable lessons from their mistakes.

The Trojan War

The fateful series of events leading up to the great ten-year siege of Troy began when Eris, the ornery minor deity of discord, found that she had not been invited, as the major Olympian gods had, to a sumptuous banquet celebrating the wedding of the sea nymph Thetis (mother of the hero Achilles). To exact her revenge for this slight, Eris flew over the banquet hall and tossed in a golden apple. The apple was marked "for the fairest goddess of all"; not surprisingly, each of the goddesses present thought the bauble was intended for her. Eventually Hera, Aphrodite, and Athena stepped forward and asked Zeus to choose which of them should get to keep the golden apple; but Zeus, who did not relish having to deal with the scorn of the two losers, wisely refused to act as judge.

Zeus claimed he had a better idea. There was a young man named Paris, he said, a prince of the powerful city of Troy (on the northwestern coast of Asia Minor), who was known to be an excellent judge of beauty. Zeus persuaded the goddesses to go to Mt. Ida, near Troy, and seek out the youth. The three competitors soon found Paris tending sheep on Ida's slopes. Not long before, his father, King Priam, having heard a prophecy that the young man would one day bring about Troy's ruin, had ordered Paris out of the city.

Paris was very surprised when the three goddesses appeared before him. Wasting no time, each attempted to bribe him into choosing her. Hera promised to make him the ruler of Europe and Asia; Athena said she would make him the victor in a war in which his Trojans would defeat the Greeks; and Aphrodite offered to make the most beautiful woman in the world fall in love with him. It was a difficult choice. But in the end Paris opted for love, and Aphrodite, having won the contest, received the coveted golden apple.

As everyone at that time knew well, the most beautiful of all mortal women was Helen, wife of Menelaus, king of the Greek kingdom of Sparta. She was so attractive, in fact, that all of the Greek kings and princes had once professed their love for her; and when she and Menelaus were betrothed, her father had made them all swear that they would help Menelaus if one of them broke up his marriage. Aphrodite led Paris to Sparta, where he became a guest of the unsuspecting royal couple. A while later, after Menelaus had left on a trip to Crete, the Trojan prince convinced Helen to run away with him, and she and Paris escaped one night, leaving behind the queen's nine-year-old daughter.

When Menelaus returned from Crete, wrote the ancient myth-teller Apollodorus of Athens, and

> learned that Helen had been carried off, he went to Mycenae [located northeast of Sparta] to urge Agamemnon [king of Mycenae and Menelaus's brother] to gather together an army to go against Troy and to raise troops throughout Greece. He himself, sending a herald to each one of the kings, reminded them of the oath they had taken to come to his aid in case anyone wronged him in regard to his marriage. And he advised each of them to watch out for the safety of his own wife, telling them that the insult was shared in common by all of Greece. (*Library* 3.10.9)

Odysseus's and Achilles' Reluctance

A number of stories were told of the preparations for the Greek expedition against Troy. One of the them concerns Odysseus (whom the Romans called Ulysses), the wily king of the island kingdom of Ithaca (off Greece's western coast). At first he did not want to waste his time and resources in a war over another man's wife, especially now that he was very happy with his own wife, Penelope; so when the call went out for the Greek forces to gather, he ignored it. Eventually Agamemnon, who had been named the leader of the Greek host, sent Palamedes, a Greek known for his cleverness and wisdom, to Ithaca to persuade Odysseus. When Palamedes arrived, the Ithacan king pretended to be mad. Mumbling incoherently to himself, Odysseus harnessed an ox and a donkey to his plow and sowed salt into the sand on a beach. But Palamedes easily saw through the ruse and placed Odysseus's young son Telemachus directly in the plow's path. The plowman immediately veered away, of course, an act that saved the boy but at the same time showed that Odysseus was perfectly rational and in control. Giving in, Odysseus assembled twelve ships and some six hundred men and sailed with Palamedes to Aulis, on Greece's eastern coast, where the Greek forces were gathering. (Odysseus, who also known for his cleverness, later exacted revenge on Palamedes by forging a letter that made him appear to be a traitor; Agamemnon swiftly had Palamedes stoned to death.)

In the meantime, another well-known Greek attempted to avoid the expedition. He was Achilles, Thetis's son, and widely seen as the greatest warrior in Greece. When he was an infant, his divine mother had dipped him into the River Styx, which had made his body invulnerable to wounds, all except the heel she held while lowering him into the dark waters. It was essential that Achilles join the expedition in order to fulfill a prophecy declaring that Troy would never fall in his absence; yet an oracle had issued another prophecy, this one warning that he would surely die in a war against the Trojans. Trying to keep her son from going on the expedition, Thetis sent the young man to live with his uncle, who disguised Achilles in women's clothes.

But just as Palamedes had sought out Odysseus, the wily Odysseus now tracked down the reluctant Achilles. Odysseus learned that Achilles was hiding in his uncle's palace and went there disguised as a peddler. The Ithacan king carried a tray displaying numerous women's items, such as ribbons, perfumes, and makeup; but mixed in with them were a sword and a small round shield. When Odysseus showed these wares to the royal princesses, he noticed that one of them ignored the women's articles and picked up the sword instead. Achilles had revealed himself, as Odysseus had expected he would. And now the latter persuaded Thetis's son to go with him to Aulis.

The Sacrifice of Iphigenia

When Odysseus and Achilles arrived in Aulis, a thousand ships had gathered there. After a great deal of expensive preparations, it was finally time to depart for the voyage across the Aegean Sea to Troy. But the Greeks soon discovered that it was impossible to leave the port because of a powerful north wind that kept on blowing day after day. A soothsayer finally communicated the words of the goddess Artemis, who was enraged that Agamemnon had recently hunted down and slain some woodland creatures sacred to her. To appease her, she said, he would have to sacrifice his eldest daughter, Iphigenia; otherwise, the ships would never make it out of Aulis. Agamemnon loved his daughter; however, as a king and the commander of so large an army, he held the expedition's importance above hers and decided he had no choice but to do as the goddess bid. The Athenian playwright Aeschylus captured the horror of the poor girl's last moments:

> "My father, father!" she prayed to the winds; but her innocence failed to move the kings, who were filled with a passion for war. Her father called his henchmen on, saying a prayer as he did so. "Hoist her over the altar like a yearling," he said, "and give it all your strength! She's fainting. Lift her, sweep her robes around her, but slip this strap in her gentle curving lips and gag her hard so that her cries will not curse the house of Atreus [Mycenae's royal family]." And the bridle choked her voice, while her saffron robes poured over the sand and her glance was like sharp arrows of pity, wounding her murderers. (*Agamemnon* 227–241)

When the sacrifice was completed, Artemis withdrew the winds, allowing the Greek armada to sail forth for Troy. But Agamemnon and other members of his royal house would later pay a terrible price for the young girl's untimely end.

Zeus Intervenes

When the Greeks reached the flat and windy plain of Troy, which separated the city's towering and well-fortified walls from the beaches, they were confident of a swift victory. After all, they not only greatly outnumbered the Trojans, but they also possessed many distinguished war leaders. In addition to Agamemnon, Menelaus, Odysseus, and Achilles, there were Ajax, a prince of the island of Salamis, renowned for his enormous size and strength; Nestor, the king of Pylos and a wise old sage; the skilled warrior Diomedes, king of Argos; and Patroclus, Achilles' brave friend and attendant.

Yet the Trojans had their own heroes. First and foremost among these was Hector, Priam's son and Paris's brother, the most fearsome warrior in the Aegean

sphere next to Achilles. Other Trojan assets included Troilus, another of Priam's sons, and Aeneas, reputed to be the son of the goddess Aphrodite and a mortal man named Anchises. Not only did the Trojans fight bravely and well under these leaders, but Troy's massive walls proved a formidable barrier, and the initial Greek attacks were repulsed with heavy casualties. Consequently, Agamemnon's forces settled down, constructed a more permanent camp, and laid siege to the city.

For nine long years the war dragged on with neither side able to achieve a clear advantage. And during these years, many of the Olympian gods took sides in the conflict. Because Paris had helped Aphrodite acquire the golden apple, and also because her son, Aeneas, resided in Troy, she backed the Trojan cause, as did the war god, Ares. Naturally enough, Hera and Athena, still resentful over losing the Judgment of Paris, favored the Greeks. By contrast, Apollo sometimes helped one side, sometimes the other; and Zeus attempted to remain neutral, although he sometimes found himself drawn into the action.

One of these times was in the tenth year of the siege. Achilles and Agamemnon had a terrible quarrel, after which Achilles retired to his tent and refused to come out and lead the Greeks in battle as he had so often done. Believing that her noble son had been gravely insulted, Thetis approached Zeus and asked him to help her exact revenge. "O Father Zeus!" she cried out, according to Homer,

> "If ever I have served you by word or deed, grant me this boon: give honor to my son! He of all others is to die an early death, but now see how my Lord Agamemnon has insulted him. . . . Satisfy my son, Zeus Olympian most wise! Let the Trojans prevail, until the Greek nation shall satisfy my son and magnify him with honor!" Zeus the cloud-gatherer did not answer, but long sat silent; so Thetis clasped his knees, clung

Achilles (holding the lyre) informs Agamemnon, leader of the Greek expedition, that he will not come out and fight.

fast to him, and cried out once more: "Say yes now, and promise me faithfully! Or else say no, for no matter how you decide you have nothing to fear!" (*Iliad* 1.600–614)

Although reluctant to take sides, Zeus gave in to Thetis's request. Knowing full well that the Greeks would be at a distinct military disadvantage without Achilles in their ranks, he urged Agamemnon in a dream to attack while Achilles was indisposed. Agamemnon did so, and a great battle ensued. At one point during the fighting, the ranks of the two armies separated to watch an individual combat between Menelaus and Paris, whose rivalry for Helen had instigated the war. Paris's skills as a warrior were much inferior to Menelaus's, and the Trojan prince would surely have been killed; however, at the crucial moment Aphrodite intervened and saved him. Then mighty Hector entered the fray and led the Trojans in an irresistible offensive that drove the Greeks back nearly to their beach encampment.

Patroclus's Moment in the Sun

Pressed hard by the Trojan forces, the Greeks were now in a perilous position, and in despair Agamemnon proposed that his own army give up the fight and return to Greece. The events of the following day only seemed to confirm that this would be the best course. The Trojans crashed through the stockade protecting the Greek camp and forced many of the Greeks to retreat to their ships. Hector was seriously wounded by the powerful Ajax, but the healing god, Apollo, soon revived the Trojan champion, making him stronger than ever. "Aflame from head to foot," is how Homer described Hector at that moment.

Picture a wave raised by a gale and sweeping forward under the scudding clouds. It breaks on a gallant ship . . . and the crew, saved from destruction by a hair's breadth, are left trembling and aghast. This is how Hector fell upon the Greeks, striking panic into their hearts. And they stampeded, as cattle do when a savage lion finds them grazing. (*Iliad* 15.722–732)

Triumphantly, Hector led his men to the Greek ships and shouted,

Bring fire, and raise the war-cry, all of you together. Zeus is repaying us for everything today: the ships are ours! They came here against the will of the gods, and they started all these troubles for us. . . . [But] all-seeing Zeus is backing us today and sweeping us on! (*Iliad* 15.832–841)

At this fateful juncture, with the Greek cause seemingly lost, brave Patroclus approached Achilles, who was stilling brooding in his tent and refusing to fight. If Achilles would not enter the fray, said Patroclus,

at least allow *me* to take the field at once with the Myrmidon force [Achilles' own hand-picked and much-feared warriors] at my back. I might yet bring salvation to the Greeks. And lend me your own armor to put on my shoulders so that the Trojans may take me for you and break off the battle, which would give our weary troops time to recuperate. Even a short breathing-space makes all the difference in war. The Trojans themselves have fought to the point of exhaustion, and we, being fresh, might well drive them back to the city from the ships. (*Iliad* 16.43–53)

Achilles agreed to Patroclus's request, and Patroclus, wearing his friend's armor, led the Myrmidons and other Greeks against the Trojans. Thinking that mighty Achilles him-

self was attacking them, the fearful Trojans began to fall back; even Hector could not withstand the force of the seemingly rejuvenated Greek army. However, the overconfident Patroclus eventually found himself face to face with Hector, who was much the superior warrior. Hector slew Patroclus and stripped off Achilles' armor, and, after a desperate struggle for the body, the Greeks bore Patroclus back to their ships.

Achilles Versus Hector
Hearing of his friend's death, the grief-stricken Achilles became a changed man. His mother, Thetis, rushed to Hephaestos, god of the forge, who swiftly created a new suit of armor for Achilles, this one even stronger and more beautifully ornamented than the one Patroclus had borrowed. Then Achilles went to Agamemnon and patched up their feud; wasting little time, he led his Myrmidons and the other Greeks in a mighty charge against the Trojan ranks. Many of the gods, backing one side or the other, joined in the fray and, in Homer's words,

drove the two hosts together and made the bitter strife burst forth. The father of men and gods [i.e., Zeus] thundered terribly from on high, and Poseidon made the solid earth quake from beneath and shook the tall summits of the hills; Mount Ida shook from head to foot, and the citadel of Troy trembled, and the Greek ships as well. Meanwhile, terror-struck in the Underworld, Hades, lord of the dead, cringed and sprang from his throne and screamed, fearing that the god who was rocking the ground above his realm, giant Poseidon, would burst the earth wide open and lay bare to mortal men . . . the houses of the dead. (*Iliad* 20.65–78)

Finally, unable to withstand the Greek onslaught, the Trojans fled back into the city; that is, with the exception of Hector, who stood alone outside the gates, waiting to face Achilles. Hector did not have to wait long, for moments later Achilles rushed at him. The greatest Greek warrior looked so magnificent and fearsome in his armor that he resembled "the god of war, the fighter's helmet flashing . . . and the bronze around his body flared like a raging fire or the rising, blazing sun." (*Iliad* 22.159–161) Seeing this formidable and frightening apparition bearing down on him, Hector momentarily lost his nerve. He turned and ran. And as thousands from both sides looked on, Achilles chased him round and round the city's walls. "On and on they raced," Homer recalled,

> passing the lookout point, passing the wild fig tree tossed by the wind. . . . Past these they raced, one escaping, one in pursuit, and the one who fled was great but the one pursuing, even greater—their pace mounting in speed. . . . Like powerful stallions sweeping round the post for trophies . . . so the two of them whirled three times around the city of Priam . . . while all the gods gazed down. (*Iliad* 22.173–175, 188–199)

Finally, Hector stopped running and faced his pursuer. "No more running from you in fear, Achilles!" he declared. "Three times I fled around the great city of Priam. . . . Now my spirit stirs me to meet you face-to-face. Now kill or be killed!" Achilles answered him, saying,

> Come, call up whatever courage you can muster. Life or death—now prove yourself a spearman, a daring man of war! . . . No more escape for you. . . . Now you'll pay at a stroke for all my comrades' grief, all of those warriors you killed in the fury of your spear!" (*Iliad* 22.296–300, 317–321)

With a thunderous crash of bronze on bronze, the two heroes came together in mortal combat. Cheers went up from the watching Greeks and Trojans, each side urging on its champion. Achilles was first to hurl his spear, but he missed; then, in a

mighty heave Hector let loose his own spear, which hit his opponent's shield dead center but glanced off. Cursing, Hector drew his sword, and, in Homer's words, "swooped like a soaring eagle launching down from the dark clouds to earth to snatch some helpless lamb." (*Iliad* 22.366–368) Achilles charged too and searched for an opening somewhere on Hector's splendid body where he might thrust his spear, which he had managed to recover. Finally, Hector's throat was momentarily exposed and

> there, as Hector charged in fury, brilliant Achilles drove his spear and the point went stabbing clean through the tender neck; but the heavy bronze weapon failed to slash the windpipe—Hector could still gasp out some words, some last reply. . . . At the point of death, Hector, his helmet flashing, said, "I know you well—I see my fate before me. . . . But now beware, or my curse will draw god's wrath upon your head, that day when Paris and lord Apollo—for all your fighting heart—destroy you at the Scaean Gates!" Death cut him short. The end closed in around him. Flying free of his limbs, his soul went winging down to the House of Death. (*Iliad* 22.384–388, 418–427)

The Wooden Horse

With the greatest Trojan warrior now lying dead in the dust before his horrified countrymen's eyes, mighty Achilles completed his vengeance. He stripped off his opponent's armor, tied the corpse to the back of his chariot, and triumphantly dragged it around the city walls. In time, however, as Achilles' anger and blood-lust subsided, he agreed to give Hector's body to the grieving King Priam. The Trojans then conducted a solemn funeral for Hector; meanwhile, the Greeks held final rites for brave Patroclus.

The war continued, however; eventually Achilles, like Hector, met his end in combat. As Hector had predicted in his dy-

The Greek warrior Ajax bears Achilles' corpse off the field after the latter's death at the hands of the Trojan prince Paris.

ing words, Prince Paris, who was an expert bowman, killed Achilles with an arrow that Apollo guided to its target: Achilles' vulnerable heel. Yet in his turn, Paris met a similar fate when the Greek warrior Philoctetes, using the hugely powerful bow given to his father by the legendary strongman Heracles, felled and killed the Trojan prince.

The killing then went on and more men from both sides made the dreaded journey to Hades' subterranean realm. Eventually,

though, the crafty Odysseus announced to his colleagues that he had a plan that would end the killing and bring the Greeks resounding victory over the Trojans. The Roman poet Virgil tells how, at Odysseus's direction, the Greek commanders

had a horse constructed with ribs of interlocking planks of firewood. It stood high as a mountain. . . . They then drew lots and secretly hid selected troops inside its dark void, till its whole huge cavernous belly was stuffed with men at arms. . . . And thus far sailed the Greeks and hid their ships on [a nearby island's] desolate shore. (*Aeneid* 2.15–26)

Seeing the beaches empty and the Greek ships gone, the jubilant Trojans flooded forth from their city and danced on the windswept plain where so many valiant men from both sides had died. When they saw the huge wooden horse standing on one end of the plain, they wondered why the Greeks had built it. Then a Greek name Sinon stepped forth. He claimed that his countrymen had left him behind, angrily proclaimed that for this slight he no longer wanted to be a Greek, and finally explained that the great horse was intended as an offering to the goddess Athena.

Troy's Fall

Unfortunately for the Trojans, their leaders gullibly accepted this story, which Odysseus had carefully coached to Sinon, and they ordered that the horse be dragged into the city. When it would not fit through the gates, the Trojans tore down part of a towering wall, and through this breach they transported the prize into the heart of Troy. There, they celebrated into the night until Troy became, in Virgil's words, a city "drowned in wine and sleep." And it was then that Odysseus sprang his trap. He and several of his comrades crawled from their hiding place in the belly of the horse. "They killed the sentries, they flung wide the gates, they admitted all their comrades," who had sailed back under the cover of darkness, and "they all joined forces." As a great slaughter began,

> cries of agony arose louder and louder. The clamor swelled and the horrible clash of combat. [The Trojan prince Aeneas] started out of sleep and climbed to the rooftop. . . [and] saw only too clearly the naked treachery of the Greeks. . . . Men shouted, trumpets pealed. . . . Who could unfold the horrors

of that night? Who could speak of such slaughter? Who could weep tears to match that suffering? It was the fall of an ancient city that had long ruled an empire. The bodies of the dead lay through all the streets and houses and the sacred shrines of the gods. . . . Bitter grief was everywhere. (*Aeneid* 2.266–268, 299–310, 362–368)

In a night of unspeakable butchery, the city of Priam fell to the triumphant Greeks. They slew the king and most of the other Trojan leaders, save for Aeneas, who, bearing his aging father on his back, and aided by his mother, Aphrodite, escaped into the countryside. The Greeks proceeded to loot the city, to burn it, and to carry away the surviving Trojan women as slaves. Meanwhile, Menelaus reclaimed Helen, whose matchlessly beautiful face, the bards would one day sing, had "launched a thousand ships." The prophecy that old Priam had feared and attempted to avert—namely that his son Paris would bring about Troy's utter ruin—had finally and appallingly been fulfilled.

The Wanderings of Odysseus

Though the Greeks were victorious in the Trojan War, thanks in large degree to the help of various gods, many never made it home from the Trojan shores that had been their home for ten long years. The principal cause of this misfortune was an act of sacrilege against a prominent goddess. While the Greek soldiers were sacking Troy, they went on a rampage; during the commotion, one of them broke into the local temple of Athena, goddess of war and wisdom. The intruder, Ajax the Lesser, dragged away and raped the Trojan king's daughter, Cassandra, who had invoked the goddess's protection by throwing her arms around her statue.

Athena was determined to make the Greeks pay for this outrage. She convinced the sea god Poseidon, who had sided with the Greeks during the war, to help her mete out their punishment. Poseidon proceeded to produce a tremendous storm that struck the Greek fleets as they were sailing homeward from Troy. The tempest was so violent that Agamemnon, king of Mycenae, lost many of his ships; Menelaus, king of Sparta, was blown off course and ended up in Egypt; and hundreds of Greek sailors drowned.

One of the Greek leaders, though, suffered much longer than any of the others. Wily Odysseus, king of Ithaca, was condemned to wander to many distant and exotic places, and it was fully ten years before he saw the shores of his native island again. In the tenth year of his travels, shortly before he made it home, Poseidon, who was still angry with him, wrecked Odysseus's small boat, and the man washed ashore in the land of a friendly people called the Phaeacians. The Phaeacian king, Alcinous, threw a banquet for the visitor, who told his host the story of his eventful and perilous ten-year journey.

"For nine days I was chased by those accursed winds across the fish-infested seas," Odysseus began, as Homer tells it in the *Odyssey*. "But on the tenth day we made it to the country of the Lotus-eaters, a race that live on vegetable foods." The local inhabitants, he went on, gave some of his men some potent flower food, which made them feel lazy and forgetful and lose their desire to continue homeward. "I had to use force to bring them back to the ships," Odysseus recalled,

> and they wept on the way, but once on board I dragged them under the benches and left them in irons. I then commanded the rest of my loyal band to embark with all speed on their fast ships, for fear that others of them might eat the lotus and think no more of home. They came on board at once . . . sat down in their proper places, and struck the white surf with their oars. (*Odyssey* 9.83–104)

The One-Eyed Giant

Next, Odysseus recalled, "we came to the land of the Cyclopes, a fierce, uncivilized people, who never lift a hand to plant or plow, but put their trust in Providence." The Cyclopes' society is very different from that of civilized peoples, the storyteller explained. They "have no assemblies for the making of laws, nor any settled customs, but live in hollow caverns in the mountain heights, where each man is lawgiver to his children and his wives, and nobody cares a jot for his neighbors." (*Odyssey* 9.94–105)

Because the one-eyed Cyclopes were so uncivilized, and also very large and powerful, the Greeks wanted to avoid contact with them. But Odysseus's men needed food. So he took twelve of them ashore and it was not long before they found a huge cave in which many sheep and goats were penned. But before the men could gather up the animals and depart, the Cyclops who lived in the cave returned home. This crude giant, whose name was Polyphemus, barred the entranceway with a gigantic rock. When he asked where the strangers had anchored their ship, Odysseus shrewdly answered that it had been wrecked in a storm and that he and these companions were the sole survivors. Polyphemus then abruptly grabbed two of the Greeks

> and dashed their heads against the floor as though they had been puppies. Their brains ran out on the ground and soaked the earth. Limb by limb, he tore them to pieces to make his meal, which he devoured like a mountain lion, never pausing till entrails [insides] and flesh, marrow and bones, were all consumed, while we could do nothing but weep and lift up our hands to Zeus in horror at the ghastly sight. . . . [After the Cyclops went to sleep] I thought I would draw my sharp sword . . . creep up on him . . . and stab him in the breast. . . . But on second thoughts I refrained, realizing that we

would have perished there as surely as the Cyclops, for we would have found it impossible with our unaided hands to push aside the huge rock with which he had closed the great mouth of the cave. (*Odyssey* 9.288–305)

The next morning, the Cyclops killed and ate two more of Odysseus's men and then left for the day, securing the great rock in the doorway so that the Greeks could not escape. When the giant returned that evening, he made still another meal of two men and then began to guzzle wine. In time, he demanded to know the Greek leader's name. Giving another shrewd reply, Odysseus claimed his name was "Nobody."

Later, the Cyclops fell asleep and Odysseus and his remaining men sharpened a wooden beam and heated it in the fire. Lifting the pole, Odysseus recalled, he and his men

> drove its sharpened end into the Cyclops' eye, while I used my weight from above to twist it home, like a man boring a ship's timber with a drill. . . . In much the same way we handled our pole with its red-hot point and twisted it in his eye till the blood boiled up around the burning wood. The fiery smoke from the blazing eyeball singed his lids and brow all round, and the very roots of his eye crackled in the heat. . . . He gave a dreadful shriek, which echoed round the rocky walls. . . . He pulled the stake from his eye, streaming with blood. Then he hurled it away from him with frenzied hands and raised a great shout for the other Cyclopes who lived in neighboring caves along the windy heights. (*Odyssey* 9.380–403)

But when the other giants appeared outside the cave and asked Polyphemus what was wrong and who was hurting him, he remembered the name Odysseus had given him and called out, "Nobody!" Hearing that "nobody" was hurting their neighbor, the other Cyclopes, confused and a bit irritated, returned to their homes.

Angry Winds, Cannibals, and Pig-Men

The next morning, the blinded Polyphemus had to roll back the huge rock to let his animals out to graze, and this allowed the Greeks to make good their escape. The enraged Cyclops cried out to his father—who, unfortunately for Odysseus, happened to be Poseidon—to punish these men who had deceived and disfigured him. (Poseidon heard this plea and later caused Odysseus considerable trouble.)

In the adventures that followed, Odysseus told the Phaeacians, he slowly but surely lost all of his companions. First, they came to the floating island of Aeolus, god of the winds. When Odysseus appealed to him for help, the god gave him a large leather bag which, he explained, contained most of the violent winds that tended to blow sailors off course. As long as these winds stayed inside in the bag, the west wind would carry the Greeks homeward. Thanking Aeolus, Odysseus and his men set out; within a week they actually saw the hills of Ithaca on the horizon. Happy but exhausted, Odysseus fell asleep. Unfortunately, while he slumbered some of his men could not contain their curiosity about what was in the bag. Imprudently, they cut it open and let loose a violent gale that blew the ships all the way back to Aeolus's island. The god was naturally angry and ordered Odysseus out of his sight.

Forlornly, the bedraggled sailors set out again for home. After six days, they came to the island of the Laestrygonians. Eleven of the twelve ships in Odysseus's small fleet anchored in the harbor, but the twelfth vessel, commanded by Odysseus himself, anchored outside the harbor as a precaution since there was no guarantee the place was safe. This turned out to be a wise move, for the Laestrygonians turned out to be giants; even worse, they were cannibals, who swarmed by the hundreds down to the harbor and attacked the anchored ships. Odysseus told the Phaeacians,

> Standing at the top of the cliffs, they began pelting my fleet with lumps of rock such as a man could barely lift; and the din that now rose from the ships, where the groans of dying men could be heard above the splintering of timbers, was appalling. One by one they harpooned their prey like fish and carried them off to make their loathsome meal. But while this massacre was still going on in the depths of the harbor, I . . . yelled to my crew to dash in with their oars if they wished to save their skins. With the fear of death upon them, they struck the water like one man, and with a sigh of relief, we shot out to sea and left those frowning cliffs behind. My ship was safe. But that was the end of the rest. (*Odyssey* 10.125–136)

Having lost eleven of his twelve ships, Odysseus continued wandering, tossed by the winds from place to place, never sure where fate might lead him and his remaining men. The last ship eventually came to the island of Aeaea. Here, a landing party went ashore to look for food, and the men found a quaint cottage in a lovely clearing in a forest. Numerous wild animals approached them, all of which, rather strangely, greeted them warmly, licking their hands and whining with pleasure. The reason for this eerie display, it turned out, was that the beautiful woman who lived in the cottage, whose name was Circe, was a sorceress. She invited the men to dine with her, and all but one of them, Eurylochus, did so. He then watched in horror as his companions turned into pigs. It was now clear that the other creatures wandering the area had once been humans themselves before falling under Circe's magic.

Eurylochus raced back to the ship and told Odysseus what had happened. Drawing his sword, Odysseus headed for the cottage; but on the way, the god Hermes appeared and warned him that Circe was very powerful. The deity gave Odysseus a special herb that would protect him from the witch's spells. Thanks to the herb, the leader of the party was able to get the best of Circe, who agreed to change his men back into human form. Now that the sorceress was no longer a threat, the Greeks took advantage of the pleasant island and its plentiful supplies and stayed almost a year.

The Spirits of the Dead
The Greeks finally told Circe that they had to move on and find their home. She was sad to see them leave and gave them some helpful advice. The only way they would be able to reach home, she said, would be to consult the old Theban seer Tiresias, who would tell them what they must do. There was only one problem, namely that Tiresias was long since dead and dwelled in the Underworld.

Circe conjured up a wind that blew the Greek ship to a remote shore of the Ocean, the wide river running around the outer edge of the earth. Following the sorceress's instructions, Odysseus proceeded to establish a connection with the realm of the dead. "I drew my sharp sword," he recalled,

> and dug a trench about a cubit long and a cubit wide. Around this trench I poured libations [liquid offerings] to all the dead, first with mingled honey and milk, then with sweet wine, and last of all with water. Over all this I sprinkled some white barley, and then began my prayers to the helpless ghosts of the dead, promising them that when I got back to Ithaca, I would sacrifice a young cow in my palace . . . and heap the pyre with treasures, and make Tiresias a separate offering of the finest jet-black sheep to be

found in my flocks. When I had finished my prayers . . . I took the sheep and cut their throats over the trench so that the dark blood poured in. And now the souls of the dead who had gone below came swarming up . . . fresh brides, unmarried youths, old men with life's long suffering behind them, tender young girls still nursing this first anguish in their hearts, and a great throng of warriors killed in battle. . . . Panic drained the blood from my cheeks. (*Odyssey* 11.23–42)

Trembling but stalwart, Odysseus greeted several shades (souls) as they rose up from the Underworld. Among them were Elpenor, a crewman he had lost on Circe's island; Odysseus's mother, Anticlea, who informed him how she, thinking him dead, had died of grief, and told him that his wife, Penelope, and son, Telemachus, were still well, though troubled by his absence; Alcmena, mother of the great hero Heracles; Agamemnon, leader of the expedition to Troy, who had been murdered by his wife on returning to Greece; Achilles, one of the greatest heroes of the Trojan War, who told Odysseus that he would rather be a servant in the house of some poor man rather than king of these dead spirits; and many others.

Finally, Odysseus met with Tiresias, the prophet. Tiresias's shade told him that the rest of his journey would be hard, mainly because Poseidon still held a grudge against him. Eventually sacrificing to that god would help soothe his anger. Tiresias also warned Odysseus that once he returned home, his troubles would not be over. His wife, the faithful Penelope, was beset by a pack of rich, noble suitors, each of whom demanded that she marry him. He must dispose of these scoundrels before he could know peace and happiness again with his wife.

The Wrath of the Gods

Having learned what he could from the dead Tiresias, Odysseus set sail with his remaining men. They soon had to sail past the island of the Sirens, women whose seemingly beautiful songs lured sailors to their deaths. Odysseus told his men that Circe had warned him about the Sirens and had advised him on the best way to avoid their deadly trap. As they neared the island, the men should stuff their ears with beeswax; that way they would not be able to hear the Sirens' song. Meanwhile, they must tie Odysseus to one of the ship's masts to keep him from being bewitched and swimming to the island.

The plan worked and the ship made it past the Sirens' lair. However, the Greeks next had to face the perils of Scylla and Charybdis, a fearsome monster and a giant whirlpool infesting the shores of Sicily's Strait of Messina. "My men turned pale with fear," Odysseus recalled,

and now, while all eyes were fixed on Charybdis . . . Scylla appeared and snatched out of my boat the six ablest hands I had on board. I swung around . . . just in time to see the arms and legs of her victims dangled high in the air above my head. "Odysseus!" they called out to me in their agony. But it was the last time they used my name. . . . Scylla had whisked my comrades up and swept them struggling to the rocks, where she devoured them at her own door, shrieking and stretching out their hands to me in their last desperate throes. In all I have gone through as I made my way across the seas, I have never had to witness a more pitiable sight than that. (*Odyssey* 12.243–261)

Though they had managed to get by the Sirens, Scylla, and Charybdis with only minimal losses, unfortunately the Greeks now sealed their own doom. They stopped on the large island of Thrinacia (an ancient name for Sicily); there, while Odysseus was asleep, his men slaughtered and ate some cattle belonging to the sun god, Helios (also known as Hyperion). Helios told Zeus about this blasphemous act. And in anger the king of the gods hurled a thunderbolt at the ship, destroying it and everyone onboard, except for Odysseus.

After clinging to a broken mast and drifting for nine days, Odysseus washed ashore in Ogygia, a remote island ruled by the nymph Calypso. She fell in love with him and made him stay with her for seven years. Eventually, however, Zeus sent his swift-footed messenger, Hermes, to tell Calypso that she must let her captive go. Reluctantly, she helped Odysseus construct a small boat, stocked the vessel with food, and sent him on his way.

No sooner had Odysseus made it out into the open sea, when Poseidon caught sight of him. Still fuming over the blinding of his one-eyed son, Polyphemus, the sea god created a storm that wrecked Odysseus's boat and tossed the man across giant waves, until he finally washed ashore on a beach on the friendly land of the Phaeacians. His first sight, on waking up, was the lovely form of Nausicaa, daughter of King Alcinous, at whose banquet the shipwrecked man had told the tale of his harrowing adventures.

Ithaca at Last

After a short stay with the kindly Phaeacians, Odysseus was delighted when King Alcinous offered to help him return to his beloved island of Ithaca. But when, after ten long years of trials and tribulations, he landed there, he found, just as Tiresias had warned that he would, his palace and family sorely troubled. Because most Ithacans assumed that he had long since died, his faithful wife, Penelope, was beset by over a hundred suitors. Each of them wanted to marry her for the money and titles he would get.

For a long time, Penelope had managed to keep the suitors at bay with a clever ruse, telling them that she needed to complete a tapestry before she could choose one of them as a husband. Each day she would work on the tapestry, but each night she would unravel her day's work, so that the

work dragged on and on. Unfortunately, the suitors eventually discovered the trick and forced Penelope to finish the tapestry. And now she was expected to announce her choice for the new Ithacan king.

After an emotional reunion with his now grown son, Telemachus, Odysseus, disguised as beggar, entered the palace banquet hall where the suitors were gathered. Not realizing his true identity, they mocked him and threw food and other objects at him. This went on for several days. Meanwhile, with the aid of Telemachus and some trusted servants, Odysseus planned to kill the suitors. Penelope herself suggested the right moment to put the plan in motion when she confided in the old beggar, completely unaware that he was really her husband. She had chosen a way to decide which of the suitors to marry, she told him; she would stage an archery contest. Her long-lost husband, Odysseus, she explained, used to set up twelve axes in a row, with the holes in each lined up. Then he would shoot a single arrow through all twelve axes without touching the metal blade of a single one. In a few days, she said, she planned to present the suitors with Odysseus's mighty bow; and if one of the suitors could accomplish the fantastic shot, she would agree to wed him.

The Suitors' Fate Is Sealed

On the appointed day, servants set up the twelve axes in the palace banquet hall, and the suitors eagerly jostled for their chance to shoot an arrow through them. What the suitors did not know was that Telemachus and the servants had stealthily removed all of the weapons from the hall. Odysseus, still dressed as a beggar, told a servant woman to lock the doors. Meanwhile, each of the unsuspecting suitors attempted to string Odysseus's mighty bow; however, none could manage it, for only its true owner possessed the heroic strength required.

It was then that Odysseus suddenly threw off his beggar's clothes and revealed himself to the startled men. Grasping the bow, he easily strung it, then fitted an arrow to the string and let loose the shaft, which flew in a perfect path through the holes of the assembled axes. At first, the suitors stood dumbfounded; then Odysseus told them,

> You yellow dogs! You never thought to see me back from Troy. So you ate me out of house and home; you raped my maids; you wooed my wife . . . with no more fear of the gods in heaven than of the human vengeance that might come. I tell you, one and all, that your doom is sealed. (*Odyssey* 22.36–42)

Now the men realized that they would have to fight for their lives, and they searched wildly for weapons, to no avail. Aided by Telemachus and two loyal servants, the Ithacan king began to kill them one by one. Homer dramatically describes the death of one suitor, Eurymachus, this way:

> He drew his sharp and two-edged sword of bronze, and leapt at Odysseus with a terrible shout. But at the same moment the brave Odysseus let an arrow fly, which struck him by the nipple on his breast with such force that it pierced his liver. The sword dropped from his hand. Lurching across the table, he crumpled up and tumbled with it, hurling the food and wine-cup to the floor. In agony he dashed his forehead on the ground; his feet lashed out and overthrew the chair, and the fog of death descended on his eyes. (*Odyssey* 22.79–84)

Eventually all of the suitors lay dead in the blood-soaked room.

Husband and Wife Reunited

The honor of their royal house restored, Odysseus and Penelope were finally re-united. During the twenty years they had been apart, both had been forced into situations in which they had to employ considerable cunning and resourcefulness. They had also displayed great perseverance and loyalty, as each had never stopped believing that they would be reunited in their marriage bed. Over that bed lingered a secret known only to the two of them; and now Odysseus revealed that special knowledge to her, so that she could be absolutely sure in her heart of hearts that it was he who had returned and not some imposter or ghost. "Inside the court there was a long-leaved olive tree," he began,

> which had grown to full height with a stem as thick as a pillar. Round this I built my room of close-set stone-work, and when that was finished, I roofed it over thoroughly, and put in it a solid, neatly fitted double door. Next, I lopped all the twigs off the olive, trimmed the stem from the root up, rounded it smoothly and carefully with my ax, and trued it to the line, to make my bedpost. This I drilled through where necessary, and used as a basis for the bed itself. . . . There is our secret, and I have shown you that I know it. (*Odyssey* 23.176–187)

On hearing this, Penelope's heart melted and her legs grew weak as she fell into her husband's arms. At long last they held each other again, and they were so overwhelmed with joy that they both shed tears and were reluctant to end the embrace. To prolong this touching scene for the lovers, since the night was quickly fading, bright-eyed Athena stretched forth her hand to delay the coming of the dawn. And in the following days, all hearts in Ithaca were filled with joy.

CHARACTERS IN GREEK AND ROMAN MYTHOLOGY

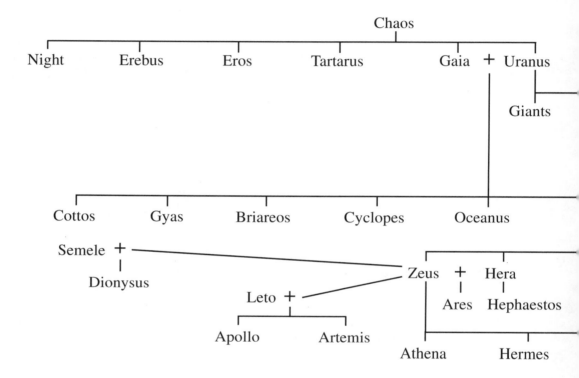

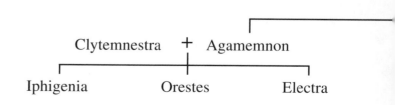

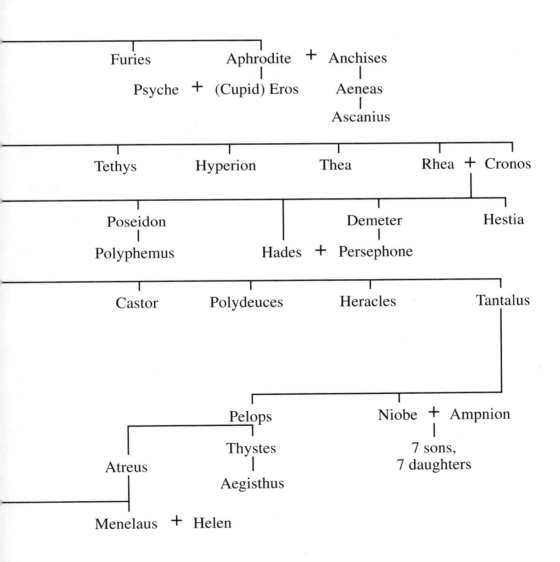

FOR FURTHER RESEARCH

Ancient Sources

Aeschylus, *Oresteia*, published as *The Orestes Plays of Aeschylus*. Trans. Paul Roche. New York: New American Library, 1962. Contains *Agamemnon, The Libation Bearers, Eumenides*.

———, *Prometheus Bound, The Suppliants, Seven Against Thebes, The Persians*. Trans. Philip Vellacott. Baltimore: Penguin Books, 1961.

Apuleius, *The Golden Ass*. Trans. P.G. Walsh. Oxford: Oxford University Press, 1994.

Aristophanes, *Birds, Lysistrata, Assembly-Women, Wealth*. Trans. Stephen Halliwell. Oxford: Clarendon Press, 1997.

———, *Clouds, Wasps, Peace*. Trans. Jeffrey Henderson. Cambridge, MA: Harvard University Press, 1998.

———, *The Complete Plays of Aristophanes*. Trans. Moses Hadas. New York: Bantam Books, 1962. Contains *Birds, Frogs, Lysistrata*, and others.

Aristotle, *Complete Works*. 2 vols. Ed. Jonathan Barnes. Princeton, NJ: Princeton University Press, 1988. Includes the *Poetics*.

———, *The Philosophy of Aristotle*. Ed. Renford Bambrough. New York: New American Library, 1963. Includes the *Poetics*.

Catullus, *The Poems of Catullus*. Ed. and trans. Guy Lee. New York: Oxford University Press, 1990.

Euripides, *"The Bacchae" and Other Plays*. Trans. Philip Vellacott. Baltimore: Penguin Books, 1965. Contains *Bacchae, Ion, Trojan Women, Helen*.

———, *Medea and Other Plays*. Trans. Philip Vellacott. Baltimore: Penguin Books, 1963. Contains *Medea, Hecuba, Electra, Madness of Heracles*.

———, *Orestes, Iphigenia in Aulis, Electra, The Phoenician Women, The Bacchae*. Ed. David Grene and Richmond Lattimore. New York: Random House, 1959.

———, *Three Great Plays of Euripides*. Trans. Rex Warner. New York: New American Library, 1958. Contains *Medea, Hippolytus, Helen*.

———, *Three Plays*. Trans. Philip Vellacott. Baltimore: Penguin Books, 1968. Contains *Hippolytus, Iphigenia in Tauris, Alcestis*.

H.G. Evelyn-White, trans., *Hesiod, Homeric Hymns,* and *Homerica*. Cambridge, MA: Harvard University Press, 1964.

Francis R.B. Godolphin, ed., *The Latin Poets*. New York: Random House, 1949.

Rhoda A. Hendricks, ed. and trans., *Classical Gods and Heroes: Myths as Told by the Ancient Authors*. New York: Morrow Quill, 1974. Contains excerpts from Valerius Flaccus's *Argonautica*, Diodorus Siculus's *Library of History*, Apollodorus's *Library* and *Epitome*, and others.

Herodotus, *The Histories*. Trans. Aubrey de Sélincourt. New York: Penguin Books, 1972; also trans. Robin Waterfield. New York: Oxford University Press, 1998.

Hesiod, *Works,* in *Hesiod and Theognis.* Trans. Dorothea Wender. New York: Penguin Books, 1973. Contains the *Theogony* and the *Works and Days.*

Author's Note: The following noteworthy translations of Homer's *Iliad* and *Odyssey* are listed in chronological order of publication. In a poll conducted during the 1980s of seventy-eight professors then teaching Homer in well-known colleges and universities, more than three-quarters of the respondents indicated their preference for the 1951 Lattimore translation of the *Iliad;* Robert Fitzgerald's and E.V. Rieu's versions scored second and third place, respectively. Regarding the *Odyssey,* Fitzgerald's translation was most preferred, with Lattimore's and Rieu's versions tied for second place. Since that time, Robert Fagles's translations of the two epics have gained wide acclaim.

Homer, *Iliad.* Trans. W.H.D. Rouse. New York: New American Library, 1950.

———, *Iliad.* Trans. E.V. Rieu. Baltimore: Penguin Books, 1950.

———, *Iliad.* Trans. Richmond Lattimore. Chicago: University of Chicago Press, 1951.

———, *Iliad.* Trans. Robert Fitzgerald. New York: Anchor-Doubleday, 1974.

———, *Iliad.* Trans. Robert Fagles. New York: Penguin Books, 1990.

———, *Odyssey.* Trans. W.H.D. Rouse. New York: New American Library, 1949.

———, *Odyssey.* Trans. E.V. Rieu. Baltimore: Penguin Books, 1961.

———, *Odyssey.* Trans. Robert Fitzgerald. New York: Anchor-Doubleday, 1962.

———, *Odyssey.* Trans. Richmond Lattimore. New York: Harper, 1965.

———, *Odyssey.* Trans. Robert Fagles. New York: Penguin Books, 1996.

Horace, *Complete Odes and Epodes.* Trans. Betty Radice. New York: Penguin Books, 1983.

———, *Satires, Epistles, Ars Poetica.* Trans. H. Rushton Fairclough. Cambridge, MA: Harvard University Press, 1966.

Bernard M.W. Knox, ed., *The Norton Book of Classical Literature.* New York: W.W. Norton, 1993. A collection of excerpts from Greek and Roman poetry, drama, and historical writing.

Naphtali Lewis and Meyer Reinhold, eds., *Roman Civilization, Sourcebook I: The Republic* and *Roman Civilization, Sourcebook II: The Empire.* Both New York: Harper and Row, 1966. Contain excerpts from Ovid's *Fasti,* Livy's *History of Rome from Its Foundation,* and numerous others.

Livy, *The History of Rome from Its Foundation.* Books 1–5 published as *Livy: The Early History of Rome.* Trans. Aubrey de Sélincourt. New York: Penguin Books, 1971.

Lucretius, *On the Nature of Things,* published as *Lucretius: The Nature of the Universe.* Trans. R.E. Latham. Baltimore: Penguin Books, 1951.

Ovid, *Metamorphoses.* Trans. Rolfe Humphries. Bloomington: University of Indiana Press, 1967.

Ovid, *Ovid: The Love Poems.* Trans. A.D. Melville. New York: Oxford University Press, 1990.

Pindar, *Odes.* Trans. C.M. Bowra. New York: Penguin Books, 1969.

Plato, *Complete Works.* Ed. John M. Cooper. Indianapolis: Hackett, 1997.

———, *Dialogues,* in *Great Dialogues of Plato.* Trans. W.H.D. Rouse. New York: New American Library, 1956.

Pliny the Elder, *Natural History.* 10 vols. Trans. H. Rackham. Cambridge, MA: Harvard University Press, 1967; also excerpted in *Pliny the Elder: Natural History: A Selection.* Trans. John H. Healy. New York: Penguin Books, 1991.

Plutarch, *Parallel Lives,* published complete as *Lives of the Noble Grecians and Romans.* Trans. John Dryden. New

York: Random House, 1932. Contains the lives of Theseus, Romulus, Pericles, and numerous others.

———, *Parallel Lives,* excerpted in *Fall of the Roman Republic: Six Lives by Plutarch.* Trans. Rex Warner. New York: Penguin Books, 1972; *Makers of Rome: Nine Lives by Plutarch.* Trans. Ian Scott-Kilvert. New York: Penguin Books, 1965; and *The Rise and Fall of Athens: Nine Greek Lives by Plutarch.* Trans. Ian Scott-Kilvert. New York: Penguin Books, 1960.

Sophocles, *The Complete Plays of Sophocles.* Trans. Richard C. Jebb. New York: Bantam Books, 1967.

———, *Oedipus the King.* Trans. Bernard M.W. Knox. New York: Pocket Books, 1959.

———, *The Three Theban Plays: Antigone, Oedipus the King, Oedipus at Colonus.* Trans. Robert Fagles. New York: Penguin Books, 1984.

Statius, *Works.* 2 vols. Trans. J.H. Mozley. Cambridge, MA: Harvard University Press, 1961.

Virgil, *The Aeneid.* Trans. Patric Dickinson. New York: New American Library, 1961; also trans. David West. New York: Penguin Books, 1990.

———, *Works.* 2 vols. Trans. H. Rushton Fairclough. Cambridge, MA: Harvard University Press, 1967.

Modern Sources

Manolis Andronicos, *Delphi.* Athens: Ekdotiki Athenon, 1993.

R.H. Barrow, *The Romans.* Baltimore: Penguin Books, 1949.

David Bellingham, *An Introduction to Greek Mythology.* Secaucus, NJ: Chartwell Books, 1989.

Walter Burkert, *Greek Religion, Archaic and Classical.* Oxford, England: Basil Blackwell, 1985.

T.J. Cornell, *The Beginnings of Rome: Italy and Rome from the Bronze Age to the Punic Wars (c. 1000–264 B.C.).* London: Routledge, 1995.

Leonard Cottrell, *The Bull of Minos.* Athens: P. Efstathiadis and Sons, 1983.

J. Wight Duff, *A Literary History of Rome.* New York: Barnes and Noble, 1960.

John Ferguson, *The Religions of the Roman Empire.* London: Thames and Hudson, 1970.

John B. Firth, *Augustus Caesar and the Organization of the Empire of Rome.* Freeport, NY: Books for the Libraries, 1972.

J. Lesley Fitton, *The Discovery of the Greek Bronze Age.* Cambridge, MA: Harvard University Press, 1996.

Robert Flaceliere, *A Literary History of Greece.* Trans. Douglas Garman. Chicago: Aldine, 1964.

Jane Gardner, *Roman Myths.* Austin: University of Texas Press and British Museum Press, 1993.

Michael Grant, *A Guide to the Ancient World.* New York: Barnes and Noble, 1986.

———, *The Myths of the Greeks and Romans.* New York: Penguin Books, 1962.

Michael Grant and John Hazel, *Who's Who in Classical Mythology.* London: Weidenfeld and Nicolson, 1973.

Jasper Griffin, *Homer: The Odyssey.* New York: Cambridge University Press, 1987.

Edith Hamilton, *Mythology.* New York: New American Library, 1940.

Martin Henig, ed., *Pagan Gods and Shrines of the Roman Empire.* Oxford: Oxford Committee for Archaeology, 1986.

M.C. Howatson and Ian Chilvers, eds., *The Concise Oxford Companion to Classical Literature.* New York: Oxford University Press, 1993.

Peter Levi, *A History of Greek Literature.* New York: Penguin Books, 1985.

J.V. Luce, *Lost Atlantis: New Light on an Old Legend.* New York: McGraw-Hill, 1969.

Georg Luck, *Arcana Mundi: Magic and the Occult in the Greek and Roman*

Worlds. Baltimore: Johns Hopkins University Press, 1985.

Evi Melas, *Temples and Sanctuaries of Ancient Greece.* London: Thames and Hudson, 1973.

John D. Mikalson, *Athenian Popular Religion.* Chapel Hill: University of North Carolina Press, 1983.

Mark P.O. Morford and Robert J. Lenardon, *Classical Mythology.* New York: Longman, 1985.

Jennifer Neils, ed., *Worshipping Athena: Panathenaia and Parthenon.* Madison: University of Wisconsin Press, 1996. (*Note:* The author's spelling of the great Athenian festival is an accepted variant of *Panathenaea.*)

R.M. Ogilvie, *The Romans and Their Gods in the Age of Augustus.* New York: W.W. Norton, 1969.

John Pinsent, *Greek Mythology.* New York: Peter Bedrick Books, 1986.

Stewart Perowne, *Roman Mythology.* London: Paul Hamlyn, 1969.

H.J. Rose, *Religion in Greece and Rome.* New York: Harper and Brothers, 1959.

W.H.D. Rouse, *Gods, Heroes, and Men of Ancient Greece.* New York: New American Library, 1957.

M.S. Silk, *Homer: The "Iliad."* New York: Cambridge University Press, 1987.

Michael Stapleton, *The Illustrated Dictionary of Greek and Roman Mythology.* New York: Peter Bedrick Books, 1986.

T.B.L. Webster, *From Mycenae to Homer.* New York: W.W. Norton, 1964.

Michael Wood, *In Search of the Trojan War.* New York: New American Library, 1985.

INDEX

Abas, 62
Acastus, 11, 156
Acca Larentia, 73
Achaea, 141
Achaeus, 72
Acharnians (Aristophanes), 179
Achates, 11
Acheron, 141
Achilles, 11–12
  and Ajax the Greater, 16
  and the Amazons, 18
  and Briseis, 25
  and Hector, 39–40
  and Memnon, 51
  and Patroclus, 57
  and Peleus, 57–58
  and Thetis, 117–18
  and the Trojan War, 273, 275,
    276–78
  and Zeus, 123
Acis, 93
Acontius, 12
Acrisius, 12, 62, 255
Acropolis, 141–42, 144
Actaeon, 12, 76–77, 266–67
Admetus, 12, 75, 220–21
Adonis, 12–13
Adrastus, 13, 66, 271
Aeacus, 13, 171
Aeaea, 142, 282
Aedon, 13
Aeetes, 13–14, 154–55
Aegean Sea, 142, 251
Aegeus, 14
  and the Minotaur, 144–45
  and Pallas, 57
  reunited with Theseus, 249
  sword of, 248
Aegimius, 14
Aegina, 66–67, 142
aegis, 142
Aegisthus, 14–15, 29, 245, 246
Aegle, 99
Aegyptus, 31
Aeneas, 15

in Carthage, 225
in Crete, 150
and Dido, 33, 225, 228–29
and Evander, 90
and the Golden Bough, 230
and Latinus, 48
and Latium, 157
parents of, 19–20
prophecies to, 226
and Rome, 164–65
and the Sibyl, 66, 229–30
travel to Italy, 225–28, 229
and the Trojan War, 274
and Troy's fall, 225–26
in the Underworld, 230–31
and Venus, 119–20
at war with the Latins, 231–33
see also Aeneid
Aeneid (Virgil), 172–74, 215
  and Dardanus, 32–33
  Evander in, 90
  Jupiter in, 102
  Portunus in, 112
  Venus in, 119
Aeolus, 15, 41, 281
Aepytus, 51
Aeschylus, 174
  works by, 174–75, 186–87, 197,
    206, 209–13
Aesculapius, 73
Aeson, 46, 58
Aethiopis, 186
Aetolia, 142
Agamedes, 71
Agamemnon, 15
  and Briseis, 25
  and Cassandra, 27
  and Chryseis, 28
  and the Curse of the House of
    Atreus, 29, 245–46
  and Mycenae/Mycenaeans, 159,
    160
  sacrifice of daughter, 77, 246,
    273–74
  and the Trojan War, 275

Agamemnon (Aeschylus), 174–75
Agapenor, 15
Agave, 265–66
Agenor, 264–65
Age of Heroes, 144
Aglaia, 93
Agrius, 131
Ahura-Mazda, 105
Aias. *See* Ajax the Greater
Ajax the Greater, 15–16, 69, 274
Ajax the Lesser, 16, 27, 279
Ajax (Sophocles), 16, 175, 212
Alba Longa, 142, 165
Alcestis, 15, 16
  and Heracles, 220–21
  and Thanatos, 116
Alcestis (Euripides), 175–76, 188
Alcinous, 16, 280
Alcippe, 76
Alcithoe, 52
Alcmaeon, 16–17
Alcmena, 17, 36, 88–89, 122, 216
Alcyone, 17, 111
Alcyoneus, 131, 222
Alcyonian Lake, 158
alphabet, the, 265
Alpheus, 143
Althea, 50, 91
Amalthea, 124
Amazonomachy, the, 17–18,
  251–52
Amazons, the, 17–18
  and Heracles, 221
  and Hippolyte, 42
  and Theseus, 251–52
ambrosia, 142
Amores (Ovid), 206
Amphiaraus, 18–19, 66
Amphilochus, 53
Amphion, 19, 267
Amphitrite, 113
Amphitryon, 17, 19, 36, 216, 217
Amulius, 19, 252, 253
Anchises, 19–20
  in *Aeneid*, 173–74

PICTURE CREDITS

ABOUT THE AUTHOR

Historian Don Nardo has written numerous volumes about ancient Greece and Rome, including *Life in Ancient Athens, Life of A Roman Slave, The Age of Augustus, Greek and Roman Sport,* and *The Greenhaven Encyclopedia of Ancient Rome.* He is also the editor of *Classical Greece and Rome,* the second volume of Greenhaven's ten-part World History by Era series. Mr. Nardo resides with his wife, Christine, in Massachusetts.